UNWRITTEN LETTERS
to Spring Street

JACQUELYN FRITH

Clink
Street

London | New York

WRITE WHAT MUST NOT BE FORGOTTEN

-Isabel Allende

-Chapters-

- CHAPTER ONE -

Flores Sea

- 29 NOVEMBER 1943 -

Jack hesitated for a moment, breathing heavily. Through his mind passed a lifetime of consideration and terrifying visions. Within a few frantic displaced seconds his thoughts swung from demanding he leap into the boiling sea to distractedly wondering if he would survive the fall. His mind swam with images of home and his family, and of all he had endured, all he had survived. Now all to be washed away. Disconnected to the unfolding horror before him, he pondered in that single blink, the dark depth of the water and worrying height of the deck, the inevitable long plunge and the lurching list of the ship. He was not aware if he spoke yet he noticed his mouth flapping open like a fish suffocating in air. Frighteningly, his thoughts became magnetically absorbed by the ominous throb and sucking power of the ship's propeller. Its laborious heaving rumbled unseen, deep under the ship, vibrating the metallic hulk and pulsing every cell in his body. He breathlessly imagined himself exposed, drowning, being helplessly drawn face to face with its hypnotic danger as a second explosion abruptly caused its shuddering halt, shattering his thoughts. He gathered himself, his mind wild and alight with indecision. He hardly noticed peripheral flickering fire and spectres of men leaping in the edge of his vision as he swayed unsteadily, terrified to make his choiceless decision. Then, clear through the cacophony a solitary voice pierced his frightened deliberation. "Abandon ship!" it screamed in Japanese. Jack didn't understand the words but heard their desperate meaning. He had fumbled to the conclusion that the unknown ocean depths and sickening fall were marginally safer than the imploding deck of their torpedoed ship.

Off guard and caught in immobile motion as the voice rang out, Jack startled into action. He began the deep inhale, the drawing of breath in preparation for his plunge, but was cut short as a final fireball explosion rocked the ship, sending a bellowing reverberation along its length. The concussive blast hurled Jack overboard so ferociously he had hardly taken breath in his lungs and had no understanding he had fallen until he was deep underwater, falling in a cascade of light and fire. The slowing of time and the drawing out of each action happened simultaneously. The fearful hesitation, decision to jump, shout to abandon ship, inhalation, explosion and plunge, all punctuated by wrenching doubt. And yet throughout, not once had he considered the temperature of the water. It had been hot and clammy as the ship lurched somewhere on the Flores Sea. Sweat had clung to him like a damp rag, and Jack could not have imagined the sea would be so numbingly cold. Darkened time washed over him and he was lost.

In that same moment the ship shuddered, the inky sea swallowed him instantly, just one greedy gulp and he was gone. He could not grasp he was underwater or that he was sinking as he dropped down and down, a falling deadweight. The slight impact of his thin body slicing the thick surface of the water disassociated itself from the sharp sting of salt clenching his eyes shut. He keenly sensed the cold, oily sensation of water as it slid over and completely covered his parched sunburnt skin but he watched from another place, some other life. A moment earlier he'd watched himself arc overboard, bare feet high in the air, buckled knees bent, hands rounded as if still gripping the gunwale rail. Jack had watched himself, mute and expressionless as the rail fell away, disappearing into sparkling black, as the ocean submerged him. The thick water thundered round his ears like a steam train in a tunnel, all oil and smoke and exploding fire, and *hell* it was cold.

In truth, he had considered the jump rationally and somewhat calmly despite the brevity and chaos. Inevitably he had made daily life and death decisions during his captivity. It was a necessity to judge situations quickly, those long months, those longer two years. His life, all their lives hung by the fragile thread of pause, reflection and considered action and still that was not enough to save many. The men had existed in a shifting, semiconscious hellish state, it took but a small step, some unremarkable adjustment to make life unbearable. And now, their worsening nightmare had unravelled and spilled into the sea. A new terror heaped upon their already overburdened and miserable existence. Empty stomachs had lurched metronomically as the ship had ploughed on, indifferent to unspoken suffering. The single screw churned as the funnel had belched choking black smoke. Pumping forward through the dark sea as they pressed, cramped and trapped in its damp holds, gripped by multitudinous fears. Of the four stifling storage holds concealed in the belly of the four and a half thousand ton metal ship, the rear two were wedged to overcapacity with five hundred and forty-eight pained men. A sick draft of far east prisoners of war. Five hundred and forty-eight souls, starved, diseased and weakened, rolled together in despair as the ship rattled endlessly on and on. Their ship seemed sure to be attacked. The huge belching target churning from the funnel signalled their position clearly to the Allies. Jack had noticed with sickening alarm as he'd embarked, that the ship was not marked with red crosses indicating PoWs, or a hospital ship. As he'd shuffled on board, carrying one end of a stretcher, he'd briefly hunkered below one of the damaged fuselage from enemy *Zero* aircraft lashed to the deck. Who would imagine this ship was a sick draft, carrying desperate Allied PoWs? The hellship that had brought them, some seven months and a lifetime before, to the hell-island had been similarly unmarked. But then, Jack had not fully realised the terrifying significance. On this, their return journey it was their collective, immovable fear as the ship wheezed on through the dark water. Its old bones creaked until inevitably in a heart-stopping rush of shuddering explosions it was shot from beneath them. Its heavy lumbering carcass disappeared with more than half their brothers into the black ocean depths in a matter of minutes.

Moments earlier the stifling hold had been an insufferable imprisonment yet had held a tentative safety. Now the entire ship had become a deathly prison, dragging his brothers away and down. They didn't have a chance, Jack could do nothing to save them, or himself. And *still*, he thought *bloody hell*, the sea was so cold as he drifted down into the murk. Blinking, he saw vivid visions of his young life exploding in front of him. He watched, paralysed and dumbstruck. So touchably real, that in one splintering second he swore his brother, George had just pushed him into the cool water at Hyde Municipal Baths, as he had so often in their boyhood. Jack gasped for air, hearing his childish shriek cut short as he splashed into the clear water, all legs and arms. Protesting mutely as streams of air rushed from his gaping mouth he heard George's muffled laughter from the edge of the water, his outline rippling through the glassy surface. He watched old men in baggy bathing suits shuffling along duckboards, towels rolled underarm, jowls dripping and their sagging bodies bristling with water. Jack floated down, open-eyed and open-mouthed awaiting the dull bump of the pool bottom. He watched multicoloured shafts of stained-glass light dance through the Gothic windows of the grand old Victorian building, illuminating the thin water in a spectacular firework display. George threw himself in, legs folded under his wrapped arms as he landed harmlessly on Jack, cushioned by the air he brought into the water. They wriggled, play-fighting and swimming until surfacing, gasping, spluttering and laughing soundlessly, their eyes creased closed. Opening his creased eyes, the expected dull bump was a hard crate, sinking in the water beside him and banging his side painfully. Multicoloured shafts of light burned within the sinking ship like cold silent fireworks. Jack frowned in confusion touching his mouth with fingertips, tasting not sour chlorine but heavy salt, sickly and thick with oil. His mind spun. Looking frantically around, this was no childhood pool. No soft light reflected here and no shouts echoed dully in the water. He shook away George's familiar face and stared hard into the gloom swallowing the sinking ship. He demanded his mind respond, demanded it grasp that this was the deep, dark ocean and he was *still* falling into its cold depths.

Wild thoughts gradually subsided, and his mind calmed as he reconciled himself to the situation, and gathered himself. His mind quietly said he'd been lucky to be on deck as the torpedoes hit. Jammed together in the hold of the transport ship more than twenty-three hours a day, he had been waiting to take the temporary relief of his few minutes permitted on deck as they lurched heavily through the sea, moments from catastrophe. He had waited achingly in the slow stream of unsteady men climbing from the hatch, stumbling upwards and forwards. His desperation for a moment of fresh air on deck was given and he waited to use the insanitary arrangements. A drum in the corner of the hold on the outbound voyage was now considered too disgusting and disease hungry for even their captors, and open boxes had been hung over the side of the ship. The precarious perched positions and lack of dignity afforded, starkly matched the PoWs' precarious and undignified existence. Food was delivered via a bucket lowered twice a day, once in early morning and once late in the afternoon, accompanied by a shout of *makan* which announced a meal. The descending bucket was usually filled with infested rotten rice and filthy water, not nearly enough for more than a handful slopped into each tin canteen. These tiny portions the men ate and drank quickly as if at a banquet, such was their hunger and thirst. The creaking, sinking ship had been a coal transporter, and the PoWs had been loaded as cargo, forced down into the depths some four days earlier, man upon man pressed into glistening filthy holds, less valuable but more troublesome than the black fuel. They were quickly rubbed sore with coal-dust, it covered ulcerated skin, filled noses and caught in the throat. There was barely room to breathe in, let alone to move, or stretch or lie. The men were so tired, so desperate to get off that hell-island that they didn't complain, couldn't complain. They would not dare. Each had personally learnt the hard lesson that silent rebellion and tiny gains were the only collective victories keeping each man fastened to sanity. The PoWs had all become ill long before boarding. Most were walking skeletons barely more than sunburnt skin taut over bone, quietly staring through stark eyes. Watching and breathing slowly. A sick draft from hellish island to god only knew where. Each man had quietly, resolutely descended into the sparkling blackness, trying hard *not* to wonder if this could be the beginning of the journey home. Instead each filled their thoughts with other imaginings. Anything that could be cradled like a precious bubble of normality in the mind, to keep from drowning in despair. But still, *home* permeated Jacks thoughts despite the pointlessness.

Some poor souls had been so deathly ill before boarding they were now beyond help. They lay out, stretchered on deck, maybe thirty of them, all angular joints and rasping coughs breathing their last in the stinking heat. All the men on board were ill. They lay silently in the deep hold, some so weakened that inevitably they did not wake at the dawn shout for *makan*. Each of these poor men was gently lifted. Every hand, no matter how weakened themselves, offered up support and a last human touch. Thus, the sorry soul would rise slowly to the hatch as softly as the others were able. They had been ordered to unceremoniously throw the dead overboard. Instead, they were offered to the sea with all the care the sickly men could muster, gently letting them drop as quiet, heartfelt farewells were spoken. The PoWs attempted to offer their brothers the respect they had been denied, as they slipped away. That ominous morning two lives had passed, one silently and the other with low groans, a last splutter but no final words. They had both already been lifted up as Jack had begun his ascent into the glaring light of the open deck for his turn at the precarious box. He'd reached up, grasping the rim of the hatch watching the white bones of his knuckles pushing against his scarred skin, as he heaved himself into daylight, blinking and squinting. The warmth of the sun on his face seemed so long ago, but it must have been only a matter of moments since he had stood frozen in indecision. And still, he rolled over and over, down and down in the dark freezing sea. Folded in a protective ball, his cushion of air and bubbles flying from him like shooting stars, as the attack replayed and raced in his mind, flashing by in fractions of seconds, oblivious to the swirling sea he drowned in.

The torpedoes had scored a direct hit, not long after what the PoWs dryly called breakfast. The sun had settled comfortably above the horizon, its warmth steaming moisture mistily off the deck and burnishing the ships peeling hull. Most of the men were awake, night-time and darkness brought little sleep. The men simply hunched against each other, tired worn shoulder to bruised jutting cheek. Jack had planted his bare feet unsteadily on the deck as the sun began warming his face and he had glanced around, orientating himself before taking the few steps to the gunwale. A few enemy soldiers leant there, looking out to sea, joking with each other and smoking cigarettes, flicking the butts into the white frothing side-wake. Three tired and harassed looking Japanese crew had hurried past, clattering tools and stacking painting gear for some task or other. The six or seven PoWs who had already climbed on deck were holding the rail tight, swaying as they staggered on stiff limbs toward the hanging boxes. Jack stretched out a hand to grip the rail as he reached it, leaning into the rising swell knees bent, as he looked out to the horizon. Blinking in the glaring sunlight, he felt its heat permeate his bone-tired body as he gathered himself to move. He was about to turn when two white lines tracing fast, fizzed through the water, catching his eye. He had never before seen torpedoes but knew instantly what they were. The terrifying foaming slashes coursed directly for the ship. Fear gripped his throat closed. The two lines were suddenly staggered by another two behind, and all four closing frighteningly fast. Jack turned, mouth agape, terrified the attack would go unnoticed as the shrill jabbering shrieks of Japanese erupted, raising the alarm. Instantly the Japanese scurried like rats in a panicked scramble to turn the ship. It was too late. Jack watched the first torpedo whizz by in a foaming blur, but the second slammed into the ship with a sickening thud. It resonated the vessel like a gong for a moment before exploding. Everyone and everything amidships was thrown in the air, and he was surrounded by a huge pulsating fireball. Instinctively he covered his ears against the almighty roar of the explosion. Pieces of ship and fragments of aircraft fuselage sailed through the air around him. It seemed to happen slowly, silently as he instinctively tried to curl into ball. He watched as some of the Japanese and PoWs immediately leapt into the sea, their mouths silently shrieking.

Soldiers, officers and civilian crew, and prisoners of war alike stood stunned and dazed, looking around dully. Jack heard nothing except his own blood pounding and a singing-ringing concussion noise in his ears, all around was slow muted chaos, as if it was too much for his mind to process. With the impact he'd fallen to the deck, hands thrown out in front as the ship shook and an instant later rocked, by the massive explosion. He was on hands and knees reaching for the rail as the ship had shuddered. The explosion knocked him upright, his feet leaving the deck. Terrified he'd go overboard he hung onto the rail, as he came crashing down again onto his knees, still unconsciously cradling the smooth metal. The explosion seemed incredibly close, underneath and all around, engulfing him in ear-splitting sound and roaring fireball. He was in the centre of the storm but in his own silent bubble observing distractedly as the ship lurched to and fro. It was a matter of moments before the third and fourth torpedoes closed in. Jack didn't feel anything of the strike of the third, he wondered if it had missed the ship. But the fourth found its target, slamming home under the main mast. The impact was thundering and even closer. It shook the ship from stern to bow, rattling everything loose. The explosion a second later was muted, as if imploding deep underwater, the searing pain of bursting appendix deep within. It snapped the ships back and collapsed the aft deck. The ship stopped dead in the water and the propeller wheezed to a stop with a final shuddering throb. There was a horrible yawning groan as the ship seemed first to swallow the fireball then spit it back out as it split apart. The stern lurched down into the sea as waves surged over onto the deck. Prisoners were heaving themselves from the nearest hold, turning quickly to help those behind, as Japanese soldiers rushed forwards to free a lifeboat. Cargo broke loose and slid down the deck, crashing into obstacles. Everything not fastened securely slipped into the burning, boiling sea.

It had taken mere moments but the screaming chaos seemed endless. Everything around him was terrifying and violent. Jacks mind could not absorb it and his eyes involuntarily blurred. The horror of the deck dissolved into a swarm of colour and silent activity, like a melting oil painting lying exposed in the rain. He stared hard, trying to refocus his vision, but could only see a swirling painting of relentless colours, and smoke and fire. He blinked hard and looked to his hands. He watched calmly, as his grip relaxed and readjusted on the rail, "This must be how it ends," a part of his mind quietly observed. Another part of his mind tugged at his sleeve. It forced him to shift his eyes from his hands, moving his gaze along his thin sun-cracked arm. He saw his elbow resting on his knee, his feet tucked underneath him. He blinked hard and suddenly saw himself and the scene with clarity, his eyes refocused and his vision cleared. He sagged onto the rail gripping the metal underarm and drew a breath. Moving his slight weight onto one knee he attempted to stand. He had long since been barefoot, trading boots for a small amount of food and a tattered shirt. Pushing himself higher he held the rail with both hands, his head bowed. His straggly hair flopped down covering his dark eyes, creating a screen through which he swiftly looked left then right, taking in the situation to his overloaded senses. He watched men swarming overboard, plopping into the sea like pebbles into a frothing lake. The ship listed horribly, smoke billowed from every available opening. Forked tongue flames licked the air from the huge open wound in the deck. Jack looked down at the water. It was littered with debris and seemed a long way down. Waves massaged the hull, the dark water frothing white as it struck the metal. The sea lolled and rolled, and the ship sagged heavily and broken in it. It was then that Jack considered jumping and had failed to immediately decide. It was then he hesitated. The ship was certainly going to sink beneath him, taking him down with it. He *had* to jump he reasoned. But, god the sea looked wild and it was such a terrifying leap. Suddenly with a fearful shiver he saw himself as one of his unfortunate brothers, slipping overboard, unburied at sea, dropping dead into the water. It filled him with horror. He was utterly lost in the chaos of indecision when sound had returned in screaming, frightened shouts and bursts of frantic activity all around. It was now that a Japanese soldier howled the belated order to abandon ship. Jack spun and saw through the clearing smoke, the aft hold and the deck collapsed around it. He couldn't see any life inside. The packed, squirming mass of men trapped in the hold was calmly silent, no one moved in its interior. It was darkly still in the midst of the screaming melee. He swung back around, looking into the hold he had climbed from moments, and a lifetime before. Four or five thin men climbed from it, turning to reach down. They wore only tattered shorts and their exposed ribs expanded as they panted heavily. Bending, reaching downwards they pulled at outstretched hands, helping up those they could. Slowly men appeared out of the deathly hold, dazed and blackened with soot. Jack wiped his brow with the ragged end of his shirt front and began to turn toward them, to help. He was distracted by the pull of his hand, and found himself still gripping the rail tightly. Something about it looked odd. He realised it was not horizontal, the ship was listing some thirty degrees. "What the *hell*?" He muttered as he looked up and down the length of the ship. It was undoubtedly going to sink, and soon. The bow was rising from the sea, pointing skywards as the stern slipped deeper underwater, dragging the limp belly of the ship with it. Jack tried to unclench the railing, knuckles again trying to burst through thin skin as time continued slowly. He watched a man emerge from the hold into chaos, panic and fear and blood on his blackened face. He stared through the fire and smoke, looking at Jack momentarily. His eyes were wild and his mouth chattered as he ran past and leapt. He coursed through the air and crashed into the sea below, disappearing into the blue. And still, only a few elongated minutes had passed since Jack had seen the white traces and the first torpedo had struck. He turned to those at the hatch, but as he moved the final massive explosion deep within the ship had finally, senselessly, flung him overboard. Cartwheeling over the railing and weighing nothing Jack looked like a rag doll, the ship a toy bobbing in bathwater. He had no sense of why he was in the air, there was nothing, but waiting. He finally crashed unknowingly into the sea amongst the debris, as his mind screamed, "God the water's cold."

Sinking into the gloom Jack felt the numbing water permeate his body. Such unexpected cold sucked away his heat, and took his remaining breath. He fell for so long in its glassy grip he thought he would never surface. As he sank he looked wide-eyed, down and around, casually, as if he had all the time in the world. He was terrified, unnerved by the dark void below and above, suffocating and close. He watched an eternity of swirling dark blue under his motionless feet. He saw air bubbles leave him, disappearing from every fold like sand shaken from clothes on a beach. He listened to the pound-pound, pound-pound of his rapid heartbeat bursting in his ears, drumming each second into an hour. He watched the ships aft hull lolling underwater, a huge ripped gash in its side. Cargo dropped out into the sea, falling away into the void beneath. Air bubbles streamed from the ships torn wound and oil leaked from somewhere. Somehow it was still bleakly lit from within. A tepid orange glow like an ember, as if still alive deep in its heart. A dying creature gasping its last breaths. All around him, men floated silently like suspended still puppets lost underwater. Their mouths open, their life gone. The ship groaned painfully as it broke apart. Jack saw muted flashes of inner implosions as pockets of air dashed for the surface from the flickering fire. The dark enormity of the ship's hull tapered down to the depths, its bow still gasping above the waves. He distractedly thought it strange that he didn't *feel* the wetness of the sea, he felt only a numbing cold, a dampness sucking at every pore, draining away life. Noises from the ship became muffled, overtaken by a singing, cracking and clicking in his ears from underwater pressure, from drowning. Darkness began to slide over him like a velvet sheet, as sparkling light danced in the last bubbles of trapped air leaving his ragged clothing. They streamed upwards, drawn magnetically to the surface as Jack dropped quietly and steadily downward into the gloom, swallowed in the great maw. He closed his eyes and drifted down.

Jack convulsed silently as he tried to take an unconscious breath and sucked in only salt water. He shuddered, feeling a sharp ache in his side, his lungs complaining. Suddenly and urgently, for the first time he felt a surge of panic and the suffocating fear of drowning, and he strained for the surface. He was shocked to see shadow above as dark as the bottomless pit beneath him. Startled into conscious reaction and an overwhelming desire to survive, he began to kick. Glancing to his feet, he noticed their movement, somehow graceful like little fins against the weight of water. He felt he had held his breath for hours, but it must have been not much more than a minute. He had lost all idea of time. He opened and closed his mouth trying to breathe but no air escaped. He tasted only sea, thick and clagging despite being mere water. Looking up, his path from the surface was completely gone. There was no trace of his effervescent descent. He felt struck by the conviction that he must not, could not, drown. Not *now*. The chaos of falling and sinking had been muted as if happening far away to someone else, but now he felt alive and invigorated, even if he had little strength. He kicked, seemingly endlessly in nothingness, feeling like he wasn't moving. Desperately he pulled at the water with his arms, his muscles complaining as he clawed, but he seemed frozen and trapped in place. He struggled on and on, alone in the claustrophobic dark. Surely the surface must be nearing. He was sure the water seemed lighter now. Yes, he could see sunbeams slicing down from above. His mind blinked into a parallel life. Shafts of sun slicing through heavy curtains on a summer's day. Tiny dust motes swaying lazily in the beams of light. He almost sighed with the promise of warmth, just outside as he felt the cool shadows of his house, beckoning him home. His eyes widened as he strained to focus. They looked so much like sunbeams, these tiny particles floating in an almost silent sea. He stretched out a hand to touch, but could not reach. Again, his mind tugged at his sleeve. "*Come on, Jack!*" it whispered. He turned his head and his mind returned him to the water, to the drowning sea. Frantic now, he scratched at the water, his mind screaming, "I must get to the surface. I can't drown, not *now*." He tried to fight the drowsiness folding in on him, and he began to feel peaceful. He no longer sensed the cold. A corner of his mind now told him to give in, to relax in the darkness. Let go and disappear into the black. Again he closed his eyes. Something caught in his throat. His reflexes coughed and gagged on the slick taste of oil in the salt water, rallying him. Again he fought against nothingness. Kicking, gasping, retching and convulsing he reached out for the elusive surface. Almost imperceptibly the water seemed lighten. Yes, it was brighter as he neared. "Is this the surface?" His mind urgently asked. He tried again to take a breath, feeling he *must* be about to break through. No, he was still under. He choked on mouthfuls of water as he tried to breathe. A surge of fury that he would die for nothing after everything he had survived, gave him the energy to kick again with ebbing strength, but still the surface eluded him. He kicked once more in frustration. The muffled sea seemed strangely louder but he felt quiet and calm. The cold that permeated his thin body had receded and he felt warmer. He realised it was over. It was finally over. He could not breathe. He stopped kicking, and drifted. Slowly, sleepily, blinking in the salt, he dreamily looked about. The ship, huge and gasping for its own breath broke silently apart, its broken stern sliding away and down. Only the point of the bow still precariously remained above water. Here and there were men, still reaching for the surface from the depths. Two uniformed men fell into the sea from the protruding bow beyond his sight— the last to escape the dying ship. Enveloped in exploding fireworks they fell through bubbles of air, kicking out like frogs alongside debris and cargo that slipped away. Jack burst to breathe. His mouth opened and closed as a heavy fog crept in around him. His glazing eyes finally, eventually, closed. His mouth opened and he slipped away. In that instant he heard an ear-splitting crash as he exploded through the water's surface, as if smashing through a glass window. Jack gulped at lungfuls of air, his mouth wide, coughing and heaving up seawater as he went under again. Thrashing wildly he quickly surfaced, bobbing like a cork. Then still gasping, he starfished out on the surface. Breathing deeply, catching his breath, his eyes bulging as slowly his bursting lungs eased. He squinted in the brilliant gleaming sunlight that he had left only moments before and wiped at his face and eyes with his ragged shirt. The moving, dispersing layer of oil on the surface left an acrid smell and taste which had caught in his nose and in his mouth. There were slicks of it here and there and he moved quickly away from the edge of the closest pool. The chaos he had briefly left remained. Sound returned like a hurricane to accompany the turmoil and disorder of his numbed senses. The muted time underwater had seemed to last an eternity of gasping cold darkness, now the thought of it disappeared, as if it had occurred in the blink of an eye. There was now only the swashing commotion of light and colour and sound above the surface. He turned in the water, eyes gleaming, aware his next struggle awaited.

The sea sagged with oil and small fires flickered across the debris. Metal protruded from floating barrels, broken crates and destroyed jetsam from the ship, bumping the men in the water as they struggled to remain afloat. Jack felt grateful to be alive, to able to breathe, but soon faced new concerns as he wearily trod water. Despite the plunge he didn't feel injured, but it was hard to be sure. He was in shock. Moments later a dull ache in his side rose to a sharp pain. He felt around his ribs under his tattered shirt and found no wound. "Perhaps a broken rib," he muttered to himself. Jack glanced around looking for something to hold onto, he knew he couldn't tread water for long and was already weakening. Suddenly, he noticed someone close by, a head bobbing maybe ten feet away. Jack decided there might be safety in numbers. He leant forward to swim to him. The thick green-blue swell rose him up and lowered him down as he made his first stroke forward. As his face touched the surface of the water he felt himself pulled back into cool clear chlorinated water. Young Jack moved forward, pushing his arms in wide breaststroke circles. He rolled over and kicked off from the smooth white and green tiles on the wall of the pool as his pale teenage legs frogged out propelling him forward, the water-filtered light dappling his muscles. He shook his head as he heard muffled sounds of children shrieking with laughter, splashing into the pool. Their young voices echoed in his mind as he lifted his face from the sea. Some four feet away bobbed the oil drenched face of a man, unblinking and nodding. Kicking out Jack moved toward him, keeping his head above the water to avoid drifting back to the childhood pool. He made a last pull against the sea causing a small wave to splash the man, alerting him to Jack's nearing presence. The man had blood smeared down one cheek, and his glassy eyes darted about unfocussed, settling on Jack's face as he spoke. Jack hardly recognised his own croaking voice as he asked, "Are you hurt badly? Can you hear me?" Jack pulled the last stoke to him, and reached out grasping his shoulder. His wake caught up with them and swirled around in tiny eddies. The man shook his head dimly as his eyes left Jack's face to focus on something over his shoulder. Jack turned, as two thin men swam up behind, then another joined the band. The small group grabbed at a passing plank of wood, and the five moved close clinging to it. They each looked hollowed and terrified. In unspoken agreement they held on, gathering passing flotsam to cling to. Each man was silently grateful to not be singularly, completely alone on the swaying ocean. Jack looked round the group for a moment and realised he recognised all of them. He looked from man to man, each thinned face wore the same protruding cheekbones and prominent noses, scarred by malnutrition. Each hollowed eye apprehensive and filled with dread. Jack saw the deep creases that cut lines into each young brow and their weathered shoulders like polished horse-chestnuts. He knew these faces, he knew these fears. Each glassy eye carried a ghost within, the horrors each had witnessed. The two-year burden each had endured fused with their unfolding nightmare. The visions were written on each face as clearly as if drawn in Indian ink.

The sea was littered as far as the eye could see with shouting men and bobbing flotsam, cargo from their disappearing ship, dispersing and moving ever further apart. Jack heard shrieks in Japanese, Korean, Dutch and, English. Everywhere soldiers, crew and prisoners splashed wildly, screaming for help, hundreds of arms waved in desperation. Their escort ship, a minesweeper, seemed to sit in stunned apathy. Then, as if roused by the screams for help it moved forward, circling the debris field. The survivors quietened, believing rescue was imminent, but the minesweeper put on speed, powering away from the melee, to the wails of those left in the water. The shouting was interrupted by the splitting groans and final creaking of their stricken ship. Every face turned as it spluttered its remaining pockets of air as if expelling its last breath. There was no one on deck now as it broke apart. Splitting completely across its core, unseen under the water it filled with seawater, fatally sucking it downward. The bow pulled upright, it stood at ninety degrees out of the sea, tall and terrifying as it showed the red-orange belly of the water line and its broken hull. The name etched at the bow stood out in the sun, bold and clear, すえず丸. The dying ship held its breath for a moment, vertical and hesitant. As if casting a last glance across the ocean. As if it knew its fate. The men watched horrified as it descended, bubbling and choking into the water. It was a little distance off but Jack was terrified it would suck his small group down. He motioned to the others to move away and they kicked out, but they were overcome with exhaustion and made little headway. He had known the ship would sink but even so, he watched transfixed in horror and disbelief as it disappeared beneath the hypnotic motion of the sea with a final gurgle. The bowsprit slipped beneath and the ship was swallowed without a further moment's drama. It disappeared, the sea was utterly indifferent. Jack almost expected to hear a plop, but there was no noise once it was gone. Aside from flotsam littering the sea and the men bobbing amongst it, you would not know the huge ship was ever there. The gathered men watched the receding ripples return to amalgamous ocean, and shared a breathless moment of calm and hushed bewilderment.

Jack turned to the group of bobbing men. The first man he'd swum to still bled from an open cut to his temple. Distractedly Jack observed the thin blood as it meandered a path from gash, around his hollowed temple, over his cheekbone and down his lined face, navigating the bristles of a stubby beard to his jaw. There, the blood mixed with beads of sweat and salty droplets from his wet hair. The weak solution hung for a moment at his jawline, then trickled drop by drop into the sea and were lost. The man noticed Jacks gaze and touched his temple, looking hesitantly to his fingers at the watery blood sliding down to his palm. He spoke quietly, "I'm all right, I-I think," before drifting off. Clearly, he was not. The men gently cajoled and he nodded agreement as they dressed his wound as best they could, using strips easily torn from shredded clothes. Pressing down with the small bundle of rags they held it in place, as they wound a strip round the back of his head, then to the front, tying a small knot at the side. It was a lopsided arrangement, loosely covering one ear with the dirty shreds of material. But he was grateful as he silently submitted to the care, his eyes closed, teeth clenched and resolute. He thanked them quietly, acknowledged in return with nods and kind murmurs. Immediate first aid completed, they looked again to each other and considered the situation. It was clearly worsening. They held tightly on to the loose planks, kicking intermittently as the waves rolled around them, ebbing and flowing. Across the surface of the sea hundreds floated. Some clung to ropes tied to life-rafts, some hung onto half submerged life-planks. Stretching for miles, their heads bobbed on the surface like frightened apples. Many floated silently, and from a distance it was impossible to tell who was still alive. Everything was bumped by spewed loose flotsam of the ship's cargo, nets, crates and a multitude of indistinguishable debris, floating across the surface of the sea. Everything heavy had sunk deep into the ocean. As the swell raised their bodies they surveyed the scene. The debris was spreading across a huge area, and everything, everything was lapped by the blossoming oil slick.

Their escort ship, the minesweeper, returned and circled the debris field, leaving a rolling wave that made the flotsam bob frenetically. Everyone watched expectantly as it slowed, then suddenly put on speed and moved away. The men gasped, unable to do anything but watch its receding smoke. With their ship sunk, and their escort minesweeper gone, time trickled on and on. Jack's small group could do nothing but grip the planks and listen to the creak of ropes, tied at one end. There was nothing but jostling debris and terrified men, alone in the sloshing roll of waves and beating sun. More than an hour had slowly passed since their ship had sunk, yet no ship came to their rescue, and the minesweeper had not returned. To Jack it felt like days. He felt vulnerable and stared hard at the sea. He couldn't shake the gaping awareness of the vast water all around him. He felt acutely exposed as he sensed his cold feet kicking occasionally and numbly beneath him, floating in nothing but the endless blue chasm. The unknown depths terrified him and his stomach contracted. He wanted to hold onto something solid, he felt an urgent need to get to more solid wreckage. He felt a strong primal survival instinct to get out of the water. He was sickeningly and deeply afraid and began to shiver uncontrollably as panic washed over him like a wet suffocating cloth. Gasping breathlessly, choking, his lip twitched and his teeth chattered as his leg muscles tightened, cramping painfully then numbly. He felt as though he hadn't blinked for a long time. "Control yourself, calm down," he muttered to himself. Jack leant backwards slightly, touching the water with the back of his head, wetting his sodden hair as he tried to regain himself. He became absorbed by the rhythmic motion of the waves interspersed with shouts in different languages. The English and Dutch voices softer, more familiar and somewhat comforting as they called to each other. The Korean and Japanese voices barking, and angry. He supposed it was because that was all he'd had ever heard from them. The shouting, in every language, that had been at first frantic was now quieter. Here and there came sorrowful whimpers of the dying. He looked around at the men dispersed in mayhem, desperately clinging on and trying to remain buoyant. They seemed to drift further away and as his group topped a wave Jack could see the debris now stretched over a huge area, and was clearly dispersing. Some objects were so distant it was hard to make out what was floating junk, wreckage from the ship and which were men. It was an impossibly terrifying sight. Jack looked back to his little group, trying to push aside his fears. He felt gripped by inaction and decided he must do something. "We should gather together. Does everyone agree?" he called out loud, trying to keep his voice sounding strong and calm. In the absence of any other plan they decided to swim to the nearest group. Struggling from one piece of wreckage to another, they gathered men who held on to their loose raft as they went. Fighting the heavy swell they began to form a larger group. Each new man was as glassy eyed, each face equally filled with dread, their clavicles arched out of the water, bony as the next. The injured were tended to using what could be found floating in the debris. Cut and wounds were bound, and splints were fixed on broken bones with bits of rope, string and drifting wood.

A few feet away a circle of perhaps ten men floated. One of Jack's group called out and they waved back. Both groups began to kick out, splashing towards each other. As they moved they pushed debris away from their paths. There were so many planks of wood, the smallest of which were discarded, but the larger pieces were gathered up to build a bigger makeshift raft for the injured. In amongst the floating mess were men, dead and floating in the open blue. There was nothing to do for them, they gently pushed them aside. They were obliged to focus on their own survival. As the two groups neared each other, two dead Japanese were noticed in between. They were easy to recognise. They were not emaciated and ragged, they were clothed, fattened and looked healthy despite being dead. Conversely the prisoners looked almost dead despite being alive. As Jack began to move one away, pushing him gently aside by the shoulder, the body turned angrily. Jack started. The Japanese solider had only been resting on planking next to a dead Japanese comrade and Jack hadn't noticed his quiet breathing. His rounded face contorted as he tried to grab at a startled Jack. Suddenly, Jack recognised him from the PoW camp on the island, the *bastard*. He looked quickly to the other men, their eyes in silent agreement as they in turn looked around, scanning the area. There were no other Japanese here, no one would see. Quickly the fat soldier was shoved ahead with all the strength of rising indignation. As Jack's group joined the other men they gathered on the merciless soldier as he inhaled deeply to shriek. Someone quickly hit him hard with a small plank. The blow to the side of his head made his eyes wobble, and he quietened. Looking around furtively and huddling close to him so no one could see, they pushed his head beneath the water. They gathered round, stuffing his mouth with ragged sleeve as he went down. He wriggled mutely as they held him tight. One man would not have had the strength, but there were about twenty men now in the rapidly growing group. They had keen hold of him, the splashing of gathering hid the act in the commotion. He kicked lamely once, then twice more and stopped struggling. They pushed his body down with hands until he sank lower, then pushed down with feet on his shoulders. He slid away, and they watched him go, slipping into darkness, open mouthed and empty eyes. His fat hands outstretched, gripping nothing, unable to cause more suffering. As he disappeared, merging into the darkness of the deep sea, the men joined together spitting after him, "Bastard." The now expanded group quickly shrugged off the moment. It was not revenge but retribution, for the endless suffering and deaths he personally had caused so many of their brothers.

The new larger group looked around at each other, nodding as each recognised another, grimacing in shared acknowledgement of the dire situation. Jack knew most of them. Those he didn't were the RAF men brought from another island. The only difference was that those with clothing left, wore remains of blue coloured rags to Jack's green. They all wore the same hollow eyes, telling the same story they all knew. Two were injured but grimly said they were all right. The group knitted, arms around each other giving the false sense of security of better safety in bigger numbers. They formed a large circle, gripping tightly and bobbing to and fro in the rolling swell. And then they waited.

The day drifted on, and the hours floated by in a staring, salt-burned, rocking of the sea, punctuated by occasionally moving a painful limb or adjusting a grip on a rope or plank. Jack felt utterly parched, alternately drowsy and wildly frightened. Over the endless hours several groups floating here and there merged into larger circles as the men tried to rescue and help each other. Each time the group expanded the men shouted for a commanding officer, knowing there were few of them, and fewer commands they could give. No higher ranking PoWs were found for some time, but the men knew their orders were to 'stay alive' and 'help each other'. These had been their orders since February '42. Larger groups drifted together as they gradually realised there were many survivors, many more than at first seemed. They floated in tens, twenties, forties and more to a group, gathering together in larger and larger numbers. "There must be hundreds of us," someone said as they surveyed the scene. The littered surface now covered a greater expanse of sea, spreading across perhaps two miles. Jack could see the outline of bodies on life-rafts, masses of wet persons on life-planks, clinging to ropes attached to two lifeboats in the distance, and another lifeboat a little nearer. In amongst, individuals still bobbed between the spewed contents of their sunken ship. Jack's group continued to grow, until they were a band of about fifty and finally a CO joined them. Conversation quickly spread round the circle as to what could be done. The CO hushed the group calmly, calling out for them to gather closer together. The men quietened to listen but the silence was abruptly broken by the chugging return of the minesweeper. Someone near to Jack said it must have given chase to the submarine that had torpedoed their ship. "Probably dropped depth charges, maybe sunk it," said one. "Must have seen it off. It'll have been one of *ours*, of course," another said. The thought suddenly absorbed Jack, that somewhere, not far from him was an *Allied* vessel. People from his *own* familiar civilisation. Out there, perhaps under his feet, slid a sleek cocoon of rescue. The idea filled him with emotion, and his throat tightened. Scanning the sea he imagined the dark shape moving through the water carrying a slice of home, a submerged bubble of safety lurking in the deep. His excitement vanished as he immediately realised he was unable to reach it. With sinking sadness he spoke to himself, "Its sanctuary might as well be on the moon."

Jack and the men watched the minesweeper circle slowly around the debris field and collectively their shoulders relaxed a fraction. He looked gratefully to each near tearful man, as they realised they were finally, thankfully, about to be rescued. It had been at least five hours and they were exhausted. As the minesweeper chugged nearer the men paddled and swam toward it, but it began to move away. The men shouted, but the crew on deck ignored them. They were busy pointing, looking through binoculars for something, or someone. The Japanese crew saw the bobbing lifeboats populated with Japanese soldiers and pointed, chattering excitedly as they moved off toward them. The men shouted out in alarm but the minesweeper moved quickly away, and to the nearest lifeboat. A panic seemed to break out in the overfilled lifeboat as the minesweeper approached rapidly on an intersecting course. The tiny boat became overshadowed by the hulk of the minesweeper. The crew hanging onto ropes around the boat quickly let go as it met the hull of the ship with a splintering crack, sending the occupants overboard with loud squeals. It was difficult to see what had happened from Jack's low position in the water, but he made out wet bodies climbing up onto the upturned hull of the lifeboat as the minesweeper stopped in its own frothy wake. The PoWs watched anxiously as rigging was thrown down the minesweepers flank. Rescuers clambered down, hanging on with hooked elbow and bended leg. Hands outstretched, the rescuers leaned down to hands reaching out from the water. They clasped wrists tightly as they were pulled to safety, their wet clothes sagging heavily as each was lifted. Jack squinted. "Wait a minute!" called one of the men. Suddenly the PoWs clearly saw these were not *their* men being rescued, these were not fellow PoWs. These were all soldiers wearing Imperial Japanese Army uniforms.

The PoWs and Japanese survivors had all been floating alone in the sea for five or six long hours, but the PoWs were already ill, malnourished and weakened by their treatment in captivity. And still, the minesweeper continued, slowing here and there, plucking only Japanese from the swell. As they watched their enemies being pulled from the water, the PoWs looked to each other, mouths open in question, confusion grappling with fear. "Perhaps, they are just rescuing their own first?" suggested Jack drowsily. "Seems about right, they'll be loath to rescue us, they'll make us wait." Each time the minesweeper neared the men reached out, waving frantically, hoping hands would pull them from the water, terrified they would be left. Each time, it passed them by. Then, the men huddled together again and continued to wait. A few PoWs were so close to the Japanese soldiers they were able to grab on and cling to the rigging, trying to climb to safety. Jack watched as they were violently pushed down, shoved with boots, fists and rifle butts. The thin men fell back, splashing into the water with frightened shouts. "They are just rescuing their own first," Jack muttered again to himself, shaking his head. He didn't believe his own words. The PoWs steeled themselves for a long wait for their turn to be rescued. Each time the minesweeper neared they futilely shouted out. Each time the engines powered up, churning the sea into froth as it moved away, again and again, ignoring their wretched screams for help. Jack watched the minesweeper moving from group to group, as time slipped by and the men waited on and on.

The rescue of Japanese went on for hours, as the day beat on relentlessly. The sun arched higher then began to descend as the men became ever more desperate, their mouths and bodies ached thirstily. In the flotsam they looked for anything to salvage, to make any use of. A small tin can had floated past but they had no way to open it. All Jack could do was shake it, holding it against his ear as its contents sloshed tantalisingly without yielding. Someone held onto it as they called to others for help. Jack became so tired, so numbly cold he didn't think he could stay awake any longer. He felt all was lost and he could not go on, his lips cracked painfully against his bristling and swelling tongue as it stuck dryly to the roof of his mouth. Then, from nowhere a banana and a cocoanut floated into his view at the same time, some lost cargo from the disappeared ship. The floating treasure was quickly grabbed, the banana disappearing amongst those worse off. Jack was grateful to be given a morsel. As someone pasted a soft chunk onto his lips he thought, 'God it tastes like nectar.' His mouth burst into bloom as he pressed the small lump of delicious mush with his tongue. It passed through his mind that he must have looked like one of those most sick, to be given it. Thankfully the cocoanut's outer skin was damaged, so someone was able to pull the thick green skin and fibrous husk from it, laboriously screwing holes into two of its three dark circles with a small bent nail released from a floating plank. Jack was given a dribble of cocoanut water and again his mouth and body responded gratefully. He felt the tiny drips of liquid coursing down into his shrunken stomach, igniting his body with a tiny burst of energy. He opened his eyes, thanking the blurred face in front of him. Others weren't so lucky. Even after all they had endured before, and survived that day, some could not be helped and had quietly slipped away. The man Jack had first found, whose head had been dressed so carefully, passed away early on in the day. It must have been worse than it looked, or more likely *he* was worse than he looked, and the injury took his last reserves. He bore it quietly, but had lost too much blood, it soaked through the rags he'd been patched up with and there was nothing anyone could do. The men closest by watched him, and listened as he spoke softly of home, of his family, his wife and his young son. Then he spoke no more. They held his hand a moment longer then let him go. The PoWs were sadly too accustomed to the injustice of surviving one unimaginable horror only to be taken by something seemingly insignificant and pointless. They observed again the unjust decisions of death, and spoke the man's name aloud as they always did, and let him float away and down. As they watched him go their spirits sank lower, their despondency palpable in the salty air.

Jack felt he must keep busy if he were to avoid that fate, and as if he caught the thought, their CO suddenly called the men, to gather together. The CO spoke firmly, "We are not being rescued just yet. The Japanese are taking Japanese first." He roused the men, "Come on, did you think they would help us first? Put us in the captain's bunk?" A few managed a mirthless grin, as he continued. He asked, "Each man to work as best you can, to gather all survivors together." He said, "No man is to be left alone," and that, "all wreckage must be checked for anything useful or edible, and we must make rafts, so 'buddy up,' and keep watch on each other." The words had a great effect and the men felt spurred into action by the new tasks. Having something to work to and the effects of the small morsels brought Jack a little energy where he thought he had none in reserve. They set to work, taking more than an hour to comb all the flotsam they could reach. All the while the minesweeper continued, moving in circles, gathering their own and pushing PoWs back. Over the endless hours of the faltering day a dozen life-rafts were salvaged as they were vacated by departing rescued Japanese. The men gathered the worst-off, lying them out as best they could onto the rafts. Others were helped onto discarded drifting life-planks which were smaller and left their legs dangling in the water. There simply wasn't room or enough rafts to hold everyone. The CO ordered they share the use of the best life-raft, taking turns getting out of the water for a short time. He ordered a rotation so each man could briefly rest. Over the waning afternoon, the two remaining intact lifeboats and a few more life-rafts were emptied by the rescued Japanese and eventually all the PoWs had gathered from the widely spread shambles, into a single meandering group. They formed into a long line of floating men, lifeboats, life-rafts, patched together rafts and assorted flotsam. In all, a straggling line of about two hundred and fifty men, perhaps more.

Gathering together, searching the wreckage and making life-rafts had occupied Jack wholly, giving him short bursts of adrenaline-fuelled energy. As the tasks concluded and the men quietened to wait, his energy quickly waned. He was utterly spent, witheringly dehydrated. He could feel himself slipping into delirious beckoning sleep. He floated, head resting on his arms on the edge of a life-plank as the sea lapped him, lolling his heavy head. He felt like a child being rocked back and forth, into a lullaby-inducing sleep. Again and again he closed his eyes only to be washed over with cold saltwater, choking and stinging his eyes, rousing him again. He again sensed the dark gaping void of ocean beneath him and began to feel pulled towards it. Someone noticed Jack fading, and pulled at his shoulder, lifting his head. A voice called out, shouting he "had a man here who needs to get out of the water." "Who said that?" Jack wondered, not understanding they had meant him. He found himself being pulled aboard a lifeboat by other PoWs. Once his body was over the side, they released him and fell back to their sitting perches with a succession of thumps. Jack looked around and realised he was sitting in the prow of a lifeboat. Leaning forward to retch, head in his hands he watched the water drain from him, pooling in the shallow murky sea sloshing inside the boat. It felt good to be out of the water but he quickly began shivering with hypothermia. He was severely dehydrated, having lain by now, some six hours in the cold oily salt bath, it had sucked away moisture and wicked warmth from him. He slumped backwards and felt the sun pressing heavily on his brow. Sweat formed and sat damp and clammy at his hairline. He didn't have enough moisture to bead or trickle. Achingly, his body dried in the descending sun, his skin cracking in the light breeze as his shuddering slowed. The fear of helplessly bobbing in the sea receded and he felt a little calmer, replaced as it was by a new gnawing weight in the pit of his stomach. The men continued to watch nervously, hopeful of eventual rescue. Jack realised there was nothing to do but close his eyes and join the others in endless collective waiting. His eyelids slid over his pupils, cleaving the world horizontally in two, framed only by the dark shadows of his eyelashes as they brushed closed, shutting out the last of the terrible panorama. It left him a pale yellow glow, edged with red as light permeated his thin-skinned lids. He heard chattering and twittering, the song of garden birds, and the fragrance of summer flowers floated to his senses. He tilted his head a fraction toward the light as he embraced the imaginary respite to elsewhere. He let go, allowing himself to fold into it completely.

The torpedo attack and subsequent struggle in the sea was 29 November 1943. Jack knew that for everyone else in the world it was simply one of many dark days in the never-ending depths of a second world war that had raged for over four years. Millions like them scattered across the globe fighting to survive one horror, and then another, until it was finished. His torpedoed ship sank in less than twenty minutes, taking perhaps three hundred of his friends and brothers-in-arms to the ocean depths. Some two hundred and fifty prisoners of war survived and floated, alone and terrified on the Flores Sea.

Jack had turned twenty-three only two weeks earlier. He had left his home almost exactly two years previously, to play his part in the war that consumed the earth. He'd barely had the chance to fight as he became a prisoner of war along with thousands of others. By the time his ship sank, he had been in Japanese hands for one year, eight months and twenty-one days. Throughout his captivity, during each and every one of those long, terrible days Jack Frith wanted to write letters home, to Spring Street.

CHAPTER TWO

13 Spring Street

The broad back of Spring Street arched like a bowed old man with houses stacked all along his tired cobbled spine. Jack listened to his work boots crack clacking as he trudged up from Lewis Street, watching the sun set into puddles of oily Manchester rain. The view, if he had stopped to look, ebbed and flowed up and down the hills of Manchester's working-class towns-within-a-city, rows and rows of back-to-backs groaning on the vine. When he closed his eyes he was there in an instant, like slipping into a well-worn coat. Warm and familiar the shape enfolded his outline and he was home. The smoky hearth enveloped him in sooty warmth as the family gathered, his mother cooked hot dinners that were simple yet filling, and as always a fire crackled in the grate. The familiar collective smells soaked through him and warmed his soul. He often bathed gratefully in these comforts. He recreated the scent in his nostrils as clearly and precisely as imagining any family photograph. His house at 13 Spring Street was the very picture of home.

He knew all the families along his street, as children they had grown together. They'd known all the same games, played out together and run amok at all the same places. Later he had watched as they'd marched away from him and signed up for the war. Rubble heaps of bricks and broken windows where old houses were only half knocked down made for hazardous yet convincing castles, defended with courage and stern-chinned bravery to the last. Lacking money, imagination had to do. The reservoir, a bicycle ride away, was perfect for cooling, if dangerous, skinny dips on hot summer days. Jack remembered the dark, still depths had terrified him. He had not dipped his head under since he'd been dared some summers ago to dive in 'open-eyed.' "Scaredy cat, scaredy cat! You can't do it!" the other children had sing-songed, while sitting safely in the grass. His best friend, Harry had caught his arm, "You don't have to do it you know." Jack had shrugged, "Can't back down now, kid!" Jack leapt confidently from rocks, laughing with a courage he hadn't felt, arching through the air and splashing headlong into the dark pool. But as he descended into the gloom he'd looked around and found it silent and unnerving. The water tasted mossy, and sinister shadows tinged with green loomed in the echoing darkness. It was breathless, quiet and still like a damp, dimly lit cave and it had frightened something inside him. He'd looked down at his pale feet in the darkness and gasped. 'Something's down there,' he thought, panicked. He spluttered, trying to surface, swimming frantically, clawing at the water as if chased by something monstrous from the depths. He'd leapt from the water panting, to the safety of the grassy verge. His friends had stood laughing as he, indignant and embarrassed, sat down with a thump and began to dry himself angrily with his thin towel. Harry approached him, "Are you all right, kid?" As soon as Jack pulled the towel from his wet hair and stood up in the warm grass he grinned at Harry, and laughed. He felt foolish for being spooked. But as they'd cycled away hooting and shouting on to their next adventure, Jack had looked back nervously at the menacing black water. He never forgot the still darkness. A fear of the depths had gripped him.

Jack's childhood was not often foolish antics and childish games. His family, like everyone else's on his street, found money was scarce. As the 1920s had rolled into the 30s life seemed hardly changed, nor much improved from his grandparents deprived generation of the 1880s. The family was as poor as the house was sparse, filled largely with heirlooms and hand me downs. Number 13, Spring Street was small, even by small terraced house standards. A downstairs sitting room straight off the road with only a turn of the steep staircase shielding passers-by a view all the way through to the back gate. The room was mostly a thoroughfare, the straight backed two-seater chair used only to welcome visitors as they sipped cups of tea. A tall hatstand and mirror heavy with coats, stood by the door and the fat armchair facing the fireplace was his father's favourite spot to squint at headlines and pictures in his newspaper. An open doorway at the far end of the sitting room led to a smaller room, the dining room which adjoined a compact galley kitchen tucked into an outhouse-sized annexe. The heavy, painted back door, always somewhat ajar, led from the kitchen out to a paved yard crisscrossed with hanging washing lines, a tin bath and two mismatched old bicycles. These home-built, salvaged bikes had been painted and repainted, so the many scratches and chips resembled rainbows of their previous colours, their previous lives and owners. In the corner of the yard a weathered pot held a tired strawberry plant, which struggled bravely to make blossom, while a tall wood container held heavy soil and small potatoes, harvested from a hatch at the bottom. Three wooden doors in a narrow brick outhouse led first to the outside, and only wc. Second along was a compact store shed filled with lengths of wood, near empty paint tins and dusty cobwebs, and at the end of the row a smaller painted door concealed the coal shed. The contents blackening the walls and filling the space with sparkling dust. Back through the house the dining room was snug, filled by a drop-leg dining table, surrounded by dark wooden chairs, their knees huddled under a brightly coloured tablecloth, which hung in a tasselled vee at either end. Standing heavily against the far wall was the heirloom sideboard, with fat rounded feet. Covered with photographs, each frame stood on a crocheted doily, tucked behind each were an assortments of letters and papers jutting out at all angles. A bowl of bits and bobs occupied the far end. On the opposite wall a tiled fireplace stood guard over the room, it seemed to sit cross-legged with broad arms and hunched shoulders, watching the occupants of the room go about their daily activities. Its brown glazed and cream tiles clashed with the tufted green and black hearthrug butting up against it, but neither seemed to mind. The mantlepiece was scattered with more letters, tattered photographs, an empty pipe in a tray and squatting in the centre, a black napoleon-hat clock. It ticked quietly to itself, tinging the half and quarter hours religiously. At the far end of the mantle sat a framed picture of Jack's parents, smiling broadly on their wedding day, in tones of grey. Jack's mother, Florrie, smiling shyly in a neat dress, short coat and flowered hat, standing slightly behind her new husband, her small hand in the crook of his arm. His father, John Robert, stood, chest puffed out, chin jutting, filled with pride. Florrie was busy every moment of each day, she took in washing and ironing, sewing and odd jobs to make ends nearly meet, somehow finding time between cooking for the hungry family, cleaning everything to sparkling shine and keeping all in repaired shirts and mended jumpers. She was the heart of their family in every way. His father, whom they called dad, now worked for *Imperial Chemical Industries*, in the *Rexine* Division, the leathercloth works that filled the skies above the town with thick industrial smoke. Despite his being partially blind since Passchendaele, due to the 'Hun stuff' he had risen from labourer to dyer and recently to the position of foreman. *Rexine* was a man-made fabric they called leathercloth. A cheap substitute for leather, it was used as a covering material for furniture, motorcar seats, bags and trunks and for bookbinding. John had worked for years in its noxious manufacture, mixing the powdered pigments with synthetic oils to colour the cellulose nitrate coating. This was mixed with polyvinyl chloride and the goop applied in several layers to cloth, each being stretched and dried out before the next application. Embossing was done with heavy engraved steel rollers, usually to imitate the grain of leather, but sometimes with wild abstract patterns. Jack's father considered the chemical work unpleasant and hard graft, but he was paid as well as a sighted man, and was promoted more than he'd expected given his impairment. Despite coming home stinking to high heaven and tired out, it filled him with a warm, manly sense of providing for his family, as he kept his wife and their three children clothed, housed and well fed.

Each of their three children had been welcome additions, although Jack was a 'bit of a surprise' as his father, John had put it. John Frith had married his childhood sweetheart, Florrie, in 1912, they'd welcomed daughter Gladys on Valentine's Day, 1914. The happy occasion occurred in the shadow of looming war, the anticipatory bubble of which burst in August. At twenty-five years old, John signed up as Florrie knew he would. He was ready to help the war effort, and anyway it would all be over soon it was said. It'd be a short war. A war to end all wars. John had felt encouraged by that and wanted to take part for his family, and for his King and for his Country. The reality, he discovered, was quite different. As he sat entrenched on the Western Front in freezing mud early the next January he pondered deeply but privately, his swift decision and whether he would see his wife and young child again. In the midst of the war, their middle child George, arrived in 1916, conceived after John had been invalided home. He had been a casualty of an early gas attack, a terrifying new German tactic. The chlorine temporarily took his sight but John soon recovered and returned to the front line dodging bullets and bombs for two more years before being sent home on permanent convalescence in 1917. This time he had narrowly survived a mustard gas attack at the battle at Ypres which left his left eye swollen, cloudy and glazed for the rest of his life and the right constantly winking in the twilight of blurred peripheral vision. He was grateful to not have to return to that awful place and readily understood that although it had taken some of his useful sight his life had been spared, whilst those around him had perished.

John Robert chose to shoulder his condition stoically, never complaining about his situation or the difficulties and frustrations it caused him. Then, the last of the three siblings, the 'surprise' as John had said, and 'gift' as Florrie called him, baby Jack arrived with a gurgle on 15 November 1920, all giggles and fluffy hair. As children the three had their own circles of friends, in part due to the age gaps between them, but once at home they formed a strong pack and were the best and kindest of friends. Jack attended Green Street School and was known as a bit of a scrapper, despite hardly ever getting into fights in his later years there. He was somewhat short for his age and when he first started school he'd been pushed about a few times. It didn't *seem* too serious, a bump here, a nudge there. His books would fall to the ground or he would be pushed into someone else, causing his embarrassed apologies. He was shoved in the dinner queue one lunchtime causing his gravy to slop over his plate, splashing onto the chequered tile of the dining room. He was scolded for it by teachers uninterested in his brief protestations of innocence. Jack had been incensed, causing the roots to take of a deep dislike and simmering distrust of those in authority who abused their power. Then, as bullies are prone to do, they pushed Jack a little more. He had been on his way home as they'd pulled his satchel from his shoulders, throwing it into a puddle. Jack silently bent to pick it up and received a boot to his rear, landing him in the gritty rainwater grazing his knees and palms. He cried indignantly. Just once he cried. He ran home, breathlessly afraid of being chased. When his mother looked at his hands and saw his bloodied knees her face flushed with rage. She swept him up to her and held him close, tears escaping her angry eyes as she closed her arms around him. She was not angry with him of course, she was furious someone would push her boy, her baby boy.

He was asleep, tucked warmly in bed when his father came home. Jack woke on hearing the low rumble of voices downstairs. He crept to the top of the stairs to listen. They sounded angry and Jack worried he would get in trouble. In the morning his father beckoned him with crooked finger. Jack followed him into the sitting room and as he dropped into his stuffed armchair his father spoke. He wagged a finger, "Son, there is nothing much worse than a bully. They never pick on someone bigger, never someone stronger. It's because they themselves are cowards. You mustn't let them push you, son. You must push *back*. You give one of them a smack on the nose, just the once and they won't bother you again. Yes, you might get a smack in return, but it will only be one. And one bloody nose will be worth it. They'll leave you be. Do you understand me?" He smiled, placing his hand on his son's shoulder and squeezing gently. Jack nodded dully, feeling the end of his nose gingerly and worrying less about his own nose than the idea of bopping someone else's. The next week, two bigger boys slyly followed him as he ran to fetch a kicked football, booted to the back of the playground near the dustbin sheds and bicycle racks, out of sight of disinterested teachers. They'd shoved Jacks shoulder, looking down at him menacingly as they demanded he hand over his pennies. Jack's blood rose unconsciously. Unbidden his bicep bulged and his knuckles tightened. He watched in surprise as his fist moved back then swung through the air toward the bigger boy. Jack looked on as his small knuckles connected with the boy's nose with a horrible squelch. The boy went over and smacked onto the ground, his nose a red welt. The other boy startled and retreated as Jack, equally as surprised, stood over his foe. The boy on the ground scrabbled to gather himself, crawling to his feet. Jack was stunned, but defiant as the other kids gathered and looked on in surprise. He beamed, his father had been right, and he knew no one *would* bother him again.

Jack was a little annoyed later to get into trouble for the punch, from the teachers. It earned him a crack on the palm with a wooden ruler, detention and lines repeated endlessly in chalk across the vast blackboard, until the light dimmed outside the window. Nevertheless, the pride in himself could not be extinguished. Despite his new found authority in the playground, Jack never bullied nor pushed anyone. He did not let it go to his head, he knew all too well what it felt like, but he grew to dislike authority of any kind. He keenly felt the injustice of the fickle teachers. They chose their favourites and he sensed their adult pettiness even as a child. He soon felt caged and restricted at school, and despite not enjoying lessons he loved the outdoor games, especially football. He was scrappy on the field, running and tackling fearlessly as if each Schools Knockout match was the FA Cup. Mud-smudged and mucky-kneed, Jack happily sat cross-legged on the front row showing his toothy grin as the local paper photographed his team. They'd made the final and had beaten their rivals at Flowery Fields School, winning the 1933 Schoolboys' Shield.

Jack had looked wistfully to the ever-nearing end of his schooldays, he smelled the chance for freedom, and how he longed for it. To do as he chose and go wherever he wanted. He had lost himself in the idea of it before realising with a shudder he would actually have to find a job and work the moment he left school. He felt suddenly caged by his future self. And as children will do, the three siblings grew up and away. First, George started at the *ICI Rexine* works with their father and Jack dreaded the idea of joining them. Then, the family of five became four as their sister Gladys married and moved to her own family home. It was the September Jack left school, and just over a year later their sister had a daughter, Carole. Jack was delighted by the little bundle and played with her whenever he could. He thought she was the most wonderful thing he'd ever seen. He sang to her and twirled her around as she grew, to Gladys' laughing shouts to stop.

As a man, as he had been as a boy, Jack was short at five foot four, but he was strong and wiry. He left school behind and was fit from working a dozen jobs and odd ends of money-making schemes. He had worked hard, pulling sacks of coal onto carts, heaving crates, rolling barrels, hefting timber and anything he could, carrying anything for money. He ran along the canal towpath, calling out for odd jobs to passing barges and he cycled for miles to the smallest of jobs. And he swam. Long easy strokes up and down the cool clear municipal baths. It was an escape, a slice of the freedom he longed for. His father had tried to coax him into a job at the *ICI Rexine* works, but Jack still did not like the idea of it. He saw himself as a young man with his whole life stretching ahead of him and despite his somewhat poor prospects and modest education, he wanted *something* more. He admired his father and brother for their care and provision for the family, but he did not want to become an anonymous man in a long line of sons shuffling along in their father's footsteps, emerging from the factory gates day after day as the sky darkened, until one day he would appear at the gates an old grey man, retiring to his grave. He talked to George about his worries, "It's not that I'm not grateful for the chance of a proper job, I just don't want to be tied to it. Not yet. I want to do something more." He'd argued. "What *do* you want to do?" George had asked, intrigued. "Well, I want to see the world." George laughed, stopped and apologised in the same breath, protesting, "No, sorry, I understand, Jack." Jack ignored the chuckle, "What if I joined the navy, or the army? I saw an advertisement hoarding today, it said 'see the world', underneath it said, 'and get paid for doing it'." A light seemed to blink on in George's eyes, causing Jack to stop to ask, "What?" George blushed, "Nothing, nothing. Anyway you're too young, you have to get some muscle on your skinny self first!" Jack fake fainted, falling backwards dramatically. George laughed, offering a hand to help him up. They laughed as they made their way home in the dimming light. It was only a matter of weeks later when George spoke to Jack, telling him of his decision to join up. "You were right. It *is* a proper job. I'm sorry Jack. I've signed up. I leave in a week," Jack watched his brother, open-mouthed, as he continued. "I'll have leave and I'll be seeing you. But, like you said, it's a chance see the world. And, it's a *proper* job."

Jack nodded dully, closing his mouth, "Aye, you said that." Jack felt his own chance of escape slipping away. And the family of four became three. Jack had shaken his elder brothers hand and now stood at the door waving glumly to George as he left to begin his barrage balloon training at RAF Cardington.

1938 drifted to its end and 1939 rolled over on the calendar, and the year seemed to speed by. As Jack neared his nineteenth birthday he became reflective. He felt his eighteen and three-quarter years had been a blur, as if the months and years had been speeding up, faster and faster until the spinning calendar came to a shuddering halt one dark, rainy September day in 1939. It had been suspected of course, rumours of impending shadows haunted the country, but now it had arrived. Jack huddled with his parents, leaning toward the crackling radio, listening as a *new* war was declared. "But it couldn't happen again..." His father had slapped his paper onto the hearth, rising from his chair to lean heavily over the fireplace as the solemn monotonous toned words echoed around the stunned sitting room, "...I have to tell you now, that no such undertaking has been received and consequently, this country is at war with Germany." The crackling of the radio faded in his ears as Jack saw the potential of his life gutter and blow out, leaving his hopes smouldering with the realisation instead of future hardship. The family again gathered to listen as the King called upon, "...Ah... my people at home and my peoples across the seas... to stand calm, firm and united in this time of trial." They exchanged deeply concerned glances as the King warned, "Ah... the task will be hard. There may be dark days ahead and war can no longer be confined to the battlefield..." His mother held the two men close, her husband and her youngest son as she wept for a moment then turned, bustling away to the kitchen.

Jack expected sudden and great changes, but nothing seemed to happen except that the news weighed heavily on his father. His eyes saddened and his brow was troubled. He began for the first time to speak of *his* war, the Great War, the War to End all Wars. He had not spoken of it previously. Now, his abstract half-stories filled the house with shelling and dark skies, lightning flashes of exploding bombs, fountains of mud raining down, row upon row of men walking, tin-helmeted, rifles in hand, rearing wild-eyed horses, miles of mud-seas stretching in every direction, the choking yellow gas rolling over barren wasteland, and the sodden infested trenches which offered precious little sanctuary from any of it. Initially, the effect of these stories had made Jack strangely, and somewhat unexpectedly interested in the prospect of adventures overseas, but as he listened more closely, and his father's stories darkened, he became disturbed by his father's retelling of the rising ominous shadow of war, the dreadful waste and the sickening pointlessness of it. His father withdrew further and his face aged visibly. The declaration of war changed him as it had changed everyone. The faces of people on the street changed, all talk was of what was happening, or *not* happening as was the case, and inevitably, worrisome talk turned to what might be to come. Jack felt the sad burden it placed on the little family in Spring Street as it weighed on families all over the country. He felt uncertain what to do but decided ultimately he must do his bit and would sign up straight away. Yet, he was anxious not to simply 'throw his life away in the first round, as cannon-fodder,' as his father called it. John had spoken gently with his youngest son, his eyes glistening, "Our sort go down first, we're expendable. Yes, we will defend the country, we *will* answer the call, but there has been no call. No, you must not go, son. *Not yet.*" Even as Jack listened, wide-eyed and promising with hidden crossed fingers not to sign up, he knew he would, and sooner rather than later. His mother wouldn't listen to a word of it as Jack had tried to persuade her, following her around the house and into the kitchen. She directed him back to his father knowing he would be equally adamant that Jack should wait. They had discussed it and agreed. "But, George enlisted a year ago, and he's all right," and "But, I'm nearly twenty!" Jack had protested, backing away from his mother's waving hand, and following his father out into the yard. His father had nodded, offering reasons and alternatives, "You know, you could join me at the factory, they are making munitions now. You'll be doing essential war work. If that isn't doing your bit..." he had trailed off. Jack frowned, "I want to be doing *actual* essential war work!" His father did not reply. He made his way back into the house, slowly lowered himself into his armchair and tapped out his pipe until it was empty. Jack waited for a reply but his father calmly filled his pipe, lit it and quietly blew little puffs of smoke across the room. He looked to Jack and slowly shook his head. There would be no further discussion, his answer had been given and Jack knew there was little point protesting further.

George in the meantime, had completed his training as Barrage Balloon Rigger at RAF Cardington earning the rank of Leading Aircraftman as war had been declared. He was quickly posted to Glasgow, attached to 'City of Glasgow, Balloon Squadron No.945' where he and his men worked steadily fixing the fat barrage balloons over the city's most important areas. They moved the *Fordson Sussex* anchoring trucks into strategic positions, hoisting great clouds of defensive balloons over the shipyards, railways and warehouses in staunch readiness for anticipated attack. The balloon crew of two corporals and ten men worked hard, with much to cram in to every day. Their day started with two hours of guard duty, then breakfast. Only then did they start their daily balloon routine. The corporal would check the operational orders to fly, alter height, close-haul or bed the balloons. Hauling down a balloon was very labour intensive, and the men preferred it when the daily orders did not include moving a balloon any great distance. Daily inspections of all the equipment was essential, as was balloon maintenance, repairing and topping up the gas. Maintenance tasks were shared as it took hours to clean, check and test everything. George had settled into the job and army life well, but the endless waiting for the war to actually start he found nauseating.

Christmas 1939 passed, his first of the war, away from the warmth of his family, and he was lonely and miserable in snowy Glasgow. His heart felt bleak as January 1940 rolled in, bone chillingly cold. The wind in blew off the Clyde, freezing Glasgow over in glassy iced sheets. George stood stamping his feet, watching his breath billow through his cupped hands one morning as they struggled to re-position an unruly balloon. The gear had iced up and the men poured warm water over the mechanism to free it. Suddenly, one of the young recruits lost his grip on the pulley handle and it span out of control, slipping and trapping his fingers in the ropes with a yelp. He would be all right, it didn't seem too bad an injury on inspection. George took him, nursing his swollen hand in a wrapped cloth and grimacing, to Bawhirley Hospital to be checked over. There, whilst sitting idly waiting in a corridor, twisting his folded cap in both hands, George noticed a young nurse passing by wearing a sparkling white apron and folded headdress. She carried a metal tray of bandages and assorted rattling implements. He must have been staring, because she turned to look back at him as the waft of her enclosed him, she smelled of soft soapy flowers. "Those are the bluest blue eyes I have ever seen," he muttered quietly to himself. He smiled weakly as she turned her gaze away and continued on her way. George gathered his courage and returned the next day to look for her, on the pretence of checking on the young recruit, but found the lad had already been discharged with only a bandaged hand. Scuffing his boots, George wondered how to meet the pretty young nurse with the kind eyes again when suddenly she was there, walking toward and past him. This time he quickly stood, shyly calling out. The voice he emitted was croakingly hoarse, only managing a strangled cough at first, but it was enough to make her stop. She turned and smiled. George blushed, looking up and down the hospital corridor nervously before blurting out an invitation to accompany him to a dance that Thursday. She replied in soft Scottish tones, "Aren't you going to ask my name first?" He laughed self-consciously, blushing a deeper red. He seemed stuck for words so she replied kindly, blinking softly, "It's Elizabeth, and yes, since it's my birthday on Thursday, I'll go to a dance with you." George seemed to start, suddenly gabbling, "You're pulling my leg, it's your birthday?" She looked puzzled, and he held up his hands, "No, no its fate! You see, it's mine today!" He smiled, his shyness overcome a little, but his cheeks still flushed. After agreeing they'd meet under the old clock on High Street at six o'clock, he watched her walk away. She turned a corner looking back briefly with a smile, then she disappeared. He turned on a heel and practically skipped down the hospital steps. He almost danced back to his balloon squadron.

For Jack, back at Spring Street, the first few months of 1940 dragged on miserably. He grew ever more restless and frustrated with himself. He was itching to join up but reluctantly carried on running odd jobs and watching as almost all the lads from his neighbourhood gathered and disappeared into the offices, signing their names at the bottom of the enlistment forms. He listened intently with his parents in late May, as reports of a stranded British Army at Dunkirk drifted daily through the radio. Each report becoming increasingly frightening. He followed the radio closely and news in early June of the evacuation of most of the soldiers left Jack as relieved as the rest of the country and increasingly disgruntled with himself and by extension, his family for not allowing him to be part of the war effort. They knew him too well. His father especially worried about his keenness, he knew they only held their youngest son by a thread. His father spoke softly and gently to remind him, "George is doing the family bit for now, son. You'll have your chance, but you're needed at home." He asked Jack to "wait till you are called up," to "wait until you are twenty-one." Jack quickly counted on his fingers, "That won't be 'til November 1941, the end of next year! It will all be over!" His father would sigh and Jack would look at his boots as his father would thank him for staying, "I'll be glad if you'll stay son. If you go we will only have my wage," and "I'm getting on, think of your mother," and so on until again Jack relented. After conceding Jack would settle down for a week or so. Then the cycle of discussion, frustration and eventual relenting would begin again.

In the summer heat of August 1940, Jack was up early helping with the local milk delivery, running errands and fetching parcels for his mother, he'd just returned as the postman stopped off with the usual three or four letters. Today, there was one addressed to Jack. He tore at the flap, discarding the others onto the dining table. His eyes scanned to the bottom of the familiar handwriting confirming it was from his brother, George. He waved the paper in the air, moving around the table and blurting excited stunted sentences to his parents as his mother tried to take it from him to read properly. "George is being posted to Belfast... he's been promoted to Corporal.... er... he's met a girl... Her name is Elizabeth, and she's a Fever Nurse. And–" Jack stopped suddenly, his face full of surprise, which quickly folded into a grin, "They're getting married," he announced. Jack looked to his mother briefly, then continued, "We're invited obviously, but it'll be a small wedding... in Greenock... they'll be reading the Banns soon." Finally his mother grasped the letter, re-reading it and dabbing at her eyes with the end of her apron. The news jolted Jack, and his thoughts turned from excitement for his brother to his own future. He often went out with his pals, sometimes a pint, sometimes for walks, to the cinema, maybe to the park. But after working all his odd-jobs, his family, and generally trying to keep out of mischief he hadn't had too much time for meeting many girls or being too serious with those he knew. He was approaching twenty years old but still felt like a child, perhaps because he was the baby of the family. It didn't help matters that his mother told him off rather often, clipping him round the ear for swearing or other misdemeanours. He shook himself, and decided to get on with it and ask a girl to a dance or perhaps the cinema. He'd liked a girl, Irene for a while. She only lived two streets away and he decided it was about time he asked her to go out with him. Sitting at the dinner table on Sunday teatime he broached the idea with his mother, who frowned as his father raised an eyebrow and peered across the table. Jack pointed with his fork, his mouth half full, "I'll tell you what, I swear that next time I see her I will walk right up to her, and well, I will just *damn* well ask her." His mother automatically shouted, "Jack! Language!" He reached forward for the salt, narrowly dodging her swipe and returned to spearing a potato, "I'll tell you what else, I think it *is* time I came to work with you dad." That stopped his parents mid-mouthful and they exchanged glances as Jack looked to his next potato, pressing peas against it with his knife. He had grown tired of running errands, that had made him feel childish too, like a newspaper boy. He had liked the freedom in the sense that he could cycle here and there, collecting threepence for delivering something or other, but he was ready and keen to take things more seriously. Dad chuckled over his pipe, "A steady job *and* a girl, ha-ha, yes, that will certainly make you serious!" Jack rolled his eyes and agreed to see his fathers foreman at *ICI Rexine* works. Except of course, they no longer made *Rexine*, they made munitions. His father cajoled him again hoping he'd completely emptied his mind of joining up. "This'll be doing your bit, won't it, kid?" Jack had rolled his eyes again, but as he saw the burden seemed to lift from his father, he nodded and smiled, "Yes, dad, it will."

In late September, Jack was called into the office of a stern-jawed manager, his father had ushered him in and waited outside. Jack sat nervously as the foreman told him about the job and asked him a few questions. It was a done deal. They shook hands as Jack was offered the job. The following week, Jack stood, his head turned slightly to the left to show his good side, a card pinned to his lapel as his was picture taken for his official work identification card. He watched as 1st October 1940 was stamped over his photograph, then signed his name neatly underneath. He peered at his small square portrait. He'd worn shirt and tie with a thick mother-knitted jumper under his jacket, and they'd given him a long black apron to wear over the top. He had combed his thick hair back but still it had tried to escape. He looked closely at the card pinned to his jacket, it bore the number '295'. He was not keen to be numbered, there was something about it he didn't like. He knew it wasn't a popular opinion, his family said *everyone* had to get in line, and number off. But still, Jack couldn't take to the idea that people should be boxed and allocated, like cattle or goods. Despite misgivings about being sucked into factory life he was not ungrateful for the job, he felt finally at the beginning of his adulthood. He worked hard, long days but, as he had dreaded it would, work soon echoed school with an eerie familiarity. He later felt it perhaps helped him survive, working hard at unpleasant jobs, under constant scrutiny, having to find clever ways to make ones own tiny freedoms and personal victories. He would reflect sadly on the easier life he'd felt so stifled by. Once his freedom was gone.

In his new working life at the factory, he would wake early, leaving before the rest of the house to cycle down Spring Street, bumping the cobbled turn onto Lewis Street, up onto Hoviley Street and out onto the main Talbot Road. He imagined this half hour as his own private moments of liberation. If he was especially early he could take his time, looping round the streets, weaving through the few trees at the edge of his path. These were his own slices of freedom, his own world to do as he chose. As soon as he punched in, it would begin, "stop talking," "carry that," and "bring this" and "go here" and "go there." He detested that part of the job, but refrained, almost always, from giving cheek. He found that a word or two thrown back to a superior in jest, or even sneaking a cigarette earned him docked wages and threats of sacking, instead of the lines and rapped knuckles of school. The humiliation was the same, and being constantly 'told' irked him endlessly. As the munitions work became increasingly mundane, he found he spent his time lost in thought. He wondered about each cartridge as he loaded them into boxes, imagining where each might end up. He was often to be found gazing out of the window, needing to be nudged back to the job by colleagues. The job he realised quickly, as he knew he would, wasn't what he was cut out for at all. 'On the upside,' he thought, 'it not only paid enough to properly support the family, it also gave enough money to enjoy a little of the freedom he so keenly wanted.' He could afford to have a couple of pints with best friend Harry, who also hadn't signed up, not yet. Best of all, he could go to the cinema rather than trying to sneak in after the picture had started, as he and his friends had done. He couldn't do that when out with Irene. He had taken her on a few inexpensive dates, he now wanted to hold the door for her as he bought two tickets for the good seats. His father asked if it were getting serious, but Jack had shrugged, embarrassed. Irene knew all Jack's family and he hers. They sometimes walked round and picked up his sister Gladys' little girl, Carole, on the way to the cinema, treating her to a bag of sweets then taking her home. "I am nearly four!" she would exclaim as Jack laughed, carrying her on his shoulders. But no matter the distractions of work, of money, family and friends or even his girlfriend, Jack's thoughts were constantly drawn to joining up. His hesitation was now only torn between his absolute promise to family and his gnawing sense of duty.

Jack had been at the munitions factory for nearly a month when the family boarded a bus to Glasgow, then another on to Greenock for George and Elizabeth's wedding. There had been much discussion about who would be able go as the travel costs would not be small, but Jack had insisted and saved for his own fare. Gladys had married locally and it had been a grand day, and now he wanted to see his brother go the same path. It was early in the year for such a wintery day, and the weather cooled further still on their journey north. Flurries of snow drifted so gently they appeared to be moving upwards, not falling. The delicate blossoms gathered first on hedges and the side of the lane, then quickly drifted into layers of powder snow. By the time the family, dressed in their best, took their seats in the chill of the chapel, a white sparkling blanket had spread over the churchyard and roof and bright white lace glittered at the high windows, as if it had also dressed for the occasion. Mother had made her best fruitcake, scraping together ingredients she could still get and using some of their small savings. Elizabeth wore a cream fitted dress with slim belt and a two-flowered corsage and a dainty netted hat. She arrived with her sister and mother and, as her father had passed two years before, her brother Butler took her arm for the short steps down the aisle. She had smiled brightly as she entered the chapel, her blue eyes flashing in the pale light. George, nervous but grinning waited at the front in his RAF uniform, alongside a beaming Jack. George watched Elizabeth's progress towards him, their eyes never breaking their locked gaze. As they met they smiled affectionately, blushing together the same shade of pink. Elizabeth stifled a giggle which caused the vicar to ahem. Later, the family threw tiny handfuls of rice confetti, George and Elizabeth dodged underneath as they ran outside. The couple smiled shyly as half a dozen pictures were taken in front of the church gate, then the family gathered to take drinks and eat the cake in celebration. The snow continued to fall, drifting deeply, stopping buses and trains and their return journey home. In all they stayed for three days, lodging with Elizabeth's family, the Norrie's, all over Greenock.

It was icy cold but finally stopped snowing on the second night, leaving a bright fresh day and a thick, deep carpet of snow. George and Jack decided to walk down to look at the Clyde and the shipyard. Jack had never seen ships towering over the street like that before, huge and to him, somehow ominous. They seemed to peer across the street, looking into the windows of the warehouses opposite and standing sentinel over the unseen occupants. He found them strangely terrifying, their huge bulk exposed, their massive propellers silently waiting. He didn't mention his fear to George as he craned his neck to see shipwrights clattering and riveting, painting and building. There weren't many working in the freezing conditions but it was essential war work and had to continue no matter the weather. The war was moving on apace and Jack's thoughts filled again with enlisting. He turned to George as they stopped their crunching snow tracks to look out to the ships bobbing at anchor on the Clyde. "I need to be doing something more, I can't simply wait to be called, I must play my part now!" he said earnestly as George put out a cigarette under his boot. He looked sympathetically at his younger brother, whose eyes shone with expectation. Jack had always looked up to him, even though *he* was the more energetic and adventurous brother, he'd always watched George, waiting to see approval in his expression. George kicked a snowball and sighed, "It'll probably be over soon. You're just not needed, not yet. You need to stay with mother and dad, look after them. You're needed there more," he pointed southwards in the air indicating Hyde, then paused, "–You know, once you're in, you can't change your mind." Jack frowned, in every word he'd heard disappointment. He had hoped to find an ally to argue his case at home. Jack's mind was in turmoil, war or not, he wanted something *more* from life. He wanted to make his mark, to find someone special, and in the future have a family of his own. But, George wouldn't be drawn further so Jack dropped the subject, and asked him about Elizabeth, as they began walking again. "I expect you'll be having some *wee bairns*, then," he said pushing George with his shoulder. George blushed, laughing, "All in good time! Anyway, we're to Belfast next." "You're back home, at Hyde for Christmas though?" asked Jack, alarmed, "We wouldn't miss it for anything!" laughed George, as they trudged back up the hill to the warm Scots hearths of the Norrie family, as heavy snow flurries again began to fall.

December 1940 brought a brief, but warm and happy family Christmas in Hyde. Jack would remember it fondly, too fondly, later. He would have to push away thoughts of home and think only in fragments of those happier times, otherwise it overwhelmed him. George and Elizabeth had stayed only a few days, bringing news they were expecting a baby. Jack was delighted, whooping and shouting he was to be an uncle again. And again he tried pressing George about signing up. George eventually agreed if he could not wait any longer he should perhaps try to persuade their mother first, then move on to talking to their dad. As an adult, Jack did not need their permission, but neither did he want their disappointment. He saw the smart blue RAF uniform on his brother, saw the life he was making and he decided he must go, and as soon as he possibly could. He felt conspicuously out of uniform at twenty years old, despite working in essential war industry. He told his dad almost every morning he felt he was dodging his responsibility. Then, as it happened, it wasn't George, nor his parents permission, that finally caused Jack to march into the enlistment office.

George and Elizabeth were long gone to Belfast, he to No. 968 barrage balloon squadron and she to stay with the maiden aunts in Magherafelt. Spring had begun in earnest in Manchester. Ice dripped from the trees and brave buds appeared everywhere, as news of tragedy came home. Jack had many friends who had signed up and gone. But, his best friend, Harry had been especially keen to go despite his own family discouraging it. Most families Jack knew bore scars of the previous war, which showed in a reluctance to let their precious boys disappear the same way. Jack and Harry had often talked about going together, but then talked each other out of it because their mothers would *play hell*. Harry thought Jack should look after his family, and Jack had responded similarly. Then, Jack unexpectedly met him one afternoon. Harry had been beaming broadly, his eyes sparkling with adventure, his lank frame wrapped in a neat, brand new uniform. He had gone and joined up anyway. Jack had felt even more determined, but his family again dissuaded him. He must continue doing his bit in essential war work, the family needed him, and their last backstop, that George was already serving, giving their family's bit. As always Jack had exhaled deeply and backed down. But that spring morning the last straw was laid upon his back and he refused to delay. Determinedly he strode away to sign up on 10 April 1941. He paused outside the enlistment office, housed in the post office building. He stood, one foot on the step, looking into the shadowy rooms beyond the heavy door. Hesitation briefly flooded him, he pushed it aside and stepped up. 'He would not turn away, not now,' he thought as he disappeared into the darkened interior. Earlier that morning Harry's sister had dashed to their house in tears, rushing into the sitting room and standing in the middle of the room blurting news between sobs. Jack's ears had thundered with fragments of the story as each word hit him like a bolt of lightning. Harry. had. been. killed. in. action. Jack could hardly catch his breath. Harry had been aboard HMS *Bonaventure*. It had been sunk on 31 March. Torpedoed by an Italian submarine, off the coast of Crete. Harry was not among the 300 or so survivors rescued by HMS *Hereward* and HMAS *Stuart*. Jack was stunned, the war *had* come home. He shook his head trying to rid his mind of the terrible news. He couldn't imagine such a fate, unknowingly torpedoed, invisibly

45

sunk from below. It seemed so pointless. And a waste, a futile waste. Harry's death had gained no ground, there was no victory, just a total senseless waste. Jack's empty chest exhaled as he threw his shoulders back in fury. He deeply wanted revenge on their enemy, he felt he had to do *something* to make Harry's loss worth something. As Jack marched home from the recruitment office his chin determined and resolute, he nodded to everyone he passed. He was certain it was the right thing to do and now he'd done it, he couldn't believe he had waited so long.

Jack had signed up to the Territorial Army. Filling out his form was a squat man, who'd lifted his bald head to peer at Jack over half-moon glasses as he asked each question in slow monotone. "Name?" "Jack Frith." "Address?" "13, Spring Street, Hyde, Cheshire." "Are you a British subject?" "Yes." "And your parents nationality at birth was?" "My father and mother are both British." "Your date of birth?" "The fifteenth of November, twenty." "And are you married, widower or single?" "I am single." The questions went on and on. Had he ever served in the forces? Did he have national health insurance? Yes? What was his membership number? Was he insured under the Unemployment Insurance Act? Eventually, the bald man leaned across the table, spinning the form around to face Jack and proffering a fountain pen after pushing the lid firmly on its end. Jack spread a hand over the paper and took the pen in the other. The nib gushed a drop of ink as he pressed it too hard onto the paper. The bald man leaned across, his glasses sliding down his nose as he offered a square of blotting paper. He'd only written the 'J' of Jack, and grinned sheepishly. Lifting the blotting paper Jack pressed lightly, going over the 'J' and finishing his signature without incident. He dotted a hard full stop after his name in subconscious completion of the deed done. The bald man took the form and signed his own name, whilst indicating Jack should wait in the next room to be called for his medical. Jack rose quickly on hearing his name called and found himself standing in a row of men undressed to their underwear and socks. Most were about his age but a few wore greying temples and peppered moustaches. One or two looked much too young to be trying their luck. Self-consciously Jack stepped up onto heavy enamelled scales as a nurse moved small weights back and forth, before settling on a number. She wrote 111 lbs on the reverse of his form, which was attached to a buff-coloured clipboard. Next, he stood heels to a metal plate as his height was measured, the sliding scale pressed into his hair, taking at least half an inch off the total five foot four and a half written onto his form. Jack blushed as the nurse pulled a tape around his chest and asked him to expand. He inhaled deeply to be measured and frowned as she said thirty-three inches. She held the tape in place asking him to breath out, he released the air and she wrote 'two inches expansion'. The nurse looked him over peering closely as she moved his chin to the right. She nodded as she noticed a small mole on his left cheek and noted it on his sheet. "Thank you. You can get dressed now." She pointed with a flick of her pen to a curtained screen without looking up. Jack blushed again and gathered his clothes, pulling on his trousers and hopping about behind the screen. When he emerged a doctor called his name. Jack crossed the room to him as the doctor spoke, "Certified A1, good luck young man." He smiled. Jack returned the smile as he shook the doctor's outstretched hand and pulling his cap on his head he dashed home to tell his family. He knew very well, they would not be smiling.

As expected, his decision was not greeted with excitement at home. Mother was worried to have 'both her boys away' and in the 'thick of it'. She had sat heavily at the dining table, her eyes brimming with concern and trepidation. His father had remained silent, his eyes lost in images from his war and terrible imaginings of his young son in such hell. Jack told them he would send part of his army wage and they were not to worry, it would all be all right. He said he couldn't stay at home and have his brother and all his friends going to war without him. They didn't object further, what more could they say, there was nothing to be done now Jack had signed the papers. His mother must have quickly written to George, as Jack received his letter only a few days later. George did not to try to dissuade, he knew it was too late for that, but instead offered advice. He told Jack to as keep safe, keep his head down but said he hoped to visit before Jack was posted. Then, the day after another letter arrived which turned his mother's face as pale as the sheets she'd been pegging out in the spring sunshine. Jack took the letter from her, reading it slowly and carefully. It was from George. He and Elizabeth had been walking home along a busy street as the Belfast Blitz had begun. Jack's eyes ran about the page as he breathlessly read it out loud. It had been the Tuesday after Easter, 15 April. They'd been to the cinema but left early as Elizabeth, cradling her small baby bump, had felt quite tired. George helped Elizabeth into her coat and they'd walked arm in arm, chatting and chuckling. They stopped, looking wildly to the skies as the wail of the city's air-raid sirens sounded the alarm. The buzzing drone of hundreds of aeroplanes overhead began almost immediately. The city held its breath then lit up, roaring with fire and explosions as bombs fell indiscriminately everywhere. They had looked to each other momentarily, then they ran. George grabbed two dustbin lids which they held over their heads for protection against flying glass and debris as the world exploded around them. They ran to three shelters before finding one with room, just a few streets from their new married quarters at Victoria barracks. There, they waited it out in the dim earthy garden bunker. They huddled with strangers around a faltering candle as soil drifted down, dislodged by exploding nearby bombs. The muffled booming caused each face to flinch in terror. Elizabeth buried her face in the folds of George's coat, and he wrapped his arms around her and the bump protectively. They felt they'd hardly breathed as they waited in flickering shadows for a rumbling eternity in the *Anderson* shelter. They emerged blinking, to a cratered street. Fires raged in pockets everywhere and the sky was shadowed with flashing orange smoke. George had written the letter as soon as possible to let his family know they were all right, he hoped to beat the newspaper reports he knew would frighten his mother. Jack put down the pages of Georges letter and gulped, wiping his nose he went to fetch a newspaper. The family read eagerly from the newsprint. Their father said how terrible to think of them there, in the middle of the worst blitz outside London! Jack read snippets out loud. A thousand killed, another thousand injured. More than half the houses damaged. Hundreds of thousands of people had fled the city. Jack's mother all the while had her eyes fixed on him. She shook her head and Jack knew she was thinking both her boys were now in this indiscriminately insane war. Conversely Jack had been relieved to hear his brother and sister-in-law were fine, repeating to his mother, "They're all right, they escaped!" But inside he felt deeply uneasy, as if the shadow of the war was closing in on them, drawing nearer all the time. His concern when George had joined the RAF, had been that he might be killed in action. But his fear had assumed that terrible fate, if it happened, would lie somewhere overseas in some nameless place, some dangerous foreign place fighting some foreign enemy. Jack had been relieved George had been posted to Scotland, and then on to Belfast. He thought he would be safe on home shores. How wrong he had been. As his mother left the room Jack he turned to his father, "You know, in this war, it's *bloody* dangerous everywhere and anywhere you go!" His father had nodded thoughtfully and distantly as his mother called from the kitchen, "Jack, watch your language!"

Jack's first taste of army life wasn't the gritty baptism of fire he'd expected, but a rather damp and drizzly Royal Artillery army camp near Crewe where he had been posted for basic training. He took the first train of the day, already full of early morning fresh faced boys. Jack thought they looked hardly older than children really, until he caught his own clean-shaven pink reflection in the window as he hefted his small brown suitcase onto an overhead shelf. Jack offered a light to a chap standing at the end of a carriage. He had weaved down the train to have a smoke and noticed the man patting his pockets while an unlit cigarette bobbed at his lips. They'd gathered around the blossoming flame, leaning in turns to catch the paper ends in the phosphoric flash. They leant back against the clattering carriage as the embers glowed with each inhale. "Thank you, I'm Harold," "Jack," replied Jack stretching out a hand in greeting. They shook, and spoke for a while as the train rattled on. Harold Guest was a quiet man, gentle with warm eyes. He was slow to anger and fiercely loyal. He and Jack got on well being 'practically neighbours' as they'd said laughingly, Jack being from Hyde and Harold from some eight miles nearer Manchester at Miles Platting.

The train full of young men had chattered excitedly as if off for a day at the seaside but a quiet gloom settled as the train slowed its approach into Crewe station and reality arrived. The young men filed into a large building at the camp, settling on rows of long benches in the mess hall. They were given strong tea and jam on thick doorsteps of bread, as their new life was briefly outlined by the booming voice of the sergeant standing on a small dais at the front. No one spoke.

In dripping rain, the line of new recruits jogged single file, carrying folded piles of clothing topped with a pair of boots from stores as they peeled off a dozen at a time into a row of long Nissen huts. Inside, each was lined on either side with a row of single metal beds piled with neat stacks of sheets and army issue blankets. Beside each bed stood a tall locker, into one of which Jack hung his woollen suit and jumper, placing his boots together at the bottom. It appeared as though a flattened, headless man now occupied it. Jack pulled the green itchy army trousers on, and sitting on the end of his bunk pulled on his new army boots as he looked about the hut. A man at the next bunk nodded in greeting, "Hello," he called out. Jack stood, offering his hand to shake. "Jack," he said in introduction, gripping firmly. "Henry, pleased to meet you." Henry Milner was a genial chap from Mansfield, with a kind face and ready grin. Slim, firm jawed and strong spirited, like Jack he had not wanted to shirk what he saw as his obligation to do his bit. He was called up and immediately felt the strong pull of duty. Henry and Jack shared brief details with each other, of home and family before turning their thoughts to what might lay ahead. They both took pride in carefully combed hair and joked of their arrow straight Brylcreem partings, laughing as each offered tips on making a neater line. A shout from the end of the hut, warning they had ten minutes before first briefing returned Jack's focus to finishing getting himself dressed and ready. He turned to a small mirror hanging on the inside of his locker door and placed his cap at a jaunty angle almost on the side of his head. Jack craned his neck, peering to look from all angles, tweaking and pulling it this way and that unsatisfactorily, until he gave up. Closing his locker door revealed the man sitting on the next bunk, folding his own civilian suit. Jack recognised him from the train and leant across clapping him on the shoulder. "Harold!" Jack exclaimed. The man turned and broke into a wide grin. "Young Jack, how are you?" "Can't complain, I didn't see you there, but I'm glad it's you." "Likewise," replied Harold. Jack turned to Henry, who had disappeared halfway into his own locker. He bumped his head on a shelf as Jack called out. "Henry, this is Harold." "Just a second," came the reply, his voice muffled by the contents of his locker. Henry emerged with a wrapped package. "Wonder if we can find some tea from somewhere, my mother sent me with this." He peeled back the brown paper to reveal a small brick of fruit cake. Jack laughed, reaching into his locker, pulling out a greaseproof package, "Snap!" He said as he revealed his own heavy curranty loaf. Both were startled by Harold whose loud laughter had turned a few heads in the hut. Harold leant over his bed to his own locker and pulled from it a similar looking paper parcel. "Triple snap," he gasped between bouts of chuckles. "Well, I think we'll be all right for cake won't we! We just need a brew now," Jack said, looking about and smiling. The three new friends burst out laughing again, relieving a little of the weight they carried.

Over the next few weeks Jack and the recruits learnt general warfare tactics, how to maintain, fire and best use different types of weapons, rifles, shotguns, pistols and bayonets. He learnt how to plant mines, throw bombs and grenades, as well as how to handle larger machinery and guns. After weapons training and shooting practice Jack was issued with a .303 Lee–Enfield rifle. He'd held the heavy rifle, stroking the smooth wood as he imagined when he would first use it against the enemy. The recruits marched for miles, yomping across fields and streams on long cross-country runs, returning to barracks every day shattered, muddy and ravenously hungry. The men became a tight knit group and began to rely on one another. Jack slipped in a muddy scramble over a wall, Henry was running close by and stopped, grabbing an arm to help Jack up. "Come on kid, there'll be no biscuits with your tea if you snooze along the way," he laughed kindly. Jack grinned, scrambling up with a grunt. Running ahead a little, he turned, jogging backwards as he called out, "Aye, but there's plenty if you get there first!" He turned to run, as Henry put his head down, running to catch up the few paces. The two raced, nudging each other and laughing breathlessly back to barracks. The men were taught to dig trenches and build defences. Jack imagined he would face a war like his dad had fought. He presumed he'd soon be somewhere in Europe, dug deep into a trench watching for the enemy and waiting out a war of whistle-screaming bombs and rifle pot shots while the sky flashed with near misses. During training they had covered what to do in a gas attack, shrapnel attack, bomb attack and artillery bombardment, and of course close physical fighting with enemy soldiers. The hand-to-hand fighting Jack found easiest to master physically, but it had filled him with anxious thoughts about being in such near contact with the enemy. He touched his nose distractedly as thought of the punch he'd landed at school, and how unpleasant it had sounded. He was not afraid, but the immediate proximity to some other human being, each of them fighting for his very life, each struggling to survive invaded his mind with doubt. Again his father's war crowded in, and Jack thought of Harry and the futility of fighting a faceless enemy, he wanted to avenge his friend but worried about taking a life that was not responsible. He worried the soldiers on the other side were equally fresh faced as he. Most of their training had been condensed into four weeks, after that there were two weeks practicing general orders. Marching and saluting endlessly and they were shown how to wear their uniforms correctly. Occasionally they marched in uniformed parades about town, which bolstered Jack's sense of courage and trepidation. His official posting was confirmed in mid-July. He had been ranked gunner and assigned to the anti-aircraft regiment, the 77th Heavy Ack Acks where he was put into 239 Battery. Four weeks of advanced artillery training followed, learning specifics of handling and firing the heavy anti-aircraft guns. When training was complete the men stayed on barracks continuing drills, exercises, parade marching, weapons training and practicing artillery manoeuvres for weeks before being granted leave, for nearly a month until late October '41.

Jack travelled home to see his mother and dad, hanging on as he swung about in the carriage aisle of an overcrowded train, his heart pounding to see his family and friends again. Spring Street seemed oddly smaller as he strode up its brow in uniform, passing the hunched terraces with each front door open at least a little. It seemed a long time since he had walked his street and he immersed himself in it completely. The smell of baking wafting from the half-open doors, children's laughter as they played in the street, the snippets of a wireless radio programme floating from a sash window, and the low cries of babies in their prams on the narrow pavement. The sights, smells and sounds merged to create the flavour of his home, and he knew he would miss it terribly. He briefly pondered what might await him, what smells and sounds would fill his senses wherever he was bound for. For now, he soaked the favour of his street into his bones, as if it might protect him on the streets he was to travel. Leave was all too brief. Just a few months later he wouldn't be able to remember in any detail what he had done there. He recalled simply an abstract feeling, of enjoying time with family, mother and dad, sister and niece, seeing friends and taking Irene to the cinema. They'd walked arm in arm in the park and sat on a bench to talk of the future. They had spoken of what might be to come. Jack had been concerned for her and said not to wait. Irene had replied she would write every day, and that she *would* wait for him. She had pinched his arm where she linked him and frowned. Jack had smiled. "All right then, love." He remembered the time was tinged with the knowledge that his future was uncertain, as if he were preparing to drop off a cliff. He could not plan to meet friends the next week, or arrange go to football the week after. He did not know what the future would bring but he remembered his eagerness to get started.

The time at home had felt almost surreal. A lulling waiting time, a deeply held breath before the plunge. He felt all dressed up with nowhere to go. He'd said goodbye to his sister, Gladys and her family at her home a few days before boarding the train. She'd stroked his cheek once, whispering, "Be careful." His mother pressed her wet cheek to his face at the train station, she could not speak. Her eyes shone as she stepped back, grasping his father's arm for support. Jack held out a hand to his father who held it tightly, his jaw gritted. No words were exchanged. His father's clouded eyes had warned 'be careful' as his mother expression had told him, 'come home safe'. Jack had replied with a smile and a nod that it was time. His father reluctantly let Jack's hand slowly slip from his, as his mother caught his sleeve, squeezing his arm. Jack smiled at her, as he hefted his bulging kitbag onto his shoulder and turned away, mingling then disappearing into a sea of khaki which slowly merged and boarded the train. Jack stood up on the carriage step, searching the waving crowd for Irene but he did not find her face. He turned and ducked into the carriage. Florrie craned, looking for him as suddenly he appeared. Pushing down a small sliding window in a nearby carriage as he leant out to find them. Now they spoke. They rushed to him, all chattering at once. "Write whenever you can," his mother called, her voice cracking. "You hear gunfire, you get down. Do you hear?" his father shouted as the train began to rumble,

"Keep your helmet on, always. Do you hear me, son?" His advice became desperate as the train emitted a long high-pitched whistle and a fog of steam engulfed the crowd on the platform. Jack called out through the mist, "I will. Yes, I will, of course. Don't worry, I'll be all right. Goodbye mother, bye dad. I'll be seeing you." His last words were lost in the swirling smoke of the train as it shunted, clanked and moved rhythmically away, chugging behind great white plumes as it disappeared. John and Florrie stood blankly watching the empty track until the last wisps of smoke completely dissipated and no trace of the locomotive could be heard. They turned, heavy hearted to discover they stood alone on the platform.

Jack spoke quietly of the parting to Henry and Harold as they sat on the end of his bunk back at the training camp. They had experienced their own regretful goodbyes with their own families but were, like Jack, keen to get stuck into the task they had trained for. Still, Jack saw in their eyes the same concerns as his own, the lurking shadow of the unknown. He chose not to voice the trepidation he felt, that whatever awaited them would be immensely difficult. He couldn't entirely place the feeling. It was akin to butterflies, like some huge adventure but with potentially serious consequences. He found himself lurching between looking forward to going and a sickening nausea of what might lie ahead. Most of all he couldn't stand the anticipation of waiting. Jack did not have too long to wait. Two weeks of marching drills and weapons practice later the 77ths were mobilised and ordered to proceed to Gourock for movement overseas. He sorted through his kit once again, checking everything. He had three fat packages he hoped he would never need containing large field-dressings alongside a tin holding a basic medical kit, canteen, mess tin and spooned-fork utensils. Into a pouch he tucked his few photographs and a notebook. He folded his spare shirt, trousers and socks, spare underwear and rolled up his gaiters and stuffed it all down his kitbag, which he heaved onto his bed. On top he laid his thick greatcoat. Around his neck hung two identity tags, a green octagonal one and a smaller red one hung from the green, strung on cotton cord. They read, 'FRITH, J. 1794521. C.o.E.' He looked closely at his name and number before tucking them inside his shirt with a sigh, where they pressed lightly on his chest. Kitted out in battledress, with his various small packs and pouches slung from webbing, Jack lowered his steel helmet on to his head, and pulling the chin strap taut and glancing into the mirror on the door of his locker. He immediately saw his father staring back. Not his father as Jack knew him now, but the young man that peered wide-eyed and shocked from twenty-year-old photographs, wearing *his* uniform and trapped in *his* war. It shocked Jack, quickly he pulled the helmet from his head and fastened it to his kitbag which he slung over his shoulder. He lifted his greatcoat, tucking it under his arm and followed the line of strong young men from the hut, all talking in excited whispers as they formed up outside on the parade ground. There, they quietened down as their commanding officer approached with their orders. Jack exchanged glances with Harold and Henry. They were finally for the off.

- DECEMBER 1941 -

A cold, sleet ravished Gourock docks greeted Jack as he arrived by lorry transport. He had felt queasily sick lurching around in the back of the truck, huddled against the other men and rolling kitbags under the flapping tarpaulin roof of the six-wheeler *Albion* truck. They had pulled up and poured out. Jack vomited over the back wheel as he hit the ground heavily with his boots. Henry slapped his back, "That bodes well," he laughed nodding to the rolling ships out on the Clyde. The smell of sea and oil caught in Jack's throat as he wiped his mouth and looked round at the bleak docks. The pitching of the toy ships, the wind squally and cold, the dark swell of the sea the same colour as the grey ships hulls all permeated his senses and made his stomach retch. He looked out to the gathered ships as they swayed like drunks on a slowly moving ocean. Waves of nausea engulfed him as sheets of sleety rain moved across his view, veiling the ships behind their cold curtain. In contrast, the dock was abuzz with light and activity. Men hoisted pallets for loading, army vehicles chugged about as navy personnel shouted orders. Added to the bustle were endless streams of soldiers forming up as they arrived in their thousands. Jack noticed the *Empress of Australia* moored alongside the dock, taking on supplies. A huge ship, she loomed over the tiny figures standing, directing proceedings on the quayside. Harold nudged Jack, "You know the *Empress of Australia* was the Royal Yacht for the King and Queen two years ago. Took them on a Royal tour of Canada! That'll do for us won't it?" he nodded, smiling. Jack shook his head, "I don't know how you remember all these things!" he laughed. "But, yes, that'll do us all right!" They watched from within the midst of the organised chaos as kit and supplies were loaded. The atmosphere was frenetic, crates were dropped, some of the cargo going aboard seemed damaged, other supplies were bashed about. Everyone seemed in a hurry. "I hope that's not our gear," said Jack. Harold shrugged, "We don't know which one we're going on do we–" he was interrupted by a shout. They craned to listen, cupping hands to ears and turning to others who seemed to have heard. "We've got more supplies to gather, there's a mess hall apparently." "Good, I'm famished," nodded Jack. His friends shook their heads as Jack slapped his belly, "I thought he was sick!" laughed Henry. They turned from the dock, marching into a long low building alongside the quay. Jack and the rest of 77th HAA, 239 Battery joined their comrades from 240 Battery arriving from Chester and 241 Battery, come up from Donnington. They were issued long sand-coloured shorts, thin shirts with roll-up sleeves and cloth buttons, and Wolseley helmets, which they tucked into kit bags. There were injections and tablets given as the men considered their likely destination. "Not France then!" said Jack, to anyone listening. "Maybe North Africa?" suggested Harold with a shrug. "We're headed to the Middle East, Basra I heard," said a man nearby quietly, as he rolled up his sleeve and offered his arm to a nurse readying a needle. Jack moved up the line to the nurse, nodding at the news and repeating, "Basra?" He winced and moved from the nurse rubbing his arm. Joining a queue for hot tea and food, he looked himself up and down while he waited. "Basra? Middle East?" He muttered. It suddenly seemed very real. Jack stared at his boots, sparkling new and shiny, and smoothed the jacket of his smart green uniform. He ran a hand through his new haircut and patted his soon to be full stomach and frowned. He moved with loaded tray to sit on a bench at a long trestle table with Henry and Harold. They chewed thoughtfully, each in quiet contemplation. No one spoke, but the air was full of breathless trepidation. Jack felt his moment had finally come and he was ready, wherever he was going.

The gathered convoy had largely been loaded with supplies and artillery and now only awaited troop deployment. The smart well-fed men, bulging kitbags slung over their shoulders, headed back to the ships on the dock to embark. There, a few families had gathered and were waiting to wave them off. Jack looked across the sea of faces, his eyes scanning the crowd. He had already bid farewell to his parents and sister, they could not be here. No one he knew could be. He stopped short as he saw two people standing closely knitted together looking this way and that, between them a small baby. Jack blinked. He had seen George's familiar face before Elizabeth's, then his eyes fell to the child. He moved to them quickly, dropping the kitbag at his feet and grasping them all in one embrace. George was now a Corporal, and had been granted longer leave after serving continuously for seven months with his new posting to No. 952 Balloon Squadron at Sheerness, protecting the approaches to the River Medway and the Royal Navy dockyard at Chatham. He had travelled up to Greenock to be with Elizabeth, who had stayed there with her mother, and together they had taken the three-mile bus journey along the coast to Gourock, in the hope of seeing him off. The three stood beaming at each other. Jack felt his throat knot so he turned to the child. "Well, well, what a handsome little chap!" The baby boy gurgled, his bright blue eyes shining. "This, is Iain George," said Elizabeth, her soft Scottish voice cracking as her lip trembled. Jack leaned down and kissed the baby on the top of his bonneted head. "I'm glad to have had the chance to have met him, kid," he said to Elizabeth, then turned to his brother. Jack and George shook hands and shared a knowing look. Nothing was left unsaid in their exchange, but in any case Elizabeth spoke for them, "Watch yourself now Jack, go carefully," she said, her eyes moistening. George nodded in agreement, as Jack cleared his throat and replied, "I will, don't worry. I'll be all right kid, cheerio then." She smiled, patting at her cheeks with the back of her gloved hand. George clamped a hand on Jack's shoulder and tried to raise a smile but in the moment could not, he simply squeezed his younger brother's shoulder and flexed his jaw. Jack returned the expression with equally furrowed brow, he felt nervous but didn't want to let it show. He didn't want his brave face to slip, when he didn't feel at all brave. Jack nodded to them both as he picked up his gear. It was time. He stood up, straightened his shoulders and without looking back, strode away gritting his teeth to convince himself, 'I'll be all right.' He walked up the gangway and onto the ship, and was lost into the hundreds of others on deck. George and Elizabeth watched him go losing him the crowd, as they strained to catch sight of him again. He suddenly emerged leaning over the gunwale, waving energetically. The small family on the quayside waved back, their eyes brimming. Jack stood proudly on the deck of the *Empress of Australia* and gripped the rail with both hands. He inhaled a lungful of salty sea-mist and grinned. He felt the pull of sheer adventure, of the unknown and he was excited. The faceless fear remained but he pushed it to the pit of his stomach and puffed out his chest. This was his chance to prove himself. To defend his country and to make a man of himself. He would not let anyone down. He would fight. A bloody nose from these *Nazi* bullies would be just fine. For Harry and everyone else who had not come home. He imagined telling his children and his nephews and nieces his own war stories, as his father had done. He would lean back in his old armchair as they gathered round perhaps with grandchildren, grandnieces and grandnephews and he would talk of these days. He would hold a finger in the air, his eyes misting and say, "We sailed from Gourock on a cold early December night, bound for who knows where..." They would listen attentively, eyes wide and mouths open. The ships horn bellowed and Jack returned his thoughts to the masses on deck. He blew a kiss to the tiny figures of his brother and family below and closed his eyes as the engines pulsed. The ship shuddered and slipped slowly from its mooring to join the gathered ships anchored on the Clyde.

The *Empress of Australia* sailed in convoy from Gourock late on the 7th of December 1941, joining ships from Bristol and Liverpool. The complete convoy, codenamed WS14 for Winston's Special Convoy Fourteen, were to assemble off Orsay Islet on the West coast of Scotland. As WS14 departed Gourock, charting a course almost due south to traverse the West coast of Africa, the men below decks and their superiors above were unaware of events unfolding some seven thousand miles away. The *Empress of Australia* left Scottish waters and quietly moved into convoy formation in the Atlantic, while hundreds of Japanese planes screamed from the skies above Pearl Harbour, dropping bomb after bomb, lighting up the ships moored there. The docks were ablaze as bombers and fighter planes came in waves of attack, each bearing the beady red eye of Imperial Japan. Aboard the *Empress of Australia* the men settled into bunks for their first night at sea. They joked with one another, spoke of home in low murmurs and forged friendships, unaware of the deadly Japanese attack that would imminently throw all their lives into chaos. Even as the first day dawned on WS14's journey, discussions in Whitehall were taking place at the highest level to decide which ships amongst the convoy would remain bound for destinations in the Middle East to shore up Allied action, and which must be sent to the other side of the world to tackle the new wound opened up there. Unaware of any change, or threat to their mission, the twenty-nine transport ships and seventeen escorts of WS14 moved in tight formation led by the *Troilus, Warwick Castle, Orestes, Abosso, Duchess of Atholl, Durban Castle, Highland Princess* and *Empire Pintail*. The second line comprised the *City of Pretoria, Empress of Australia, Scythia, Strathallan, Athlone Castle, Highland Monarch* and *Clan Cameron*. They were followed by the third line of the *Empire Curlew, Empire Oriole, Oronsay, Reina Del Pacifico, Cameronia, Empire Peregrine, Empire Egret* and armed merchant cruiser *HMS Cilicia*. The rear formation was held by *Empire Condor, Andes, Orcades*, HMS *Engadine* and *Empire Widgeon*. The sailing positions remained in place until docking at Freetown two weeks later. The convoy had been escorted by various ships as they travelled around the bulge of north-west Africa. Each had escorted for several days before handing over. The destroyers *Beverley, Croome, Lancaster, Newark, Sherwood, Westcott* and *Witherington* with auxiliary ships *Ulster Queen, Foxhound, Gurkha, Nestor, Vanquisher, Volunteer, Badsworth, Beaufort* and *Witch* and battleship *Ramillies* all shared escort duties for WS14, as it moved into warmer southern waters.

The bow of the *Empress of Australia* towered above the swell as she lunged through deep waves. She crashed down almost level with the sea, then lurched up high again as she powered forward. The sea foamed, spraying the ships deck white although the ocean seemed black, tinged with deep green, a measure of the great depth of the Atlantic. Deep below deck the men lurched together, conditions were cramped and sweatily damp. A few men vomited loudly into bags and containers. It had seemed a dream to board the luxurious vessel, but the majority of the ranks quickly discovered there were no state rooms for them. They lay in tightly packed bunks, coughing and grumbling to each other through the night. Despite the lurching voyage, and their sea-sickness, the men were healthy. There were beds and warm bedding, lamps for reading and plenty of food and entertainment. As they had embarked, Jack's boots had stomped down the steep ladder in a slowly moving line to the lower decks. He peered below, one arm holding his balance on the ladder rung as he scanned the men's darkened, nervous faces. Under a swinging lamp a card game was pushed from view, some men already lay in bunks, reading. There were short bursts of laughter here and there as he made his way down, stepping onto the deck. Some were deep in conversation others kept to themselves writing journals and thin papered letters. A hanging banner bearing neat sewn lettering, *Royal Artillery 77TH H.A.A.* slung across a bulkhead. The 77th was made up of Jack's Battery the 239th and the 240th and 241st Batteries, each armed with eight 3.7 inch guns. Jack had looked amongst the sea of men for familiar faces and found Henry and Harold and started to make his way through to them. Henry was hunched over, expertly pressing a tin-opener into a can of condensed milk. He turned the can in his hand and pressed another *vee* in the lid. When he completed the task he lifted the tin to drink. He pursed his lips, bending his elbow and turning the can around as he found it lifted silently from his hand from behind. Jack slurped a little of the milk and handed the can back, his mischievous grin wrapped in milky moustache. "Oi!" shouted Henry, laughing as he recognised the face. Jack laughed, "Sorry I've only had a bit!" "That's all right then, good to see you, Jack." laughed Henry. Harold reached for the can, "Thanks very much, didn't realise we were sharing," he said as Henry held it up out of his reach, "Oi!" Henry said again, "I *wasn't* sharing!" He laughed and passed it to Harold. The three friends laughed as Jack slapped his belly, "We had better find out what the grub is like on board, three strapping lads like us will need good dinners won't we!" he said as his friends grinned. Jack threw his kit bag onto the nearest empty bunk and rubbed his hands together. They stood, Jack shedding various pouches, knapsacks and excess equipment and went with his friends in search of the galley to investigate what and when their meals would be. Unfortunately, for the first few, long days Jack became one of the weary sea-sick, unable to keep much food down and spending his time sipping at his water bottle whilst leaning wretchedly over the ship's side. A week later his stomach had become accustomed to the lurching roll and settled to the motion of the sea. In the long days aboard as the weather warmed on their approach to the equator, Jack explored the decks as much as he was allowed and one afternoon came upon a wood panelled smoking room. It was exclusively for officers, but as he peered through the bevelled etched glass he saw it was unoccupied. He turned the brass door handle and stepped inside. 'I can say I was just looking,' he thought to himself. Jack looked around the dark wood-lined room, with its plush leather armchairs and decided to enjoy the moment. He might not have the chance again. Taking a cigarette from a crumpled packet and pushing it between his lips, he lit it in the first flash of the match. He puffed out a cloud of smoke and leaned against the oak wall, which creaked as his weight braced there. The smoky, dimly lit room smelt of liquor and cigars mingled with polished leather and old oak, and Jack embraced the luxury that was not his. He chose to leave before his excuses ran out. He did not want the moment to end in being hauled out and reprimanded. He resumed his walk along the deck in the sunshine, listening to the thudding of his heavy boots clumping along the wood, smiling to himself for getting away with the moment of indulgence.

The three friends often wandered the ship 'looking for trouble' as Jack called it. Really, they were just looking to fill their time. They told each other all their stories and jokes, laughing as they strolled the decks as if on a cruise as the journey's long days grew into longer weeks. The men had plentiful entertainment and the 77ths put on regular concerts. There were also games, mostly draughts, dominoes and lotto, the latter being the only game they were formally allowed to gamble on. Jack spent much of his free time writing letters home, to his mother and dad, to Irene and to George and Elizabeth. Less than a week after leaving Gourock, on Friday 12 December 1941, Jack had lain on his bunk and penned two sides to George and Elizabeth, adding his young nephew to his salutation. He wrote of this and that, promising George he would look after himself. He spoke of looking forward to seeing his nephew grow up into a big fellow, which caused a lump at his throat and he could not help but write morosely, *'I wish I could see you all, it may be 3 years before I get the chance again.'* He shook himself, adding, *'still, its no use moaning, its got to be finished hasn't it.'* He realised he'd run out of news, and reflecting had made him homesick, so he signed off quickly.

With all my very best love, cheerio, your loving brother, Jack

He added a row of x's, then another underneath, then decided to add a row for his nephew. He held the piece of pale blue paper at arms length and decided to add a new, separate set of x's, jotting to the side, *'special for Iain.'* He grinned to himself and folded the letter. He slid it into a top pocket as a thought struck him that it would take some weeks to arrive, so pulling it from his pocket, he unfolded it and added. *'A merry Christmas and a happy new year to Betty, George and Iain'.* He refolded it, pushed it back into his pocket and went in search of his friends.

The three friends sat together often, talking of this and that as Christmas approached and as the evening sing-songs turned into Christmas carols, and Jack's thoughts turned again to home. He felt they had been at sea for a lifetime as he watched the endless expanse of ocean and the ever changing ships in their convoy. Several ship and escort changes had occurred en route, some were detached, others had engine trouble and fell behind. Their orders were adjusted accordingly and the ships sailed in different formations. Eventually the convoy was escorted into Freetown on the 21st of December by four destroyers. No one was granted shore leave, they were to simply re-stock and refuel. The mooring was brief, just a matter of days before sailing early on Christmas Day, destined for Capetown. No matter their location nor destination, the men enjoyed a heartfelt and warm Christmas celebration on the ship somewhere out to sea, of roast turkey and plum pudding. The three friends carried their full bellies to their bunks and Jack pulled a small saved wedge of his mother's Christmas cake from a chipped flat tin. He unwrapped the greaseproof paper as the festive scent of orange and clove unfurled in his nostrils. Such is the power of smell, his mother appeared before him, her hazy image flickering in the half light below deck as she smiled at him. Jack's eyes shone damply and he smiled to himself as he got up to share the cake, her image disappearing through him in wisps. He turned, to be greeted with Harold and Henry holding two similarly wrapped chunks of their own mothers' Christmas cakes. They laughed as they had back at basic training months previously. "I *knew* there was good reason we should stick together," laughed Harold. "Happy Christmas lads," said Henry, "–And to you," Jack replied, looking to both. Harold raised his cake, "Yes, happy Christmas to us, and to our mothers and all at home." They grinned as they ate. Jack clambered back onto his bunk. Leaning back with his hands folded behind his head, his boots crossed he smiled almost contentedly, "Ahhh, we had better stick together hadn't we, even if just for the cake!" he grinned to himself as he dozed off.

- JANUARY 1942 -

Jack came to as the ship rocked slowly, sickeningly, up and down in the heavy swell. He jumped up banging his head on the bunk above as he had done almost every morning. Rubbing a burgeoning familiar bump and grimacing, he asked, "Where are we?" Harold replied as he pulled on a shirt buttoning it quickly. "We're coming into Capetown, I heard we're not stopping. Somethings happened. I don't know what. Someone said we aren't going to the Middle East now either." Henry had woken on hearing the tense voices and sensed the change in atmosphere. "What's happened?" he said as he pulled his shorts on hastily. "We don't know, were going up to see now," said Jack as he tugged his bootlaces hard, winding them round in double knots. WS14 arrived at Capetown on the 5th of January 1942, for supplies and refuelling. The convoy stayed four sweltering days leaving on the 9th of January. Taking the lead was the *Highland Monarch* carrying the Vice Commodore, flanked by the *Clan Cameron*, the *Warwick Castle* carrying the Commodore, and either side the *Orcades* and outlying, Jack's ship the *Empress of Australia*. These lead ships were trailed by ten others, in two waves of formation. The convoy again regrouped at Durban on the 13th, where various ships re-joined and others detached, some troops were re-shifted, including

RAF aircraft men from the *Esperance Bay* to the *Dunera*. The whole convoy was then reorganised into columns in addition to the formal rows of formation so each column could more easily peel off into three new smaller convoys. Each headed now for separate destinations still unknown to the men below decks. The two left outlying columns departed for the Gulf of Aden and the central three detached and headed for Bombay. The two right flanking columns also disengaged from the convoy with orders to reinforce the troops at Singapore, now threatened by advancing Japanese. The *Empress of Australia* now led the right flank of the Singapore detachment. The pace on board changed dramatically as the men ran endless drills and exercises as best they could on a bustling ship preparing for battle. They talked of what they little they had heard of the Japanese attacks and advances. There had been an invasion, spreading across a huge area quickly, and they were to reinforce Singapore. It shouldn't be too difficult nor take too long as they were told the island was a fortress. Jack had reacted to the change in destination with concern, largely worrying over the extended voyage. He was sick of the ship and wanted to get on firm land to start doing the job he'd trained for. They had been kitted out with sandy shorts and thick puttees for the dry heat of the Gulf, Jack now wondered if they were at a disadvantage going into what he assumed would be completely different terrain. He'd never been so far from home in his life and had no idea what to expect. As WS14 had split into the three smaller convoys bound for different destinations each gained a new codename. Jack's sub-convoy was re-designated DM2. The *Empress of Australia* circled a great arc out to starboard from her front-right outlying position, as the *Warwick Castle* mirrored the manoeuvre to port. Both rounded to bring up the rear, re-positioning either side of the *City of Canterbury*. She had remained in her rearward position alone as left flanking *Troilus* and right flanking *City of Pretoria* turned white foam in the sea as they moved apart to allow the rear *Malancha* to move up between them. They were joined by the Commodores' ship, the *Dunera* and this line of four ships became the front leading line, ahead of the three rear vessels. The DM2 convoy refuelled at Addu Atoll on the 26th of January, as the *Empress of Australia* had been running low. On the 28th, DM2 was re-joined by ships detached from the Bombay convoy that had previously been part of the original WS14, the *Nova Scotia, Dilwara, Esperance Bay* and *Empire Condor*. Five escort cruisers joined them three days later, along with two destroyers a few days after that. As the now larger new convoy approached their destination, the Bombay convoy along with the *City of Canterbury* detached for Singapore, leaving the remainder to now sail for Java. The detachment would arrive only days before the Allied surrender of Singapore and all the troops were taken prisoner. Meanwhile, Jack's *DM2* convoy of six remaining troop transport ships and seven escorts arrived at Batavia, Java on the 3rd of February 1942.

Jack had lain drowsily in a bunk drifting in and out of disturbed sleep. His body seemed to sway in rolling motion. He had half woken with a jolt, sweating and confused. *Where am I, and what is that noise?* Disconcerted he'd been unable to disentangle himself from slumbered imaginings. What *were* these dreams? Not drowsy disconnected confections of semi-conscious reverie but the touchable visions he witnessed while the body was completely unconscious. Were these lucid realities he inhabited nightly, simply his mind breaking down the narration of his waking experiences? Understood only as crumbled smatterings of abstract images, strung together with matters occupying his daylight thoughts. Did his mind filter these dappled fragments, and knit them together into credible threads to weave the turmoil of his life into order? What did the mind achieve during its time of unconsciousness? While bodies rolled to and fro and twitched, while mouths dribbled onto pillows and limbs entwined sheets, while fingers absently scratched unseen itches and experiences percolated into dream. He recalled lying paralysed, subconsciously awake as a child, as frightening night-time shadows danced against the sheets like paper puppets. Prowling amongst his senseless thoughts, consciousness invaded like a finger pressing on taut fabric. His eyes danced behind his lids as it bowed inwards pressing on his mind, prodding his unconscious to surface. The sounds of the living, voices and noises were woven into his fictions as he emerged from sleep. Notwithstanding his knowledge that he was safe in his home, he clutched at the sheets, fingers clenched in fear. *Where am I, and what was that noise?* He screwed his eyes, choking as he emerged from the subterranean void. He rose from the horizontal like a body lifted from water. An unseen gossamer sheen slid from his face and ran down his neck as he fought for consciousness. As his mind rose his face twitched, his fingers clenched and unclenched. He reached out into emptiness. There it was again, that noise. A constant thrumming. He recoiled, rolling his head from side to side unable to place the sound. It resonated, becoming louder like an irritant fly buzzing about his ears then moving away. His senses struggled to focus, his mind on fumbled alert. Still his thoughts returned to wonder 'Where am I? Was it the ticking of a clock? Was it birds singing the alarm?' Blinking while closed, his eyes rolled in circles beneath their lids as his thoughts finally and abruptly, surfaced. He was soaked with sweat as he wildly reached out, grasping at air and panting deeply as he remembered where he was. He remembered. He dully remembered the thrumming beating noise was *not* the pot-bellied alarm clock sitting snugly on his warm bedside table. *Not* the lung-bursting morning song of English garden birds announcing the fresh new day. The piercing thrumming, that resonating sound was the rasping whine of cicadas and the painful sorry wheeze of men. Men who slept morosely, packed tightly together, rasping desperately to survive. He remembered the whine of cicadas was the constant audible reminder, the backdrop to this hell-hole. He remembered he was *not* encased in the sheets his mother had starched in the yard that smelled of the North winds of home. This was *not* the ship he had lain bunk to bunk with his fresh-faced brother soldiers on their two-month voyage. This was a festering Japanese prisoner of war camp. Grossly overcrowded, built for hundreds and now housing thousands of pained souls in the sweltering heat of Batavia. He and his military brothers had now endured almost a year at the mercy of a merciless enemy. He wiped the sweat from his feverish brow with the back of his bony hand and remembered, terribly and tearfully, that he was *not* home. He tried to calm his breathing and his racing mind as reality urgently gathered around him.

- FEBRUARY 1943 -

The place was Tandjong Priok prison camp. It was still dark as he'd awoken, startled by the misplaced sounds of home. He both despised and loved the double-edged freedom of his dreams, their ability to transport his mind without body, with such ease to anywhere he would rather have been. It was simultaneously magical and cruel. Morning often broke this way, pushing aside reflections of wished for escape and reluctantly accepting the daily truth of his dire situation. Thinking and dreaming of home had at first been a torture of its own in the early days of his captivity. Now, just over a year later, he felt it tethered him to sanity. It was a guiding light and his hopeful aim. He planned to get there, to get home. Every morning he had woken, he hoped might bring him another day closer to that goal. He held his head in his hands, how long would it take? Nearly a whole tortuous year had already slipped by.

- FEBRUARY 1942 -

Jack had landed at Batavia, disembarking from the *Empress of Australia* with the 77th HAA, expecting a fight but found himself descending into chaos. As their convoy had approached Tandjong Priok harbour, Jack stood alongside the men of 239 battery looking over the side as a loaded ship, the *Duchess of Bedford*, moved quickly away. She put on speed, heading out to sea crowded with women and children, refugees escaping the escalating madness first at Singapore, now imminently set to engulf Java. The *Empress of Australia* anchored outside the harbour awaiting permission to take a mooring as the dock was slowly cleared for the convoy's arrival. Finally the 77th disembarked and the lads spewed off the ship, rifles to one shoulder, kitbags slung from the other and helmets clamped on heads as they formed up on the quay in a sea of disorder and confusion. The ships had had to take turns docking and unloading. Some of the disembarked men immediately had to resupply themselves and re-board for a dash to reinforce Timor. The need for organisation at the port showed no sign of occurring, and by mid-February the harbour would be packed with almost one hundred and fifty ships. As Jack's ship emptied it quickly refilled with evacuees, sailing for Colombo as the men tried to organise supplies they'd hastily unloaded onto the dockside. As daylight failed, troops were still marching to temporary barracks all over the city, leaving kit, artillery and cargo littering the quayside.

The men wanted to fight, they were more than ready. After two months rolling and retching at sea they were ship-weary, eager to stand on solid ground and hungry to engage their enemy. The men of the 77th stood at the docks as commanding officers strained to take stock of the chaotic situation. Eventually it was decided the three batteries were to be split into two, 240 and 241 Batteries would travel quickly to Soerabaya to defend the Dutch Naval port there. Jack's 239 Battery would stay and continue unloading, and defend the docks at Batavia. The situation beggared belief, as Jack's battery took stock of their supplies, it quickly became apparent much of their gear and equipment was missing. They set up a temporary base in adjoining warehouses, and worked hard but it was a hopeless situation. More than half their guns had the wrong ammunition. Supplies had initially been split as the convoy split on leaving South Africa. There had been further unnoticed confusion at each stop on the convoys journey. Kit had been misplaced or re-loaded into the wrong ship, and maddeningly not all heavy artillery had travelled with its corresponding ammunition. There stood at Batavia dock hundreds of airmen without aircraft, anti-aircraft batteries without artillery, drivers without vehicles and overall a lack of food, quarters or proper organisation. There had been no GHQ set up on Java. The entire operation fell under ABDA-COM, the American, British, Dutch and Australian Command, which had stretched itself, overseeing operations from Mandalay to Darwin. ABDA-COM had set up its south-west Pacific command only the previous month in Batavia, moving again a few days later to Bandoeng. Ultimately, in reality the Javanese army and the Allied troops disembarking into the Dutch colony, fell under local command of the Dutch, the British chaffing under an unfamiliar yoke, with ABDA-COM blindly overseeing proceedings from one hundred miles away. Masses of equipment filled the dockside and warehouses but much did not correspond to the arriving troops, the cooks, drivers and clerks. 239 Battery unloaded ship after ship of useless equipment as the days wore on, as slower ships in the convoy arrived alongside ships retreating overrun Malaya and Singapore. The *City of Canterbury* was anchored for two days before moving slowly into harbour to a mooring. The 239 men unloaded her cargo including much needed *Bofors* guns. As each ship was unloaded supplies, guns, artillery and vehicles piled up at the docks. Various units not yet deployed and lacking their own equipment, gathered to search for supplies, taking a first-come first-served approach, ransacking cargo and taking what most closely resembled equipment they'd trained with. Various regiments raided off-loaded kit, including the 77th's *Bofors*, weapons, motorcycles and ammunition and rations. Men of 239 were forced to track down their *Bofors* and retrieve them. Fortunately they hadn't gone far as their gun tractors could not be found. The warehouses on the dock became filled to capacity and guard patrols had to be put on. Equipment had at least to go to its correct unit, as hastily appointed quartermasters tried to sort kit, allocating to the most suitable. Even the uniforms they wore, as Jack had feared, were not suited to the climate. Most were kitted out for the Middle East. Some tropical supplies had been brought aboard but not everyone was reissued properly, a situation made worse by the clouds of mosquitoes that infested the swampy docks. As the harbour flooded with ships, equipment and stores and outgoing troops, as well as incoming masses of evacuees from Singapore and Malaya, the situation deteriorated further. Along with the wrong equipment, the wrong troops swarmed the dockside. Most difficult to reconcile were the hundreds of RAF aircraft-men and pilots disembarked with no aeroplanes. These men could not be spared for the impossibility of immediate retraining as infantrymen. Pilots and crew were much needed elsewhere. Many were simply re-boarded and sent on their way. In the midst of melee Jack watched as the *Empress of Australia* sailed from the harbour two days after it had deposited him, leaving him with a surging feeling of isolation and abandonment in insanity. He watched the familiar deck crowded with unfamiliar faces and for a moment his heart wished he were aboard. It seemed only moments since he'd stood there waving to his dear brother and his family. He suddenly, achingly wished he were returning to England on the next tide. Jack shook his head and turned away, he knew he must buckle down to the job at hand. He'd felt ready for a fight despite the general unreadiness of the situation, and tried to dig in for a long haul. Once unloading was completed as far as possible, 239 Battery set up a defensive perimeter, siting their guns, but quickly found themselves as every other unit, desperately short of ammunition.

As if the situation wasn't miserable enough, the end of the first weeks unloading had been swept with endless torrential rain in the simmering heat. Jack had never experienced the like. For him, rain came with a biting northern chill and rain fell similarly icily. To be soaked through but remain swelteringly hot felt so strange to him and was little relief in the sweating job they'd undertaken. At the same time, the first of many Japanese air raids began on the port of Tandjong Priok as 239 Battery scrambled to ready their anti-aircraft guns, reserving ammunition for the best chance of success. The combination of missing equipment, lack of supplies and fewer than needed troops, the chaos of their arrival and deployment and the hot hailing rain and the heat, compounded by endless bombardment from Japanese planes made for a purgatorial existence. Elsewhere, misery also attended 240 and 241 Batteries as they encountered tragedy before even reaching Soerabaya. The packed carriages of their train ploughed into a goods train sitting idle on the tracks, sending three carriages over an embankment and smashing four more to pieces. Twenty-one were killed and some forty more were injured.

Back in Batavia, there followed another week of disorganised chaos. The men had little time to prepare for the anticipated Japanese invasion as colonial civilians desperately tried to leave their sinking island. Food supplies were initially lacking and, with no place to set up a mess and nothing to stock it with, local hotels were paid to supply meals to each regiment at great expense. Eventually, a food supply depot was set up and local food bought in and prepared directly. At the end of the second week the men were paid a few guilders and set about spending most of it on local food and drink. Jack got a pass and sat outside a local bar, Dutch beer in hand. He briefly felt a rising glow which disappeared as news began to filter through, — Singapore had fallen. The men ran back to their units, knowing they could soon expect an influx of refugees and, hopefully retreating Allied servicemen to bolster their numbers on Java. The loss of Singapore was somewhat expected, but a shock when it came. Doubly so as Malaya was abandoned and evacuated the following day. Each man knew what these losses meant. The Japanese would be coming for Java next.

In the following days Jack and 239 Battery were met, at the dockside as expected, with endless arriving civilians and retreating military as the

Orcades docked from Sumatra. It seemed the whole of Java was awash with people on the move, as retreating ABDA armies filled the country from Sumatra, Singapore and Malaya. These troops unloaded as a long shuffling line of silent men, passing Jack in single file with staring eyes and bandaged brows who jumped when spoken to. Jack guessed some ten thousand RAF crew must have passed through Tandjong Priok that week. Jack's job remained confined to the disorder of the dockside, unloading and re-loading, watching weary troops disembark then almost immediately standing back as frightened evacuees hurried to re-embark. They carried their worldly possessions in knotted bundles and held their children tight as they stumbled aboard. The scene unfolded in thickening mud from incessant downpours, breeding waves of blood-thirsty mosquitos, under strafing fire and intermittent bombing by the Japanese. Under threat of this advancing enemy, and in worsening conditions on Java ABDA-COM now decided the situation had become hopeless and began preparations to evacuate non-essential men. Leaving the men of three light artillery regiments, the 21st LAA, 6th LAA and 48th LAA, with the 77th the only heavy artillery ordered to remain in support of the beleaguered Dutch forces.

Unspoken was the knowledge that the inevitable was approaching, death or surrender. As remaining ships filled with departing higher ranking officials bound for Australia and Ceylon, Jack could not help but wonder if the situation was as hopeless as it seemed. He thought, 'If there were no hope at all, why would the whole of the army not be evacuated? There were still plenty of ships with room aboard in the harbour, still chance for so many to get out. Why not leave Java altogether and make a stand elsewhere, with the right troops and the right artillery?' Yet, as the ships left port, with most not nearly full, Jack felt his opportunity sail away with them. Just a week earlier Tandjong Priok had been filled with more than a hundred ships. Now, as rumours increasingly spread of imminent Japanese approach the need became desperate, and every ship was ordered to move out. Surplus men and airmen, many of the drivers, clerks and cooks, along with refugees and newly arrived evacuees from Sumatra, Malaya and Singapore were all turned around and sent back out. Then, the harbour was closed to all ships in preparation for defence against invasion. Meanwhile, at the opposite end of Java, ABDA-COM departed. Officially handing over to the Dutch on the 25th, just over three weeks after DM2 convoy had arrived. ABDA-COM shut down rapidly, packing up in a frenzied burning of papers and hastily gathered sensitive documents, maps and equipment. Command departed for ships at Tjilatjap in a charge of cars, brim full of officers that swept past worried onlooking locals, to their escape. A few officers felt obliged to decline the opportunity and took up arms, standing beside the remaining men in the face of imminent Japanese invasion. Later that same day, as ABDA-COM's ships disappeared over the horizon, reports came in of a potential Japanese force off the coast of Borneo. That evening in Batavia, fierce artillery fire broke out as the Japanese launched a massive air attack, injuring half a dozen manning the *Bofors*. Jack was in the midst of the defensive fight back against the Japanese as news came through of ABDA-COM's departure, and the officers being evacuated from the other end of Java. Disbelief merged with incredulity. He felt he stood on a sinking raft of an island, with their superiors stepping off the other end, rocking their delicate island raft, failing to aid either stability nor buoyancy. Jack and 239 Battery hunkered down amongst the dock warehouses for the night amid sporadic fire. As dawn broke, intelligence reports began to filter through of second invasion fleet in the East, one that could attack by early morning. The Western invasion force, that could easily land face to face with 239th without warning had not been sighted for days, the radar trackers had lost it. Eventually, it was picked up again on the 28th, closing in on the island. There were simply not enough units nor resources to defend the whole island, but both Tandjong Priok at Batavia, and Bandoeng, being sites of expected Japanese attack, were manned, armed and as ready as they could be. All intelligence on previous Japanese invasions suggested the Allies should expect a two-pronged attack. Then, suddenly 77th HAA were issued new orders. 240 Battery were to move quickly to Tjilatjap to defend the port, 241 Battery were to gather in Soerabaya to defend the docks. Jack's 239 Battery were ordered to remain in position at Batavia and continue preparations for invasion.

Jack was on night-watch on the quayside and felt the suffocating anticipation of eerie calm before deathly storm. He looked beyond the still water of the harbour to the peaking sea, which he could only just hear crashing on the low seaward wall. He was unable to prevent his mind from imagining a thousand Japanese ships materialising, drifting through the gloom and darkness toward him. He constantly rubbed the visions from his tired eyes, until a hand on his shoulder told him he was relieved and he fell exhausted into his bunk in the dawning day of the 1st of March.

- MARCH 1942 -

It was almost midday when Jack woke to raised voices. He swatted a fly from his clammy cheek and sat up. Fragmented news was coming through that the Japanese had landed at dawn near Kalidjati, but reports were intermittent and patchy. Jack dressed quickly and joined the men gathered outside around the open-shuttered radio room. He tucked his shirt into his shorts, looking about anxiously as everyone shouted at once, "Whats happening?" "My god, where are they now?" "How many are they?" The clamour only quietened on the arrival of the CO. Jack waited alongside his brothers, tense and silent in the dripping heat for confirmation the Japanese had landed *somewhere*. They had landed on Java, at Kalidjati, and were now on the move. "Where is that?" asked Jack rubbing his temple as orders were issued to prepare for a second front invasion at the port, "Kalidjati? More than a hundred miles east," replied someone as he hurried past. The men dashed to positions, gathering equipment and loading guns in readiness. For the rest of that day, and the day after, a dozen men and Jack lay, rifles in sweaty hands, in scrub to the side of the warehouses they had only recently filled with unloaded cargo. Two *Bofors* were concealed with another dozen men in thicker scrub and bushes nearby. Jack's small pocket of men were replicated in groups lying in wait all around the port and harbour. They listened to the slosh of the tide in sickening wait, as oblivious clouds drifted across the sky. Jack inclined his ear to every sound, as if he'd be able to make out gunfire a hundred miles away. As the second day wore on each man became more concerned, hushed talk turned to irritation, "*What* are they waiting for?" "Why doesn't someone *tell* us where they are, they could've landed *anywhere* by now!" The 2nd of March drifted into the third as endless rolling watches rotated, each man unable to rest between shifts. Late that sweltering, still afternoon came the urgent order to withdraw to Bandoeng, a journey of over ninety miles. Batavia was to be declared an open city by Dutch command. The remaining RAF and the men of 239 Battery would have to leave the civilian population to the imminent Japanese invasion, to hope and pray for the best. 239 was the only battery to have retained heavy artillery and it was an immense task to simply up sticks and traverse the muddy country roads. Meanwhile reports came in of Japanese moving rapidly across the island, as Allied forces attempted to establish a new base at Bandoeng. 239 Battery struggled cross-country and arrived wearily at Bandoeng on the 5th of March, joining the rest of the remaining Allied force, some ten miles from the advancing Japanese front. No sooner had the British arrived than the Dutch commanders declared Bandoeng would immediately be made an open town. Dutch command stated that this action would effectively end Allied resistance to the approaching Japanese force. They'd argued there could be no guerrilla war as the Javanese could not entirely be trusted to support Allied action. Discussion, often heated, burned on as midnight of the fifth rolled into morning of the sixth. In the blossoming light of early morning, the RAF were ordered to withdraw from Bandoeng immediately with 239 Battery to follow by noon. Jack and the men again packed up what little had not already been jettisoned, as the Dutch attempted to negotiate some semblance of honourable surrender with the Japanese. Many now took the small window of opportunity to try for the coast, to get away, perhaps to Australia. Of those on the run, most were tracked down in jungles and forested hillsides, but a few reached the ocean, bargaining for transport with locals. Some made it off the island before the devastating Allied capitulation. The British officers and their men argued they were wholly against any surrender as word travelled through the ranks of the immediate laying down of arms.

The Japanese would accept nothing of negotiations, demanding only the formal arrival of the Governor General and his commander in chief at Kalidjati airfield would satisfy their *honour*. The irony of their dishonourable demands was lost on them as the Japanese commanders threatened failure to comply would result in total destruction of Bandoeng and its civilian population. The only option offered the Allies was to surrender unconditionally. As the Dutch Commander agreed to complete surrender, so British, Australian and American forces on Java reluctantly capitulated as one. The men of 239 Battery were not aware of developments as they had already retreated from Bandoeng, heading south dragging the remaining *Bofors* behind their three-ton trucks. They choked along deep rut-mudded roads, rolling and sticking, their wheels spinning futilely as snippets of news filtered through their wireless. A rumour the Allies had been ordered to capitulate was met with disbelief and shouting amongst the men. The possibility that their army had simply unconditionally surrendered seemed absurd, but it filled the men with horror, and wild ideas of slinking into the forest to lie in wait for their enemy. However, without supplies, low ammunition nor the will from their commanding Dutch officers putting such suggestions into practice was impossible. Instead, on the 7th of March the men of 239 Battery set about digging in to make a last stand on Java. In the darkness, an officer and a couple of the men cautiously crept back up the road to scout out enemy approaches. They stopped abruptly on hearing voices and approaching boots. Standing silently, poised to fire, they were relieved to find it was an Australian officer who breathlessly informed them he had been searching for them. He had brought the news the Dutch had *already* capitulated the previous evening at 6pm. The Battery was undone, and ordered to re-join the Allied forces, now converging on Kalidjati. A few days later, Jack and 239 Battery reluctantly marched across the airfield and stood to dusty attention alongside the remaining units and regiments of Java. The Allied formal surrender was accepted by the Japanese in the fading light of 12th March. Jack's damp face twitched in the ebbing heat as Japanese officers strutted to and fro. They ceremonially signed fluttering papers on a table dragged out of the mess hall. Jack's stomach fell heavily in sickening anticipation. Bile rose in his throat as he swallowed hard, trying to contain his anger, afraid of nothing but losing control and becoming overwhelmed. It suddenly felt to him a futile five weeks and three days spent manhandling cumbersome equipment, pointlessly moving about the inhospitable countryside, and growing ever more weary and demoralised. Now, cut off and taken captive Jack felt deep despair for the first time. He knew there would be no Dunkirk for them.

The prisoners were transported back to Batavia by train. Jack wondered what awaited them as he slumped amongst the cramped men. He hoped to write to his family soon. And, as ever he wondered when the next meal would be, if there even would be a next meal. The men lurched into the capital and were trucked to a crumbling prison which ran alongside a decaying Dutch-built canal in the north of Batavia. The place overflowed with prisoners and Jack struggled to stay together with men he knew but quickly became separated in the chaos. He stood for a rambling roll-call, feeling lost and abandoned. He swayed in the line, his stomach groaning, as he thought of his mother. His mind often drifted to her in hunger, as her Sunday dinners materialised in his mind's eye, the smell rose in his nostrils as he stared at the hard ground. His thoughts turned to Irene. She seemed to appear in his mind as evening fell, as he thought of their dates. Walking arm in arm to see a cinema show at dusk and their brief kisses under the glowing streetlamp at the end of her road. He roused quickly as he was push-marched into a darkened cell. He sat in a corner and leant his back against a cold wall, shoulder to shoulder with a man either side. He had to pull his knees up under his chin as a man in front perched on the floor, similarly cramped. The man to his right turned his head, looking Jack squarely in the eye. Jack squinted, blinking back in the gloom. The man ever so slightly nodded. His arms were folded over his knees, his hands clutching his elbows. He extended a hand to Jack by simply turning over his palm as he released his elbow. Jack reached across, took the hand and shook it. "From bad to worse, wouldn't you say?" Jack turned, it was a recognisable voice. It was one of the chaps from 239 Battery he knew, George Brennan. "George?" Jack whispered, "Where have you been?" George returned his stare to the floor between his feet. They spoke softly of the unravelling situation and both agreed the predicament was bleak. They knew each other's faces but had not spoken at any length and now swapped their stories. "You're only a week younger than me. When did you say you were born? Twenty-third of November 1920? Mine's the 15th, so that's erm only eight days!" "-you're not far from me either, Ramsbottom to Hyde. We were practically neighbours!" Noted George as he reeled off his service number. Jack stopped short, "What? What did you say?" he said, eyes bulging, "George Brennan, one-seven-nine-four-five-ten, why?" Jack extended his hand then tapping his chest he spoke softly, "Jack Frith, one-seven-nine-four-five-*twenty-one*." They looked at each other, then smiled briefly. George replied, "Must've been stood just ahead of you in the line..." his voice trailed off as Jack's face reddened. He felt fired up, and hissed, "I'll be damed if my family would know I am a prisoner after only a few weeks of fighting. We will escape and..." George placed his hand on Jack's elbow, "You know that's impossible, kid." Jack suddenly turned to George, an idea in his eyes. "What say we swap service numbers? The Japs won't know the difference. At home they won't know we're prisoners will they? It'll mess up the Jap paperwork too, won't it? What do you say?" George scratched his head, "I don't know, what if they realise-" "How can they?" interjected Jack, George's frown turned to a mischievous grin. The following day the men waited in columns, moving slowly forward, toward rows of Japanese soldiers seated at small desks stacked with reams of papers. Jack stepped up, repeating his name and the service number of his friend. He could not help himself, he smirked a tiny smile. A guarding Japanese soldier leapt forward, slapping him hard across the face. Jack righted himself and stood firm, his chin jutted and his cheek blazing. George stood in a column to the left of Jack and had seen the slap as he'd stepped up. He felt furious, causing him to forget himself as he tried to catch Jack's eye, just as the Japanese soldier asked his name and number. George repeated his own, off-pat then hesitated. He had been distracted and in the moment realised with a cold chill he'd repeated his *own* number. George stood silently for a moment, causing a guard to push him hard. George shook himself and stumbled on his way. Back in the cell, they agreed to stick to using the same number, "We can't change now, but they'll never know will they?" Jack spoke quietly to avoid drawing unwanted attention to their conversation, "I'm sorry, kid," said George, "I got distracted. Are you all right?" Jack felt his cheek, still hot and stinging, "I'm all right." George continued, "We'll have to be careful not to stand together in line, we don't want to repeat the same number one after the other, agreed?" "Agreed," nodded Jack.

As the first week in the camp came to an end men began falling ill and rapidly losing weight. They could not stomach the poor food. Their rations suddenly consisted of stale rice with a few pieces of indistinguishable vegetable added to the evening meal. Most still had a little money and were able to buy a few items of food which they shared amongst small naturally formed groups. Added to the worsening conditions and illness that quickly spread through the camp, a few days later working parties began. Jack, along with most of the able-bodied men were rounded up, packed in the back of a truck and sent out to repair the aerodromes, filling in craters made by Japanese bomber 'planes only a matter of weeks earlier. Over the following weeks and months Jack worked across most of the small airstrips around Batavia, filling craters and stamping down the loose earth in the heat of the day with only a few minutes morning and afternoon break, and a slightly longer noon-day rest from the back-breaking work. Jack knew he had a strong constitution when it came to food and it now served him, protecting him a little from the illnesses that struck down many around him. He could stomach the coagulated rice with a sprinkle of sugar the Japanese served up, along with the eggs he bought with his dwindling funds. The rations were small however, and despite his attempts to supplement his diet, he found he was almost always hungry. As the day's slop spattered his mess-tin he found he didn't even look, he simply ate whatever it was as quickly as possible.

It wasn't long before all talk turned to plans of escape. Each man's idea was thoroughly considered but, ultimately rejected. The men were alone on an island swarming with Japanese soldiers, and a population whose allegiances were largely unknown, and whose language none of the men spoke. They were surrounded by a sea of hostility with any journey being thousands of miles to Allied land. There was also simply no access to any kind of transport, nor could they rely on the hospitality of the local people, as any help given would no doubt attract dire consequences for aiding prisoners of war. The talk of escape boosted morale while it lasted, until each avenue was one by one deemed hopeless and all plans and hopes were finally extinguished. A week later, while spirits were still low, the Japanese soldiers ransacked the small cells, searching for anything they considered illegal, confiscating everything from the camp wireless to clothes, equipment, money and a variety of personal items. Jack buckled mutely, as soldiers up-ended his kit bag and precious photographs of his dear family were spilled onto the floor and trampled under their two-toed boots. A few days later Jack caught a fever. He sweated heavily, hallucinating he was swimming in the dark reservoir pool of his youth, gasping for air and clawing for a surface he could not reach. He was unaware of his reaching out and shouting as his army brothers tried to soothe him and help him rest, but there was little they could do. It was days before the fever broke and Jack came to. He found himself briefly unable to place his location until the walls of the cell emerged from the haze and he slowly began to recognise his miserable prison surroundings.

Over the following months the men became hungrier as rations shrank and supplies seemed to run short. Still, the working parties went out. The commanding officers of 239 Battery and others had tried to keep up morale, keeping as many men off the working parties as they were able, negotiating for supplies at the risk of bashings from the soldiers, and trying to keep their two Dutch doctors in basic supplies to aid the sickening men. It was a daunting task as they tried to pull the men away from despondency, looking for ways to keep them occupied in the camp during their brief free-time and scant rest days. They organised football matches between the men who were well enough to play. The men were keen to show their grit, and developed the games into a sort of football league. Generally they were just a few chaps pitted against other batteries, all matches obviously being friendlies. Jack occasionally played but became frustrated, he was not as strong now. He had been a good striker at Green Street school, now his feet ached and he tired quickly. The matches gradually became shorter and several 'half times' interrupted each game. The Japanese soldiers seemed bewildered by the effort spent jogging about the patch of scrub in the prison, kicking about the balled up cloth, wrapped in rubber. They seemed irritated by the morale boost such games brought and delighted in withdrawing permissions at random for any requests, leaving the men mutely frustrated. Then, without warning they would again be allowed to buy various small packets of food, sometimes a pineapple, sometimes tobacco or tinned goods, all at black market prices and all under the whim and watchful eyes of the Japanese soldiers. Jack could feel his body weakening as his weight dropped little by little and the work intensified. Eventually the football games were rarely played as the working parties increased yet more. No man could spare the energy needed for such exertions. One morning, at roll call a buzz circulated, whispered from ear to ear, of a planned move. Jack paled as he heard the rumoured destination was thought to be the mosquito-infested swamp docks of Tandjong Priok. It seemed hardly a moment since he had lain there amongst the warehouses, awaiting these Japanese soldiers. At least he had been a free man then.

- MAY 1942 -

The new camp at Tandjong Priok, on first impression seemed better than the overcrowded cells of Boei Glodok, but Jack quickly realised the little extra space would only last until all the prisoners were corralled from all over the island. Jack stood in line at roll call, turning briefly to nod to George Brennan, as they took care to ensure they did not line up together. Desks had again been set out and Japanese soldiers were taking down names. As the men shuffled forward, Jack pushed a little ahead whilst George hung back. The soldiers pushed through the lines, shoving the men about, pulling by the elbow and putting them into different lines, all the while shouting incoherently. George ended up some seventeen men ahead of Jack in the same straggling line. Jack strained to see what was going on. He watched as George moved back down the line. As he passed, George held up a small rectangle of wood secured about his neck with string, a number was stamped on it. Jack frowned, George replied with a shrug, as Jack moved a step forward. At the head of the line Jack again repeated George's number, more hesitantly this time but aware he couldn't go back now. "Jack Frith, one-seven-nine-four-five-*one-oh*," he repeated, forcing himself to check the last two digits in his mind as he uttered them. The squat figure of the Japanese soldier squinted at a list of names, then nodded as he checked the large flapping folio, finding Jack's name and marking a number next to it. A second soldier checked the number and confirmed with a nod, rolling an adjustable stamp onwards one digit and thumping the right-hand corner of a large rectangular index card with the number. Jack recognised his own name in the top left corner and halfway down blinked as he saw the name, 'Frith, John, Robert' typed there. Something caught in Jack's throat as these words, the name of his dear father, swam in front of his eyes. He could hardly focus for the water filling his vision as the solider barked at him to lower his head, prompting a guard nearby to push his neck down with a grunt. Dazed and reeling, Jack felt the string slide down his neck and a small rectangular piece of wood tap lightly on his chest as he lifted his head. He was pushed away by the guard. Stumbling back, Jack muttered to himself, "So, do they know...where I am?" He realised his family might now know he was a prisoner of war. He looked down to the tag, his fingers finding the rough wood. Lifting the tag and tilting it into the sun, he recognised he had become Japanese prisoner of war number '3310.'

The dilapidated camp, using the dockside warehouses damaged by the Japanese aerial bombardment, buzzed with a million mosquitos. The men who were already ill were now threatened with rampant malaria to add to their misery. Conditions again worsened with the outbreak of a major dysentery epidemic affecting three quarters of the men. Jack sat briefly in the shade of a crumbling warehouse as his stomach turned. The churning contractions made him fear the worst, that he too had succumbed. Much to his relief, he decided after a latrine visit, it must have been the slight increase in rice quantity that caused his stomach upset. Nevertheless, he knew he had lost weight. He bent his arm, flexing his bicep muscle which appeared like a tiny bird breast on an otherwise thinning arm. The food might have slightly increased in the new camp, but the guards were certainly much worse. Bashings became a frequent peril to avoid however impossible that was. It was as if the Japanese had been briefly preoccupied with organising themselves, but now settled into their malevolent roles as captors. The aggression escalated immediately on arrival at Tandjong Priok. A smash to the side of a man's head causing the pulsating sensation of trickling blood, the blunt crack of a rifle butt to a jaw that brought stunned ringing to the ears. A jab. A kick. A punch.

Each immensely painful to the unprepared man. Each victim unable to retaliate. Thus, each cowardly attack was borne mutely, stoically. Jack considered whether there were too many prisoners for the soldiers to bash *everyone* everyday and tried his best to avoid conflict where he could. He quickly recognised, with ringing ears, that keeping a low profile afforded no protection.

Soon, new working parties were assembled and as work began Jack found himself unloading ships and clearing debris at the same dockside where only a matter of weeks earlier he had unloaded the *Bofors* and kit of his own Battery. Aside from longer working days, poorer provisions and the ever watchful squinting of the Japanese soldiers, it had initially felt eerily familiar. He found porting the cargo from ship to dockside, pulling at ropes and manhandling crates all day in the heat, deceptively similar to army life and at first had to keep looking to his ragged string and the wooden tag suspended there to remind him it wasn't some wretched hallucination. The working parties sent out to the docks, were pushed harder each day, loading and unloading cargo and supplies. It was heavy, dirty and dangerous work and they returned filthy and exhausted to the camp at dusk. Jack often thought to himself if he'd worked like that for *Rexine* leather-cloth works or the army he'd have been factory manager or promoted to colonel within a fortnight. Each day dragged endlessly on and on. Every evening Jack returned to camp, ate a cup of mouldering rice slop, and come darkness lay down in the gloom amongst a melee of equally exhausted and filthy men. It seemed obvious to the men but the Japanese soldiers seemed unable to connect the terrible state of men returning from the working parties and the cases of serious illness affecting those same men. It was quickly realised they *had* made the connection they were simply indifferent to the suffering they caused. In a surprising concession the men were briefly allowed to swim in the sea to clean themselves. No warning was given, the working party was simply marched to one end of the harbour as the sun drifted slowly towards the horizon. As Jack plunged into the water weeks of accumulated sweat and grime were freed from his body and swirled around him. Briefly underwater, he looked about and saw the blurred underbellies of the ships moored there, until visibility fogged with the cascade of men entering the water and he sank down. As he descended it felt dark like the reservoir of his youth and he kicked out, surfacing quickly, spitting the seawater from his gagging throat.

The initial restraint of the soldiers at the docks, where they'd simply ordered the men to work while they settled down to card games, only occasionally looking to check on their charges, disappeared within a few days. Jack soon witnessed the first very bad bashing. A man had accidentally tripped with a heavy shoulder-load of cargo, spilling the load all across the dock and knocking into several men in the line. No one had been hurt but the mess would take some sorting out. The man had looked up a bit dazed and sheepish, but full of humour at his Chaplinesque stumble. The Japanese soldiers had descended like demons on him, beating him mercilessly as he curled foetally bracing his arms around his head. Jack started forward but was held back by men around him. Other PoWs had started forward and were similarly held back. Jack felt a rising rage he found difficult to contain and had to look away in impotent fury, angry tears brimming. When the soldiers moved off, screaming for work to continue three PoWs rushed to the prone man. They carefully lifted and carried him back to camp, into the makeshift hospital.

A year slunk by as his life fell into a monotonously dangerous routine. Jack had continued work at the dockside, hauling back-breaking cargo every day. He soon ceased marking the days. The scratched five-bar gates on the beam in his hut weathered as he missed days, then weeks at a time. Then, a year had drifted by, as he became suspended in a sweating void of time. Jack watched as prisoners departed for other occupied lands, shipped away as if a forced army of prisoners were gathering elsewhere. Every day he descended into the holds of each metal ship to retrieve supplies he was not able to possess but so badly needed. He sadly manhandled crates and barrels into the same warehouses where he'd stacked ammunition the previous year. It was late in the afternoon as he stood frozen in the doorway of a warehouse at the end of the dockside. He hadn't been to this far end of the dock, to this warehouse for month. His mouth gaped open as he stared unblinking at great stacks of unopened, crumbling *Red Cross* parcels. He wept as he placed a hand on a brown papered, shoebox-sized package. They were tied with string and addressed,

```
PRISONERS PARCELS,
BRITISH RED CROSS
AND ORDER OF ST JOHN,
WAR ORGANISATION.
```

They were stamped all over, but the rest of the printing was foreign to him. The only word he could decipher was 'soap'. He recoiled in realisation of the significance. These parcels were clearly intended for them, the prisoners. The Japanese were not only withholding them but stockpiling them, but to what end? Jack reasoned it must be to both deny the men essential supplies and to use as stores for the Japanese. He reeled as a further ramification hit him, clearly those at home did know of their captivity and importantly, aid had been sent. The latter realisation gave him a tiny, warm glow of hope as he wondered if there might be some sort of liberation plan. He wondered then, how the war was progressing. Whether Allied troops might at that very moment be on their way. He wondered if it meant his family knew he was a prisoner. His head dropped to his chest. In that moment he wished he had not used the wrong service number. He worried his family, instead of being told of his survival albeit as a prisoner of war, they might have been notified he was 'missing in action'. His heart ached for them. Perhaps they thought he was dead. He wished he could shout out for them to hear! How he longed to see them, how he longed to go home. His eyes brimmed with painful tears. He stopped himself suddenly hearing the sound of boots. Quickly, he darted through the open doorway, picking up a sack and hoisting it onto his shoulder as he blended into a line of men moving alongside the adjacent warehouse. He looked sideways as a Japanese soldier peered into the warehouse, shrugged and closed the door.

Jack's work at the dock sometimes enabled him to obtain a few food items. Only those small enough to be concealed in a shirt sleeve or long short pocket. For this purpose he'd tried to hold onto items of clothing as he shared his spoils with his immediate group of friends, who in turn helped him keep his shirt in buttons and shorts in patches. These were mostly men of 239 Battery that had come through the endless trials of the long year together, including Henry, Harold and George. They also worked on the dockside, but in separate areas. Whilst moving supplies, Jack found the holds begin to feel claustrophobic. He felt their heavy walls closing in on him as he sorted and stacked cargo, attaching hooks to netted sacks and tying thick ropes around crates ready for hoisting. The very thought of the sweating supplies in the damp holds would wake him at night in the camp. He'd leap up panting, having dreamt he was trapped and suffocating, slowly drowning and unable to reach the surface. Sometimes he dreamt he hung suspended in deep dark water, watching shadows of ships passing around him like circling sharks.

As 1942 drew to an end, and their first Christmas as prisoners of war approached, the officers managed to procure extra rations and the men had Christmas Day itself off the working parties. Jack thought of the previous Christmas Day at sea off the African coast and wondered inevitably of what his fate would be by the time Christmas 1943 came around. He wondered, "I could be home?" Then, darkly, "Will I still be alive?" Jack sat heavily against a wall and slid to the ground, his precious mess tin in hand, as a game of football got underway. The food for their Christmas lunch had included an extra ration of rice, some vegetables and sugar and, amazingly, a blob of jam. Jack ate it all, trying to savour every bite. He stirred the jam into a blob of rice he'd separated out and saved for the purpose and tried to imagine he was eating his mother's rice pudding. He rolled the thin sweet mixture around his mouth, startling as he found he'd salivated at the taste of sticky fruit. The image of his mother and home made Jack feel a little better, as he tried to send them unconscious thoughts of him. He pictured them all sitting at the table at Spring Street, and wondered if they heard him. He realised his mother would no doubt be upset that day. He imagined suddenly they were soberly raising a glass in his honour, wishing him home. The vision evaporated as his chest heaved in sadness. He stood, hoping to shake away the emotion as one of the commanding officers passed and tapped his shoulder, "Come on Jack, we need you. Centre forward, son..." The idea of football helped him push family from his immediate thoughts. He joined his brother prisoners and set about defending the honour of his country, in the first England vs Holland prisoner of war Christmas football match. It was an energetic game considering their condition. Despite their surroundings, light-hearted banter resounded around the hard-earth pitch. Jack was delighted to score England's equaliser ending the game dramatically in a draw as incredulous and confused Japanese soldiers looked on. They simply could not comprehend European spirit in the face of adversity.

- MARCH 1943 -

The months rolled on, and the first year of captivity officially passed on the eighth of March. The year had changed Jack dramatically. He walked slowly across the hard baked earth of the parade ground in the sole-thinned boots to wait for *makan*, standing quite still in the line. A slight figure, his baggy shorts and thinning shirt hung around his weakened body, metal mess tin limply held in his bony hand as he waited. He hoped there would be an extra ration today. Around his neck rubbed a taut string, strung through by the worn and smoothed piece of wood. The number etched onto the wood still showing his prisoner of war number, **3310**. He detested being numbered and imagined himself every day come wars eventual end, pulling it violently from his neck and throwing it to the ground in disgust. He stood in the line, a faint grin appeared and disappeared as he imagined doing such a thing. He'd imagined the consequences, causing his grin to fall away. He stepped a pace forward as the line moved and inclined his head to the sky, closing his eyes to the bright sun. He swore he could hear the faint chirrup of birds. He transformed the sound into English garden birds and looked to imaginary fluttering wings in the trees against a pale blue English sky. He imagined he felt a weaker sun on his face and raised his chin a little to the non-existent cool breeze while the birds burst their tiny bird-hearts in morning song. He found it peaceful, being lost in his minds thoughts and he chose to stay, anchoring himself to the sound. He startled as he heard a gravelly screech and turned to look as the birds scattered, flapping from the canopy. The screech was his own bicycle hard-breaking in the dry mud of a back lane near his home. His *home*. He looked down at himself, his carefree self before the war. He'd been a young man, baggy shorted and shirted, his sleeves rolled up, wrapped in striped tank top and weighed down by nothing more than heavy boots, as he dangled astride his oversized grid-iron. The wind flapped his unruly hair and his cheeks flushed as he shouted to his brother, George, "Come *on*, I can't wait *all* day!" His brother was a way behind on his old clanking bicycle. Jack chuckled out loud, eyes screwed shut and suddenly his laugh seemed conspicuously loud. He opened his eyes to search the real scene, careful not to break his daydream. No one had noticed, the line of thin men had not moved forward and no one had seemed to hear nor turned to look. Jack slunk back into his thoughts, hoping they would still be there. He found George as he shouted back to Jack. He was panting, trying to keep up. "Don't worry, there's plenty of time, kid!" George called. Jack smiled muttering to himself, "Aye plenty of time," shouting back with a grin, "but not plenty of leg power! Come on!" George laughed. Jack slapped a pedal with his sole and it span back creating dust as he wheeled off down the lane, George pedalling hard to catch up. Jack threw his hands in the air, hooting loudly and laughing as he freewheeled ahead of the dust cloud created by his hard tyres. The wind blew through his dark hair and his shirt sleeves unravelled and flapped. He was breathless but felt free as a bird. He heard his own laughter echoing around him as he blinked, squinting in the familiar glaring light. He wiped sweat from his burnt brow, licking his lips dry of salt from his own perspiration. Jack exhaled deeply, as thoughts of home and his brother faded. He sighed, and held out his battered mess tin, feeling the weight increase a little as a rice blob landed in it. Carrying his tin to a stack of wood near the perimeter wall he settled there, pushing his sharpened spoon into the grey mixture. As he chewed on the gritty tasteless slop he turned the spoon over and over in his hand. One side displayed his initials, 'J. F.' And, on the other 'Hyde,' his distant home. This single word represented another world, entirely separate from the miserable void he inhabited. He closed his eyes and tried again to bring the other world into focus.

He knew it will be difficult to take himself there. He folded his arms and leant back on the creaking wood, resettled his bare feet and tried to plunge into home. "Picture their faces, picture them, describe them," he told himself. George, would be twenty-six by now. Jack had turned twenty-two the previous November, there in the camp. He closed his eyes and tried to see George. Suddenly, he was there. He looked thinner and taller than Jack, wearing long trousers that were too big for his lithe waist. He was wrapped round with a thick leather belt that seemed to hold both him and his trousers up. George pulled a thin hand through his slick black hair and shook his head, smiling. Jack heard him at his ear, "You're always in a hurry, Jack!" Jack startled, his eyes began watering. He turned to look, opening his eyes, "George?" But, there was no one there. He closed them again and pedalled away, shouting for George to follow. It seemed like yesterday. He moved his head and saw the back alley of their cobbled Spring Street in Hyde. Jack free-wheeled past the bosomed mothers in aprons and headscarves. They whipped their cold, wet washing onto their lines, wooden pegs squeezed between pursed lips. They always looked as if they were about to scold someone. Jack swerved through the back gate hardly slowing and screeched into the backyard whilst George followed behind. Their mother stood on the back step. Hopping off his bicycle as he approached, George neatly stepped beside it for the last strides to the yard gate and quietly wheeled it through. George spoke first, "Sorry we're late," nodding accusingly at Jack, who opened his mouth to protest as their mother cut them both off. "Never mind, you're here now," George pulled her leg, "Aye, but only just," Their mother gave him a hard stare. Jack chuckled. George never was any good at pulling a leg. His honest face blushed at his attempt, and he quickly replied to her stare, "Sorry, I was just joking..." Mother cut him off, "Hmm, Jack's influence no doubt! Anyway, never mind and come on with you. Dad will be here any minute!" She turned and disappeared into the shadowed doorway. George leant his bicycle over Jack's protectively and closed the thickly painted yard gate on its iron latch and followed her into the house. Jack desperately wanted to follow, he was deep in home now, his mind filled with the hanging layer of factory smoke and Manchester drizzle, whilst his body sat in the sweating heat of Batavia. Jack pressed his eyes further closed and tried to conjure up the memories, some like yesterday, some as if they'd happened a lifetime ago. He scratched at his neck, slapping a mosquito dead and pushed his mind to find them again. He thought he heard English birds singing, but couldn't now tell if he was dreaming. He opened his eyes and looked to the remaining grains of rice occupying his tin bowl. It was no use, they had gone and he couldn't find them.

Jack found he was now often too exhausted to think absently, for his flights of fancy. It had been a harrowing year of lost souls and waning bodies. He had been able to keep his mind clear in these places, in the passing of days by visiting in his thoughts whenever he could. It gave him slices of normality as he refused to accept this nightmare reality would never end. He refused to feel beaten, he refused to give in. He had wanted to fight on with his brothers but they were undone by their Dutch superiors. He'd defended the island and held on but when called to surrender he'd had no choice. Now, the Japanese said their surrender was dishonourable, and that the men deserved no respect. Jack had gritted his teeth in the early days, hoping for a chance to prove them wrong. But they were a monstrous machine, squashing men down, taking every ounce of dignity. They had deliberately weakened the men, so they'd have no will to fight. The men did their best to sabotage and disobey in secret, but they had to keep in mind that a man could be killed for failing to salute or bow low enough, or for looking at a Japanese soldier the wrong way. Jack chose his battles with great care. But, as the first year ticked by, he felt weakened and strained, and he began to drift, almost unbidden from hazy daydream to sickening reality in alarming cycles. He unconsciously plodded on, simply surviving as he ambled back to his bunk in crowded, darkened rooms. It prodded his memory, of playing outside in bright hot sun as a child, then going into the house, finding it dark and still as his eyes struggled to adjust. He remembered feeling with patting palms, along the wallpapered hall into the back room as he stepped gingerly around the sideboard he knew was there but could not see. His eyes blurred and his view fogged as he felt along a wall of peeling paint in the dilapidated camp building, finding the open door to the cramped sleeping quarters. He didn't know where he was, and let out a manic giggle. He found his bunk and sat heavily, his body weary and his head spinning. Someone jumped down from the bunk above as Jack rolled from his bunk ledge onto the floor. He gazed about, lolling and semi-conscious as the pair of boots landed heavily near his face. The thud of boots and a shout 'hello' announced the arrival of his dad and sister Gladys. Jack stood with his brother. They nudged each other as they listened to the thud of working man's boots clodding through the front door and into the hall.

Mother flurried her sons away and they obeyed, stepping to one side in readiness to greet their dad. The door opened, revealing his startled face. His face broke into a grin as their mother beamed at him. The little family grasped his hands, shaking them excitedly from wrist to folded-sleeved elbows, congratulating him. Mother called first, "Happy birthday, Dad," as they all chorused. "Happy birthday, Dad." The merry shouts echoed in the air, as if spoken aloud in Jack's mind. He wondered deliriously if he had said it out loud. "Happy birthday, Dad?" "What did he say?" Asked one of the men leaning over Jack. "He must have hit his head," said another as they lifted him limply under his arms and ankles, back onto his bunk. Jack mumbled, his eyes watering, "Happy birthday, Dad," as someone pressed a cup of liquid to his lips. Jack's body responded and he opened his eyes. "Too far, I've gone too far," he murmured, "I have to come back." He squeezed his eyes tight shut and mustered something from within to remove the images from his mind. He opened his eyes fully, to remind himself where he was. Lying in his bunk in the camp at Tandjong Priok. He could still hear their voices, now only a whisper, "Happy Birthday..." and he let them fade.

- 7 MARCH 1943 -

In Groton, Connecticut a newly completed *Gato* class submarine rolled down the slipway, gathering speed as it splashed heavily into the water amid cheers from the throng gathered on the quayside. The soaked red, white and blue bunting sagged heavily as it hung from the stern of the USS *Bonefish*.

- APRIL 1943 -

Jack had been granted several days rest on the Dutch doctor's orders and felt good deal better, although not actually well. The men he'd shared his stolen food with had all gathered to take care of him, sharing rations as he built up his strength a little. By the time he returned to his first working party, tasks at the docks seemed to have dried up. Men were now being gathered in large numbers, grouped together and shipped out to god only knew where, leaving an even more fragmented group of men behind. Many officers seemed to have disappeared first, and each time a group were taken the remainder had to reform a chain of command. It seemed arbitrary who was selected, the Japanese simply walked the line at roll call, ticking off names and numbers. Those left behind assumed the destination must be other camps. As no one returned, it was concluded the transports were permanent moves. Then, at the end of the first week of April, four thousand prisoners of war were lined up and given inoculations that made them queasy and lethargic. It had begun. The transport of four thousand men to the spice islands of the Moluccas had begun. The following day a thousand names were ticked off, including Jack's, and allocated the transport code A-3, bound for Liang. These thousand Liang men were made up of five hundred RAF, three-hundred and twenty Royal Artillery including the 77ths and a tank brigade of Kings Own Hussars. All four thousand spice islands men left Tandjong Priok for the train station. Each was issued with two kilos of rice and two small loaves. Pairs of Japanese soldiers pushed through the men, poking at the mens' feet with long batons, shouting and gesticulating to crates of rubberised boots they carried between them. For once, having a smaller frame was useful for Jack, as the boots that were too small for the others fit him quite well. Nonetheless, Jack found the two-toed boots a strange and uncomfortable fit. The train journey was intolerable, with dozens more men crushed into each carriage than capacity allowed, en route to Spoorwegstation the main station at Soerabaya. The journey took thirty-six horrendous hours. On arrival, the men largely fell from the carriages, many were carried to the temporary camp. Twenty dysentery cases were identified and taken off the transport, replaced with reserve prisoners. The first victim of the transport passed away due to heart failure the following morning, most likely due to the stressful pressure and lack of water during the journey. He'd felt horribly faint and ill as they'd fallen from the train and his heart simply gave out.

In the early morning of the next day the men marched exhaustedly down to the harbour as the sun began to rise. The orange flecked sky and scent of a fresh day merged with the spray of salty sea, filling Jack's lungs. A man near Jack leaned across pressing against his shoulder as they marched. "I heard someone say the Japs have said we are going to a holiday camp!" Jack frowned, "Ha! righto! I don't think so. Do you?" The man leaned away from Jack as if he'd crushed a believable dream. Jack blinked hard as he looked at the man, whose face was twitching excitedly. Jack shook his head, clearly he'd had begun to lose his grip on the situation. Anchored in the harbour were five ships, the *Kunitama Maru, Amagi Maru* and the *Matsukawa Maru* alongside the *Mayahashi Maru* and the *Nishi Maru.* The latter two ships would carry the thousand men to Ambon. The former would take men on to Ceram and Haruku. As a mass of swarming bedraggled ants, the four thousand formed up at the quayside at Soerabaya. The port bustled with movement as two of the ships, the *Mayahashi Maru* and the *Nishi Maru* slowly moved to dock at the quay, the others remained at anchor. The scene reminded Jack of visiting Greenock with his brother some two and a half years and a lifetime before. It brought back the mixed emotions on departing Gourock in the sleet, now nearly a year and a half ago. It seemed impossible to Jack that the men formed up on the quayside could possibly fit into the ships gathered. Yet, the thousand men were split into RAF and army, and Jack found himself with four hundred Royal Artillery and Kings Own Hussars. Before they were allowed to board, the men were lined up in rows and ordered to step forward one at a time. At the front of the line stood a soldier with clipboard beside a small table with a box on top. Inside were rectangular cards stacked end on end. As he approached the soldier pulled at the string around Jack's neck, which gave way, snapping easily. Jack had previously had to re-tie it often, but had hoped he'd be the one to pull it off. The soldier hung another cord around Jack's neck, tossing the tattered string into a box on the ground. From now on Jack was no longer prisoner **3310**, he now became prisoner **13208**. Jack again saw his name on the card, there was a momentary flash of recognition as he glimpsed his home address. There wasn't time to read each word, but the familiar '13 Spring' and 'Hyde' jumped at him. It took a moment to understand why the words looked familiar. He frowned, how could *Spring Street* be a real place that still existed somewhere in the world. How he longed to run along the cobbles to his house. To breathlessly arrive at the half-open front door and push it wide open and run inside to the embrace of his family. The thought caught in his throat and his eyes watered. Between the rows pushed medical orderlies with small boxes of glass rods. They told the men to drop their trousers, as they were to be tested for dysentery. The tests were clearly pointless, the rods were pressed into each man's behind then the next, without ever looking or cleaning them. If one man had the disease, now they all surely would. It was a test of indignity, and for the amusement of a deranged enemy rather than serving any medical purpose. Jack and the men were ushered forward and sprayed with disinfectant as they approached the gangplank of the *Nishi Maru*. Jack struggled to keep hold of his kit-bag as he was jostled up a rickety gangplank and onto the deck. Once on board they had then to slosh through a shallow cattle dip. Pushing and shoving was involuntary as men in outer lines were shoved and jabbed at by the Japanese soldiers. Like a flock of starlings avoiding a predator the crowd of men surged this way and that, struggling to remain standing. They made their way across the deck towards ladders descending into the blackness of the holds. The ship's cargo had been loaded by local men, who had made platforms within the hold to increase the numbers who could be pressed in. Jack felt someone fall heavily against him and instinctively reached out as he felt himself falling. His arms were caught by the strong bony grips of the men either side. He rose, catching their faces in the low light, recognition spreading across all their faces as they grinned a shared grimace. These were his two old friends of 239 Battery. "God, I thought you'd had it, Henry," Jack exclaimed tactlessly. "Well, nearly, once or twice, but I'm all right," came the reply. "By God, it's good to see you, present situation excepted!" replied Harold nodding. Despite their moving about, the three men looked at each other gratefully and accepted that whatever was to come, it would only be made better with familiar and trusted friends at one's side. As each man tried to make a small space for himself, Jack looked around in the gloom. He recognised faces he thought he'd not seen since the *Empress of Australia*. In truth, they'd all been held at the same camps together, except they'd been lost on different working parties and had grouped into small survival circles. The hold was cramped and an inadequate transport for the weary men. There was barely room to sit, no indication where they were going or whether there would be any food or water.

Any proper sanitary arrangements were lacking, truly it was a *hellship*. As the men reacquainted themselves with each other they wondered what was to come next as the days intense heat dissipated with the arrival of a tropical rainstorm.

It neared the end of April as the hellship convoy finally set off, escorted by a small launch and two destroyers. The route hugged the coasts of successive islands as the men tried to work out where their destination might be. But that did not concern them as much as the sparse rations. The food, as ever, consisted of rice slop in a thin watery soup. It was little more than water, sometimes with partially cooked vegetables floating in it. Fish had previously been cooked in the water, but had been lifted out, obviously destined for the Japanese soldiers. The fishy residue left the water unappetisingly greasy without the benefit of actual fish to eat. A few days into the voyage it was announced 'today is Hirohito's birthday'. Curry powder was then added to the 'soup'. The spicy taste was something of a change but not helpful in the tropical heat, for thirst nor the upset stomachs it caused most of the men. The following day the men were 'washed' with a seawater sprayed from a hosepipe as they stood, largely naked on deck. The men were allowed a few minutes on deck each morning and afternoon. Jack and the men took this as a very welcome breath of fresh air, as the hold now stank due to the lack of proper latrines. A drum had been placed in the corner of the hold for the purpose, but it quickly reeked, attracting hordes of flies. The convoy had set off with sick aboard, and the numbers of ill men grew as the days passed. Two Dutch doctors were amongst the prisoners, and they helped as best they could despite having no real medical supplies. The Japanese said they were being generous in granting permission for the men to smoke around an ashtray on top of one of the hatch covers, but few had any tobacco. On the fourth day at sea, three ships from the hellish convoy diverted and sailed away, leaving the *Mayahashi Maru* and the *Nishi Maru* to sail alone toward Ambon.

As the *Nishi Maru* docked, its engine idling, at the small port at Ambon, the Commander of the Prisoner Escort ordered the prisoners on deck. A short, squat Japanese officer came aboard and nodded to a subordinate who translated the words he read from a long sheet of paper. He held the paper in both hands and glared at the PoWs as he began to shout his demands. "Ahhh, regulations for prisoners. One, the prisoners disobeying the following orders will be punished with immediate death." He paused for a reaction, looking across the bowed heads of the PoWs. "Those disobeying orders and instructions. Those showing a motion of antagonism and raising a sign of opposition. Those disordering the regulations by individualism, egoism, thinking only about yourselves, rushing for your own goods. Those talking without permission and raising loud voices. Those walking and moving without order. Those carrying unnecessary baggage in disembarking. Those resisting mutually. Those touching the boat's materials, wires, electric lights, tools, switches, etc. Those climbing ladder without order. Those showing action of running away from the boat. Those trying to take more meal than given to them. Those taking more than two blankets." His narrow eyes scanned the silent men. "Those losing patience and disordering the regulation will be heavily punished for the reason of not being able to escort you." His round face ran with sweat which he ignored as he pressed on. "Two, be sure to finish your 'nature's call', evacuate yourself before disembarking. Three, meal will be given soon. One plate only to one prisoner. The prisoners called by the guard will give out the meal quick as possible and honestly. The remaining prisoners will stay in their places and wait for your plate. Those moving from their places reaching for your plate without order will be heavily punished. Same orders will be applied to handling plates after meal. Four, navy of the Great Japanese Empire will not try to punish you *all* with death. Those obeying all the rules and regulations and believing the action and purpose of the Japanese Navy, cooperating with Japan in constructing the New Order of the Great Asia which will lead to world peace, will be well treated." He folded the paper and watched the PoWs for a reaction. They stood motionless and expressionless as the engine chugged to a stop, vibrating the ship as it coughed then ceased, leaving only the sound of the swashing sea on its hull.

- 22 MAY 1943 -

The family gathered around the table for breakfast in the small sitting room at Spring Street. George had arrived the previous evening, staying for one night on his way to Greenock. He had five days leave from retraining as a Flight Mechanic at No.1 School of Technical Training at RAF Halton. He stared at the crumpled telegram, his eyes darting from his father to mother. "It came just now," said his mother. George unfolded the page and read it aloud slowly.

```
Jack Frith, Royal Artillery, 1794521.
Previously reported missing, now classified.
Missing believed Prisoner of War.
```

Bittersweet tears ran down their faces. His mother managed to speak, high-pitched and faltering, "So, at least, at least he is alive, at least he is not, not..." she trailed off, sobbing. George laid a hand on her shoulder gently. His father squeezed her hand, "Yes, he'll be all right now, he will be looked after. Don't worry. There's the Geneva Convention. They have to look after Prisoners of War." George exchanged glances with his father, who looked away. George wasn't sure if he had seen his worried expression. Rumours had trickled through of ill-treatment by the Japanese, but like most wartime rumours were patchy and unclear. "All we can do is wait," George said, putting as much confidence into his tone as he could. "And hope," replied his mother. "Wait and hope." They nodded in agreement as they held hands around the table. His father let go first, and clasped his hands together. "For what we are about to receive—" he said aloud, his thoughts entirely preoccupied with his youngest son.

- CHAPTER THREE -

Ambon Island

- OCTOBER 1943 -

The matches rattled scratchily in the box as the squat Japanese soldier shook it against his ear. Jack followed him warily through squinted eye. Realising he was being closely watched, he closed his eyes. The soldier leant towards Jack, an ugly curl at his lip as he slid open the matchbox, pushing the inside box with extended thumb through the hollow outer box with slow deliberance. Retrieving a match with his dirty, fat fingers he struck it against the rough outer edge. Scraping noisily it travelled along the coarse surface. It scratched, flickered and burst into flame. The sharp, hot smell from the red bead of phosphorus filled Jack's nostrils with smoke as it exploded into life, before settling into a round glow of yellow flame on the end of the matchstick. Instantly intoxicated, Jack inhaled quietly as he sucked in the smoky scent. The glowing light flickered on his eyelids as he saw candlelight dancing on the mantlepiece in the small sitting room of his home. He looked to the grate below, it was stacked and ready. He inhaled the musty smell of coal as he twisted sheets of newspaper, its ink staining his hands. Kneeling in front of the fire he'd built, lit match in hand he touched the papers edge in two, three, four places and settled back on the heels of his boots to watch it catch and take. It was scent more than anything else that took him home so vividly. The flame burnt steadily, licking the kindling wood, warming the coals. He placed another coal on the catching fire, rubbing his hands together to clean off the ink and sparkling black dust but it remained, glistening on his damp palms. Smoke curled from the paper, thickening around the coal and belching upwards, as it chugged up the chimney and out into the cold night Manchester air.

Closing his eyes he spread his blackened hands over his knees to wipe them on his thick woollen work trousers. His hands searched, but he felt only his thin, bare legs. His aching body sagged as his mind roused, reminding him he lay in the sickly heat of the camp hut, and his throat released a pained groan. The squat Japanese soldier had watched Jack intently, touching a small candle with the light from his match. The candlelight grew steady, illuminating Jack's outline with flickering shadows. The soldier watched Jack's hands clutch at his knees as he moaned softly. Seeing the PoW was alive he kicked Jack sharply with the rubber toe of his boot. Jack jumped quickly to sitting position. Opening his eyes wide, Jack habitually nodded, bowing reverentially in his half aware state. The soldier sniffed the air, and reluctantly moved away to other figures, faded silhouettes lying in the half-light of his quivering candle.

Jack rolled onto his aching side as the bamboo rasped under him. He could not stay long. Peering through slatted gaps, the sun began its early morning creep through the wafting trees. He gazed in wonder as the amber light slunk along the bare earth, touching everything in its path with golden warmth. Jack lay still closing his eyes for one more moment. Reclining onto the woven slats gave the illusion of comfort, yet nothing could have been further from the truth. His tired, thin body sagged, touching the splintering bamboo at aching heel and calf, fleshless bottom, pointed shoulder blade and the back of his bony skull. He felt draped like a discarded doll, his thin blanket half underneath him to soften the surface, as he drifted momentarily. He watched the sun meander up the bamboo hut wall, as sudden shafts of light sprang through the gaps, slicing beams across his eyes. The effect jolted him wide awake in a bright sea of red, glowing and hot. He sat upright, but couldn't see anything but long thin beams, burnt into his retina. He blinked rapidly and the glow fizzled to yellow then blurred to a disappearing stamp of light, fading with each wink of his eye. He didn't know what had woken him or again where he was for a tense moment. He squinted hard at his surroundings, he had played this game so many times before. Blurring his vision, imagining a different scene and taking himself elsewhere. He inclined his head almost imperceptibly to align his eyes into the thin glow of light. The slanting beams drifting through bamboo became slices of light through the thick curtains of home and he returned there again. Standing silently, wearing the remains of his tattered uniform. Thin and aching he stood perfectly still in the sitting room of his home. He was out of place and out of time. His arms hung heavily at his sides as he felt his shallow hot breath in the calm, quiet room. Only the dull tick of the mantle clock punctured the air. Sweat still clung his thin shirt to his body despite the cool of the room, and he felt the soft hearth rug beneath his bare feet. He looked about, his mouth parched as his stomach turned with the thought of his mother's hot cooked dinners. With thoughts of his mother. If only he *could* transport himself there in the blink of an eye. It was quiet and still, darkness fell between gaps in the fabric as motes drifted within the beams. His hand reached out, stretching in front of him. He watched his gnarled fingers straining to grasp the material, trying throw wide open the familiar curtains, just out of his reach. He stopped short, inert and interrupted, what was that noise? *Twitch, twitch*, the incessant buzz of insect life crowded his ears, filled his mind. His fingers clenched as the ticking mantle clock turned to cicadas and he returned to the damp, sweating jungle of Ambon.

Jack exhaled deeply, looking around in the morning light inside the hut. He lay in his festering bunk, a bony arm outstretched, still dreaming of home. The dream vanished into the delirium of the camp. The situation was dire, one could hardly imagine a more hellish place. He refused to give in, nor give satisfaction to his captors. He looked around at his brothers in the hut, and did not pity himself. He knew there were those worse off. Those in the sick hut and those interred at Boot Hill. They had not heard the sludge of feet carrying their bamboo stretchers through the mud, the work of the spade nor the words mumbled by men desperately sorry to bury their brothers yet tearfully grateful it was not them. Not yet. Dozens of them lay there, silently sleeping under the coral-flecked earth.

Jack rose stiffly, joining the bent-kneed shuffle of men to the end of the hut, eyelids drooping, his energy already spent. "I could walk this path in my sleep," he muttered to himself. It was twelve of his slow aching paces from the end of the hut to the water pipe and tank, then four more paces to the tea kitchen. The tea kitchen was in fact just the end of a bamboo water pipe spluttering into a battered boiling pot. Twenty-two paces took him to the latrines and forty-three dragging footfalls to the gate and guard house. He knew each step, each rock and weathered tree stump in this earth. Jack counted each as he plodded along every day. Every man did. It had been one long year, seven tortuous months and two aching days since capitulation. He had survived over a year on Java at two equally horrendous camps before being moved, he had hoped on to a better camp. His hopes had not been fulfilled. This camp was far beyond his worst imaginings.

Jack was just one, of a thousand men transported to languish on the paradise hell-island these last seven months. Seven long months struggling to survive on this island, Ambon Island. He didn't remember its name from geography class at school. He had never heard of it. No one had. He imagined himself a tiny curled-up speck, sitting atop an infinitesimal dot amongst a thousand other dots. All afloat on a vast expanse of blue on the map back in his schoolroom. The island was part of a group of tiny islands, the Moluccas, sat in the archipelago of the Netherland East Indies, nestled between the bellies of Borneo and Celebes to the West and New Guinea to the East. He could hardly believe it had been nearly seven months, 'My god, it may as well have been seven years for the toll it had taken,' he thought. Each day stretched to exhaustion with back-breaking work in blazing heat, scant food and only a dribble of water. Heaped onto the straining back of each day was uncontrolled, untreated disease and relentless, never-ending mindless brutality at the hands of the Japanese soldiers and Korean guards. Each day stretched indefinitely into an infinity of horror.

- APRIL 1943 -

A thousand men, these thousand prisoners or war journeyed from Java in the holds of the two ships, the *Mayahashi Maru* and the *Nishi Maru* early that April, in swirling monsoon tides that lashed the decks and pitched the ships. Empty bellies had retched but there was nothing to vomit. They lacked food and clean water, even sanitary facilities, save for a disgusting drum for that purpose in the corner of the hold. Conditions had quickly become unbearable. Previously the hold of the *Nishi Maru* had carried coal, and Jack and the men soon became covered with glistening sparks. The soot sticking relentlessly to each sweating body. The dust caught in their throats causing lungs to rake and cough. Man after man joined the chorus, like a terrible wheezing symphony. They sloshed around in the famishing hold, thirsty and alternately trembling with cold or shivering in sweat. They had endured the year of hardship in captivity on Java, and had been selected to go to "a new camp, a better camp." Jack recalled thinking that to be sent elsewhere might offer a reprieve. "Certainly it could not be worse," they had all agreed. Instantly they'd regretted even considering the thought. Jack had pushed it away, refusing to acknowledge the creeping hope that tried to slink back into his mind. "Change is not necessarily for the better. The unknown in our situation must surely be a change for the worse, as each change so far has been," he had said. He'd tried to steel himself for whatever was to come, yet conditions on the island were so much worse than even his most pessimistic imaginings.

Seven months previously the sickening voyage had ended at a small quayside at Ambon. His first view of the island had been welcome relief, simply because it was land, but as always, it was the briefest, flickering moment of respite as one nightmarish situation slid into the next. The *Nishi Maru* had pitched up at Ambon dock, slipping between what appeared to be two islands, later revealed to be a wide strait bisecting just one. The island narrowed to a sliver and isthmus that tenuously joined the two halves. Jack had looked back and forth to either side. The left, mountainous forest, its curved back arched against the sky like a stretching cat. To his right endless cocoanut trees punctuated by a clearing for the small dockside. The dock was surrounded by a ramshackle collection of buildings, only one of which looked as if it could withstand a sudden gust of wind. Ropes thrown ashore to the handful of disgruntled and nervous looking native men brought Jack the uncomfortable twin emotions of relief that the hellish voyage was over and a deep dread, trepidation of what awaited. They had spent the journey arched and braced against each other in the dark cramped hold, coughing and trying to relieve the discomfort of bony spine against bony spine, now it became achingly painful to unfold the body to creaking standing position in order to climb out into the sunshine and the unknown. The men unloaded themselves, falling and stumbling down the gangways onto the quayside, leaning on each other, retching and stretching as they gathered the strength to stand to, for the demanded roll call. And there they stood, a thousand broken trees after a storm, tattered and angular.

Jack had bartered his few remaining items of any value before he left Java, anything to aid his unknown future. He now mostly wore the last remnants of uniform that had not yet worn through, and a relatively new shirt. The shirt had been given to him at Tandjong Priok, by a CO who for some reason had several in a canvas sack. Jack had not asked where they'd come from. He was just grateful to feel the thicker cotton of an unworn shirt and to be cushioned by sleeves was a long-forgotten luxury. It had two buttoned breast pockets, and felt extraordinarily comfortable as he'd sweated through his previous shirt until it was little more than seams. He could hardly remember the comfort of socks, and the boots he had marched onto the *Empress of Australia* from the sleety dock at Gourock, over a year and a half ago, were long gone. Their soles had first worn to wafers despite his repairs, then the leather had simply evaporated into the heat. He had been issued a canvas pair with rubber soles and separated toe, for the journey. They were cooler than the leather and more suitable for the climate but were infinitely less comfortable, particularly the parting of his toes which felt completely alien. Jack's kitbag now only held the 'Thinnest Blanket in the Far East,' a torn vest, his thin, seamy shirt and scuffed HAA cap. A cotton pouch within held a battered tin mug, misshapen bowl, a dented canteen and a sharpened spoon onto which he'd etched his initials, and home, 'J. F.' and 'Hyde'. He had salvaged one photograph, but it was badly creased and faded. The bulk of his kit had been confiscated along with everyone else's, leaving him few personal items and only the one memento of home. The paucity of possessions and supplies made his tattered kitbag light to carry, but lumpy as any sort of cushioning pillow.

As on Java, the men would have to set up a way to trade the remainder of any possessions with the locals to supplement meagre food rations. It was a dangerous activity, to be caught would mean a vicious bashing or worse. Trading was almost as dangerous for the Javanese as for the PoWs, but still they had bravely offered sporadic exchanges and sometimes left a few morsels despite the risk. It would be much harder on this tiny island, especially as the men had practically nothing left to offer, and the Ambonese would be seldom seen after the PoWs' arrival. Now, as the men stood swaying in the heat on Ambon dockside, listening to the barking orders of the commanding Japanese and sounding off, they saw an opportunity to gain a few supplies. Once the thousand men had been counted off, the soldiers screeched new orders to unload the ships cargo, pointing and pushing the nearest group, in which Jack stood, back towards the holds. First, they were to pile their deflated kitbags on deck, then climb down and unload the cargo. Underneath the cacophony of Japanese commands, the quiet murmur of a passing message rumbled, travelling from mouth to ear. The cargo, someone had discovered, was mostly food supplies. There were sacks of rice and sugar, and importantly, many of the hessian sacks were already torn. As the soldiers watched from the quay, smoking cigarettes and flicking butts into the narrow sliver of sea between ship and dock, the men set to work hoisting the supplies. Sack after sack of edible goods, as well as bamboo lengths, attap and artillery shells came out of the hold, rising like some cruel magic trick. Cruel, because it had been unknown to the weakened hungry men that stored just under the boards beneath their feet was all the food they'd needed.

Alarmingly, it had all been pressed in, alongside and against, masses of ammunition that would have sealed their fate if the ship had been attacked en route. Nets of oranges had split during the voyage. The rounded fruits had bounced down and come to rest amongst the bombs. The oranges, broken and squashed, had rotted into a slime which covered the shells, making the unloading of the slippery bombs particularly dangerous. Jack now recalled as he manhandled the slithering cargo, that he had imagined he smelled a ripe citrusy aroma, but had dismissed the idea as olfactory hallucination. He had sniffed the air, thinking of cakes and marmalade his mother made and had searched with his nose for the source. But, he had lost it amongst the oily, dirty ship, the salty sea spray and the stench from the latrine drum with its buzz of flies. Before the hessian sacks were heaved up from the depths of the hold, the small rips were enlarged, allowing the contents to pour freely. Each man silently and secretively filled his pockets with sugar before stuffing the holes and hefting the slightly lighter sack onto his back. Hoisting endless crates and heaving each sack down the gangplank in a steady stream and back up for the next, the day dragged on. It was no feast, they gained only a handful of sugar, pushed deep into tatty pockets. Furtively licking his fingers Jack nevertheless hoped that it would be lifesaving fuel for whatever was to come next. The line of tired men continued up and down, unloading and stacking supplies, without food nor water, and only a few minutes rest each hour as the sky began to darken. Those most exhausted, closest to collapse, were quietly swapped in the hold by other PoWs, so they could rest a little, hidden in the darkness. The Japanese soldiers were indifferent, it appeared as if the PoWs continuously unloaded the holds. As long as supplies kept coming, moving along in a long line of huge leaf-carrying marching ants, each struggling with loads as large as themselves, the soldiers simply stood back, watching and waiting.

By twilight much of the cargo was stacked high on the quayside as the rumble of approaching trucks caused the last unloading to stop as everyone looked on. Half a dozen heavy wagons shuddered to a halt in cloud of dust, their engines rattling to a knocking standstill. The men looked to each other, wondering if the transport would be taking them to a camp. Soldiers silhouetted in the dusty headlight beams began shouting excitedly at the pause in work, and the ant trail resumed. They followed the pointing demands of the soldiers and the shoves from their rifle butts to form new lines going from the stacks of supplies to the trucks. There were fewer in each line struggling with more work for the already exhausted men. "Why do it twice?" they said amongst themselves, "We should have unloaded directly onto the trucks, why do it all twice?" They glumly agreed with the pointlessness of the doubled task. It was almost dark when the ship was unloaded completely. The men were utterly drained, there had been little rest since the trucks had arrived. With the darkening sky the soldiers had become agitated, demanding work speed up. Finally, as the last truck drove away piled high with goods the soldiers ordered a stop, and the men collapsed as one onto the dockside. Jack slumped onto a heavy metal mooring post bracing his feet on its base. Nearby two men dropped to the ground and for a moment it seemed they might not recognise each other. Henry was the first to realise, raising a hand which Jack grasped without a word. He then realised Harold sat to the other side of him and releasing his grip, they also clasped hands. No words were necessary. There were no words. Their expressions spoke to each other, and for a time they simply looked on, nodding. They hoped that wherever their night's rest was, that it wasn't far, "Perhaps," they asked each other, "theres somewhere just outside the dock. Perhaps there's a town?" They quietly passed amongst the small groups, some hidden morsels.

Dabbing at the stolen sugar and finishing dribbling dregs from shared canteens Jack watched as a cooling breeze moved the dark silhouettes of cocoanut palms. He listened to the sea lapping against the ship's hull as it rocked gently at its creaking mooring. The men hoped, rather than assumed the trucks would return for them, but as the breeze turned into a stronger wind, there came no indication from the Japanese soldiers as to what, if any plans had been made. The bedraggled men could only wait, and wait, as the soldiers came to their decisions, or received their orders. Suddenly the Japanese soldiers began shouting excitedly "*Speedo, speedo!*" The men rumbled and rolled to their feet, forming up in straggling lines. "We're walking then," someone said. Replies were murmured, their faces in the dusklight full of concern. The soldiers directed them back onto the ship, ordering them back down into the dark holds. A scuffle broke out in the centre of the men. Someone cried out they didn't want to go back down there, the terror of their voyage clear in his voice. Those around him held him tight, helping him up the gangplanks, as the soldiers peered angrily into the mass of men to discover the commotion. Those helping him looked placidly blank, shrugging and bowing their heads to cover the man's sagging, weeping body. Crouched again in the glistening black hold of the ship Jack and the thousand men passed a long night swaying at the dockside. Jack pulled his knees up under his chin, raising his eyes to the square of sky framed by the hatch. Stars clustered in the darkness, flashing and twinkling, diamonds thrown on dark velvet. Jack stared into the ink, as clouds rolled across his square cinema screen and drops of rain began to fall. He tried to watch a single drop, tracing its barely illuminated path in a fraction of a second as it descended. A vertical raindrop landing silently on the backs of men huddled below. Quickly the drops grew into a downpour and the men leant back automatically, their heads raised and open mouthed to catch the fresh drink. It stopped almost as soon as it had started. Just a cloudburst and the men, now damp with sweat and rain, tried to settle for the night. "I'd have preferred to lie out under those cocoanut trees than in here," called out Jack in the darkness. "Or just sleep out there. On the quayside, at least there's room, and air!" came a reply from the darkness. A murmur of agreement rumbled round the dank space, then quietened down. The silence was punctuated as someone quipped, "Or the Ritz... I don't mind either way!" Muted chuckles echoed sadly and briefly around the damp void, as the hatch was moved over the opening, leaving the hold in claustrophobic pitch dark.

The morning air was fresh and misty from the nights rain but began to warm even at the early hour, as the men formed up on the quayside, retching the clagging coal dust from their throats. Jack glanced about for trucks but there were none, he realised that wherever they were headed, "We're walking then," he murmured to those around him. Tired men nodded agreement in reply, and sighs of resignation rumbled around as the Japanese soldiers demanded the men count off for roll call. Eventually they had a figure after restarting several times, it had seemed to take an age in the rising steam of the quay. One thousand ragged, tired and hungry men marched off the dockside at Ambon, in two long columns side by side. Jack found himself towards the back. The Japanese soldiers had left a bucket, containing sticks of festering dried meat for the men to take as they began the march. The meat sat the rising sun, stinking and sweating and attracting flies. The smell of it turned every passing stomach, no one took a piece. If the men had known how long it would be before there was anything to eat, they would have fought for even a single bite of the disgusting meat. As they marched through the collection of buildings around the dock and out onto a main dust road, locals watched from shuttered windows and behind trees. The dust road veered to the left up a gentle slope to a newly constructed narrow concrete bridge. Jack hoped rather than assumed because they were walking that the camp couldn't be too far away. His thoughts were broken as someone began to hum defiantly. At first just a low murmuring tune, Jack looked nervously to the soldiers flanking the columns, but to his surprise they seemed to ignore the humming, making no move to stop the sound. Boldly, the men began whistling. Someone interrupted with a big band tune, *Little Brown Jug* and it quickly spread through the column. Those at the back whistled the trumpets, others rasped the higher notes. It was favourite of Jack's, he'd loved leaping around the house to Glenn Miller and he managed a brief smile, which soon disappeared as they clattered over the bridge and out onto the main road hugging the coast.

They marched on for some three miles, the dust rising from their boots as the sun rose. Someone toward the front spotted a camp and called out, prompting a whisper that rustled back through the lines, "We've arrived at camp!" They could not halt until there was a Japanese order, but no call came. The men looked about expectantly, slowing their pace a little, assuming they'd be stopping any moment. As they approached the camp a couple of Japanese soldiers stopped and stood to near a gate. Instead of directing them inside, they motioned to continue past. The men in unspoken reluctance continued on. As they passed, they saw the camp was crowded with Allied soldiers, who now approached their fence line. Gripping the wire in clenched hands, their faces sunburned and shining they nodded to the passing men. All eyes met one another, observing each others plight. The marchers continued on as the captive men stood watching, each group wondering who was worse off. One man in the camp shouted out to the marching column, in a strong Australian voice. "You're nearly there, mate," he laughed kindly. The men grinned and someone called back, "How's the hotel?" "First-class mate," came the reply. Another adding, "The room service is terrible though." The darkly humoured banter trailed off as the Japanese spun round, moving closer to the marchers, looking for those calling out and barking commands to hurry. The Australians' expressions rearranged into frowns of concern and shared pity, tinged with determination and a solidarity with the Britishers. They returned the expressions as they passed, their eyes left in silent salute.

Whistling and humming had long run dry as the water supply drained away, and the warmth of the morning became the suffocating heat of midday and still no rest, nor food or water was given. Many had been issued the same rubber and canvas boots as Jack, others wore thin plimsols but some went barefoot. A few men were shirtless, they'd tied them around their heads to shield against the beating sun, as nearly all lacked any cap or hat. There was, by now little noise apart from the shuffle of feet. Just the scrape of boots, and coughing. There was always coughing. Marching under the intermittent shade of cocoanut trees was at once dreadful and beautiful. Jack plodded monotonously on, losing himself deliriously in the heat and scented air. The island was fragrant with frangipani, lilies and hibiscus growing thickly and fervently in the oppressive humidity. Their scent drifted to his nostrils, buttery and at the same time citrusy, it was like nothing he'd smelled before. But it was the heavy aroma of clove-spice that permeated the island, flooding his senses, pungent and intoxicating, sweet and sharp in equal measure. Nervously watching the thousand marchers pass, native women wrapped in swathes of bright cloth flattened harvested piles of cloves with their soft palms, leaving them to dry on thin woven mats at the side of the road. Beads on their slender brown wrists clattered and rattled as they patted the buds apart, ensuring each single head felt the sun burning down, sucking away their juices. The buds dried and shrivelled, moisture invisibly leaving the soft green heads as they turned into hard black shells. Jack had smelled them before he caught sight of them. Ragged and exhausted as he was, the seasonal familiar scent caused him momentarily pause as it caught his olfactory attention, as the men stumble-marched forward. The women sat back on their heels in the dust, watching and wiping their hands on their skirts as the glorious smell of his mother's Christmas cake arrived in Jack's nostrils. He was taken home in an instant as the festive scent filled his head, his lungs, and his heart completely. He inhaled deeply, following it through the back door, through the small familiar kitchen and into the sitting room at Spring Street. He could almost taste the sticky cake, the tang of orange against clove, could almost hear someone stoking the fire, the clack of the poker hitting the grate through the brittling coals. Home percolated through him. He felt the warmth from the fire, heard the creak of coals as they fell through smouldering ash in the grate, and the comforting smell of Christmas and the smoky fire enveloped him. He fainted headlong into the room, tightening his squinting eyes as he stumbled, trying to inhale the flavours. He looked around the room, filled with a fine lingering mist from the flickering hearth. Above the fire sat the fat mantle clock, along the mantelpiece resided the photographs, tucked-behind post and the assortment of books. There were the stacks of newspapers heaped nearby, the scuttle of earthy smelling coal, the log pile leaning against the scuttle. He observed it all, every detail, and he bathed in it. The table was set with clean cloth, plates, sliced meat, a piece of cheese and a three-quarter loaf of bread, upended. Tea cups jostled with the large teapot suffocated in a thick tea-cosy, mist escaping its snout. Mismatched spoons for mother's homemade jam and chutney laid alongside bone-handled butter knives and a single silver spoon for the sugar bowl. He folded himself into the heavy sooty warmth of the small sitting room and refused to leave. The mist of blueish smoke from the hearth fire stirred in eddies around his mother as she moved slowly through the room. Jack watched her, breathlessly. She took a butter knife, using it to peel back parchment paper around a moist and heavy fruitcake. Folding away the paper with the knife she slid it onto a large patterned plate. She turned to him and smiled, her eyes piercing him, as she disappeared in the blue smoke. He opened his eyes, his arms outstretched, hands reaching for her, as he fell. Tears rolled down his crumpled face as he landed heavily on the dust road. The man to his left quickly helped him up, with an eye on an advancing soldier. The man heard him sob, and placed a hand on his shoulder. "It's all right, look we're stopping now. Keep your chin up lad. It's all right." Jack nodded, not looking up, his eyes filling again. He slid the back of his hand over his cheeks, wiping away his sadness as he lowered his head. He watched his wobbling boots making dust clouds on the hard road, as the mist of home disappeared in their haze.

The day dragged on as the sun rose higher, and the water supply ran as dry as their tongues. There were only a few minutes rest each hour of hard marched slog, they marched then briefly slumped panting at the side of the road as the sun first stood above them, then slunk down their backs, burning their necks as it arched over the sky into afternoon. The air was still. Not a wisp of breeze eased their overheated bodies. Blisters formed and burst, and sweat dripped. The brief stops did nothing to rest aching limbs, numb with exhaustion. Each step somehow appeared after the last, disconnected to each man's intent. Jack looked down, blinking as he watched his own foot move forward, creating a tiny dust cloud around his rubber boot as he planted it on the road, then wobblingly his other foot appeared and numbly stomped the ground as the first again lifted and swung through. He carried on, unaware how he managed to keep moving. With each step the possibility of collapse became more imminent. Those with water canteens had passed them around giving to those without, but there had been hardly even enough to wet the lips, all had now run completely dry. Jack tried to eat a little of the sugar from his pocket but his mouth was stiffly parched, his swollen tongue scratched at the grains on the dry roof of his mouth, unable to moisten them or swallow. All along the road Japanese soldiers shoved their rifle butts in the men's backs. They descended like flies, prodding with bayonet and kicking anyone who stumbled or fell. The marchers lifted any who tripped, helping as much as they were able. As a long line of staggering, supported wretches they straggled on for fourteen more miles as the sun arced down, dropping to the horizon, as the light drained from the sky.

Jack had listened to the sea most of the day as they'd passed alongside, the waves sometimes crashing on rocks, sometimes gently lapping on sand. Suddenly, ahead the sea seemed louder as they were ordered to a stumbling halt. The men looked to each other quizzically yet grateful for a respite, however brief. Some of the men began to collapse, slumping to the side of the road. They were quickly descended upon by the soldiers, shoving and barking at them to get up. They were ordered over a small rise, and down onto a long, thinly curved beach. On the brow of the rise they could see the sea lapped both sides of the narrow strip of sand bisected by their winding dust road. It was the isthmus of the island, the thread holding the two halves together. The men now collapsed onto the sand, lying flat out for in exhaustion until the soldiers began barking their next commands. Jack pulled off his boots gingerly. He had thought the rubber might adapt, rounding to each curve of his foot, but the relentless march and sweat had rubbed his skin into the hot rubber, leaving red raw blisters. He was attending to his swollen feet when surprisingly, the call came for food. The shout started a scrabble for tins and bowls and a jostling for a better place in the gathering line. Two of the men had been ordered to manhandle the large steaming stewing-pans. Grasping a handle either side, they carried one out of a small cook tent. Heaving it onto a trestle table next to four other similar vessels, Jack noticed each pan had collected a mist of tiny flies. The command to line up and bow deeply was followed quickly, as a slop of mushy boiled rice and filthy maize fell into each receptacle with a splatter. Jack looked for a moment at the disgusting slimy mixture, dirty and foul smelling as it fell from his homemade spoon. Each man looked briefly to another before gulping it down. They were ravenous and every grain disappeared in moments. Jack licked his bowl, looking through his raised eyebrows over the rim as incredibly, a man flopped heavily next to him with a cup of tea grasped tightly in his fist. Poured directly from a large kettle taken off the back of a truck, the tea was offered to wash down the slop. Jack watched as the dark, clear liquid splashed into his own tin mug. He secretively pinched a tiny thumb-full of sugar from his pocket, swilling the mug in small circles to dissolve the precious sweetness. He sipped at the mug, letting the warmish drink soak his tongue. It tasted heavenly to him and he lingered over each drop. Closing his eyes, he let it trickle round his mouth, hesitating before swallowing to savour the sensation.

The men washed their cups and bowls in the lapping tide then lay on the sand, curled on their sides with rolled shirts or elbows beneath their heads as pillows. The contrast with the night before could not have been starker. Jack almost felt settled, as he scooped sand from under his hip for comfort. However, all was relative. Having a little more space to spread out, on damp sand amongst the buzz of flies and mosquitoes, watched by a ruthless enemy was infinitely better than the crush of a filthy coal hold in the choking darkness of unknowing, under the same oppressive yoke of their captors. Jack lay out on the sand listening to low murmurs of conversation amongst the men, as the waves lapped with a swash-swish onto the shore, the surf sucking grittily at the sand as it retreated. He rolled onto his back, folding his hands behind his head, to watch the clear twinkling night sky. The moon, huge and tinged with blue, rose over the horizon and hung in the sky illuminating the ragged men below in eerie light. Jack stared wide eyed, at the orb for a time, then clambered to his feet, hands resting on the back of his hips as he walked slowly toward the shore. As he stopped at the tides edge, someone nearby began, low and slow, to sing.

...Blue moon,
You saw me standing alone,
Without a dream in my heart,
Without a love of my own...

More whispered voices joined the slow song, in the stillness of quiet night. They sang softly, and Jack listened as the sobering words drifted mournfully across the beach. His heart ached for home.

...Blue moon,
You knew just what I was there for,
You heard me saying a prayer for,
Someone I really could care for...

Jack returned to his place and dropped into a foetal ball, as the men around him rolled over, curling up to try and sleep. He lay still, watching the moon until his eyes would stay open no longer and the exhaustion of the day pulled him into unconsciousness. Despite his fatigue, he slept badly, rolling, twitching and slapping at mosquito punctures through to the early hours until he awoke with a start. He had been dreaming. He was running, to where he couldn't remember, feet pounding the earth, men shouting, a commotion in the darkness. He looked around, his eyes failing to adjust. The moon had set and the beach was dark with shadows and the deadened rumble of voices. It took a moment to realise his feet were wet. The tide had come in, rising quietly up the sand

and catching those nearest the shore. The men gathered their soaked gear drowsily. They trudged up the sand to the cackle of a few soldiers sitting smoking outside their dry tents. Damp, itchy and hollow-eyed, Jack found a gap between two men at the edge of the beach, under a straggly, stubby tree. He lay down gratefully as they nodded, clearing space for him. His eyelids dropped over his eyes as he fell into the gap, and he passed into fatigued twitching sleep almost immediately. It rained heavily in night, a tropical downpour, warm but relentless. The tree gave a little shelter, holding back the worst of the deluge, funnelling rainwater into steady streams between its branches so the men had only to avoid its flow. The deluge woke them and they filled their water canteens until the torrent became a trickle, then fat drops which landed monotonously with melodious splats. The raindrops sang them back to unsettled sleep in the early hours. Jack felt he had barely closed his eyes, as dawn broke. He felt as fatigued as the evening before, as orange light burst through the trees and raced across the beach.

Jack rubbed his eyes, and began lining his boots with leaves from the shrubby tree. With boots pulled painfully on he stretched himself and moved to wait in line to collect the morning slop. Breakfast such as it was, was the same mush as the night before, only now it was more congealed and more foul smelling. But, as the days destination and duration was unknown, each man ate every scrap. The soldiers screamed the order to fall in, and the thousand weary men began the second days trudge. They reasoned the march would last at least the whole morning otherwise they wouldn't have camped out, they would have been pushed on. The sun climbed again as they stumble-marched along the dust road that gradually thinned to a track. They followed it as it briefly wound inland, emerging from thick foliage, parallel to the sea. Their route hugged the sea for the rest of the march. The previous day the calm sea had been on their left, and Jack had been able to look across to the other part of the island. Now, the water lay to his right, clear open ocean, crashing and rolling with the fresh morning tide. Jack glimpsed it first though the trees then in full splendour as they emerged from the wooded interior. It was dazzlingly beautiful. He shielded his eyes as he gazed upon the ocean, the colour of lapis lazuli until it met the snow-white coral sand, where it lapped in shades of azure. Weary as he was, he could not fail to be mesmerised. He blinked hard as his boots shuffled forward, his outstretched hand now on the shoulder of the man in front, the hand of the man behind gripping Jack's shoulder in turn. He had felt tired but more determined at the beginning of the day despite the lack of rest or proper food. The feeling had quickly drained from him as the morning stumbled on. The soldiers would not let the men pause to refill canteens in the many trickling streams they passed. The heat sapped the energy from each man, wicking away moisture, emptying canteens of precious rainwater and numbing their limbs. As the heat increased more men staggered and fell to their knees. Those who could, helped sling their limp bodies between them and they carried on. No man collapsed consciously or willingly, knowing the soldiers would leap upon them, poking sharply at the fallen with bayonets, kicking hard with their boots and screaming like crazed banshees all the while. As the hours drifted by in a semi-conscious blur of heat and dust, the soldiers too, began to fade. Despite better health, an uninterrupted and comfortable night's sleep in dry tents, and bellies filled with food and thirst slaked, many Japanese soldiers now began to sway and stagger. Some meandered to the edge of the road and stumbled into the shallow ditches. Their comrades angrily helped them up while casting furtive glances to the column of marching, watching men. The oppressed men felt that whatever the cost, they would show their captors they could complete the march. They felt as a matter of pride, of honour, they would not give in, they would show them their mettle. The thousand men continued, swaying like drunks, their chins jutting and determined. They stumbled on for fourteen more miles, each walking man holding up another, until sweating and panting they were ordered to halt. It was almost dusk. Trees wafted gently in a light breeze as the weary men began to sit, assuming it was another short rest stop. Someone noticed a pile of sweet potatoes at the roadside and in one ravenous lunge each man descended, grappling to get hold of one. The potatoes had mostly turned bad, but the men bit at the parts that were not yet too rotted, chewing at hard chunks, hungrily eyeing the vegetables for their next bite. Meanwhile, the soldiers had gathered in a clearing to the right of the road and began barking new orders to waiting guards. Those soldiers exhausted by the march were now drinking water as they pulled off their boots. They had been helped into the shade of a long bamboo and attap hut, that the men now noticed in the haze of their weakened state and desperation for sustenance. Jack and the thousand prisoners of war were herded into a clearing in front of the hut and ordered to get up and stand to, for roll call. As they numbered off, row upon row, Jack realised this must be their new camp. They had finally arrived at 'Sub-Camp III'— Liang camp, such as it was, late in the afternoon of 3 May 1943.

Jack stood wearily as he took in his new surroundings. Thick trees edged the clearing, creating a darkened interior cut by slices of dappled light filtering through the leaves. Ground had been cleared as a gathering place for roll call, but the area circling it as far as he could see, was punctuated by rocky coral outcrops standing jaggedly within the thick forest. He looked around for where they might shelter, as the laborious task of roll call continued on. There was nothing constructed around the clearing except the soldiers' bamboo hut and another to one side only half completed, its roof loose and tatty. Soldiers began erecting tents. Clearly the huts and tents were reserved for the Japanese. Jack and the men noticed a pile of familiar kitbags and realised they were their own. They had been piled on the deck of the ship and the men had been given no access to their scant possessions. They were left for two days in the pouring rain before the soldiers ordered them to load the dripping kitbags onto a truck, heaped on top of supplies. The soldiers now saw the men looking across to their kit, and shouted they were not to retrieve them. Jack wondered what state his belongings would be in, 'probably everything will be soaked through, and ruined' he thought. He startled as a shout echoed from deep inside the long bamboo hut. The hut door swung theatrically open, held by a saluting guard, as a rather pear-shaped, squat Japanese officer with a pinched face stepped casually down the planked steps to the ground. Lieutenant Colonel Sanso Anami strutted across the hard coral earth of the clearing, distain written clearly on his face. Anami looked along the swaying lines of ragged prisoners, squinting through peevish eyes. He stopped abruptly, his hands behind his back, making his rounded belly protrude all the more. Jack's eyes followed him back and forth, careful to avoid his gaze. Suddenly Anami opened his mouth, barking,

"あなたが働くかどうかは気にしませんあなたはここで死にます"

An interpreter dashing alongside began repeating Anami's words to the men, "Ahh, I don't care if you work or not, you are all here to die. None will leave this island alive." Anami's narrow shining eyes widened as he searched for the impact of his words on the men before him. The prisoners lowered their heads, looking briefly sideways to each other to confirm what each had heard. No one dared speak. Jack closed his eyes, bristling with the urge to shout out. Instead he clenched his fists and held fast. He knew the futility of responding. Anami turned away, nodding to his interpreter to continue, and returned to his speech. He pointed with a fat finger at the gathered men,

"おまえ たち.....Omae-tachi...."

The interpreter trotted next to Anami, listening and inclining his ear as he falteringly continued. "You, you coolies..." he prodded a finger toward the men, echoing Anami's poking in the air. "...you are all prisoners of the Japanese Army, which is now conducting a war with this place as one of its bases. Consequently food and living conditions generally are an acutely difficult problem. I myself, and my subordinates are engaged day and night in trying to overcome these difficulties. I do not want to be bothered by suggestions or protests from you. You will take your orders from me and I expect prompt compliance with them. I would add that Japanese wounded left behind on the evacuation of Guadalcanal were steamrolled to death by the Americans. I do not propose to retaliate upon you for this and I shall treat you kindly so long as you are obedient. It is the duty of you and your officers to make this camp cheerful." Anami's yapping voice finished before the chanting echo of his interpreter. The men stole glances at each other, keeping their heads low. Dread crept over Jack, 'This is definitely *not* going to be better than Java,' he thought. He needed no speech to tell him that. The two-day forced march explained the new situation clearly enough. Anami eyed the men, his bottom lip protruding, then abruptly turned, marching away to a waiting truck. He swung aboard without looking back and was driven away, leaving the camp silent with the echo of his words and the dust from the truck's wheels. Jack chanced a whisper, "I'm not surprised he's not staying here, there's nothing." A muttered reply came, "He must have somewhere else on the island." Men close by nodded in agreement, looking around at the sparse clearing framed by trees which surrounded the coral ripped earth. A soldier dismissed the men, who dispersed to huddle together under trees as dusk fell.

Lieutenant Colonel Anami dabbed at the sweat on his forehead with a large handkerchief as his truck rumbled away through the trees in its own dust cloud. He considered himself a moral man, a brave man, but he found it impossible to retreat from the hatred he felt for these prisoners of war. He blamed them for his being stuck there, on these festering fly-blown islands. His face contorted as he thought of these men without honour. They who had surrendered! It was worse than dishonourable to his fractured mind. He could see neither the stark beauty of the island nor the intense suffering he inflicted. It did not occur to him to ease their situation, despite his remarks. It had not entered his mind that to damage and destroy the enforced work-force, was unfathomably counter-productive to the Japanese war effort. Beneath it all, he simply hated them because he blamed them for his predicament. He did not have the wherewithal to examine the truth of his beliefs, to find them lacking. He simply held steadfast in his errors of judgement and knowledge, continuing his broken mission. As a younger man rising through the ranks he'd imagined himself in command, leading Japanese soldiers into battles. Watching as his men fought hand to hand as ancient warriors. He felt the glow of glory would be his. He'd imagined receiving medals, and one day his emperor would say he was the bravest man he knew. His eyes shone as he had daydreamed throughout his army training and solitary subordinate years. Then, a pilfering to his mind, matter of too much drink, a brief challenge to a superior, Anami shouting he would one day be 'the highest ranking man in the army' had led to disgrace. He was relegated to prisoners of war camp commander. To oversee PoWs on these islands, building airstrips to support the planned invasion of Australia. He was overall Commander of these island camps, but it was a periphery posting, out of the action and in charge of these, his most hated of men. His subordinates followed his lead, partly due to their fear of him, but all were loyal to the ideology of the 'Greater East Asian Co-Prosperity Sphere'. His captains Shiogawa and Ueda, and Sergeant Majors Kawai and Yamamoto supported his every decision and instruction not only without question, but with gleeful enthusiasm. The lower ranking soldiers bowed even more subserviently, First Lieutenant Iketani and the camp doctor Shimada were particularly keen to impress with competing sadistic actions. The Korean guards in turn, followed the example set. They needed little encouragement to comply with Anami's rule of terror, Fujimoto and Kimura being amongst the worst. Anami treated the PoWs as he did, because he considered them not human, but also because he was afraid of them. Deep inside he was terrified they were stronger than he and could revolt. The thought angered him despite it being confined to his imaginings. He found solace in crushing their spirit at every opportunity. Anami's disgruntled face creased unpleasantly in the bright mosquito-clouded headlights of the truck as he stepped down and stalked to the door of the Dutch colonial house he'd commandeered for himself.

Back in the darkness of the camp, the men were woken by a deep rumbling. They sat up to listen as the rattle of trucks approached. They'd been sleeping fitfully on the rough coral. Gathered in groups, and huddled together, they tried to create shelter from nothing. Some of the men assumed the sound was some passing truck and lay back down, until a shout of *makan* indicated food had arrived. Jack could hardly believe it. Like the others, he'd eaten only the maize slop in the early hours of that morning and the few rotten sweet potatoes. The latter had lain heavily, sickeningly, in his stomach. Whatever came off the *makan* truck, he knew he would eat it. Jack held out his tin bowl as a blob of mushed maize fell gelatinously from the serving spoon, followed by a splash of thin green liquid. He didn't recognise the smell or the taste, but it was warm, somewhat filling and not wholly unpleasant. His bowl emptied quickly as he knew it would. There wasn't much but it helped stave off the pangs from his stomach as he tried again to settle amongst the tree roots and coral outcrops. Despite lying uncomfortably on a thin layer of palm fronds he fell deeply into a delirious stupor of sleep as someone nearby covered him with his thin blanket. He was awoken much later in pitch dark by rain. Fat blobs landed on his face, ran down his cheeks and filled his eyes with rain-tears. Instinctively he opened his mouth, letting the water splash his tongue, swallowing and gulping, as he drank the fresh liquid. Exhaustion and hunger were familiar, but neither were cured by rest nor small slops of food nor drops of rainwater.

A damp dawn brought the bitter reality that a new, more unpleasant life at a new camp had begun. Jack looked around the clearing despondently, it was *not* some awful dream. His body was painfully tired. Sleep, such as it was, had done nothing to alleviate the aching in his bones. The earth of the camp clearing warmed in the early sun, steam rose from the ground as each weary man gathered himself for roll call, *tenko*. Their shadows stretched across the clearing, the long outlines bowing as the men coughed and rasped in the morning light. They gulped down a small ball of grubby rice and a half cup of tepid water as the soldiers began their days shrieking orders. To Jack they seemed to pace back and forth like short roosters, twitching and pecking the air. The camp staff were largely the Japanese soldiers and Korean guards who had watched the PoWs arrive, and some of the Japanese soldiers who had accompanied their hellish voyage. All their expressions revealed nothing but contempt for the PoWs. First Lieutenant Iketani strutted forward, shouting commands to the guards, who in turn barked at the PoWs. Iketani pointed to stacks of attap, lengths of bamboo and palm fronds stacked around the camp clearing, which had been brought by local Ambonese men, forced to cut the materials and transport them to the camp. Iketani was a small pinched faced soldier. His sunken-cheeked, sallow skin was marked and pitted, and his eyes, barely open, peered wildly through perfectly round spectacles as he commanded the guards into a scurry. Jack instantly disliked him.

As the men were herded around the camp clearing, the soldiers barked orders to construct huts, pointing with bayonets, and shouting for work to begin. Jack muttered to the man beside him as they heaved bamboo lengths onto their shoulders, following the pointing guards. "Why shout all the time?" he asked, shrugging awkwardly beneath the weight, "...it's not like we understand much of anything they say, is it? Shouting won't make it any bloody clearer." The nearest man lifted a length of bamboo onto his bare shoulder. "Exactly, and we're not stupid, we can see there's nothing built for us, we can see the materials here and that we will have to make our own huts." The man at the other end of the bamboo joined in, "It's because they don't think we have half their brains." Jack nodded, replying from the side of his mouth as he passed, the bamboo resting unsteadily on his damp shirt shoulder, "I'd like to brain him!" They stilled brief grins as they continued the sweating task. The men loaded endless bamboo onto their backs, moving it to various positions around the camp as designated by the engineers amongst the PoWs. A guard watching Jack, pushed him forward with a jab at his shoulder, shrieking incomprehensibly. Jack could do nothing but stagger a few steps, gather himself and continue. He desperately wanted to throw down the bamboo and lunge at the soldier, but instead he clenched his hands around the thick trunk, gritting his teeth before moving on.

Working in, by turns colossal downpours of rain and scorching heat, steam smoking from their thin damp shirts on their backs, the cicadas ticked the hours by. The huts began to grow out of the forest floor and the camp began to form. Over the ten days they had been allotted for the work, the ground had been cleared of long grasses which revealed larger coral rock outcrops. Using badly made and battered old tools, the men hacked at the smaller chunks, clearing the ground and enlarging the space within the camp. They left the largest outcrops in place, building the huts around them. The huts positions had been laid out by lengths of bamboo. The men had been given something of a free rein in siting the huts and various ancillary structures, not by any Japanese generosity, but by a wilful and complete lack of interest. The soldiers and guards were content to sit on the steps of their huts, or in the shade of a tree, watching them toil in the sun. Thus the men found they could position their huts a little further from the Japanese huts. The bamboo position markers were kick-nudged and shuffled along whenever the soldiers were not watching as closely. The PoWs wanted as much space between them and their enemy as they could. Amongst the PoWs were men with building skills and a couple of engineers. Between them they inspected the extant Japanese hut to learn its construction, then they copied the structure as closely as possible. Jack held a long section of bamboo upright with two other men, as others lashed it together with horizontal bamboo poles to form the main frames. This carcass was sheathed in attap and covered with palm fronds. It wouldn't keep out all the rain but it gave a vague misplaced sense of security once inside. The men sited the huts parallel to each other. At first the camp was only two long huts with basic ditch-dug latrines. The soldiers demanded they dig these nearer their sentry post, toward the entrance of the camp, so the soldiers didn't have far to walk to relieve themselves. The positioning meant each PoW had to pass the sentry, asking permission to *benjo* while bowing low before being allowed to use the latrines. Jack despised bowing almost more than any other indignity. It went against every grain of his being. He had tried various ways to avoid it. Not bowing as deeply, trying to slip by with someone else, or waiting until the soldiers were engaged in their own conversation so they took less notice. Nothing had worked. The only thing he managed was to each time bow a fraction of an inch less. It was a practically invisible distinction to anyone else, but it was his own personal victory, *his* seemingly infinitesimal act of resistance where none was tolerated. But, it was a risky victory.

The huts and latrines had been built in the first days after their arrival, some seven months previously. Now, the camp was surrounded by a perimeter fence. It was just a few strands of barbed wire wound around wooden posts set into little mounds of cement but, the men felt wrapped tightly by the wire and the new sentry posts in which their enemy lurked, squinting and watching from without. The main camp was now split into Japanese section at the front entrance with their stores, camp offices and barracks for the soldiers and guards, and the PoW section to the rear. An altogether more dilapidated and sickly area of ramshackle structures. The PoW assortment of bamboo and attap huts included four long sleeping huts. Jack's hut ran parallel with the straggling barbed fence, with two hundred and thirty-nine, sweating and coughing men squashed inside. There was now a latrine just outside, between Jack's and the next two huts. Behind that stood the fourth PoW hut at the very rear of the camp. On the opposite side of the camp to the sleeping huts was the sick hut. It served as the only PoW 'hospital,' and had, as a matter of urgent hygiene, separate latrines and kitchen. It was a misnomer to call it a hospital being as it was without equipment or medicines. Basically, it was simply another place to lie. No man wanted to go in there, no matter how ill he was. They fought tooth and nail to not be taken, using their last remaining gasps of energy. Only when they had exhausted themselves could they be carried in, submissive and weakly resigned. Jack thought that to go into the sick hut, was exactly what you got— sick. 'Better to take my chances outside, where I can see *it* coming,' he'd thought. He had wanted to stare *it* in the eye, and embrace *it*. If and when *it* came for him. Between the fourth hut and the wire fence was the incinerator and a small water tank fed from the PoW built pipeline which served the most important function of supplying the 'tea boiling point', or 'tea kitchen' as some called it. In reality it was little more than an area to hang a battered pan over a fire to boil the precious water trickling from the bamboo pipe. There was no running water when they'd first arrived, just a tank half-filled with buzzing liquid, dark and dripping in the shade. They didn't dare drink from it, the threat of cholera lurked ominously in the shadow of the bamboo shade atop the tank, a breathless spidery spectre hanging from its thread, waiting. It filled each PoW and soldier alike with mortal dread.

The soldiers and guards seemed to lack the most basic idea of hygiene or how to curb the spread of diseases, they seemed utterly disinterested. The illness that ran rampant through the camp in the first weeks was entirely, frustratingly avoidable. The men had all washed in the same place, within the sick-hut area. They drank the same water, and had no medicine to treat diseases they succumbed to. The lack of fresh water fuelled the diseases and the situation quickly turned desperate. The PoWs knew the problem lay with their water supply. The water tank was refilled by truck brought in drums from a village some three miles away. Sloshing about on the pitted track, half seemed to be lost on the journey. The water then needed boiling. There was barely enough for everyone to drink, hardly more than half a cup twice a day. There was simply none to waste on washing sweating, aching bodies. A few men had tried standing out in the rain, mouths open to drink at the same time, but quickly found it was a good way to catch a chill. Some caught rainwater in tin mugs, using less than half to wash their entire body. It didn't clean well, nor defend against disease, however they felt the humanity of a clean face. They wetted their hands, spilling not a drop and rubbed their faces and neck with the moisture, trying to cleanse away the day's dirt. Despite their best efforts dysentery broke out in the first week and it became a desperate requirement to have running water for *all* their needs. Fortuitously, at the same moment a small stream was stumbled upon. A working party, sent to cut more bamboo for hut building, discovered fresh running water. The clear water filled a pool where local Ambonese had washed clothes and bathed. They had deserted the site quickly as able-bodied men were gathered up and pressed into hard labour on other parts of the island. Near the camp lay some lengths of steel piping. The men asked for permission to use them to build a pipeline. The soldiers were reluctant but realised it was also to their benefit and set about taking control of construction. They demanded the men form up, selecting two dozen for building work parties. Jack was put into a group to help lay the pipeline. They first dug out the shallow natural pool to increase its flow, and began to fit together the first pipes. The route to the camp was undulating and where the ground fell away they raised the pipe up, hanging the lengths from trees by stringing them up with creepers. The pipes were carefully placed with a slight pitch, just enough to allow liquid to flow, which was a near impossible task as the gradient was such that there was practically no drop to the camp. It was six back-breaking days before the men ran out of metal pipe, and the Japanese refused permission to continue. The men knew it was a refusal to acknowledge they couldn't obtain more of the pipe. An intolerable silent standoff of sorts ensued, that the men were careful not to provoke. They could not ask questions as the soldiers would 'lose face'. The men continued traipsing to the distant end of the metal pipe to inspect the trickle that fell there. The situation continued for several weeks. Each day Jack imagined the end of the unfinished pipeline dripping pointlessly in the forest, the precious water lost to anyone but trees. The stalemate was broken by another dire outbreak of illness coinciding with someone having the idea to use bamboo instead. The soldiers agreed, the working parties were regrouped and work re-commenced. The task at hand was too important to both men and soldiers, so the latter unusually gave the men space to work themselves tirelessly in overcoming obstacles. The soldiers allowed the men to plan the route and continue on with the job relatively unhindered however, the work was inevitably slow and exhausting.

The task moved on apace when local men were rounded up to cut and ferry lengths of bamboo to the work area. Jack found himself standing in the buzzing twitching forest with his group of men, awaiting the arrival of bamboo. The soldiers paced, occasionally watching, some seemed to show genuine interest in their progress. Most sat or leant against trees, smoking cigarettes and blowing clouds of smoke into the dappled light. The men had been issued tools, mostly *parangs* — a local type of machete. Each was carefully counted and had to be returned, missing items would attract a bashing. Jack waited under the shade of the trees, deep in thick forest. He stood still, his drinking canteen slung around his neck and a sharp, potentially deadly *parang* weighing heavy in his hand. He passed the smooth handle from palm to palm, feeling the weight of the sharp blade pulling at his muscles. He became momentarily fascinated by the idea of *taking care* of the few soldiers who had accompanied them into the forest. The blade flashed in the flickering tree-light as he turned it over in his blistered hands. He glanced at the nearest soldier, standing a few feet away, one side of his face glowing in a shaft of sunlight. He wouldn't know what had happened. The next nearest soldier was another few feet on. The idea spun in Jack's mind. One leap forward, thrash the first one in a single blow, a crack to the second soldier and Jack would be off, running through the forest. Jack imagined his legs pumping, canteen banging on his chest, and his heart thumping within. He would be away...But away to where? The island was a speck in the rolling ocean, there was nothing but water for miles. Even if he survived the ocean and reached another island, surely that would also be inhabited, and occupied by Japanese. And what of the other PoWs? They would no doubt pay some price for his escape, successful or not. No, it was futile, a simple act of suicide. The idea receded in his mind's eye as the image of himself running in the forest began to fade. He came to, realising he was staring at the *parang*, lost in his hopeless plan as someone nudged him, breathing softly, "Come *back* Jack. Don't even think of it. It'll do no good..." The man prised the *parang* from his grip as Jack, unblinking, pulled his eyes to the face of the man taking the tool. Glazed and unfocused his mind returned to his forest surroundings, "I was, I was... just, thinking," he said at last. His eyes brimmed as the disappearing thud of his running boots echoed away through the trees. The man clapped his shoulder and Jack shook the idea from his thoughts as the long-awaited bamboo finally arrived, carried on the shoulders of nervous local men.

The pipeline grew, snaking through trees, the bamboo creaking gently as it carried the trickle in a steady stream nearer the camp. Finally, the last few sections were lowered into place. Jack and two others fixed the last bamboo pipe to a supporting sapling at the camp perimeter as PoWs, soldiers and guards moved in for closer inspection. A couple of men manhandled a drum bringing it directly under the running pipe as water reverberated loudly into the empty container, like distant thunder. Instinctively, Jack put out a hand to feel the fresh water run over his palm. Immediately he felt the thud of a rifle butt to his side, as he was shoved away. He backed off, eyes lowered, as a young soldier slung his weapon over his shoulder and produced a tin cup. He held it beneath the small steam, watching as it filled with the clear liquid. He looked around at the gathering, then sniffed the water suspiciously. He grinned as he took a deep drink. The parched men gasped involuntarily, they all hoped for a chance to drink. Not one was allowed. The guards jabbed the air with rifle bayonets and the men slunk back as the soldiers shouted that the area was now out of bounds. Four men were assigned to what became known as the 'tea kitchen', the fire and boiling spot at the camp end of the pipeline. They gathered firewood and kept the fire going to boil the collected water. Two others were assigned to running pipeline repairs, an Englishman and a sturdy Welshman. They fixed leaks, strung up sagging bamboo pipes and repaired damaged joints. The water was rationed, after the soldiers had taken all they wanted. A large part of the remainder was then sent to the sick hut and a rationed quantity was issued to men on working parties. The pipeline had been built in the first month after arriving at the island, and it quickly became part of life, and an essential one. Nonetheless, it was only a part of the ritual of daily life and death on the island.

The camp expanded over the months and became almost a small village for the Japanese soldiers and Korean guards, arranged such that they now had offices, doctors, medicine, food and storage, and also an air raid shelter. The men, the thousand PoWs, outnumbering their captors five to one, were housed in a space only slightly larger, but with no such facilities. Their small PoW hospital was just another hut, with no real medicines. The two medics amongst the men were as prone to illness as everyone else, yet despite the hardships they did what they could. The camp dug in, as did the daily grind. Every day was the same. Jack stood in the back row of swaying men as they fell in for roll call at six am. He jabbed at his flapping tattered shirt, tucking it into his thin shorts, rubbing at his face with the dry palms of his hands in an effort to rouse himself. The string, from which his number-tag hung, rubbed against the thin cord holding his quarter-filled canteen around his neck, scratching at his skin as he tried to push both irritants under his frayed collar. Then the order came to number off in Japanese. The men had learnt the words under the twitching sting of a bamboo sapling, "Ichi, Ni, San, Yon..." Jack had initially said the closest English words, but it became too much effort to check he wasn't observed. Still occasionally he uttered, "Itchy, Knee, Son, Won." After the daily throng to the breakfast lorry subsided and each man had eaten the small unsatisfying splat of mouldering rice in a dribble of green water, they formed up again to leave on working parties, spending the day baking in the sun while working to exhaustion. After the allotted ten days to build their camp huts had passed, new working parties had been gathered and the next miserable drudge had begun. Jack was pushed into a group of fifty men who marched out at a fairly brisk pace considering their weariness, aided in forward motion by bayonet threat and jabbering demand. They'd moved along the dusty road, turning as it split in two at a junction and followed the right fork onto a smaller track into a dense forest of cocoanut trees. In the middle of the thick plantation they were ordered to a halt. The march had taken just over an hour, and they were some three miles from the camp. Jack stood panting and looking around. He realised they were in a small clearing not much wider than the road. He watched nervously as the soldiers yapped at each other, pointing profusely and consulting a crumpled map. The ground rumbled, they turned as a truck bumped up the thin road barely wide enough, stopping with a shudder. Jack stood close by and a soldier ordered with pushing and nodding angrily to the nearest men, to unload the truck. Jack climbed aboard with three others and handed down picks, saws, shovels, *parangs* and other tools. Most looked old and too flimsy for work. He felt deep apprehension for what lay ahead. As the sun pressed at their brows and sweat beaded, their new task became clearer. A wide clearing was to be cut through the cocoanut trees, a mile and a half long and three hundred yards wide. The men looked up and down the thickly wooded area surrounding them as they stacked tools and the soldiers barked their orders. "This is going to take one *hell* of a long time," whispered Jack seriously to the man next to him, "I hope I can last that long!" the man replied, eyebrows raised. The working parties fanned out along the track, taking long saws and axes. They were soon spread out over nearly a mile.

Felling each huge cocoanut tree required four men, two on each end of a saw, pulling and pushing, grunting and sweating for the best part of half an hour until they had sliced through each heavy trunk. Every tree felled made a little more room once it was taken away. Clearing away the trunks was a huge task in itself. It took six men to cut away the palms, sawing the sharp fronds and piling them into stacks for later use as roofing and firewood. The fibrous leaves sliced at their bare hands, cutting thin sores into every crease of their skin. Once each tree was rendered down to a smooth long trunk they were next to be moved. Each trunk needed fifty men to carry the weight. Wedging bamboo braces underneath and hoisting each trunk into the air, the buckling men staggered to the edge of the clearing. There, the forest opened out onto a white sand beach. It took months of intense hard work to move and stack hundreds of felled cocoanut trees on the beach. Each tree cut and hauled along the ever-expanding line cost each man dearly. The heat was relentless, burning scalps and arched shoulder blades as they bent, contorted to their task. Each day was spent dehydrated, exhausted, achingly hungry and ever watchful of Japanese soldiers who stood in the shade. Drinking from full canteens, some enjoyed the cruelty of pouring water away into dry earth next to a gasping man. Others seemed to enjoy nothing more than to suddenly turn and bash a man for no reason. The relentless work seemed to continue without end. Once all the trees were felled in the designated area, their stumps and roots had to be cut out and the resulting holes back-filled. Jack found himself wielding a rough pick axe, only half listening in a vacant parched daze as it thudded hollowly against the stump. He lifted the pick, his ribs raising under his fluttering torn shirt, they resembled the brown protruding roots he hacked at. He dropped to his knees chopping at the stubborn roots with his *parang*, hitting the ground and stump wildly. Heaving and pulling, he wrenched the embedded heart of the tree from the earth. Every man wore the same distant daze as each day folded into the next, unchanged, unending and unbearable. Their bodies wasted as they trudged on, waning on the meagre rations, using far beyond the energy such poor food provided. Jack sweated and gasped his way through each day until his twitching dreams became endless roots weaving through the ground, surrounding him, clenching him tight and choking him. He would wake in the darkness to find he was wrapped in his thin blanket, pushing and kicking at wasted legs of men all around. It felt like drowning. He spluttered until he calmed himself and returned to fractured and fitful slumber. The days and nights churned along, every man thinning, the task seeming to go on and on. Over the dragging months the working parties finished felling the trees, clearing their stumps and moving the earth and roots away in baskets, creating the wide clearing that unbeknown as yet to the men, would be an airstrip. Jack lifted his pick and stood in the centre of a now desolate monochrome landscape, stretching away in all directions. Gone was the fertile green of the cocoanut fronds with their fibrous brown trunks, the flowering tropical oasis had been utterly obliterated. The earth was laid bare, pocked all over where the trees had stood, now only populated by bended men, arched like charcoal sticks, chopping at the ground in a vast charred white field. It reminded Jack of negatives, the inverted pictures from his father's wasteland war.

Jack and the men had wondered what the clearing was to be used for. "Perhaps we're to sow crops," Jack had suggested hopefully early on, during whispered hut discussions around a guttering candle flame. The soldiers met their quizzical glances with their next demanded order, which was to flatten the ground. The men set to, clearing the pitted surface, levelling out humps of coral, flattening lumps, and filling tree-stump craters with earth. To and fro along the long line, men collected shallow woven baskets filled with earth, lifting with handles on either side. They heaved them onto a shoulder, carrying them away to the sides of the cleared area where they tipped the soil into piles as pointing soldiers shouted and pushed at them. Snatched discussions amongst the men as they passed one another had since reached a consensus that the flattened clearing was certainly an airstrip, a runway in the middle of nowhere. Soon suspicions were confirmed as the heaps of earth piled higher and they were directed to form them into 'U'-shaped embankments, dugouts to camouflage enemy aeroplanes. Jack felt angry now he *knew* they'd been building an airstrip, as all the talk turned to its specific uses. "Must be for an invasion, for refuelling. Must be to launch an attack on Australia, surely?" was the agreed upon enemy goal. Day upon day Jack hefted earth into the baskets, exposing more hard white coral under the thin layer of soil. Like the whole island the airstrip was coral ground, sharp and impossibly hard. Chopping away with his *parang* Jack reduced the outcrops, a chunk at a time, to sand with his bleeding hands. The coral dust seemed to know how to creep into the grooves of his fingerprints and wedge there like glass shards, making each man's hands painful to the touch. The sound of chipping chipped away at Jack's ears, and his mind. The grit of it in the air ground between his teeth and rubbed at his tongue, drying his mouth. The sand-blown coral dust settled on every man and blew into their eyes. Soon, many had painfully damaged eyesight, blinded by dust and glare of sparkling white coral in the relentless sun. Each day as the march to the airstrip endlessly repeated, the men became more exhausted, the line more quietened as the men became deeply contemplative. Each day they formed up, hoarsely shouting off their numbers, readying to leave camp. Each day took more from them, thinned them, and left most barefoot and barebacked, shuffling along with burnt skin and wandering gaze. Through the months of building, they had trudged through biblical downpours, sloshing mud, the suffocating sweating heat and relentless clouds of flies and mosquitos to the ever-expanding, ever-flattening clearing. The passing of time was marked only by the rising of the sun and the going down of the same. Despite the pipeline now providing running water, the gradient was such that the fall of water was not constant and disappointingly it was not sufficient to allow rations for washing. The Japanese soldiers were disinterested in the lack of such facilities for the PoWs, until yet anther severe outbreak of illness indicated some opportunity must be made. Working parties returning from the airstrip construction grew filthier by the day. They trudged into the camp in gathering dusk, sweating, covered with coral dust and soil. Eyes caked, they blinked painfully as they lay down to rest. The PoW officers, in desperation asked again that the men be allowed a brief soak in the sea. Scepticism was finally replaced with permission as the Japanese decided they wouldn't be able to swim far anyway. It had been weeks since Jack had anything approaching a proper wash. He had made determined use of collected rainwater, and had occasionally splashed himself with stream water. At the end of the following day, after clearing hard ground Jack along with fifty or so others in his working party were unexpectedly marched down in the fading light to the shore, to ablute. Jack looked out to sea incredulously. He immediately considered the opportunity to escape. He looked out to the darkening waters and his thin aching body declined the idea. After all, where would he swim to? The men around him tentatively waded out to wash in the salty water. Clearly there was *no* possibility of escape, but still it filled their thoughts and imaginings. This method of washing became the norm most days. Fifteen allocated minutes soaking in the sea seemed something of a blessing, and the men quickly took the opportunity to heart, making the very most of it. Soon, these permitted minutes in the sea became the only part of the day in which some sense of humanity, of normality, could be felt. It was in these moments of calm that Jack was reminded of the astonishing beauty in the place. Each day he'd had to focus his mind, to last the day, to hold on until dusk for the weary march to the beach. To survive for his precious fifteen minutes.

Jack stood at the shore, the sea gently lapping his bare feet. Precariously he waded out a little way, for his minutes of imagined freedom in the warm shallow lagoon. The clear water was quickly pocketed with murky clouds of dirt as it soaked the day from his ragged clothes, forming swirls of muck and dust around him. Here, he allowed himself slices of somewhere else, whilst trying to maintain his tight grip on reality. It would have been so easy to sink into dreams, slink into madness. Some had already lost their minds, the poor souls. They blinked in the twilight of reality as their lives ebbed away with the tide. Jack took his fifteen longed for minutes and divided it first into time needed to take care of himself, washing clothes then wounds in the stinging healing salt water. The remaining minutes he took as his own, as his *dreaming* time. He first slipped under the sea, his dark dry skin soaking in the beams of ebbing sunlight as he gently rubbed the thick salty water into his parched scalp. Sand and coral specks never left the body, they found ways into every fold of flesh. He twisted grains from his ears and stubbly chin with his coral chipped fingers. His dark floppy hair had bleached in the beating sun and was now wildly tufted having been cut haphazardly. He thought of his family, muttering to himself, "What would they think if they could see me now? Would they even know me?" He pushed the thoughts aside and finished washing. He discreetly looked about for watching soldiers and, finding them preoccupied sitting under the shade of cocoanut trees on the beach, he took his chance in the melee of men washing and scrubbing their own bodies to lie out flat on the sea. Hidden in the chaos, his arms stretched above his head and his legs out star-fishing, Jack dreamt quickly and briefly. Floating, slowly moving his legs and arms, making small strokes in the water he closed his eyes. Gentle waves rolled over him as he imagined where he would go today. Gone from this war certainly, gone from captivity obviously, away somewhere. Anywhere. Perhaps, with a lover on some secluded island beach like ones he'd seen on posters at the train station. No, too much like the island he was trapped on. He pushed the idea away but the palm trees waved and the sea seduced. The scene framed around him like some mesmerising view from a beachside restaurant... restaurant. Immediately his fictions dissolved in the thought, the fantasy of food. Real food. The imminent barking order to leave and return to the camp for *makan*, to eat the tiny portion of stale, dirty rice could never compare with the meal beginning to cook in his mind. Idly, he licked his blistered lips and dreamt of all he would have, forgetting to count his moments of self-preserving freedom. The meal swam in his mind's eye, thickly cut juicy roast potatoes oozed melting butter, a balanced golden blob teetered then slid down the rounded crispness of a potato. The butter pooled, making golden eddies in dark gravy, thick with onion and splashed over the meat. Peas, verdant as a cricket green and perfectly rounded, piled against the potatoes. Delicious fragrant steam left the plate in swirls, the aroma caused his parched mouth to almost water and Jack forgot himself completely. Someone bumped him as he waded past. "Come on lad, *makan*," the man muttered despondently, Jack roused himself, splashing as he stood. The hard cricket ball of stale rice, speckled with dirt and sitting in a puddle of greenish liquid, smelt foul and diseased. It was cold, having travelled three miles from Liang cookhouse, but that was the least unappetising thing about it. Their daily diet hadn't changed much, it had lessened from 'not enough' to 'almost non-existent'. No man could continue back-breaking work on such rations and not be turned to skin and bone, and not succumb to the catalogue of illnesses that plagued them.

Food, and the lack of it, was the topic of conversation each and every single day. Mouth-watering meals would be described down to the most infinitesimal detail, taking turns to speak of meals enjoyed, meals wished for and anticipated meals once, hopefully free. At every camp on Java, the food had been the same, now at Liang here were the same rations, except that the quantity kept reducing as the men worked longer and harder. William, a friend of Jack's often said, "No matter where I am in captivity, the diet is always the same." On Java, breakfast used to be a pint of steamed rice and a spoonful of sugar. The midday meal was three quarters of a pint of steamed rice in a greenish liquid, little more than water. Then, in the evening there was one pint of steamed rice and a few of the greens that had cooked in the midday water. On Ambon the daily ration was often half that. Only those working were allocated food, so the meagre rations were also shared with those in the hospital hut or otherwise sick. The first truck of the day usually rumbled into the camp as the men waited for dawn roll call, *tenko*, to dismiss. The men surged forward to get to front of queue, as all too often the supply ran dry before the end of the line, so it was imperative to get one's bowl under the serving ladle. Jack and the men didn't call it food, they used the Malay word *makan* meaning 'to eat'. Jack often asked that to eat, when there was hardly a mouthful, hardly anything to chew, could that really be called eating? Jack had grown into a strong young man on his mother's cooking, it had been plentiful, filling and hot. Now, the malnourishing rations caused his stomach to ache as it contracted and shrank. Everything here was a misnomer. They called the morning drink 'tea' when it was merely warm water with maize, and no sugar or milk to soften the flavour. "How can it be called tea, it's just slightly warmed water with unidentifiable things floating in it?!" Jack would say, not ungratefully as it splashed into his mug. It was as if each aspect of daily life was designed to be more difficult, and more unpleasant than it needed to be. Latrines were another source of disgust for Jack and the men, that needed to be overcome. When they'd first arrived the men had been ordered to dig trenches for the purpose. The area was soon swarming with so many flies it turned Jack's usually sturdy stomach. Later they would instead use the beach when allowed to wash in the sea. It was here that Jack's friend, William, made good use of a tattered copy of *Ben Hur*, that he'd managed to conceal in the attap roof of their hut. The book brought some small relief in every sense of the word. William carefully and gently peeled two pages from the book where the preceding pages were already missing, as Jack looked about to make sure the sound of early morning tearing didn't attract unwanted attention. The two men took turns folding the precious pages into a pocket or sleeve and at ablution time took turns to read a page. Swapping when each had finished, nodding to each other at the words. Jack was lost amongst places in some other world that still read books and history. He read each page as true stories pulled from an imagined reality of what was known to have occurred in ancient Rome and beyond. They shared the escape, the prose and then disposed of the soft paper, on their poor behinds. "It feels like silk," Jack had said, "I hope Mr Wallace won't mind, we mean no disrespect do we?" William had responded kindly, "Quite the opposite, we're grateful for his encouragement and the transporting words of the story." Jack replied chuckling, "– and we are equally grateful for the lavatory paper." William had smiled.

Moments of brief amusement took on greater significance juxtaposed as they were by the stark contrast of the daily grind of their captivity. The soldiers had been clearly ordered to maltreat the PoWs, to under-nourish and withhold medicine. But, it was their capacity for unbridled cruelty that staggered Jack. For the pointlessness of it and the sadistic glee with which it was carried out. Amongst the guards and soldiers there were those who were most hated. Captains Shiogawa and Ueda, Sergeant-Majors Kawai and Yamamoto, and the Korean guards Fujimoto and Kimura being the worst culprits. The actions and inaction of the Japanese camp doctor, Shimada took an unnecessary toll of the life expectancy of the PoWs and there were many more who meted out terror for the sake of it. There were also those seemingly less dangerous, yet still unpredictable. Rather than from any sense of mercy, they occasionally chose to overlook a 'misdemeanour' due to lack of interest, or plain laziness. Jack had once tripped walking across the haphazard airstrip, falling forward and sending his basket of coral and dust into the air. He braced for the arrival of the bamboo strip he felt sure would strike any moment. He'd looked about when no shout came. Nearby, a soldier motioned to pick up the basket and clear away the mess. Jack nodded, moving quickly as the soldier reclined in the shade, simply motioning with his hand. Clearly, he couldn't be bothered to move. Jack had felt grateful but also it angered him to be subservient to his enemy.

Leniency was the infrequent exception rather than the norm. Day to day, the soldiers and guards spread over the dreadful conditions an unbearable layer of hardship. Bashings occurred regularly, for not bowing quickly enough, for not working hard enough, for stopping briefly, for speaking, or for anything they deemed warranted it. Often, simply the soldiers own boredom. Punishments were meted out for the smallest action and were unavoidable. Early on, in the first weeks after they'd arrived a man in Jack's hut was terribly ill with a bout of dysentery that had struck down many PoWs. The disease ravaged him mercilessly, thinning his body and hollowing his cheeks. He was unable to carry himself to the latrine one rainy night, and come morning the soldiers were furious on discovering the small area of mess he'd been unable to avoid causing. He was summarily dragged out to the restrained protests of the other men in the hut. The PoWs held back those most enraged with struggling arms and pleas. "You'll make it worse," and "you want to join him? There's nothing you can do." The paralysed men watched as the unfortunate's heels dragged through the earth as he was carried backwards, limp in the soldier's grip, his head lolling slackly. The men couldn't see where he had been taken, but as the working parties formed up a short time later preparing to leave for the day's grind, they saw him. He stood against a post at the entrance to the camp. His hands were tied behind the post, pulling his back taut against the wood. His head was bowed, and his chin rested on his chest. Jack squinted in horror, he couldn't make out what looked so strange about him, then it struck him as the column marched painfully forward. The man's light hair was darkened, his shadowed face was clouded by flies. The swarm had been attracted to the foul-smelling slop that had been poured over the poor soul, the contents of a latrine. A pointed lesson in futility from their captors. There was nothing this man had done, save be ill. The punishment for his un-committed crime perfectly described the irrational and unfathomable behaviour of these soldiers without honour. Each man marched silently past, unable to do anything to help him. His downcast eyes blinked sorrowfully at each reluctant and commiserate stare. Jack wished he could dash to him, cut him free, wash him and save him. His muscles tensed and a tear escaped his eye. He was unable to do a thing. To even move out of the line would be suicide. He was unable to shake the picture from his mind. The whites of the man's eyes, blinking and staring from the foul, moving blackness of his face woke him in the night. Jack thought the man had spoken his name and told him not to worry. Jack had cried out, reaching out to help. Someone leaned over him, whispering "It's all right lad," Jack, sweating and anxious, propped himself up on an elbow looking about the prone figures alongside him down the dark hut. "What is it? What's happened?" he breathed. "He's gone lad. They've cut him down. We've wrapped him and we'll bury him the morning." Jack gasped quietly. Others leant forward as news travelled down the ragged line of limp bodies, now rousing. In the morning the man was carried to Boot Hill, and laid into a shallow ditch. William said kind words to comfort both the wrapped man, and those lining the edge.

He was the first of them to Boot Hill, the makeshift cemetery opposite the camp, on a small rise. Hundreds would follow in the months ahead. They would be carried there from malnutrition, vitamin deficiency and starvation, from exhaustion and relentless beatings, and of course by disease. Invisible diseases swirled unseen around the camp, carried by the multitudinous insect life. Bedbugs and scabies, maggots, fleas, flies and lice, crawling into and infecting sores, rapidly turning them to tropical ulcers. Each malady slowed a man, causing the thousand as a whole to limp and stagger about the camp and on to the airstrip. Sores and smaller injuries also made each man vulnerable to the lurking threat from larger predators, cholera, dengue fever, typhus and tuberculosis and beriberi, that took hold of each weakened body and consumed it. So many were needlessly laid in Boot Hill for want of a little medicine. Heaped upon these deathly plagues were repeated attacks of malaria and the twin devils of diarrhoea and dysentery. Each visited every man, causing yet more avoidable deaths among them. The first man to Boot Hill was followed soon after, by a long line of ghostly departed men. Each passing was entirely avoidable. Jack found himself helping to carry a stretcher into the sick hut, after a man had collapsed in the heat and being nearby, Jack had offered his help. He paused at the threshold of the sick hut. He'd had no intention of ever entering. The front of the stretcher continued on, heaved in by the forward man and Jack had no choice but to be pulled into the dim interior filled with inert figures, and wheezing movement. An oppressive miasma hung in the air, lit by candlelight and the declining sun. Each man lying there was desperate to get out but each was unable to leave. Jack surveyed the hut, everywhere pleading eyes reached out. He looked down, his eyes beginning to brim as a man nearby gasped. Jack looked to the man's outstretched hand and without hesitation moved to his side. Taking the hand in his as others looked on mournfully, Jack realised his action was dangerous. Whatever fever or malady could easily be caught, but still he held the hand tightly, gritting his jaw to hold back the filling of his eyes. To no avail as tears splashed down his thin cheeks. Something about him reminded Jack of his elder brother and he could not help himself. As the man lay dying he spoke quietly of family. Jack promised to write to them, to visit them. "Settle now, I *will* see them. I *will* go, don't worry yourself now..." he spoke the consoling words softly. The man's grip tightened suddenly in spasm, as Jack leant forward in the flickering light. "Easy now, it's all right..." he whispered urgently into the man's ear as the breath caught in his throat a final time. His eyes widened, then dulled. Jack reached forward closing the man's staring blank eyes. He sat back on his heels and lowered his head. And he sobbed. The guttering candlelight, reminiscent to Jack of church candles, flickered off the walls of St Mary's church back home, and Jack was there in an instant. He wiped his face with the back of his hand as he observed the bowed heads and sermon issued in monotonous tones by the vicar. He bowed his head for the man, listening as the boy's choir sang out, interrupted by the muffled coughs of the congregation. As he looked around to see who had coughed, a hand clapped his shoulder, waking him. The coughing was there in the sick hut, these men all coughed. Jack cleared his own throat, stood and left the oppressive hut, blinking in the daylight.

Jack saw so many more brothers and friends pass, but he held the hand of only that one man. He could not bear the closeness, and the promises to carry their words home. He worried what would happen to the messages if the end were to come to *him*. He reconciled the passings of his friends into his uneasy and unbelievable daily routine. Every day waking at dawn, lining up for *tenko*, sounding off numbers in the line. The scrabble for the slop of rice to put in the pit of each stomach. The gathering of thinner and thinner men into working parties and the daily struggling march to the widening clearing. Each day filled with endless chipping at the relentlessly hard coral, the sun beating their backs, flies buzzing around their damp brows as they, dehydrated and delirious, hacked out the airstrip along the beautiful, paradise fragrant coast. Inevitably the working conditions and terrible treatment would take a rapid and gluttonous toll.

The morning following the death in the hut, Jack found himself lining up for *makan* with Henry and Harold. They were in different huts and different working parties so they didn't often see each other to speak to, for weeks on end. At breakfast the three sat under a tree chewing earnestly on hard rice-balls. They watched a man with battered mess tin in hand, meander past wearing a potato sack into which he'd cut armholes, he also wore a slight grin. "He looks rather well dressed today," Jack commented without humour, pointing with his spoon. They watched him go. His thin arms protruding from the sack were not much thicker than his legs dangling below as he walked by. Harold leant against Jack whispering, "That man, was a manager at Woolworth's." Jack watched him shuffling forward in the long line for rotten rice. He seemed cheered to have something to cover his bony body from the sun. Many of their clothes were shredded or worn away, particularly those who hadn't any new kit since they'd stepped off the convoy. A few were now 'Jap Happy' meaning they wore only an immodest loincloth. It was so named as it seemed to amuse the soldiers, presumably that the men had to resort to such measures. Sandals, no more than a sole whittled from scavenged wood tied on with leather scraps were worn by a few. Many now went barefoot. Jack was grateful to still have his tattered shorts that had once been trousers, and his impossibly thin ragged shirt. It flapped and fluttered, it's frayed and torn edges whistling in the breeze. Jack was loath to discard it, he felt it was a part of civilisation and clothed him in dignity, where both were lacking on the island. He did not wear it every day, in an effort to preserve it. He had long since cut the arms away, offering one sleeve as bandages to the sick hut. The other he used to make a sort of band for his brow, against the relentless sun. The rice ball now devoured, Jack bade farewell to his friends and joined the gathered men as they set out for work at the airstrip. He couldn't say what day it was. Each merged into another punctuated only by the passing of more poor souls. The work was dangerous even for a healthy man. Chipping at the coral had caused painful blindness for many, where the coral dust had scraped at their eyes and took their vision. Unable to work these men were confined to the sick hut. When it was full as it often was, they slumped outside in the sun, blinking painfully in the harsh sunlight. They lay out all day in the camp, becoming susceptible to other maladies of camp life. Burning feet syndrome, camp eyes and camp ears which pecked at their remaining resolve to fight on. The men who were still able to work, spread out along the coast chipping away at the great chucks of coral, flattening the ground, every day inching the airstrip nearer completion. They had no choice, the men had to show some willing, however every chance they could, they sabotaged construction. These small victories boosted morale considerably despite the risk. They held up work as much as possible by all and any means whilst trying to dodge bashings. They flattened the earth, disguising uneven pits by placing concealed layers of palm fronds and filling the pits loosely. A more compacted layer was patted gently on top. The idea was to damage any aircraft that attempted a landing. There were silent hoots of victory as a single propeller *Zero* swooped down to land, bounced once and promptly lost its landing gear in the pits that had

138

immediately given way. The fuselage was still sliding along the runway as they turned back to their tasks, whistling quietly to themselves. Where they could the men left sharp protrusions, pieces of bamboo or tools. Their private *modus operandi* was that, 'the airstrip must not be allowed to land planes successfully'. This they agreed as one, that if they *had* to build it, it should not be built well. The Japanese soldiers sometimes noticed poor work but so clever were the men in concealing their handiwork, the soldiers usually believed it was due to the men's fatigue and building inability. Despite not catching the men red-handed the soldiers pursued them relentlessly. Threatening and screaming, pushing and jabbing, bashing with rifle butts or bamboo lengths. By July, so many men were too ill, too malnourished and diseased to work, with many more badly injured by unprovoked bashings, that the working party numbers had dwindled dramatically. The worst of the ill men were moved to the sick hut, then often on to Boot Hill in a rolling, avoidable procession of the inevitable.

Jack felt he could better face illness, the dangers of work and the lack of provision, rather than the enemy's sadistic attacks. These were maladies that could be faced, head on. If he succumbed to disease it would have been a 'fairer fight' in his view. It would have been utterly pointless and unnecessary, but he felt these dangers were tangible. The unknown horror that haunted him was being at the mercy of Japanese soldiers and Korean guards. The former hated to be on the island and only hated the PoWs more. The latter hated being under the yoke of the soldiers as well as being trapped. Each meted out their frustrations and inadequacies on the men, who were simply trying to survive each day, each hour. A common quiet discussion topic at night was the insanity of these soldiers and guards. They wanted the airstrip built and common sense dictated that a well-fed and healthy workforce would work harder and the job would be completed faster. Jack could not fathom why they should be starved and worse, so they were no more than roaming skeletons. Weakened men could not serve their purpose. Jack believed the purpose was so they were not a threat. A healthy, strong workforce would retaliate, they would overrun their enemy. He believed the intention was to break the men physically and mentally. To kill the will to escape or fight back. Suffering was nothing new, but the determination to survive grew stronger. Jack would say, "After all, we are still alive, we've made it this far." He had wondered if he had been spared due to fate, or luck, or his sheer bloody-mindedness. No, he had reasoned, it must be down to fate. Those who had not survived were no weaker nor less determined. They were no less focussed on surviving. Their fates were individual to them and no one could say why one man survived and the man next to him had not. The exceptions to fate, he knew, were those taken by deliberate acts of the Japanese. All suffered due to these pointless bashings. In truth, Jack and the men were all too keenly aware that not one man needed to have suffered and not one should have been buried at Boot Hill.

Jack knelt on the open airstrip in blazing heat, looking furtively sideways as he hand-shovelled loose coral and earth into his basket. His mind was taut, cold clammy hairs on his arms and back stood on end in the sticky heat. In the pit of his mind a gnawing anticipation that the end, his end, could be any moment. He would not give them a reason, though they needed no reason. These soldiers were no cartoon caricatures, yet were indeed monstrously cruel dead-eyed, soulless devils. If they lost their minds, men lost dignity and their lives. There was nothing to do but endure. The men cajoled each other, helped those they could, trying to maintain some sort of humanity, even at their weakest selves. Even at their thinnest, most beaten down, crushed men, they were not defeated, and so it continued on and on.

Months before, not long after their arrival one of the PoWs had simply taken too long to get his drink, and a particularly nasty soldier had pushed him. The liquid was quite hot and he had spilt a little, which caused him to jump, raising a scalded hand in the air with a yelp. The movement of the PoW innocently raising a hand, caused the solider to react as if he'd been attacked. He screamed, and raised his rifle butt, turning the bayonet forward he prodded painfully at the PoW. There had not been many other PoWs nearby, but a few had stood, watching in silent horror. There was nothing they could do. Jack witnessed the incident, his fists clenched impotently. The soldier gave another vicious prod, pushing the PoW to the ground. He fell to his hands and knees. A circle of red rose through the back of his ragged shirt, blossoming outwards as he awkwardly grasped at his back, crying out in pain. He stood, as his eyes fell to the blood on his hands. The soldier stepped up again in preparation to jab again from the front. He screamed at the PoW to face him. The man turned and looked squarely, calmly at the soldier. He seemed stunned and watched momentarily, his slack-jawed and his small eyes bulging. They stood briefly in silence, then the Japanese soldier eyed the gathered PoWs surrounding the scene and he shrieked hysterically, bringing soldiers running. The PoW spoke gently to the soldiers as he raised both hands, trying to calm the situation. The furious soldier shrieked and stepped backwards, tripping and falling onto his backside in the coral dust, where he screamed like an enraged child. The PoW backed away a little on the approach of more soldiers, his eyes wildly darting back and forth. He wiped his brow with bloodied hand, which smeared red across his face. He looked to them, "I haven't done anything," he said quietly. They rushed forward and caught him up, marching him away to the shouts of the sitting soldier, who scrabbled to his feet and ran alongside screaming for immediate revenge. The other PoWs nearby watching mutely, now stepped back as the group passed. The PoW did not struggle. Jack looked him in the eye but he could not return the gaze. His expression was vacant, he was already far, far away. He knew he was beyond help and he knew what was coming. As dusk fell that night and the men queued for the evening mouldering slop with watered vegetable dribble, they tried to ascertain what had happened. In hushed tones in the gloom of Jack's hut to the accompaniment of the ever twitching cicadas those who had waited in the dark told what they'd heard. The man, clearly innocent of any wrong-doing even of Japanese unpredictable standard, had been horribly unlucky. That solider had been on the edge, simmering all day and he had perhaps deliberately, misinterpreted the man's simple hand movement. The previous day the same soldier had demanded a man walk faster and the man had tried, only his legs cracked with painful weeping ulcers and he'd stumbled. The soldier had pursued him, prodding and pushing until the man passed out and lay limp and breathless in the blistering sun. The soldier, a pinched and peevish looking lieutenant they knew as Iketani demanded the camp commander take action against the PoW accused of raising his hand in attack. In the officers hut, camp commander Anami had shifted his hefty weight in his chair, he was already feeling tired and ready to leave camp for his dinner, he didn't have time for this. Iketani's flushed sweating face demanded *honour* must be attended to. Anami motioned to his sergeant major, Yoshikazu Yamamoto, for the man to be brought immediately. He wanted to deal with it without hesitation, nor too many lengthy facts. Anami was hungry and absently patted his rounded belly. He sighed unsympathetically as the man was dragged in by Yamamoto and Mitarai. Two PoW officers waited quietly nearby, trying to overhear what was happening. They called out in the dusk that the man must be represented, but were ignored. Anami sniffed the air, waving at the man to step forward and stand before him. Yamamoto thrust him forward with a hard push. The man now bore a welt on his brow which had closed one eye and his wrists were tied with bamboo saplings, cutting sharply at his skin. He stood limply, hands immobile, palms half opened as he stared bleakly at the floor. Anami coughed once, and immediately burst into a short yapping monologue, agreeing with Iketani that there were few crimes worse than raising a hand to a member of the Imperial Japanese Army. The prisoner had indeed been wrong. Honour had been insulted and the man would be taken into the bamboo forest and dispatched forthwith. Iketani smirked as the man looked back and forth, unclear what had been decided, but seeing Iketani's response, he sensed the worst. He had not spoken a word in defence, nor had he been asked to. The man, a Trooper of the 3rd Kings Own Hussars, a wholly honourable and kind man, and an honest champion of the underdog, was led away. After evening *makan*, the PoWs watching the perimeter fence saw the Trooper taken into the forest by Mitarai and Yamamoto. They waited nervously in the dusk until the two returned, without the Trooper. The PoWs vowed if they survived, if they ever got off the island, they would look for Mitarai and Yamamoto and claim them for the Trooper, their friend.

Major Mitarai was hated as much as the worst of them. He was never too lazy to bash a man for not bowing deeply enough, for looking at him insolently, for simply anything he took a mind to. Sergeant Major Yamamoto had a caricature evil face, pinched and beady-eyed. He watched constantly for the opportunity to cause suffering. The two captains Kazue Shiogawa and Tadae Ueda were doubly terrifying, but they tended to issue orders and retreat to the cooler shade, leaving much of the day to day discipline to their subordinates and guards. Even so, captains Shiogawa and Ueda did not often miss roll-call and the chance to walk amongst the men, pushing, poking and striking out with thin bamboo strips. Sergeant Major Kichijiro Kawai was another much hated solider, although he was often not in the camp, something the men were grateful for. He was a soulless, merciless fiend. These, the more senior Japanese seemed to circle various camps looking for situations to complain about, for men to bash and unjustified punishments to mete out. The PoWs had concluded there were more camps, on nearby islands and the senior Japanese moved around these with equal unpleasantness. The theory was confirmed when RAF men were later brought from nearby island of Haruku. These RAF chaps had described the same process of building an airstrip on 'their' island. The Korean guards at all camps were as bad as the Japanese, as they passed on their own punishments combined with the treatment they themselves received from their Japanese superiors. Shigeru Kimura and Yoshio Fujimoto were both equally hated. A simple unintended look could end in terrible bashing, a nod or bow out of place could elect banshee screams and an unwarranted thrashing. There were others, all equally hated and all only concerned with themselves. Not *one* eased the suffering whether they were the cause or not. Each had a nickname the PoWs used amongst themselves which described each proclivity for cruelty. Of these guards and soldiers, Jack could not now remember every name. Their faces however, were indelibly etched into the minds of each man who suffered at their hands. Their twitching pinched ochre faces would never leave their nightmares. Each day the men overcame the harsh surroundings and tropical heat, lack of adequate food and water, disease and injury and pointless hard labour made indescribably worse by the treatment of their horrific captors, by simply *surviving*.

The foul-tempered camp commander Anami, not only condoned the actions of his subordinates, he ordered and enthusiastically encouraged it. Anami hated the island. He hated the PoWs and he hated the flies. His fat balding head swarmed with them drinking at the sweat on his brow and neck, he flicked and thrashed but they never left him alone. It was as if they too mocked him and the pathetic foul figure he had become.

His rage, and disappointment in himself, he meted out to flies and PoWs who had unknowingly and innocently sealed his imprisonment on the island. Each man was as insignificant to him as each fly. But, for all his brutality he *saw* the bravery amongst the PoWs. He chose to ignore it because he could not bear to see it. They helped each other, these men supposedly without honour. They shared their meagre rations generously with each other and they fed their sick brothers. They gave their own food to men who had no hope of surviving even with an extra portion, the act only left the healthier more hungry. But what *integrity*, what *honour*. Anami couldn't understand it and despised them all the more for it. He'd been lied to about these men. They were *not* without honour. These men were unquestionably honourable and deeply courageous in the face of their situation. A situation he was responsible for making so much worse. They carried on with an inner strength and dignity that made him ever more furious in his own shortcomings. He felt he might explode with injustice for himself, unable to see the injustice he served them. He tried everything to break them. What else could he do? They *must* be shown to be worthless and dishonourable, otherwise why was he there? What was the point? Yet, despite his efforts, they braved the direst of punishments and simply carried on. They died in droves, of malnutrition, of starvation and neglect, savage beatings and overwork. They simply would not die of shame, nor fear nor lack of courage. It utterly enraged him. *That* is what motivated him. He wanted to break them within as well as without. He wanted retribution for his being sent to the island instead of receiving the admiration of generals and his emperor. It sickened him to his bloated stomach, it infested him and he could not see beyond. He felt searing, agonising pity, for himself. A bead of cloudy sweat ran down Anami's temple touching his eye causing him to blink it away. He swatted at a fly on his neck. Pulling his wet collar from the sticky fat of his neck and running a finger round the damp khaki he lifted his wobbling chin in gritted grimace. He considered the command of these island camps, this posting, beneath him. Building airstrips on islands could have been a major role in this war for him, pushing the invasion of Australia and gaining air superiority. All thanks to his masterminding these airstrips. If only he could have been involved in the planning and execution of that endeavour. But his role was to simply oversee the PoWs and their work. He did not decide where runways should be sited, or when an attack might be launched, nor was he involved in greater war planning. He had not even chosen which islands. He had power over nothing except these PoWs. He was simply a janitor, a gaoler and it soured him through and through. He wore a constant expression of displeasure, his bottom lip protruded slightly, his mouth permanently downturned and sneering. His subordinates did not respect him, they were afraid of him. His underlings, Shiogawa, Ueda, Yamamoto, Iketani, Kawai and the others would cower, but like snakes they slid one by one back into the hut, pouring compliments and ideas into Anami's broken mind. They feared him, and his quick temper deeply, and there was palpable relief among all as he left to inspect progress of the airstrips on neighbouring islands.

Jack nudged the man next to him, pointing with a look and raised brow as Anami came out of the guard hut looking agitated. The PoWs had been lined up and a Japanese soldier had just given the order to sound off. The men watched Anami carefully, discreetly, as they answered, "Ichi, Ni, San, Yon..." Anami stopped and spoke to Ueda as he stepped down, eyeing the gathered men dangerously. Ueda nodded and bowed. He barked at a subordinate, Iketani, who in turn dashed to one of the PoW officers yapping in stunted English. Jack looked to his fellow men quizzically, "Someone was heard in the night, don't know what," someone shrugged. "Poor bugger," replied Jack, his face full of concern. Both Anami and Ueda were out for trouble today. No one spoke. Ueda paced up and down, Iketani on his heels, while Anami watched from the overhanging shade of the hut. Someone was going to be made an example of. Someone would have to step forward. Ueda demanded someone admit the act or *all* would be punished. Iketani chattered angrily at the men, as everyone tried to understand what had happened. Jack, weighted by the thoughts of men too sick to take further punishment, rocked slightly on his feet considering whether to step forward, to ease it for the others. He felt the weight of all the surrounding men considering the same course. He was about to burst into step, his brow sweating heavily in the morning heat, as suddenly a small quiet man whose name Jack didn't know, sputtered forward.

He spoke quietly saying he was at fault. The men around him could not speak. They all knew it wasn't him, because no one knew what 'crime' had been committed. The men were unable to argue, to speak to defend themselves or make demands. They were unmanned and impotent in useless and silent protest. They each knew nothing could be gained from a pointless struggle. Ueda was delighted to have found 'his man' as Iketani took his upper arm and moved him a few steps forward. Ueda tapped his shoulder with his bamboo stick as he strode around him. As he moved behind he used the end of the bamboo between his shoulders to direct him forward. Ueda dismissed the rest of the men and they stumbled across to the truck for the half cup of mouldering rice and warm water. They watched silently as the man was taken away. Ueda prodded the PoW forward, as the men looked on. They glimpsed him between the huts marching to the camp gate and on to the guard post. There he was badly beaten and pushed into a bamboo crate, no bigger than a crouched man. He was left there for two days, in scorching heat and tepid rain, which washed his cuts and ulcers and gave him precious drops of water to drink that he later said had saved his life. He was brought out, bedraggled and wide eyed, and dropped into the clearing. The men gathered him up and took him to the sick hut. He fought defiantly and somehow overcame his ordeal, re-joining the working parties after a few weeks, but now with a blinking twitch and clicking jaw. He later travelled on the same ship as Jack bound for Java. As they'd taken the man away, the soldiers had jostled and shoved the remaining PoWs so they could not linger. As they formed up for the days working parties, Iketani was waiting. He was a caricature of callous Japanese soldier if one were needed. He wore prominent round glasses, that slipped down his squashed sweaty nose. His buck teeth overhung his puckered lips, and his eyes were constantly narrowed. His hair was shaved at the sides, longer on top and it flopped down in a greasy curtain covering one eye. Jack had always thought he had Hitler's haircut. He'd looked sideways at Iketani as he passed, and briefly thought, 'Ha!' A small grin began at the edge of his lips, which Jack stopped quickly. He must be careful, of all the soldiers he was completely humourless and dangerously unpredictable. Iketani stood, feet apart, tapping a long baton onto his open palm.

His face screwed more than usual and his feet itching with impatience. Today was nothing different, Iketani simply waited for an opportunity to unleash his anger.

Every day, continued to unfold, achingly the same. Wearily and almost broken Jack stumbled to the airstrip. They moved forward at hacking command, trudging toward the gate, bowing as they shuffled past the guard hut, ignored and unseen, unless they failed to bow sufficiently. As the airstrip neared completion each day was filled with endless clearing of coral, and moving baskets of heavy rubble from pillar to post. The hours groaned by in thirst and sweating exhaustion, ever overshadowed by the swish of bamboo through the air and the rasp as it connected with someone. Eventually, as the sun slunk lower each day the men would be rounded up to march to the beach for the precious fifteen minutes soak. Jack found himself standing there, his feet dug into the pearlescent sand, looking out to sea as if salvation could float over the horizon and wash up on the tide. He could not gaze long, pause and contemplation attracted the unwanted attention of Japanese bayonet prods or raps from bamboo sticks. He stared briefly, unblinking into the setting sunlight. These glimpses of the ocean had always been moments of deep reflection for him. Images of the island, this beach, could have covered magazines and posters offering escapes to far off paradise. He found the irony painful. Cocoanut palms waved fondly, gently, in invitation to relax on the shore. They bowed lazily over the white powdered beach, sun-tanned trunks arched in the sun, cocoanuts bulging beneath their fronds. Jack listened to the hypnotic cascade of the sea, as it massaged the soft sand with foamy waves. It was *breathtakingly* beautiful, utterly idyllic. Shells with pearly interiors scattered the beach amongst smooth wave-worn driftwood, marking the line of high tide under a perfect blue sky. Jack waded into the water slowly and lay out on the surface. His body still and reflective in the melee of splashing, washing men. He watched the sky. It was the same beautiful blue firmament covering the whole world. Achingly, he wished it were skies filled with clean starched sheets flecked with the soot from Hyde's chimneys. For a moment he drifted, looking hard into the deep azure. He squinted to blur out the palm trees swaying either side of his vision. He turned the foreign scape into familiar scenes, factories and belching chimneys, the streets and cobbles rattling with wheels of trucks and children's laughter. His thoughts continued the journey to home, slipping quietly though the door as usual, searching for them. He turned his body in the warm salty water. He saw their faces— mother, dad, sister, brother, all clear and strong in his mind. They smiled, looking to him and beckoning him home. He let out an involuntary pained sound. *Home.* He found it impossible to imagine that somewhere in the world there were people going to church come Sunday. Drinking tea and eating his mothers fruit cake. Some wonderful place could surely not still exist where grubby boys ran down back alleys, their boots reverberating off the alley walls with metallic echoes. He exhaled deeply, "How I wish to be there, how I wish to see you all again." He turned again and lifted himself from the water, and waded to shore. A salty sheen ran down his thin body in rivulets, catching the light of the setting sun.

As he pushed the spoilt rice down, gulping at the small cup of water he tried to push thoughts of home and of family from his mind. They remained, lingering just outside the door, trying to creep back in constantly. He knew he'd left the door of his mind slightly ajar for this purpose. He did not want to detach from that life completely, from his former real life. This insanity was all that was happening now, but it was not *all* the man he was, not *all* he had been. He gave in and returned to them, thinking hard of each familiar face, but found it difficult now to bring them into focus. He thought of George's baby son, so small as he had left. He imagined for a moment the children he would hope to have one day. He thought of Irene, and stopped. He could not think this far into his unknown future. He needed to fight to stay alive for today, to ensure his future. He closed the door quietly, but could still see light through the crack.

For all the men, his brothers here in the same nightmare situation, Jack felt solitary and completely alone on the island. Each man endured a solitary prison, each escaped in their minds to home when they could. They told each other stories of their lives before, to keep the pictures and memories alive in their thoughts. Walking outside Japanese earshot they described every minute detail, their previous jobs, their towns and families, their hopes and dreams. When every piece of information had been wrung from their minds they swapped working partners and began again. Come evening all were exhausted and sick from working in the heat and most nights they lay silently in the huts listening to cicadas and tried to sleep. But, sometimes they talked, soft and low in the dark. They talked mostly of the lack of food and the terrible work, and the heat. Hanging over everything else, the heat. Sweat prickled up the body even before the sun was up. A stinking, sticky sweat that kept the body constantly damp. Eventually they would talk of home. Jack came into the hut and felt along the platform for his space. He listened as he moved and thought sadly of *his* home. He felt along the bamboo and attap, stopping at his slatted space in the bunk and lay down, crammed either side by tightly packed men. The bright sun and its reflection on the coral caused him to constantly blink in its blinding reflected light. Now, in the dark his eyes blurred and the camp hut fogged as he slipped into paralysis, unable to move or stretch his limbs in an act of freedom.

And, the next day dawned. Jack woke, the day ahead exactly the same as the day before, with one goal. To survive to wake the next day. As dusk gathered after the sweating day, Jack wiped his brow. It had been especially hot and humid. The sea foamed onto the beach choppy and roaring as the clouds swirled above crowding and hanging over the line of bedraggled men as they made their way down to the shore to wash. It was a true reflection of their spirits, overcast, heavy and bursting to let go and be soaked. Jack felt desperate that day. He had been prodded hard in his side and bashed twice, as he had staggered to lift a basket. He wished he could fly from there, escape, but there was no means, but there was still the constant thought of it in his mind, in all their minds. The soldiers knew the men were dreaming of escape and found it amusing. They pointed to the sea, laughing. The men looked to the horizon of endless water with only the mirror image of an equally hellish neighbouring island interrupting the panorama. Jack wondered how long he could go on for. They all wondered the same. All had wondered if there could be any Allied rescue. Did anyone know they were there? They wondered if they had been completely forgotten. Jack felt exhausted and lost. It was a lost world where normal activities of life were unimaginable. Who would believe the things he had seen and who would *know* what he had seen, if he didn't survive? It opened the door again to thoughts of home.

He imagined his mother smiling, his father sitting at the fireplace, pipe in the corner of his mouth and wondered what they were doing at that very moment. He imagined them huddled close, listening to the radio, ears inclined to hear the news. He shook his head, noticing the radio in his minds eye, and he wondered how the war had moved on. Perhaps the Allies were winning. Perhaps the Japanese were on the verge of collapse and their increasingly sadistic behaviour was indicative of their desperation. He clung to the idea. He felt *something* was on the horizon. He felt *something* was going to happen. It was a nagging feeling he couldn't shake. Something must change, it had to.

He carried the thought in his mind back to the camp, where there seemed to be some excitement. It was somewhat muted excitement, but *something* had clearly happened. He emerged fully from his lonely reverie realising there was a definite buzz in the air. Jack looked about to ask someone what was going on. He caught a man's arm. He said they were being allowed to send letters home. Jack staggered. Disbelief washed over him. "I was, I was just there," he mumbled, his eyes brimming. "I was there, at home!" he exclaimed, gripping the man's arm tightly. Home only seemed to exist in his imaginary world and the idea of sending a letter to reality caused his throat to tighten. He cleared his throat, "I was just thinking of them..." He trailed off as the man shook his head sympathetically, he lifted Jack's hand from his arm gently and wandered away. The idea that he could *contact* them, his family, instantly felt like a precious thread had formed, umbilically attaching him to them, invisibly stretching across thousands of miles. He darted into his hut and looked around at the other poor souls, they frowned, shaking their heads. 'No,' Jack thought, 'I don't believe it either.' He stepped out of the hut, moving to a group of men sitting on the ground around small cooking fire, and listened for the truth in the rumour. They spoke quietly, deciding they needed to know more. Someone was duly elected to find out. The nominated man nervously walked to the Japanese part of the camp, bowing, as the men gathered themselves and shuffled back into the hut. A short time later he returned. The PoWs made room on the slatting, watching him closely, their faces inclined to listen. He nodded, "It's true. We *are* allowed to write home." Jack couldn't believe it. He stood up, but the man raised a hand, so Jack sat again. "But," the man continued, "we have to strictly adhere to rules and procedures." They looked to each other. "What does that mean?" Someone asked as everyone spoke at once. For a moment Jack didn't care. He heard nothing more, as thoughts surged through his mind. He wanted to tell them, 'I am here and I am alive.' He babbled to the nearest man, "They won't know what has happened to me, to us all. Will they? They can't have been told anything. The Japs would hardly send information to our families would they?" "All right settle down," the man said, placing a hand on his arm, but Jack was completely absorbed. His eyes shone wildly as he thought of all the things he wanted to say. Suddenly, he stopped short, as the words that had drifted around the hut eventually entered his ears and his thoughts. "Strict procedures and rules? What are they? Perhaps we're only allowed a handful of words, a limit? Maybe we only a sentence, or one sheet of paper?" The man shrugged. "We don't know yet, do we." he conceded. Jack ruminated on the possibilities to himself. If I am only allowed a sentence, I must make it count. What's the smallest number of words that can say the most? If we are allowed only one sheet of paper, how small could I write? I want to say everything that's happened, the journey, the conditions, the situation. How can I describe day to day life? I will try to write all, every detail and everything I've seen, the colours, the smells, and the heat. How will I describe the heat, the lack of food, the treatment? Jack stopped, asking out loud, "We won't be able to tell them of *this*, will we?" He waved a hand round the hut. The men shook their heads, some looked away. Jack wandered away down the hut and out to the fence line to think, as the others watched him go. The sun lingered on the horizon then slipped away through rustling trees as Jack returned to the hut and lay out on the bamboo slat. He whispered to himself, in the hope they would hear him. "George, god it's hot. I am lying in the dark looking at the roof of this hut and I wonder where you are. I have no news of you and I hope you are surviving this war. I hope to see you again, and soon. God, I hope you're still in Belfast, and have not been sent to fight these damn Japanese. Sorry mother for swearing." He half laughed at his comment then his face creased in anguish at the idea of his family. His eyes filled as tears fell uncontrollably. He squeezed them shut and drifted. There was too much here, so much to say, too much. His island floating like a natural garden of Eden, and simultaneously such a place that hell couldn't imagine. He didn't know *how* he could describe it all. It was a bombardment of all his senses, of his mind and body. Beauty and tranquillity juxtaposed against hatred and despised enemy. The men, *and* also the Japanese, each despised their enemy, each other. But Jack had seen such kindness, bravery and love. A man dying in need given compassion by another man dying of the same malady. You take what mercies you find, and some comfort from the smallest act. The more he thought of his letter, the more a realisation drifted over him. It covered him like a cold, wet suffocating cloth. The Japanese wouldn't let them say anything of their capture, their treatment, their location or anything else. How could they let him write to his family? They didn't speak English properly, how could they read what they had written. Jack disbelieved the entire exercise. He became convinced it was a cruel trick, perhaps to raise spirits only to dash them. He was convinced any letter he wrote would never see home.

Come morning, Jack had answers to his many questions. The Japanese had pre-prepared sentences. These were typed on a single sheet in bold capitals and the men were allowed to copy two or three of these sentences. The rules were clear, and were barked at the men at roll call. If they didn't follow the sentences exactly, their letter would not be sent. If they tried to change any words, their letter would not be sent. If they wrote anything extra to the sentences, their letter would not be sent. If they did *anything* that looked as if they were writing in a suspicious way, their letters would not be sent. The men nodded agreement to all the rules, and the choices of sentence were handed out. Jack's mind swam as he read them,

I AM IN GOOD HEALTH
I AM BEING WELL FED
I AM WORKING FOR PAY
I AM FIT AND WELL

Jack's mouth hung open, aghast. The sentences contained only lies. Anger rose and dissipated as the men stared at the sentences and each began to think privately which selection would bring most comfort to those at home. The men collectively realised as one long sighing exhale, that their letters could never have told anyone what was happening. Such information would have served no purpose. They realised they must do their best to reassure their families, that they were alive, to comfort them and let them think they were well treated. And that *they* must carry on. It would be an exercise in futility, but Jack felt each short sentence must serve a purpose for those at home. Their families would know, they would understand the men couldn't say more. Importantly, they would *know* they had survived. Jack found it hard not to think of his mother and dad, of Gladys and George, opening the only letter from him in over a year, only to find it offered no real words, save these confected sentences of his enemy. He shook his head and read the choices again, trying to decide which *would* offer them most comfort.

As Jack wrote out his prepared sentences, copying each letter carefully despite his trembling hand, he wondered how long it had been since he'd held a pencil. He was fearful of miswriting or smudging, causing his letter to be rejected and remain unsent. He spread the thin paper out gently with his left hand, holding it flat on the rough surface of the bamboo bench as he brought the pencil to the paper. His eye was drawn to his fingers, and his hands. Like old man's hands, chipped and blistered, cracked and dirty, holding the small stub of pencil. His hand weighted the thin page, his fingertips felt softness in the rough sheet as he considered that this *very* paper would be held in the hands of his mother, his father, his family. The physical, umbilical idea of proximity was overwhelming. He stroked the paper softly, caressed it and tried to give it the life to express more than he was able to say. He wished silently, he could hide himself in a crease of the paper. A tiny speck of dust concealed there until he tumbled out of the folds into safety in his family home. Frowning at his fruitless notion, he looked back to the paper and carefully, slowly and deliberately wrote his words.

MOTHER AND DAD,
I AM FIT AND WELL,
I AM WORKING FOR PAY.
ALL MY LOVE, JACK X

- 8 OCTOBER 1943 -

Six long months had ticked by on the island. How time fragmented, how it slowed painfully when watched obsessively, in desperate captivity. Jack laughed hollowly to think how he'd felt captive in school, where he had watched the classroom clock unblinking. It hung on the wall, immobile and indifferent to his desperation for the heavy minute hand to move. It took an age for sixty echoing clicks of the second hand to finally tick the single minute over, closer to half past three. He heard the ticking, yet its leaden pointing minute finger seemed to make no discernible movement towards his moment of freedom. The achingly slow stillness, painful in its tortuous one-minute year-long click around the face. How foolish he felt now to have considered it burdensome. Jack sat alone in contemplation, with no real sense of time, but imaginary clock-watching nevertheless. Each man had aged so much in the year and a half since capitulation and the six months on the island. They seemed like old men to him, burdened by time and captivity. By the treatment and the back-breaking work. He watched them stumble about the camp, wandering to and from *makan*, lining up for work parties and sagging heavily onto the bamboo stretchers outside the sick hut and thought, 'poor sods'. He looked to his weathered hands and battered body realising he too was one of these wretched souls, inhabiting a stringy body full of pains, disease and hunger. He shook his head, not one of them were yet old.

As the airstrip neared completion the soldiers became increasingly nervous of the stark white coral revealed by the PoWs work. It was all too visible from the air, an obvious white marker for enemy reconnaissance. They'd had the idea to plant vegetation and flowers to cover the scar and that now became a task for those who were most ill, yet still forced onto working parties. Jack found himself among those planting flowers and realised again nervously he was clearly considered one of those most wearied and sick. He tried to reassure himself that the heavy labour was all but finished but he knew the work had taken a deeper toll on him. It absorbed him, wrung him out, taking so much that there wasn't much spirit left in him at the end of each day to ponder much of anything. Nevertheless, Jack found himself increasingly sitting alone as dusk grew, eating a handful of rice and considering his plight. His spirit was breaking and he knew it was pointless. He found himself not wanting to face another new day. Yet, each new day arrived regardless of his wanting to remain in permanent slumber. He awoke to dread and recognised his task was to fight on. Every day was still the same. The dreary drudgery interspersed with bashings, lessening food portions and those slipping away, escaping only in death. Each day had drifted by deliriously as they'd cut the airstrip along the coast. He now felt the monotony had made him dangerously vulnerable. He knew he needed to remain alert, and ever watchful. To have managed to survive this long to simply slip under now began to refresh his resolve. Jack looked upon the place as deathly and hellish so automatically that he often forgot it resembled a paradise. Beauty went unnoticed every day. How could he take in the middle distance when the immediate was so desperate? In the last few months he perceived it more often, as he gazed upon the clear turquoise of the shallow sea, its waves quietly lapping the beach of glistening white coral sand. The beach edged with the long brown trunks of swaying cocoanut trees, crowned with thick green fronds wafting this way and that in the cool breeze. The sky was piercing blue, merging almost imperceptibly with darker hues of the deep ocean at the horizon. Occasional snow-white clouds floated by, melting away lazily under the hot sun. This same hot sun that scored their brows and blackened their bony backs. It was as if two incompatible places existed in the same space and time.

There were few left that Jack had started out with, his brothers of 239 Battery, the men of the 77th. The Heavy Ack Ack men had been fragmented. He thought back to Christmas 1941, when they had been laughing and drinking somewhere off the coast of Africa. Inescapably he thought of the next year? He couldn't seem to see that far into the distance yet he wondered where he would be, how many would be left of his brothers, and whether he would still be there, in the camp? He squinted into the distance, trying to see his future. He wondered what of the looming Christmas, only a couple of months away. It would be no celebratory event, it simply marked the passing of time, as the previous year at Tandjong Priok had been. He caught himself wondering could he be home by then? Eating sticky fruitcake and stoking the fire at

Spring Street? The idea insistently invaded his thoughts and he could not sweep it away. His eyes brimmed glassily as he stared into space. The smells of home, the warmth of the fire, the creak of wood as it fell through burning logs in the grate enveloped him. He sank into his daydream, willing it to be made real. He almost smelled the wood fire and heard it snap. He heard the footsteps in the yard as his brother came through the back door. He turned to look and saw him on the back step. This pushed him too far, he felt a clenching tightening in his throat. Squeezing his eyes tight he mustered something from within to remove the picture from his mind. He opened his eyes and looked about. He still sat on the end of the slatted platform in the hut, his shoulders hunched and his chest sunken as he shook his head. "It won't do, pull it together Jack," he said aloud to himself. It seemed a comfort— the comforts of home, but it stretched him too far when it could not be reached. He felt his mind breaking, he was weary but could not rest. He rubbed his bony temples, and spoke softly to himself. "It's important not to let go. Got to keep the mind occupied." He hoped his words would help his body carry on. Keeping his thoughts on the important higher purpose of survival to try to keep up his spirits. He had seen men that might have survived, only their spirits were broken, and then they were lost. They had slept on and come morning could not be roused. "Sleep on brothers, I hope it is better where you are." He had said. The remaining men were a thin bleary-eyed and fragmented family that huddled together to shelter each other from the storm of each passing day. What human mind could believe this was now the order of things? How could anyone accept that this was how it was? Men starved slowly, beaten suddenly, expiring frequently, were expected to perish silently. Those whose fight was finished, granted their escape and those that were left carry their sorrow on for them. Jack added their losses and their frustrations to his own, like another heavy bundle loaded onto an already overburdened animal, as eventually he lay down to sleep.

There again, was that sound. Waking, thinking he was lost in swathes of sheets and blankets, safe at home. And again, that repetitive buzzing sound. It must be his alarm clock or a bird singing. Maybe there was a blackbird out on the sill. Then at once discomfort flooded his body. His shoulders ached from carrying, his legs stinging where they were rasped by sharp leaf edges walking through the forests. The buzzing was cicadas and mosquitoes, and the birds were real enough. There would be a surge of envy as they landed and walked about the camp, they strutted flightlessly as every man tried to capture them. What a meal they would make! Effortlessly with a single flap they'd be on the roof of a hut. Jack watched enviously, what wouldn't he give to flap his wings once and soar from there. They were disturbed by loud sounds and were quickly able to glide away over the fences. As easily as that. A beat of wing and they soared out over the edge of his existence, escaping without fear of retribution and no buck-toothed squinting enemy following. No shouting and no demand to halt. They were unchallenged and floated away, like Jack's idea of escape. On the few occasions a bird was caught Jack felt so sorry as they squirmed, desperately clinging to life as their necks were broken. He would turn his head and look away, his pity remained despite the need to eat of their unchosen sacrifice. Another new day dawned and it was hot, even for Ambon heat. Flies and mosquitoes tried their best make it yet more unbearable. They circled the dampness on Jack's forehead, rounding his neck and settling at any opportunity. The bamboo creaked and splintered as he got up from the platform. The men gathered themselves and rose like spectres in bedsheets, phantoms from their waking graves in dirty thin rags. They all wore hollow eyes that didn't make contact. There was no point looking into someone else's misery, there was plenty to go round. Iketani was already shouting, "*Speedo, speedo!*" in his fast crackling voice. The men slowly moved forward, creaking as much as the bamboo beneath their feet. They slump-shuffled, a ghostly lurching march to the open end of the hut. *Today* Jack felt a long way from Hyde, and thus the days and weeks and months had rolled by. Jack fell asleep again that evening as the rain pattered onto the fronded roof, building to a splattering hammering he didn't hear.

- 1 NOVEMBER 1943 -

Seven months after he arrived Jack climbed from his bamboo slatted bed, stood, and followed the shuffling line to the end of the hut. He wobbled on first standing, his feet, knees and hands oversized to his thin, emaciated body and his eyes bulged, unblinking in his gaunt face. Despite it, they shone with gritted determination. He had continued, walking to the airstrip and working every long day, until finally, he became deliriously ill. He'd been planting flowers on the runway as they began to swim in front of his eyes. He'd tried to stand, squinting into the heat haze as across the parched coral airstrip walked Irene. Her flowered dress fluttered in the breeze as she moved slowly toward him, her dainty hands in button-backed gloves, a small hat perched in her curls. She smiled as she stepped nearer, the heels of her neat shoes crunching to a stop on the gritty soil. She stood, her back to the searing heat of the sun, casting her face into shadow and held out her hand. Jack stood, grinning at her as his basket of flowers spun alternately with the blue of the sky as he vaguely realised he was collapsing. He woke momentarily as he was carried from the airstrip, his hand lolling and catching a leaf at the side of the track. The wobbling lurch of the stretcher woke him in delirious moments of snatched vision and sound. Clouds had drifted by, rustling trees, waves lapping, shouting Japanese voices. His mother's voice. Clear and strong, but tearful through the whistling confusion. "Jack, wake up. Jack, open your eyes." His mother vanished as the thin kindly face of the Dutch doctor peered over him sympathetically. "I thought you were gone for a moment then. Here, have a bit of this to drink." His strong accent peppered his impeccable English. He eased Jack's head up, supporting his bony skull in the palm of his hand, as Jack took a sip. It tasted incredibly sweet and flavoursome, exploding his mouth, rushing energy through his body. "What is it?" Jack asked weakly, the dark room spinning again. "Water, with a little sugar and some herbs, it should make you feel a little better." Jack had forgotten such a thing as flavour, his mouth only responded to mouldering nothingness of stale rice. His body hardly knew how to acknowledge nor recognise taste. He had been numbed by the bland need to survive. These last weeks he had been on increasingly straggling working parties who shuffled to the airstrip and knelt as, if in prayer, to plant the camouflaging flowers. He had survived the endless chipping at coral, the endless work, illness and the bashings to find himself nevertheless, in the sick hut. He had fallen ill before but had fought hard not to go into that hut. He knew most only came out to make the journey to Boot Hill. Jack lay still and accepted he must remain, he hadn't the energy to gather himself. He looked to his hands, staring hard at how worn and calloused they had become. They dropped to the platform and sagged heavily at his sides, too heavy for his scrawny arms. His feet looked equally oversized dangling at the ends of his emaciated legs, his rounded knees punctuated the straight brown sticks of his limbs. Jack's once dark hair was now blond. And all over his body his skin was sunburnt taut, scraped, scratched, bruised and parched. He felt breathless to have found himself in the sick hut, he knew it meant he was gravely ill. He ignored the distant urge to fight, the idea of letting go was stronger as it pulled gently at him. He lay deliriously for seven days, drifting in and out of consciousness, as his mind wandered between home and camp. He awoke to the hallucination of his mother tucking him in, she pushed the blanket under him and spoke softly. He could hardly open his eyes as he whispered back to her, trying to lift his hand to her. The hut doctor moved across to him as the man who'd tucked the blanket under him stepped back. Jack lay still as the doctor shook his head, calling his name. Jack drifted home, hearing his mother call his name. He looked desperately for his family in his bewildered state. In his mind he lay on a hillside above Hyde, watching as clouds rolled by, his bicycle discarded at his feet. He felt the sun on his face and dozed pleasantly. Every so often he'd felt a sharp jolt, as if stung sharply and painfully. He roused himself and jumped on his bicycle, pedalling wildly toward home. He cycled as if chased by a swarm of angry bees. Rounding the corner to Spring Street and bouncing over the cobbles, he heard his mother calling his name. His house seemed fixed, he could not seem to get closer to the door. He pushed the pedals all the more frantically. He cried out and thrashed his arms. The doctor stayed with Jack, watching him with concern, but there was nothing he could do. Gradually the imaginary clouds parted, the rattle of cobbled streets and chugging smell of chimneys faded and the cicadas returned. Rain washed over the camp and the hak-hak of angry Japanese voices rattled his attention from streets of Hyde and back to the furnace of Ambon. His fever had broken. Somehow he had survived, the doctor stared at him incredulously. The following day the doctor insisted Jack remain to gather his strength, Jack was adamant to the contrary. There was no more time for reverie, no more chance to reflect, he had to get through each day and make it into the next. Jack refused to lie down, waiting to die. He was bloody minded and gathered himself. Standing unsteadily he made his way slowly to the end of the hut. The doctor had many more patients to attend to, and yet more waiting for the space Jack had occupied, so he watched him go without further protest. Jack turned and thanked the doctor but was determined to return to his own hut and get back to the working parties despite the oppressive work. He had survived *and* escaped the sick hut. He felt a little better as a breeze kissed his cheek and he wandered wobbly across the camp to his hut. He returned to planting flowers on the runway the following day and had been back for a little over a week when the unimaginable at last happened. It was announced a sick draft was to leave the island. It all happened so quickly, in the space of three days Jack heard his name called, and found himself on Ambon quayside with five hundred and forty-seven gathered PoWs, readying to board a transport ship to Java. Jack blinked and swayed as he stood in line. He looked up at the ship and retched dryly. He saw as he boarded, a name painted on the dark hull, すえず丸.

- 31 DECEMBER 1943 -

Mother burst into tears. She handed the newly arrived envelope to Dad who stared at it, unblinking. He found the faded words hard to read but in any case he could see it was clearly a letter from overseas. George had been posted to RAF Blackpool that October and was able to visit Elizabeth and young Iain a little more often, as they now stayed with John and Florrie in Hyde. George crossed the room and gently took the envelope from his father's hands, reading the familiar handwriting. He looked closer. It seemed unusual for Jack to write in capitals but despite the tired looking text George recognised it could be no other than his brothers handwriting. He smiled momentarily as air paused in his throat. George caressed the crumpled paper knowing it had been sometime lately held by his younger brother. He slid a finger under the weak gummed edge. It lifted easily, unfolding into a single sheet. His eyes scanned the few scattered words written there, taking them in with a single glance. The page was undated, the writing pale in faded pencil, so lightly written it was difficult to read. George instantly felt its journey backwards, handing it back to the postman who pushed it back into his mail-sack. It jostled with other exotic war-torn envelopes as it travelled back across oceans, sitting quietly on so many distant quaysides. In a moment it returned to Jack's hand, who held a worn stub of a pencil in his trembling fingers. A sound escaped George's throat. He felt its journey condense then expand as it returned to him. He squinted sadly at the faded letters. He held the page in his hands and felt the proximity of his dear brother in the thin paper. He wished he could conjure him here, reaching out a hand through the letters journey, grasping his hand and pulling him through time and space. How he wished he were here. He sniffed the air to escape his emotions and to save upsetting his parents, cleared his throat and read the short lines out loud,

MOTHER AND DAD,
I AM FIT AND WELL,
I AM WORKING FOR PAY.
ALL MY LOVE, JACK X

- CHAPTER FOUR -

Yoshio Kashiki

- 4 JUNE 1949 -

An early morning chill hung mistily as Yoshio Kashiki hesitated in the open doorway of Tokyo Convalescence Hospital. His breath billowed in the unseasonably cold air but he felt warmth rising from the earth through his thin soles. He hoped the haze would burn away to reveal a fine spring day. Hovering half in, half out and afraid to make his move he gripped the doorframe tightly, momentarily unable and unwilling to let go. This had been his place of rest and recuperation, of safety and solitude. It was familiar, comforting, and it had shielded him somewhat from his horror filled nightmares. He felt certain no one here would agree with his actions, or inaction. Either now, or then. A rustling behind half turned him, jolting him into movement. He nervously realised people had begun to stir. Yoshio stepped fully down, grimacing painfully whilst keeping a steadying hand on the frame. He did not want to be seen, he did not want eye contact with anyone. He believed even a single glance would betray his plan, his mission to save his soul. If they looked, anyone would see the burning, painful flame within his eyes. He took another small step, winced then strode swiftly, albeit lopsidedly, away as he heard louder movements in the shadows. He looked back whilst continuing apace. He saw a man he did not know grinning in the retreating doorway. Yoshio's eyes unfocused and he forced a return smile. As he turned back to his path ahead his smile dropped like a dead weight and his mouth formed a hard, flat line. Sliding a hand into his dark overcoat Yoshio found his inside pocket. He smoothed a lank, creased letter concealed there. Flexing his jaw, he quickened his pace. He would deliver this *letter*, nothing else mattered.

Onto a neat desk within a bustling office, deep inside an imposing white building with towering dark arches, the lank, creased *letter* dropped into a wire in-tray. Crumpled and curled at the corners and slightly damp, it lay quietly upon a pile of unopened letters. The name scrawled in lilting handwriting on the envelope was smudged but clearly addressed to *General Douglas MacArthur*.

The *letter* was collected, opened by a secretary who read it and frowned. She stamped on a date and took it to the secretary pool supervisor. The supervisor scanned the *letter*, turning over the envelope eyebrows raised, then hurriedly took it to a uniformed man. He became increasingly anxious as his eyes darted left to right absorbing the curling text. He searched the ceiling while re-folding the letter, slotting it back inside its lank envelope. He nodded politely to the secretary, turned and walked briskly down a corridor to another office. He rapped with a single knuckle on the half glass-paned door. There was a dull incomprehensible response. The uniformed man entered and placed the envelope in a shallow wooden tray sitting on an untidy desk in the centre of an open-windowed office. Long heavy branches of soaked leaves rustled softly at the sill and a grey-green fan drifted round the ceiling, disturbing the manila scented air. A broad-shouldered captain sat at the desk, his face buried in a folder of untidy documents. He scribbled furiously onto a lined pad to the side of the papers, his head swinging back and forth whilst muttering under his breath. Stacked around the room were masses of papers, folders and documents, towers of which wobbled precariously on his desk. Two drawers of a stuffed filing cabinet hung open and batches of tied papers filled the three chairs around the room. The uniformed man waited for the captain to finish writing. Eventually he looked up, brow raised in question. The uniformed man gestured towards the letter tray. The captain slid the *letter* gently from its envelope. He searched the uniformed man's face for answers as he unfolded and looked at it, frowning. The captain stood abruptly, his eyes shining as he followed the words along the page. The crumpled *letter* looked tired and worn as if it had been folded and unfolded many times even before being sent. The neat cursive, contained only a few short precise sentences in simple English but their meaning exploded in his mind. The captain finished reading and sat heavily. He looked distractedly from window to chair to floor shaking his head, deep in perturbed thought. His black hair fell obscuring his concerned brown eyes. He slid a hand over his hair, then hastily refolded the *letter*, returning it to its envelope. He dropped it into a fresh manila folder, which he slapped closed. The captain looked up to the uniformed man, both their faces stern and solemn. The captain turned, reached across the desk almost dislodging a precarious pile of paper and taking a heavy stamp by the rounded knob, he hammered it into an ink-pad. He brought it down onto the manila folder with an official thud. He leant back revealing the word Confidential stamped there, the bright red ink drying slowly from the centre outwards. He looked again to the uniformed man, his teeth gritted and his eyes flashing with indignation. Blinking slowly as his face uncrumpled, he did not speak but reached for the manila folder. He reopened it and retrieved the *letter*. Captain Jack Sylvester straightened his tie, unfolded the page, and began to re-read the *letter* from the beginning.

Yoshio Kashiki had limped his way through the market, pushing past clusters of people huddled against the unexpected cold. The air had been a misty blue in the weak morning light. The buildings and streets were black silhouettes like watercolours made with charcoal sticks and daubs of deep ultramarine, washed out and soaked through. Yoshio brushed against dark blooms protruding from a flower stall, he hurried as the rain began. A drop, a splash on his cheek at first, a disturbance in a puddle here, a crown of water landing on a petal there. His eyes took it all in. His mind alert, his face stretched taut in fear. He felt he had scarcely blinked in the six years since. His mouth remained flat as he splashed through the puddles. He felt his exterior was wet and cold but nestled inside, warm and dry, gripped beneath and tucked under layers of clothing, lay his salvation. Written on a single sheet of paper, folded twice lengthways and snugged inside its long envelope, was the curling script of his friend who'd copied word for word what Yoshio had to say. He hoped tearfully, desperately that it would free him. Yoshio's heart was beating so violently, so loudly he thought people could hear it. Could they sense he was about to betray himself? Eyes were everywhere, a hundred faces turned to watch him pass. *They know!* His mind screamed. They see what I have hidden inside! All eyes could read his thoughts, read his *letter.*

Dear Sir

Hereby, I report to you the fact of prisoners murder case, because I read newspapers every day, but I can't find that fact in any paper, and so I think the fact is still kept unknown by anyone.

The words burned in his mind, *murder case, kept unknown*. It is still unknown. 'How can it still be unknown?' He exhaled, panting deeply. He hoped the *letter* said everything he had dictated. His mind ran over anxiously. 'I must tell them what happened. My nightmares would leave me if I tell them everything I know. Everything I saw.' He hurried on. Looking to his feet he splashed into a deep puddle. He stumbled but did not unclench his grip on the unseen paper hidden within. He righted himself and ran an unsteady step or two. Someone bumped heavily into him and he let out a cry. His mind screamed 'they've caught you!' But the heavy person simply grunted a rebuke for the collision, and dashed on. Yoshio ran again. A few steps. Looking behind in panic, 'Surely I look guilty, so conspicuous. Calm down!' He told himself. He coughed and pulled a smudged handkerchief from his pocket and dabbed at his mouth. He glanced away as he pushed it back in his pocket. He knew there was blood there, but he did not want to see. He knew what it was, and what it meant. He forced himself to slow his pace, to walk calmly. But, it was the brisk walk of the guilt-laden. He was drenched now.

The rain ran freely down his stubby nose and slid off the rounded end, falling onto his dark clothes merging and disappearing into the sodden fabric. His rounded eyes glistened, his dark hair slapped to his face. 'God, I couldn't be wetter if I was swimming'. Swimming... *swimming*. His mind's eye blinked a scene into his thoughts like a lightning bolt. A vivid flash of an image. Men in the water, arms waving, grabbing at floating debris, shouting. Hundreds of them shouting, calling out for help, their arms reaching out to him. It was only an instant but the vision echoed as he tried to shake the men's screaming faces from his mind. Like chasing bees, they followed him. He ran on, as they shouted louder and louder in his mind. A tear left his eye and ran down his face, mingling with the rain on his face. He pushed it away muttering 'the *letter* will save me.'

The detail of the fact is as follows . —
The S. S. Suez-Maru, a Japanese transport-ship , which loaded
3 airplanes, sailed from Ambon, on the 25th Nov. 1943, and she
was guarded by a Japanese 3rd-rate, submarine-patrol No. W12.

Soaked through to his skin, Yoshio's mouth was bone dry as he wiped his eyes with his wet sleeve. He moved quickly now. Puddles splashed up his legs as the whining sound of the ship's engine rang round his head, following him, chasing him. Waves crashed, the funnel spewed thick smoke, the heavy chug as the screw turned rumbled in his heart, moving the ship forward. He cringed, hunching his shoulders, tripping and stumbling through puddles as the ship exploded around him. Men lay out on deck gasping, men reached up from the holds, a sea of arms. Their mouths all open, screaming silently. They stood-to, staring at him before leaping overboard, so gaunt, so desperate. He saw the wild whites of their eyes as they looked through him. He had seen the traces in the water, the flash of the torpedoes. The morning sun had glinted off something, blinding him. Instinctively he lifted a hand to shield his eyes as he fell against a sheltered doorway. Peering breathlessly through his fingers the flash dissipated and he saw only the rain and gloom of the Tokyo morning. He exhaled gratefully as his hand slid from his face to clutch at his frightened chest to still his heart, beating hard through the *letter*.

She was torpedoed and sunk at the sea-area, which was guessed north-east of the Sunbow island at about 9.30 a.m. 29th Nov. 1943. At the same time, prisoners about 270 or 280, who were on board the ship, were killed on the reason that they could not be rescued. But, we, about 200 Japanese, who were on board the ship, were all rescued except some ones who died.

Tears ran freely with the rain down his cheeks, he cried for himself, as well as for them. He wished they would leave him. They had blamelessly tormented him all these years. Grasping him at night, calling him in the darkness, hands outstretched from the sea. He reached for them in terror, but he was immobile as they were pushed back, even as his own were saved. They reached out to him even as they were killed. They stood, arms raised, baring their chests as they shouted out. Yoshio panted loudly, his teeth chattering as he caught his breath. He gasped not from running, he was drowning. Drowning in his disease and in the ocean of men he couldn't save. He looked about him, no one had chased him, save those who peopled his nightmares. Their faces real and close, shouting and looking to him, their eyes piecing him with glazed stares. He looked away as he ran on, shaking his head, still surrounded and followed by the angry bees. He gasped frantically, I must give them the *letter*. The *letter* will save me.

I don't mean by this to inform the murderers to you, but I wish I could let the families of the Allied- Forces prisoners know the fact and mourn them.
I don't know English, so I asked my friend to write to you in English. I reported the same fact to the G.H.Q. Tokyo, in Japanese before.

3rd, June, 1949.
Yours Sincerely
Yoshio Kashiki

Yoshio slowed his pace. Panting he rounded a corner and stopped. Standing under thin newly planted trees he looked across the road to an imposing white building with towering dark arches. A row of gaping mouths ready to devour the guilty, SCAP GHQ, the general headquarters of the Supreme Commander for the Allied Powers. Yoshio took it all in. He had read it in the papers, this was where the American General had his headquarters, this was where they investigated war crimes. The weight and enormity of his mission pressed heavily. The main entrance was guarded by neatly-uniformed troops along the tree lined boulevard and the windows were thrown open allowing the occupants to breathe. It was a part of the city he didn't like to visit, it was all tidy pavements, roaring cars and symmetrical buildings. Yoshio felt like an obvious outsider in his oversized coat and dripping face. He looked around furtively wishing he was invisible as he retrieved the long thin paper envelope. He watched it intently as it emerged from his coat. As if in a dream he looked beyond it with surprise to see his feet stride toward the nearest guard. The guard noticed Yoshio's change of course and watched him approach with mild suspicion. Yoshio saw his own arm extend in front of him, the *letter* in his fingertips. Trembling slightly, he watched it intensely. He noticed the crumpled edges and the tired paper. The guard moved toward him with an aching slowness. Yoshio's outstretched hand clasping the *letter* moved towards the now outstretched hand of the guard. Their hands came together, each taking an opposite end of the envelope. Yoshio's eyes reluctantly moved from the *letter*, traveling up the buttons of the guard's uniform until their eyes met. Yoshio was unable to speak, his mouth lolled open. The guard read urgency and desperation in the stranger's eyes. He took the slight weight of the envelope and saw relief flood the stranger's face as his hand hesitated, then withdrew. The stranger looked suddenly less pained, less creased, as if some burden had lifted. He appeared to shrink as he stepped backwards, turning to leave. He stared a moment longer, whispering almost soundlessly, "It's gone. It is done." This utterance seemed to shake him free. The stranger wiped his face of tears collected there and moved away, mingling with the gathering crowds and disappearing into the misty rain like an apparition. The guard looked down at the envelope as a drop of rain landed on the name written on the front, smudging it slightly. It was addressed in slanting capitals to *General Douglas MacArthur*.

- 10 June 1949 -

Captain Jack Sylvester straightened his khaki tie, his eyes following the lilting cursive handwriting on the small creased piece of paper closely. He looked across to Isao Kondo, muttered briefly then turned back to the page. Kondo was a small rounded man with rounded glasses, nervous eyes and a toothy smile. He was happy to work for the Australian Army after the war. He hadn't believed in the damn thing from the outset. He had been terrified by the fanatical obedience of some of his countrymen and had wanted to do something worthwhile afterwards, so had volunteered as translator. Kondo had been a languages teacher in Osaka specialising in English before the war. This, he hoped would be a chance to start a new career and perhaps a new life out of the ruins of that terrible nightmare. Kondo raised his tufted eyebrows in quizzical response to the captain. The captain continued reading, occasionally tutting and shaking his head. He replaced the letter in the thin manila folder and slid out another document, inspecting it carefully. After a few moments he looked over the top of the paper to Kondo and said he needed to summon several individuals. Kondo nodded and quietly left the office. A few moments later a young officer arrived. Officer Beirne was a short fellow with kind eyes and an unkempt bob of blond hair which would have flopped over at the front if not combed back with thick Brylcreem. He had a distinctive ready laugh and walked with broad shoulders and open smiling face. "Yessir?" he asked energetically. "Thanks, Beirne, I need three demands for questioning sending out, ahh one Tamaki Shirakawa, one Masaji Iketani and a Major General Seiichi Saito." Officer Beirne began writing as the captain continued speaking. "Tamaki Shirakawa was captain of this ship *Suez Maru*," he tapped the document with his pencil as he moved on, "Also one Masaji Iketani, a First Lieutenant and the *Suez Maru* transport commander. Thirdly Major General Seiichi Saito, Commander of Java PoW Internment Camps. I have last known addresses for two but not this Iketani." Officer Beirne had expected a long list but said nothing as he noted the three names, repeating, "Shirakawa, Iketani and Saito." "Yes, thank you Beirne," nodded Captain Sylvester. Officer Beirne turned and left the room to fetch a secretary to complete the paperwork for the requests, nodding to the waiting Kondo to re-enter. Captain Sylvester looked again at the papers in his hands, spreading them across the few vacant areas of his unruly desk. Immediately after reading Yoshio Kashiki's letter he had formally requested documents pertaining to the loss of the ship, the *SS Suez Maru* and had received a thin dossier, which now lay alongside a few other papers he had acquired. Yoshio Kashiki had given no permanent address in his letter, and had not yet replied to a request sent to the hospital for questioning. The captain wanted to speak to him, gather more precise details. He wanted to ask him what else could he remember. He was certain Yoshio's letter was simply an opening gambit, that Yoshio knew much more, the captain just had to find him. It hadn't been much to go on, a date and a name but the captain excelled at these early investigations. He weeded out small details, noting names and conducting questioning sessions where he would pull out yet more tiny clues, all building his case. Thus he expanded each investigation until the evidence was gathered.

The captain had heard nothing for a few days since sending his first probing requests, until three documents arrived at once. All were from the Japanese government. First, a list of the *Suez Maru* personnel, naming Tamaki Shirakawa as captain and Masaji Iketani, the POW commander. The second document was a report on the sinking, written by Rear Admiral Saito, the Java POW Camp commander and the *same* Masaji Iketani. Captain Sylvester urgently wanted to question all three. The third document contained a list of POW casualties aboard the *Suez Maru*. The captain set about the huge task of comparing the list with known Allied casualties. Captain Sylvester picked up the second document and re-read the report of the sinking. He muttered each word as he scanned along the faded typed words. The report by Saito was dated 12 December 1943, but referred to a statement by Iketani dated 2 December 1943, only three days after the sinking. This report, so immediately after the event, bore no relation to Yoshio's version.

```
Java PW Internment Camp Report A, No. 210.
   Date:- 12 Dec 1943.
      To:-Chief PW Information Bureau
      From:-SAITO, Seiichi, Commander, Java PW
Internment Camps.
```

Subject:-Submittal of a Roster of PoW who
died from PW transport sinking.
Forwarded herewith are an affidavit and a
roster of PoW who died (all PoW on board)
from the sinking of the transport Suez Maru,
which was torpedoed while en route from Ambon
Island to Java with patients and invalid PoW
from Sub-Camp no.3.

AFFIDAVIT

The PoW listed in the appended roster were
all patients and invalids incapable of
working. While en route from Ambon Island to
Java on the transport Suez Maru, they were
subjected to a torpedo attack by an enemy
submarine in the vicinity of the Kangean
Islands, north of Bali. Two torpedoes struck
the third and fourth holds where the PoW were
located aft of the ship and the ship sank in
a few minutes. All PoW were kept in the holds
because the necessity for strict security.
Since the holds in which they were kept
exploded and the ship sank very rapidly it
is believed that all of them went down with
the ship. No survivors could be found despite
rescue attempts by our escort ship. Therefore
it is hereby confirmed that all perished.
Date, 2 Dec 1943.
Masaji Iketani, 1st Lt, Transport Commander
of the Suez Maru.

Captain Sylvester ground his teeth, turning the paper over on its back as if his file were a book, as he peeled back the next page with licked thumb. He read each document again carefully and thoroughly, his eyes darting left to right as he made notes on a separate sheet in preparation to interrogate suspects. He stopped writing suddenly, tapping his teeth with the end of his pencil. He knew this report *must* be a fabrication if Yoshio Kashiki's account were true. Reading of

Saito's involvement he knew the war crime *must* have gone higher in the Japanese ranks. Concealment of such a serious war crime it would have needed involvement from very senior authorities. He was eager to speak to Shirakawa, Saito, and Iketani as soon as possible. It wasn't that the captain hadn't handled cases with some similarities before, but his new investigation stunned him. The sheer number of victims involved, coupled with such an audacious concealment of the crime simply staggered him. He found the falsification of the official report in his hands quite shocking. Captain Sylvester felt determined, and overcome with revulsion in equal measure. When he'd investigated war crimes in Singapore, it hadn't been like this. There had been many more investigators, more support and much more time. The captain was now one of only four assigned to 'mopping up'. These last cases were supposed to be smaller, lesser crimes. They *should* have been less complex, easier to pull the evidence together and importantly, they *should* have been quick to bring to trial. Yet cases such as this, major war crimes, kept coming in. Of all the horrific cases he'd dealt with, this new investigation was a particularly bad one. He sighed and looked to the window thoughtfully as rain spotted the pane. He had hoped this was almost finished. It had been so very difficult. The job had weighed heavily, and he felt it had aged him, made him cynical and bitter. He had seen so much horror, so much unnecessary cruelty, brutality, inhumanity. He sometimes found it impossible to digest. His nerves were not as steady as they once were, he felt an angrier man now, and far, far sadder. He simply wished he was finished, he wished all *this* was finished.

- 13 JUNE 1949 -

Captain Jack Sylvester at nearly six foot, was a dark haired, broad backed Australian, his square jaw had been gritted against the horrors of Japanese War Crimes for over three years, he thought he'd seen it all but this was a particularly nasty case. Still, he was resigned to continue to the end, as best he could. He lifted his captain's cap from his desk, pinching the crown with his thumb and forefinger and placed it confidently on his neatly combed black hair. He straightened his shoulders, nodded a single resolute tilt of his head to Kondo. Sliding his papers into the manila folder, he pushed back his chair and paced to the door, hand outstretched for the handle. Kondo jumped up and followed the captain as he strode away down a long grey corridor. The captain walked with an almost imperceptible limp, caused by a badly set broken right femur, an accident before the war. He didn't allow it to slow his pace and it hardly altered his gait yet his colleagues recognised him by the irregular sound of his footsteps. The clacking of his clean polished Australian Army boots joined the click-click of typewriters from offices along the corridor and the whirr of metallic fans that moved the docile air around in warm circles. Kondo half jogged to keep up as the captain tucked the manila folder tightly under his arm, its card edges catching and creasing under his damp shirtsleeve.

Tamaki Shirakawa sat, hands in lap and tight lipped in a small square room made more stark by the sparse items arranged there. A thin legged rectangular wooden table squatted in the centre, at which he sat uncomfortably in a metal chair slung with fading maroon cloth. Two similar chairs occupied the room. One opposite Shirakawa, unoccupied and tucked neatly under the table and another alongside a square table pushed against a side wall. Their cloth once bright emerald was now faded in the strong sunlight, to a frayed dull olive. The floor tiles smelled faintly of stale mop, Shirakawa noticed the figure-of-eight dried stains made by its soggy passing as he waited. An enamelled cone light-shade surrounded a dim bulb, which gave the room a yellowish glow, sickly in comparison to the fresh sunlight attempting to crack through slivers in the closed shutters. Three vertical bars were fixed to the inside sill of the window. Shirakawa watched motes glide between the parallel beams, rolling and turning, disappearing in shadow, reappearing in the beam below, churning and tossing in an unfelt draught. Shirakawa was still a fairly young man at only thirty-five years old. Though his bushy eyebrows showed a peppering of grey and his cheeks had begun to jowl. His stomach had a perfectly rounded appearance as if he'd swallowed a cannonball whole. His hands lay with upturned palms, one resting lightly on the other in his lap, as he silently watched the dust move round the room. So lost in the motions of the motes was he, that he startled as the door cracked open.

Captain Sylvester opened the door wide and strode into the small interrogation room, startling Tamaki Shirakawa who sat up quickly, embarrassed and equally annoyed to be caught off-guard. The captain slapped his manila folder on the desk and gestured to Kondo to take up the seat at the small side table. Kondo sat, placing the notebook and pencils he carried neatly at right angles on the desk. Captain Sylvester sat, spinning the manila folder with his thumb to face him. He opened it, passing his hand over the documents he'd re-read earlier as he slipped several blank sheets of paper from it. He retrieved a sharp pencil stored in his top pocket and placed it diagonally on the top sheet of paper. He slid pencil and paper across the table towards Shirakawa who showed no acknowledgment, not once moving his gaze from the captain's face. Shirakawa was almost certain he knew why he was there. There were other possible reasons but he didn't want to admit to anything until he knew which incident would be referred to. Shirakawa just hoped he wouldn't ask about the worst that had never left his mind. Captain Sylvester nodded to Kondo, indicating he should begin translating, as he turned to Shirakawa. "Were you formerly captain, master of the Japanese transport ship, the SS Suez Maru?" Kondo repeated the question in Japanese and Shirakawa sank in his seat, looking to his feet awkwardly before nodding and murmuring "Yes." He now knew this was what he'd most feared and he bristled in anticipation of the consequences. Sweat sprang into fat beads at his hairline and he pulled at his collar to loosen its sudden grip on his drying Adam's apple. Captain Sylvester's eyes widened then squinted as he took it all in. He was well aware of the fidgeting shuffles of the guilty, their sudden difficulty in speaking and their subtle nervous responses to direct questioning. At the start of each investigation the importance of gathering evidence and questioning witnesses quickly could not be overstated. But this case was already six years old. The well-worn 'I don't remember' excuse, a standard response of the guilty could be used quite legitimately, by those responsible. In his experience it was *they* who seemed to have the most 'difficulty' remembering. The captain gestured to the sheets of clean paper and the pencil in front of Shirakawa. He spoke clearly and slowly, knowing Kondo's translation would follow, uttered between his sentences. Even so, he paused tentatively between each to make sure Kondo kept up, as he continued to watch Shirakawa closely. "As master of the SS Suez Maru, I would like you to record here a written account of the sinking of your vessel in November 1943, and everything you recall about that event. You will then be questioned about the event and about your statement. You must tell the truth according to the dictates of your conscience. You shall conceal nothing nor will you add to the facts. Do you understand?" Shirakawa listened as the questions filtered into Japanese. He nodded and twitched unconsciously from time to time, his expression glazing slightly. Captain Sylvester saw in his eyes the events of that day unfolding as clearly as if it were yesterday. He could see Shirakawa remembered every detail, every moment. He watched it play out vividly on Shirakawa's face as he winced almost imperceptibly, closing his eyes in search of respite. As Kondo finished the translation Shirakawa immediately turned and spoke to him, his eyes pleading. Shirakawa turned back to the captain repeating the words as Kondo translated to the Captain. "Yes, he will write a statement. Yes, he understands. Yes, he will tell the truth and will conceal nothing, nor add to the facts." The captain didn't need to hear the translation to see the sadness, guilt and pity moving behind Shirakawa's eyes. He knew he would write all he remembered. Whether his sadness was for those killed, guilt for his own actions or pity reserved for himself, the captain was not yet certain.

Shirakawa pulled the papers toward him across the table with the flat of his hand and turning the sheets longways he began, from the right hand edge to draw the angular strokes of the written Japanese language. Captain Sylvester leant forward watching the pencils movement for a moment. He'd seen the script often but this was his first suspect in a new case and he wanted to watch carefully to ensure the writing was legible. Satisfied, the captain then concerned himself with the official translation. He knew the backlog was running at over a month as he pondered how to speed this one up. He wanted to read what Shirakawa knew, he needed to know where to make his next move. He decided he would later have Kondo read it back to him. He knew it must still be sent for translation for it to be admissible in any trial or hearing, as an official sworn translation would be required. But right now he needed information and he needed names in order to build his case. His mind was alight with all the stages of the process. Captain Sylvester made notes on a clean page from his manila folder as Shirakawa scratched his way along his page. Further requests for interrogation would be needed to bring various suspects in for questioning and statements would need to be taken. He usually tried to interview as many as possible before there could be any discussion between them. But this case was six years old and he wondered what the guilty had already agreed amongst themselves. 'How could they think they had got away with it?' He wondered. And yet so far, they had. The captain had seen so many horrible cases but this one was callous even by the standards of the Imperial Japanese Army. He never understood their capacity for cruelty and seemingly personal vindictiveness towards the PoWs. The captain looked at the list he'd made and sighed. He pulled a fresh sheet from under his pile of documents causing Yoshio Kashiki's handwritten letter to half slide out. The triangle of paper leant out from beneath the others. Its familiar slanting letters stood out in the dull light, and the stark words caught his eye, '*killed on the reason that they could not be rescued*'. Could not be rescued? Captain Sylvester did not believe that. Not for a single second.

Captain Jack Sylvester opened the door to his office and ushered Kondo inside. He swept up a pile of documents from an overburdened chair, balancing them atop an already precariously wobbling heap of filing. The captain circled his desk gesturing the interpreter to the now empty chair as he passed before sitting heavily in his own. The captain nodded solemnly to Kondo to begin reading and leant back in his chair. His fingers steepled, fingertips resting on his pursed lips, elbows on the arms of the chair, he listened keenly. Kondo began his translation falteringly, "Ahhh... I, Tamaki Shirakawa, swear etc. etc.... ahh, I was the master of the SS Suez Maru when that vessel sank at 0920 hours on 29 November 1943, following two direct hits by enemy launched torpedoes..." Kondo rearranged his seated position more

comfortably and finding a rhythm he continued, "...At about
1700 hours on 23 November 1943, I received my
sailing orders at Ambon to sail to Soerabaya and
the ship left Ambon at about 1800 hours on the same
day. Earlier, I received orders that about four to
five hundred prisoners of war and about two hundred
Japanese servicemen were to sail on the vessel. We
also carried two damaged aeroplanes on the upper
deck. These orders were given to be by First
Lieutenant Nishikawa of the Army Shipping Command
at Ambon. Nishikawa told me that Minesweeper W12
would escort us. I am unable to recall the name of
the Master of the Minesweeper. I did not see him
before we sailed, although I later met him..."
Captain Sylvester sighed irritably. He'd heard this preamble before, laced
with hidden lies in order to make the suspect appear humane, less
culpable. 'I never met him' or 'I didn't hear what was said' and 'No one
said that to me'. The captain knew all these tricks, all the wriggling on
the hook. He didn't take anything at face value. Kondo had stopped
speaking as the captain sighed, now he watched him for an indication to
go on. The captain exhaled through his nose with a low growl and raised
his brow with a nod, for Kondo to resume. He reminded himself to try
not to become irritated with self-serving statements. He listened again
as Kondo found his place. "...After leaving the port of
Ambon we followed a course set by the commander of
the escort vessel. One or two days after sailing I
was ordered to change course and sail for Batavia,
because of the presence of magnetic mines in
Soerabaya Strait. About 0900 hours on 29 November
the watchmen on the upper bridge shouted 'torpedoes
on the port side'. It was then shortly after
breakfast and I was smoking on the lower bridge,
and my position was about seven feet away from the
watchman. On looking to port I noticed the traces
of two torpedoes. Before any action was taken by
me, I think Chief Mate Watanabe had ordered 'Hard

aport-full speed'. Two torpedoes struck the stern of the ship in quick succession. I then ordered Watanabe to investigate the extent of the damage. The prisoners of war were carried in holds three and four, aft. One or two minutes later Watanabe reported back and stated that the poop deck was considerably damaged and the mainmast had been broken off and the aft-most hold, ahhh, hold four, was immersed. I did not enquire of him the fate of the prisoners of war, nor did he report on the matter. After receiving his report, I gave orders to 'Prepare to abandon ship'. Shortly before giving this order I learnt that seawater was entering hold three. I then gave orders to set the pumps in action, however upon receiving another report that seawater was flooding the engine room I judged the position as hopeless. In the meantime, the transport commander, a first lieutenant, whose name I am unable to remember..." Captain Sylvester's face twitched involuntarily, he shifted in his chair mumbling to himself, "Name I am unable to remember.... ahem, and so it goes on." Kondo had again stopped speaking and the captain nodded, "Hmm, please, go on," Kondo nodded in return, scanning the page again for his place, then continued. "... I told him my intention to abandon ship, immediately thereafter I gave orders to leave the ship. Because the prisoners of war were in holds three and four, a great number of prisoners of war must have been killed at the time of the explosion. We had only four lifeboats, two of them with a capacity of thirty and the other two carrying twenty each. I shouted many times 'Sick and injured first!' I did not know how many sick and injured were on board but I did hear from the medical officer that a number of mild cases including himself were on board. As for the prisoners of war although I did not hear from the medical officer or anyone

else that there were sick and injured prisoners on
board, I understood that the medical officer had
included prisoners of war when he told me of the
sick and injured carried on the ship..." "Well, if that's
not wriggling on the hook I don't know what is," muttered Captain
Sylvester. Kondo paused, nodding agreement and continuing at a nod
from the captain. "...I ordered the Chief Purser, but I
am unable to remember his name, to take care of all
the important documents. Seven or eight minutes
after my order to abandon ship, this is about twenty
minutes after the explosion, I ordered Quartermaster
Shimizu to inspect the ship for the last time. Upon
receiving his report that no other men remained on
the ship I plunged into the sea with Shimizu and
Chief Engineer Mitaji and the Chief Wireless
Operator. I shared a plank about two feet square
with Mitaji and the Chief Wireless Operator. In
order not to be dragged down by the undertow caused
by the sinking vessel we swam desperately for two
or three minutes away from the ship. On looking
back I saw the Suez Maru sinking stern first. A
second later one of the aeroplanes which had been
carried over hold two floated to the surface of the
sea about five feet away from us. Had it hit us we
would have been killed or at least very seriously
injured. The other aeroplane which had been loaded
alongside the other plane, did not come to the
surface and must have gone down with the ship.
Minesweeper W12 kept circling the area in order to
prevent further attacks by the enemy. During the
course of the circling movement explosives were
dropped on two or three occasions. For four or five
hours none of the survivors were taken aboard the
minesweeper and I began to fear that none of us
would be rescued. Two or three hours after the
sinking, three aeroplanes appeared flying very

high overhead. I do not know if they were Japanese or enemy aircraft. Although I am not certain of the numbers there were at least seventy to eighty Japanese and between one hundred and forty to fifty prisoners of war clinging to numerous planks and pieces of wood. Besides these personnel some two hundred were crowded into the four lifeboats, except for two or three PoWS, all on board the lifeboats were Japanese. However, on both sides of the lifeboats a number of lifelines were attached and many PoWs and Japanese were clinging to them. Four or five hours after the sinking, it was then about 1400 or 1500 hours, the minesweeper approached the lifeboats but only the Japanese were allowed to go on board. The prisoners of war were pushed away. After the Japanese had boarded the minesweeper the prisoners were cast adrift in the lifeboats. About thirty minutes before the minesweeper commenced rescuing us, I was quite close to a lifeboat, Chief Mate Watanabe who was in charge of this lifeboat took to the sea, saying 'Captain, you take my place'. I then entered the lifeboat. I think mine was the last of the four lifeboats to be unloaded. It was then about 1600 hours when I was transferred to the minesweeper." Captain Sylvester and Kondo exchanged glances. The captain had listened carefully, weighing up the presence of lies and possibility of truths in the statement. He folded his arms and let out a deep exhale as he nodded toward the statement in Kondo's hand, for him to finish. "Er... after thanking the captain of the minesweeper and a first lieutenant whose name I am unable to remember, I checked the survivors and found about three members of my crew missing. One of the survivors amongst the crew was badly injured and he died about four or five hours later. If I remember correctly three or four Japanese passengers were also missing. I reported to the

captain of the minesweeper that three of my crew
were missing. He then told me to try and locate
them, but I was unable to do so. After ascertaining
that no Japanese survivors were floating in the sea
and about two hours after my transfer to the
minesweeper, I heard machine-gun fire. Amazed, I
went out and saw that the prisoners of war both
those in the lifeboats and those adrift and those
swimming were being massacred by machine-gun fire
from the deck of the minesweeper. The shooting
lasted between one, and one and a half hours, and
the fire was intermittent..." Captain Sylvester stood,
slowly moving along his desk. He paced thoughtfully to the window.
Bracing his hands across its frame he let his head drop between his
shoulders. "Continue, please," he said softly to Kondo. Kondo had
watched him move slowly to the window, studying his turned back and
wondered whether to go on. He was startled by the captain's quiet words
drifting across the room. Kondo looked down at the pages, his eyes
scurrying to again find his place. '...machine-gun fire...,' and
'...lasted one and one and a half hours...' jumped at
him from the page as he struggled to finish reading. "...Ahhhh he
said that at about 1900 or 1930 hours, it was then
not yet sunset, the shooting ended and the
minesweeper sailed for Batavia. On board the
lifeboat as the minesweeper approached us, one of
the ensigns shouted out that no prisoner of war
should be taken aboard. I was forbidden by the
master of the minesweeper to make any mention in my
later reports, of the murder of these prisoners of
war." Kondo stood quietly, "That is the whole statement, sir." The
Captain turned from the window, walking stiffly towards Kondo, his
hand outstretched for the document. He smiled thinly at Kondo,
offering subdued thankyous as he grasped the papers. Kondo nodded
and turned to leave. As he closed the captain's door softly behind him,
he heard low mutterings and riffling of documents, and the busy
scratching of a pencil across paper.

- 22 JUNE 1949 -

Major General Saito stood, arms behind his back, his fingers entwined, in the corner of the same interrogation room as Captain Sylvester opened the door and marched in. Kondo followed, closing the door behind them with a quiet click. The captain extended a flat palm towards the empty chair with its back to the door, offering the seat to Saito. Saito didn't remove his stare from the captain as he walked slowly around the table. His eyes finally dropped as he arrived at the chair. He sat stiffly, transferring his unflinching gaze to the middle of the table as he settled his hefty weight into the uncomfortable seat. The captain exhaled and pulled his chair out by its back, sitting with a thud and pulling himself under the table with a scraping hop, his hands firmly grasping either side. Kondo had dashed to his small table as Major General Saito sat, and now began to unload his pile of papers and pencils onto his desk with a clatter. The captain glanced across, frowning. Kondo mouthed 'sorry' and quietly awaited instruction. The captain turned to Major General Saito immediately asking, "Do you know why you have been summoned?" Kondo repeated the question in Saito's native tongue. Saito pursed his lips, eyebrows raised. His bottom lip protruded in an indifferent shrug. He did not reply. The captain continued, unmoved. "What do you know of the SS Suez Maru? Do you know what happened to that transport ship?" Saito's eyes darted upwards quickly, recognition flooded his features, and the captain knew he had hit his mark. Saito was quick to gather his composure and his blank gaze returned to the table. The captain knew how to prise truth from suspects and pressed ahead unfazed. "I am investigating a very serious war crime, you are not currently a suspect but it would be better for you to outline what you know, now!" Saito startled and looked to Kondo, as the captain continued apace, "I know you have knowledge of this ship and-" Saito interrupted in halting broken English, "Sometime, ahh December, ahh 1943, I was in South East Area Fleet HQ and I heard some ones talking there, some orderlies... they said ahh, commercial ship carrying Japanese servicemen, and ahhh Allied PoW, is sunk by Allied plane." He paused, "Of course, I know nothing of it myself." The captain narrowed his eyes, replying mildly, "You will now outline what you recall of the conversation." Saito broke into slow and deliberate Japanese, Captain Sylvester gesticulated to Kondo to copy down as the Major General spoke. Kondo wrote quickly, repeating the flowing narrative from Saito in English to the captain's attentive ears. "There were five or six of them talking, one said I heard very recently that a large ship carrying five to six hundred Japanese sick and wounded as well as three hundred Allied PoW were discovered and sunk by an Allied aeroplane. The ship was on its way to Japan." Saito continued, "I did not hear the name of the ship but then someone said it was called the Suez Maru. It was a hospital ship, so she couldn't be bombed. A hospital ship couldn't be mistaken for another because of her large red cross markings on the deck and on both sides." The captain looked across at Kondo at this final remark. They both know the Imperial Japanese Army and Imperial Japanese Navy had routinely carried wounded servicemen, as well as sick PoWs *without* marking transports as hospital ships, and *without* the obligatory red crosses. The comment irritated the captain, designed as it was to infer the Allies had deliberated bombed a hospital ship. When in fact the presence of PoWs and injured men had been concealed by the Japanese, and was unknown to the Allied submarine. Saito continued, "Someone said, don't you think it's unreasonable for hospital ship to carry Allied PoW? Another said I suppose the Suez Maru was turned into submarine fodder." The captain was impatient for Saito to divulge his personal knowledge of the incident. He was irritated by the blatant evasion thus far and he felt he had listened to enough hearsay. The captain interjected, "All right, thats enough of that. What was the Suez Maru's actual destination? What date was the sinking and what did you know of Captain Shirakawa?" Saito looked about mildly, his eyes half

closed, a hint of smirk at the edge of his mouth. He was pleased to have
irritated the captain. He responded with a shrug. "I only heard
them say it was bound for Japan. As to the date of
the sinking I only heard them say it was recently,
and I didn't know if Captain Shirakawa was on board
the Suez Maru." He went on, "After being attached to a
court-martial I heard a Lieutenant-Commander say
that Captain Shirakawa being a queer fish, must've
have then transferred to Japan by plane." The captain
was not impressed by Saito's lack of cooperation and tangential stories.
Nevertheless, he controlled his rising agitation. He slid a document
from his manila folder holding it to one side as his gaze passed over the
typed text. "You were the Commander of all the Java
prisoner of war internment camps in 1943. Yes?" Saito
was silent, he raised his chin slightly, peering at the document. Realising
he appeared too interested he quickly returned to his defiant demeanour.
The captain pressed, drumming the document with his fingers, "I
have evidence here that you falsified war records."
Saito shifted uneasily but still did not speak. "You wrote a report
on the loss of the Suez Maru in December of 1943,
along with an Army Transport Commander, named
Iketani." Saito's eyes widened, he clearly recognised that name. His
face moistened making his rounded nose shine and his cheeks glow, but
still he did not offer any statement. The captain leant forward and
began to read from the report, as Kondo translated, "While en
route from Ambon Island to Java on the transport
Suez Maru, two torpedoes truck the third and fourth
holds where the PoW were located aft of the ship
and the ship sank in a few minutes. All PoWs were
kept in the holds because of the necessity for
strict security. Since the holds in which they
were kept exploded and the ship sank very rapidly
it is believed that all of them went down with the
ship." Eyebrows raised in challenge, the captain looked across the
paper to his suspect. Saito leant nervously into the repeated whisper
from Kondo. The captain read the last line of the report, slowly and

deliberately whilst watching Saito carefully. "No survivors could be found despite rescue attempts by our escort ships." The captain gently lowered the sheet and without pause continued, "Tell me Major General Saito, what were the rescue attempts made by the escort ship? What were the names of those on board? I should like to speak with them." The captain waited patiently for a reply. Saito still retained his belief that he was too superior to be questioned. Although he knew all the terrible details of that voyage, he considered there would probably by now, be no one left alive to question what he did, or didn't know. So he chose to keep to himself. He smirked as he began to tell the captain an unrelated story. "You know..." he began slowly with a smirk, "...hearing about this Suez Maru incident revives another case in my memory. Sometime, I think in January 1942 some American PoW arrived on the SS Ashigara. A tent was pitched on the upper deck and four or five PoW came up, they were interrogated by Lieutenant -Commander Asahi. He had been in France and he treated the PoW like guests. A cook told me that Asahi ordered him to serve port, wine and whisky to these prisoners of war! Can you imagine?" Saito laughed, his belly wobbling as he pointed across the room, "He said they looked like officers, sitting there on the deck drinking wine and chatting!" Captain Sylvester frowned involuntarily, he decided it was pointless to continue. He stood, curtly thanking the Major General for attending and nodded to Kondo, who opened the door for Saito to leave. A waiting guard stepped forward from the corridor to escort Saito from the building. As he moved past, Saito turned to Captain Sylvester, a sly wrinkle at the corner of his mouth, "I am glad to be of help to you." The captain flushed angrily and responded, snapping, "Do not think I have finished with you, I may recall you for further questioning." As the door closed behind a smirking Saito, the captain thumped the table in anger. He was irritated with himself for letting Saito get under his skin, and was annoyed to have risen to Saito's parting comment. His flash of anger was gone as soon as it arrived and he sighed, "What is said is said," he spoke to no one in particular. The captain gathered up his papers and taking the rough translation from Kondo he left the room deep in distracted thought.

- 23 JUNE 1949 -

Officer Beirne knocked at Captain Sylvester's office door and entered. He began speaking immediately on seeing the captain was alone. "Sir, some others have been traced from the personnel listings we received and checked." The captain looked up expectantly. Officer Beirne continued, "Erm, one Fumio Nomaguchi has been found, they're bringing him in now. He was apparently on the escort ship, the er, Minesweeper W12. He was a Lieutenant-Commander in the IJN." A crease appeared at the captain's lip. He dropped the document he was reading into a folder, which he closed and slid to a corner of his desk. He rubbed his hands together gleefully, startling Officer Beirne. His usual slight frown turned to a wide grin. The captain was pleased to make any progress on this difficult case. He had been convinced it was too old, too cold and that enough witnesses and by extension, enough suspects, would not be found. The captain now looked around squinting, searching the chaos of papers and documents piled haphazardly round the room. Officer Beirne raised his eyebrows, wondering how he ever found anything. The captain caught his eye and his thought. "I know *exactly* where everything is Beirne, it's filed in here as much as here," he said, tapping his temple then the desk with his forefinger. "Ah-ha..." he said, reaching for the thickening manila folder, "– here it is." The captain opened the folder, "Yes, Nomaguchi, good, good. Let's just give him some time to sweat and then we'll go in." He paused abruptly, "Any word on Iketani yet?" Officer Beirne replied, "No, but we've traced others. Some were crew on the *Suez Maru*." He waved a piece of paper he'd brought with him and the captain gestured to a seat, indicating he wanted full details. Officer Beirne took the prompt. "Well, we've also traced Yoshi Nagasaki, he was only a storeman on the *Suez Maru*, but we also have a Daiso Yatsuka. He was the senior gunnery officer on board. There's Shunichiro Narishima, seaman and Hidenori Kokussen, another seaman. Saburo Maeda, a deckhand and Joji Nukui, he was ship's purser. We've one Ichiro Ehara, an apprentice machinist on board and Morimasu Kikuchi, he was one of the firemen." The captain smiled broadly and slapped the desk, "Well done Beirne, you've rounded up more than I realised. All right, get them all in..." he paused, examining a small appointments diary, flicking pages back and forth while tapping the end of a fountain pen on the desk. "All right, get them in the first week of July. We will have to make sure they don't see or speak to each other. We'll have to stagger days and use all the interrogation rooms, clear the calendar." The captain paused thoughtfully, "Wait a moment, where is Iketani? Why hasn't *he* been found yet, is he dead? What's his first name again?" He didn't wait for a reply as he rifled through pages in the manila folder. He stopped at a long list of names, down which he ran an ink-stained finger, muttering each name in turn, "ahh, Iketani, *Masaji* Iketani. We must find *him*. He was supposed to be in charge of the PoWs. Issue other request, will you? What about this Kawano, Osamu Kawano, has he been traced yet? He was captain of the minesweeper, where is he?" Officer Beirne shook his head apologetically, "I don't know about him. We haven't heard anything yet. But they'll all turn up captain, I'm sure of it. They have to be somewhere." The captain nodded in unconvinced agreement lifting his cap from the desk and sliding the manila folder under his upper arm, "Come on then, I think Nomaguchi has stewed long enough. Where's Kondo got to?"

Fumio Nomaguchi sat nervously in the chair, his feet tucked neatly under the seat, knees together and fingers clasped tightly on the table as Captain Sylvester and Isao Kondo strode into the room. He looked to them, his lip trembling. At once he began to protest pleadingly. "I don't know why I am here, I haven't done anything. Please, my mother is sick with worry." The captain sat opposite and looked him directly in the eye, studying his face. He could usually quickly determine how genuine a plea was, whether it was self-pity or remorse. He nodded to Kondo to translate. Nomaguchi's face was youthful, his rounded cheeks tinged pink and his dark eyelashes were weighted with tears. 'He must have been barely a boy six years ago,' thought the captain. "All right, settle down, I just want to ask a few questions, you're not suspected of anything. Just answer truthfully and you can go soon. All right?" Nomaguchi listened to the translated words coming from Kondo and his shoulders relaxed gratefully. He decided to trust the captain and nodded eagerly, "I will answer anything truthfully. I haven't done anything." His eyes brimmed again. The captain looked away and moved on. He nodded to Kondo to repeat his formal questions. Kondo made the quick translations back and forth. "Were you a lieutenant-commander in the Imperial Japanese Navy, aboard Minesweeper W12 as she escorted the Suez Maru, November 1943?" Nomaguchi stammered at first but quickly gained his confidence. "Yes, I was a lieutenant-commander." The captain nodded, making notes. "But I wasn't on any minesweeper. I was on Ambon Island when I heard of the fate of the SS Suez Maru." The captain studied Nomaguchi's face. "Oh? Go on, what did you hear?" Nomaguchi again faltered, then swallowed hard, finding his voice. "Well, a few days after 5 December 1943, which was when I arrived at Ambon, at the HQ of 2SEF. I heard there was a transport attached to the fleet, which was torpedoed and sunk by an enemy submarine." The captain leant forward listening intently. "Yes, what did you hear about that transport? What was its name, where was it sunk? What date was it sunk? Who was on board? What else was the ship carrying?" Nomaguchi's face creased in alarm, "I don't know the name of the ship, or the location or the date of her sinking, I don't know what the cargo was. I just heard it was hit by a submarine and the survivors were brought to Soerabaya after they were rescued by an escort warship, I don't know its name. I don't know if PoW were shipped on that same boat," he stammered. "That's four 'I don't knows' in under half a minute," the captain muttered to Kondo, who nodded. "I think, yes, I am sure that er,

Engineer Yoshio Hiramatsu, yes he would be more
familiar with matters concerning transportation
in those days. He was the SO Engineer with 2SEF. I
can scarcely remember that any PoW were shipped in
those days..." Nomaguchi trailed off, he looked hard at the floor,
his face flushed with distress. The captain turned to Kondo and shook
his head. It was clear to him Nomaguchi probably knew little further.
Moreover, he was not on board either ship, any statement would be
mere hearsay and, except for the name he'd offered, was of no further
use. The captain indicated to Nomaguchi via Kondo that he was to
write out and sign a short note of what he'd said. Kondo explained
and wrote the scant information onto a single sheet. He read it to
Nomaguchi, who nodded glumly. Captain Sylvester signed the sheet,
noting it was a rough translation as he dated it '23 June '49' in the
corner. The captain inclined his head to the door, glancing to Kondo,
who took the signal. He turned to Nomaguchi to say he could leave.
Nomaguchi quickly jumped up, gratefully nodding. He bowed, wiping
his eyes and sniffing loudly. The guard outside escorted him away as
Kondo closed the door behind his retreating sobs. Kondo turned back
to the quiet rustle of papers. The captain looked through his notes
and Nomaguchi's statement. "What was that name he said Kondo?"
Kondo crossed the room and gathered his papers, leafing through
them. "Hiramatsu, Yoshio Hiramatsu." "Yes, thank you." The captain
scribbled on the edge of one of his sheets, then pushed all the papers
back into the growing manila folder. Tucking it under his arm he strode
toward the door. "I need to see this Hiramatsu ASAP," he muttered
to himself.

- 28 JUNE 1949 -

Captain Jack Sylvester sat frowning amongst stacks of documents piled
around his cluttered office, absently tapping a pencil on the edge of
his desk. He watched a bird perched on his windowsill. It pecked at
something as absently as the captain tapped his pencil. He was currently
working on three other investigations, but felt intensely drawn to this,

his most complex current case. The torpedoed transport ship and those PoWs. Something about the emerging facts gripped him. That these men had survived years in harrowing Japanese concentration camps and deathly work on those islands, that they had survived a terrifying torpedo attack, that they had seen the gurgling sinking of their ship and then... and then. He felt outraged that the Japanese had covered their crime so completely. It might never have been known but for Yoshio Kashiki's courageous letter. The letter defied belief. He had hardly believed it. Yet as Captain Sylvester poked gently, tentatively, at the bloated belly of the story it had spilled relentlessly. An outpouring and gushing of such putrid heinous truths, he could hardly bear it. Captain Sylvester felt driven to see the case to its conclusion. He was horrendously overworked, that was not in doubt, but it was the switching between his various overloaded and complicated cases that he found so taxing. Making adjustments to each horror-filled crime, each suspect interrogated, each indignant face sneering replies to his questions with a lack of remorse. His other cases were not as complex but each still demanded careful scrutiny and probing to ensure a clear case against those suspected. He felt the weight of the souls lost *and* of the survivor's sufferings in each war crime he investigated. He carried them all with him. Compelled and determined to find truths, and the guilty to atone for the torment and grief caused. Captain Jack Sylvester was one of only four investigators and each confronted these nervous and mental strains in their own way. Nevertheless, their faces were etched with each individual they represented. Harry, Lionel, James and Jack did not often have time nor the inclination to socialise with one another but, on the rare occasions they were able to share a meal or a drink away from the suffocating atmosphere of their offices they found a little weight of their daytime activities lifted. As if by sharing their burden they decreased the pressure. After time spent together talking, taking a drink and laughing at nothing in particular, the captain found himself briefly released and able to sleep deeply for a night or two. Come the morning he would feel reinvigorated and ready to continue his gruelling task.

Captain Sylvester sighed deeply. As he leant back in his chair it emitted a loud wooden creak and the bird on his windowsill flapped away in a single beat of its wings. He watched it flap higher on three, four wing beats then soar as it caught warmer air. It banked right and disappeared into the morning haze. The captain returned to his unruly desk and examined the manila folder sitting snugly alongside his black *Corona Mk IV* typewriter. His eyes again scanned Kashiki's letter, the typed statements and his notes. He shook his head, grunting. He had never fathomed why a strong, useful workforce would be treated in such a manner. Surely it would have made more sense to treat them well, enabling them to work harder. It didn't make any sense. Even putting aside the fact that forcing PoWs to work contravened the Geneva Convention. There was deep inhumanity in the actions of these war criminals. He had found generally those two things went hand in hand— war crimes and inhumanity. The Japanese he'd previously investigated and helped convict of war crimes had never shown an ounce of remorse or any discernible sense that their actions were not only criminal but utterly barbaric and inhuman. He sighed, shaking his head free of the unpleasant train of thought. He turned his attention back to his typewriter, and pulling a clean sheet of paper through the platen roller, he readied himself to speak. He didn't type often, the secretaries copied the documents he needed, but some letters he preferred to type himself. He stretched out his hands and let his fingertips rest gently in the shallow cups of the keys. The smooth metal of the space bar was cool to the touch as he placed his thumbs lightly on it. He began the letter, inclining his ear to listen as the type-bars leapt from their places one after the other with soft clacks. Each bar completed its thudded smudged letter and returned snugly to its gap in the curve, forming a wide toothy grin on top of the machine.

Captain J Sylvester,
2 Aust War Crimes Section SCAP,
TOKYO.
28 Jun 49

```
Major H.S. Williams
C/- A. Cameron & Co. Ltd.,
36 - 1 Chome, Shinsaibashi-Suji,
Minami-Ku,OSAKA
```

Dear Major,

    Further to our telephone conversation herewith attached is a copy of letter I mentioned to you from Kashiki.

    The incident referred to in the letter actually took place!

    The fact of the sinking is in the American prepared official lists of enemy ships sunk during the last war, and has been confirmed by the Japanese authorities, who also state that PoWs were on board the ship at the time of the sinking, although the total number and nationality is 'apparently' unknown to them.

    As you know the type of information we require, I have taken the liberty of communicating with you.

    Please convey my regards to Mrs. Williams and the children.

Yours sincerely

J. Sylvester

The captain walked to his door and leaning around the frame called down the corridor for a secretary. A young uniformed girl hurried up. He gave her the letter he had typed. "I need this posting, and a copy made, fast as you can." She nodded in reply. "Of course, I'll be quick as a jiffy." She turned to leave and paused, turning she spoke, "Sorry, I almost forgot, this just arrived." She held out a long thin envelope. The captain took it and the secretary dashed back along the corridor, the captain's letter wafting in her hand. Captain Sylvester frowned at the sealed envelope, he recognised the script. It was another letter from Yoshio Kashiki. He slid the letter from the envelope as he walked around his desk unfolding the two pages. He dropped heavily into his chair. Scanning to the end of the second page to confirm the name and seeing Kashiki's signature he nodded to himself. He began reading the neat lines, reaching for a half empty cup of tea which stood stone cold on the edge of his desk.

Dear Sir

I hope you are in good health this fine spring season. The reason for this letter is that I have some information I wish to volunteer in writing. This information concerns the fate of Allied Prisoners of war at the time they were aboard the transport Suez Maru which I believe was on the high seas somewhere off the shore of Soembawa Island, about 9.30 hours at the end of November 1943. I boarded the Suez Maru at Ambon on 25 November with 200 or so wounded and sick patients while being evacuated to the Soerabaya hospital I unexpectedly encountered this incident. I was discharged from the hospital once since then but was admitted into a hospital again in June 1945, and am at present am still hospitalised.

As a result of my morbid condition and the numerous mental changes occurring during this period I have suffered a lapse of memory so I do not clearly remember the dates and place names. Nevertheless I am writing this in the hope that the true facts will be conveyed to the next of kin and that memorial services will be conducted for the dead officers and men. After a thorough investigation has been made even if it requires much trouble. Please pardon my poor penmanship and style of writing.

The captain put the letter down briefly. He clenched his fists, his jaw muscles flexing as he ground his teeth. He stood for a moment looking down at the letter on his desk with furrowed brows and sagged back into his chair, elbows on his desk, his knuckles to heavy cheekbones supporting his weary head, as he continued.

194

The transport Suez Maru, with some 200 of us wounded and sick soldiers aboard, departed from the port of Ambon on 25 November 1943, escorted by the minesweeper no W12. These two ships were destined for Soerabaya. Besides us, aboard the Suez Maru there were approximately 270 British and Dutch officers and men. All of them were prisoners of war who had grown sickly because they were forced into hard labour at Ambon. Furthermore, two damaged navy float planes are carried on the forward deck and one on the aft deck. So, figuring that this ship would naturally be attacked and sunk we were poised to abandon ship at all times. At any rate if I'm not mistaken it was on the 29th that the escort ship left us for some purpose. Then about 9.30 hours the Suez Maru while sailing unescorted was hit by two torpedoes and with her hull breaking in two where the rear mast is located, she sank soon after.

In spite of the act that the persons aboard, other than medical men, prisoner of war, command and the crew were all patients. All the lifeboats were occupied by the crew. Approximately three hours after that the escort ship finally caught up with us and we Japanese were rescued immediately. But not even a single one of the Allied prisoners of war was rescued. Soon after we went overboard navy planes came from Soerabaya to patrol the area so I believed that a rescue ship should of course come from Soerabaya. However, I did not hear anything about it aboard the ship. Meanwhile the fate of these officers and men was sealed merely by a few words like "Shall we do it?" and "Lets dispose of them," exchanged between a person who seemed to be the commander of the minesweeper and the commander in charge of the prisoners of war.

Some seventeen or eighteen seamen each armed with a rifle lined up on the foreword deck and indiscriminately shot and killed the 270 or so men who were screaming for help. After killing every single one of them, the ship left the area in the evening with us on board and headed for Java. Cruising at approximately twelve knots the ship entered the port of Tandjong Priok on 1st December, and we were admitted into the army hospital at Batavia after that. The ship's name Suez Maru was derived from the Suez Canal. The ship's captain had been rescued at that time.

I have written the above statement in the hope that the souls of those dead officers and men will rest in peace. However since I was sentenced to three months' imprisonment on the charge of ideological offences when I was in the army I was forsaken by my family and even by my one and only elder brother, and since I am leading a lonely convalescent life at present I would be placed in a much more embarrassing position if my name became known in connection with this case... Consequently I ask that my real name will never be made known if and when there comes a time where my name has to be used. To be more specific about the offence I committed while in the army. I was charged with founding a party and convicted of an "Attempted Desertion as a Party Adherent."

In closing I pray for your health and prosperity.

I remain,
Yoshio Kashiki.
Tokyo National Hospital, Ward 5.

Captain Sylvester leant back in his chair, re-folded the letter and slid it into its envelope. He lifted the manila folder from the deep drawer and dropped the envelope inside. He replaced it, sliding the drawer shut with a thud and turned a small brass key in the scratched lock. He tucked the key into a pocket and standing stiffly he lifted his cap from a sparse hat-rack near the door. He flopped his jacket over his arm and left the office. Officer Beirne stopped in the corridor as Captain Sylvester passed by. "Sir?" he questioned. The captain frowned without slowing his pace, "I am going home."

- 1 JULY 1949 -

The turning of the month brought oppressive summer heat. Captain Jack Sylvester sweated in the muggy warmth despite being largely inside, either in his office or an interrogation room during the squatting humidity of daytime. His investigation had been reluctantly sidelined for almost two weeks. Suspects and informers could not be traced or were reluctant to agree to questioning and had to be rounded up and brought in. The captain worked on other cases in the meantime but now sat at his desk working through his briefly neglected manila folder, making extensive notes. Officer Beirne entered with a short knock. The captain without the slightest inclination of his head, looked up with only his eyes. "Yes?" "Tamaki Shirakawa is back again and also Yoshimitsu Nagasaki, erm, the store man on the *Suez Maru*, he's here too." The captain looked puzzled. "Did Shirakawa say why he's come? I didn't summon him." "I don't know, he asked to speak with you urgently." The captain folded the manila folder closed and frowned. He pointed at Officer Beirne with his pencil, "Put Shirakawa in one, Nagasaki in three, I'll be there shortly. I'll see Nagasaki first, let Shirakawa wait awhile." Officer Beirne turned to leave as the captain called out, "Get Kondo from the canteen or wherever he is, as well." Officer Beirne grinned as he nodded and ducked out of the office. The captain returned to the manila folder, opening it and rifling through papers. There were several more potential suspects he wanted to question but the case was slowly gathering. He was now certain the crime actually took place but who *specifically* was responsible, who gave the order, who actually carried it out and importantly, who then concealed it, were all questions he was determined to get firm and factual answers to. He jotted down another note, slipped the paper inside the manila folder, and left the heat of his office to silently await his return.

Yoshimitsu Nagasaki sat nonchalantly in the stuffy interrogation room. A fly buzzed in through the open window and droned in orbit around the dim light. Nagasaki watched, his lip twitching. Its irritating humming as if it were running out of petrol made his teeth clench. He leapt forward to swat at it just as the door opened and Captain Sylvester strode into the room, Kondo following. The captain stopped short, brows raised at Nagasaki's odd posture. Nagasaki dropped back into the chair with a shrug. The captain took his usual seat opposite the detainee, as Kondo moved across to his side table amassing his collection of pencils and papers in a haphazard pile. The captain briefly watched him fumble about as pencils rolled off the desk and papers scattered. Kondo offered a toothy embarrassed grin as he leaned down gripping the table to gather up the errant stationary. He rearranged the papers neatly in a pile, placing pencils to the side and nodded to the captain, who rolled his eyes as he returned his attention to Nagasaki. Nagasaki bristled as the captain addressed him, Kondo echoing in Japanese. "Yoshimitsu Nagasaki, can you confirm your name and that you are currently employed as a seaman, and that you were a storeman on the Suez Maru when it was torpedoed and sunk on 29 November 1943?" Nagasaki's eyes widened on hearing the name *Suez Maru*. He shuffled his feet under the table and looked to Kondo as he finished translating. His shoulders dropped, realising he no longer held any secrets of that day. "Yes, my name is Yoshimitsu Nagasaki and I was on the Suez Maru, I was only a storeman, but yes, I was there when it was torpedoed," repeated Kondo to the captain. The captain's face betrayed no emotion but inwardly he was pleased. He knew Nagasaki needed no breaking down, he would easily offer up all he knew. It was so much easier when they told the truth, the captain thought to himself as he pulled sheets of blank lined paper from the back of the manila folder. He slid them across the desk and nodding to Kondo to begin translating he turned back to Nagasaki. With a firm tone he began, "You will swear tell the truth according to the dictates of your conscience and shall conceal nothing nor will you add to the facts. Do you understand?" Nagasaki replied "Yes." Kondo repeated the reply to the captain, who leant back in his chair, "Tell him to read out what he writes to you, I'd like to hear this without waiting a month." Nagasaki nodded to Kondo on the instructions and licking the end of the pencil he began to make small angular shapes longways on the lined paper, repeating the words as he wrote. Kondo murmured the words in English as the captain listened head inclined, his fingers steepled. Occasionally Nagasaki was stopped by the captain and Kondo translated that he was to expand on a point or clarify his meaning. The captain asked, 'Where was he at this time?' or 'Well, how many boats were there?' or 'Who was the last to leave the ship?' Until a tired Nagasaki had eagerly written out all he remembered with little crossing out, he checked and nodded agreeably with each amendment. Kondo spoke the words offered by Nagasaki. "Yes, ahh, I was a member of the crew on the SS Suez Maru when that vessel was torpedoed at about 0915 hours on 29 November 1943. At the time of the explosion I was off duty and resting in my quarters, in the bow of the vessel, just forward of hold one. On hearing the explosion, I went on deck and found one lifeboat had already been loaded. I judged that preparations were being made to abandon ship. I saw Captain Tamaki Shirakawa standing on the bridge. Everything that would float and was available I threw into the sea. This included such things as planks and life-rafts, each about two feet square. About twelve or thirteen minutes after the explosion the Suez Maru sank by the stern. I believe two torpedoes exploded in the vicinity of hold four. Until I left the ship I remained upon the upper deck near holds one and two. Three or four minutes before the ship sank, her bow was then rising fast, I plunged into the sea on the port side after adjusting my life jacket around my neck. Captain Shirakawa had plunged into the sea a few seconds earlier, from the opposite side of the ship. A few seconds later, Quartermaster Shimizu plunged into the sea. Shimizu was the last man to leave the ship. Four lifeboats were carried on the Suez Maru, with a capacity of 50-60 men each. I only saw two lifeboats, which were crowded with survivors. I do not remember seeing the other two. Shimizu and I managed to climb onto a life-raft which carried us away from the two lifeboats. I was unable to see whether any prisoners of war were in the lifeboats at that time. At a distance of about 300 feet I saw a group of between twenty and thirty prisoners of war clinging to rafts, planks and barrels. There were many others, both Japanese and prisoners of war swimming all around us. An approximate total number of PoWs seen by me at that time was about 100. I don't know how many PoWs were carried on the Suez Maru. I do know that many of them were sick and wounded, I saw them embarking at Ambon and many of them were carried on stretchers. During this time the minesweeper kept circling the sea. At about 1630 hours a small boat left the minesweeper and rescued Shimizu and myself. About one and a half hours later while I was lying in a corner of the minesweeper deck I heard machine-gun fire. Although I do not know how many machine-guns were in action, I did see one machine-gun situated on the bridge that was firing. At first, I thought it was intimidating fire directed against the enemy submarine. Seconds later looking closely at the sea I observed that it was directed either at one of the lifeboats which was carrying six or seven prisoners or war, it was fifty or sixty feet away from the minesweeper's stern, or to a number of PoWs in that vicinity. I saw in the distance the other lifeboat. It was then sinking but no one was aboard. I do not know what became of the other lifeboats from the Suez Maru. I watched the scene for ten to fifteen minutes during which time a number of PoWs were killed. I then returned to my former spot."

The captain had watched Nagasaki closely as Kondo read the statement, his jaw flexed almost the entire time. Nagasaki looked almost cheerful, a weight lifted, as he neatly copied the final sentence confirming his statement was made freely without threat or promises to influence. He signed the last sheet and the captain noted the date, 'this first day of July, 1949,' before signing in right slanting cursive across the very bottom of the sheet. Kondo tapped Nagasaki's shoulder and opened the door. A guard outside took the now silent Nagasaki away down the corridor. Kondo turned back to the room, closing the door as the captain gathered his papers and got to his feet. His face was flushed with anger and he began muttering, "Oh, I just went and sat down again in my cosy spot! Like he'd just watched a film and finished his ice cream, he went and sat back bloody down again!" The captain spun around, pointing to the ghostly scene, "He stood there on the deck of that minesweeper and watched more than two hundred and fifty men murdered in cold blood! And he tells me about it so calmly. He just stood there like he watched a brass band marching past. Did you see his eyes, it meant *nothing*. They were PoWs and it hasn't caused him a moments sorrow, hasn't stirred his conscience even once!" The captain was shouting, he pointed angrily to the window, to the unseen ocean. "He's *still* working as a seaman, sailing about as if it didn't matter, and what's worse, that's not necessarily a crime! Standing there witnessing it, without expressing the tiniest bit of revulsion, well that ought to be a class A war crime!" He picked up the sheet Nagasaki had signed and waved it in the air. "And this. This tells me no more than I already knew. It gives me no new names, it's simply another statement of 'I couldn't care less'!" Kondo listened silently, his eyes full of concern. Eventually he cleared his throat and spoke. "Maybe it strengthens the case, maybe if there were a hundred men, and they all said the same thing. That this happened and it happened like this. Then it has to be the truth. Maybe." Kondo looked to his feet, blushing as he continued, "Maybe Nagasaki doesn't matter. It is his own conscience whether it troubles him. Whether what he saw comes to haunt him or not. Perhaps it is not for us to worry about such things." The captain watched Kondo, stunned. He had seldom heard him speak much more than a sentence aside from 'Good morning and good night' and apart from translating work the captain hadn't really considered him more than an 'observer'. But here he was, a 'participant,' with opinions. The captain was surprised by the soft kindness and gentle understanding Kondo offered and found he had to swallow an unexpected tightening lump in his throat. He coughed, "Well, yes, of course, that is right," the captain admitted, stress washing from his face as he allowed a smile. He shook himself and returned to his professional persona, "Well, all right, now, Shirakawa will be waiting. Let's go and see what's rattled his cage shall we?" The captain put Nagasaki's paper into the manila folder, "I'll arrange this translation." Kondo nodded courteously and turned to leave. "Kondo..." the captain called to his departing back, "Thanks." Kondo hesitated briefly at the door, a small grin crept over his face. He turned back to the captain, nodded again. They left, closing the door gently.

The room sweltered as the day pressed on. A fat fly meandered up the wall in the sickly yellow light, buzzing erratically. Tamaki Shirakawa stood statue still, only his wet bulging eyes followed the insect weaving its way to the ceiling. "Where is it going?" He muttered. Suddenly it stopped. Wriggling a leg, tugging and pushing with another leg it tried to move away but had become caught in the edge of a cobweb. It pulled at the thread, only succeeding in getting another leg tangled. The unfortunate creature wrapped itself ever more tightly with each movement it struggled to make. Its wings whirred loudly and intermittently. Above, in the dark, the weaver of the web emerged stealthily from a crack between ceiling and wall. Silently it moved out from the shadows of peeling paint, lowering itself towards its wriggling prey. Shirakawa could not tear his eyes away, he almost moved to rescue the fly. He could carry it to the window, set it free. His legs twitched and flexed as if he were about to move but he remained still, as the fly was slowly bundled away and pulled up to the dark crevice. Shirakawa glanced to the window, picturing the fly he could have saved bumbling away safely in the warm breeze. He stared transfixed in the imagined sight, lost and glassy eyed as the door opened and Captain Sylvester entered the dim room, manila folder tight to his chest. The captain opened his mouth to speak but paused as Kondo tapped at the door, entering without waiting for a reply. He bustled to his table with his armfuls of papers, notes and pencils. The captain frowned in warning to Kondo to sit quietly before looking back to Shirakawa. The captain tried to read his face but saw nothing there. He gestured with upturned palms, "Well, what is it? Have you something more to say?" Shirakawa looked to Kondo as he translated the captain's words. Shirakawa spoke as he turned back to the captain. "I've been thinking," he started nervously, "and ahh, I want to make additions and corrections to my earlier statement." The captain settled himself into a chair and gestured to the chair opposite with a flat palm and wry smile, "Do you? hmm." The captain was well aware that a sudden attack of conscience did not definitively infer guilt, but at the very least it usually meant much more was known than was first admitted. "Of course," the captain offered gently. "Yes, ahh, yes, I think I made some ah, mistakes and I ahh, I wouldn't like there to be misunderstandings because ahh, of my ahhh, my mistakes. We are not a wealthy family, I am working in my wife's restaurant, if anything should happen to me, ahhh because of a, ahhh, a misunderstanding, then it will mean ruin for them, and for me. Ahhh so I wanted to make sure you understand, that yes, I was captain of the Suez Maru, but that I was not involved in what happened. Ahhh, you see I can tell you more, much more, I have more information that I can give you, names and such. Perhaps I can amend my statement to tell you more." The captain leaned forward, "I cannot offer you protection, nor leniency, if you are found to be responsible you will be arrested and charged." Shirakawa's face filled with concern and alarm, "But I was not responsible, ahhh I was only there, I-I-I could not have known what was to happen." He gesticulated with his hands, pointing here and there to emphasis his points before leaning towards the captain, his palms open, pleading "I swear I did not know. I was only there, I-I-I was not responsible." The captain held up a hand to halt Shirakawa. "You can tell me anything further you wish to add, I will take note of it, you may amend your statement, and when I have interviewed other witnesses, I will call on you for further questioning. If you are innocent you have nothing to worry about. Do you?" The captain finished mildly. Shirakawa did not hear the scepticism in the captain's tone nor the underlying meaning of his words, he simply sagged, in misplaced relief. "Yes, yes, thankyou, very generous. I will write all the things I, ahh, I forgot earlier." "Yes, you do that." The captain frowned, then nodded to Kondo and the pair fell into their familiar pattern of talking, pausing, translating, repeating and making notes. Shirakawa's voice was low and falteringly, anxiously eyeing the captain all the while. "Well, I wish to make the following additions and corrections to my sworn statement of 13 June." He pulled a rolled-up piece of paper from an inside pocket in his coat, holding it up and oddly grinning with nervousness. "Ahhhh, as I've thought more about it, there were probably more than two hundred Japanese servicemen in holds one and two, and about five hundred PoW in holds three and four. When Chief Mate Watanabe gave the order 'Hard aport -full speed', he also sounded a warning on the siren, to help the PoWs. When I ordered Watanabe to inspect the damage I also ordered Shimizu to do the same, to see if the PoWs were injured. It was Shimizu who reported that hold three was taking in water. It was the medical officer who hastened to me and it was he I told to abandon ship. The transport commander was sick and so the medical officer acted on his behalf. Also after I gave the order to abandon ship I stayed

there on the bridge for seven or eight minutes,
supervising matters." He pointed to imaginary persons as if he
was giving his orders. Captain Sylvester knew that such unconscious
re-enacting signalled truth and he listened closely. "Were you, as
captain, the last to leave your ship?" he asked.
Shirakawa nodded "Yes, about the same instant that I
and two others jumped from the ship I saw Shimizu
plunge into the sea from the bow." "Have you any more
information on the prisoners of war, what was their
condition and how many were there in the sea?"
Shirakawa searched the floor uncomfortably, sighed deeply and said,
"Ahh... perhaps I did not give the full picture
when I was last here, in fact I think I said that
many PoW and Japanese were clinging to the lifelines
from the lifeboats. I, ahh, I now remember that
there were about ten PoWs and around a hundred
Japanese using the lifelines." "That's quite a
difference is it not?" noted the captain pointedly. "Ahhh
yes, also just before the minesweeper came to the
first lifeboat to commence rescue operations, a
lifeboat with an emergency capacity of about twenty
led the minesweeper to pick up survivors clinging
to planks and pieces of wood. As I did not see
later or hear of any PoWs being on the minesweeper,
so I believe that only Japanese were picked up by
that boat. However, I did not see nor did I hear
from the others that prisoners of war were knocked
or pushed away from the rescuing craft. Although I
was unable to understand what they meant, I heard
the shouts of prisoners of war from time to time.
After the rescue of the Japanese survivors
commenced, their shouts became louder. During the
one and half hours that they were machine-gunned I
heard occasional agonising shrieks which shocked
me. I could not help witnessing the killing of the
prisoners of war with machine-guns because I was

looking amongst them for Japanese survivors. From time to time, here and there the sea water was coloured red from the blood of the dead and dying." The captain exhaled loudly leaning forward, watching Shirakawa. He was horrified by the description. He shook his head, asking, "Why on earth were you watching so closely, simply to look for your own men? Did it not occur to you that this was a crime, that in fact this was murder, a war crime?" Shirakawa swallowed hard, he pointed and bowed as if receiving orders, looking about him and reliving those moments. "Yes, ahh, I know, yes, I knew it was murder. But at that time, you see, ahh I had reported to the Master of the Minesweeper that three of my crew were missing and he ordered me to watch the surface of the sea and try to locate any Japanese. I was ordered you see, what could I do? For this reason, I saw the greater part of the massacre but no Japanese were found." "No Japanese were found! To hell with them!" shouted Captain Sylvester. "You regret that no Japanese were found, when all around innocent men were being murdered!" Shirakawa shook his head, "No, no I thought it was terrible, and I thought at that time that although the ship was crowded with rescued Japanese, the minesweeper could have carried safely at least a hundred or more Prisoners of War." Shirakawa sunk deep into his chair, his eyes glassy once more. Captain Sylvester looked to Kondo who tilted his head in shame for his countrymen and looked away.

The captain straightened his shoulders, tugged his shirt taut and speaking softly he asked, "So, what of your later report? You say you were forbidden to report on the matter, what actually happened then?" Shirakawa shook his head as if trying to clear the terrible scene from his memory. "The next morning, I went to the dining room and asked the Master of the Minesweeper whether the disposal of the PoW should be reported by me. He

said, 'You needn't report that matter'. Neither
did he mention the reason why he had murdered the
prisoners of war. So, I did not make any report
aboard the minesweeper. We arrived at Batavia at
about 2200 hours, I think on 30 November 1943,
maybe the day after. On arrival an officer of the
Batavia Shipping Command came on board to see me.
He said that clothing had been made available and
could be obtained at a warehouse near the pier.
Being late, I did not go to the Shipping Command
that night, but went straight to a hotel with other
survivors. We travelled on two trucks supplied by
the Shipping Command. Next morning, I went back to
the Shipping Command and I reported orally to the
officer in charge." Shirakawa's eyes dimmed. He was clearly far
away as he repeated his actions. Captain Sylvester saw he was moved
by the events he described, and decided he wanted nothing further, for
now. He dismissed Shirakawa, who stood to leave gratefully. Shirakawa
tried to shake the captain's hand, but he avoided the gesture by instead
grasping the doorknob and opening the door. Shirakawa disappeared
in a tussle of thanks, as he was shuffled out and escorted away down the
corridor. Captain Sylvester blew out his cheeks, shaking his head as he
still held the doorknob. He and Kondo exchanged solemn glances as
they left the room, as still as before their arrival.

- 5 JULY 1949 -

It was a soggy, muggily hot Tuesday morning as Captain Jack Sylvester
arrived at SCAP GHQ's tall white building cut by its deep arches. The
wet weekend slowly evaporated into the humidity of the fresh new day.
The captain had used long overdue leave and had taken three full days
off. A whole weekend as well as the Monday, to relax and recuperate
with his young wife Anne, visiting from Melbourne. It had been four
months since they'd been together. They had at first been reserved and
tentative with each other. He'd asked about her journey from Australia

and her work as a clerk. She had told him how family were doing at home and asked him about the Tokyo rain. Then they had laughed loudly together at her polite enquiry about the weather. They fell into an embrace that they hardly broke from in their three precious days. God, it had been good to laugh, and not talk about murder and brutality, but gardens and sunshine and family. They had been married for nearly four years, but hardly six months of that had been spent together, and they were eager to occupy the same house and have their own garden, to fill with children. They'd taken a taxi that morning to Tokyo airport which still somewhat resembled a military airstrip, little more than a white conning tower and collection of low buildings. They had kissed, she had cried and he had squeezed her shoulders. He waved her off, his hand high in the air long after her *De Havilland* had become a speck. Her journey would be nearly as long as the time spent with him but she said it was worth every moment of her leave. She would stop at Singapore overnight and then take just one hop of the *Qantas* 'Kangaroo Route' from Singapore to Sydney via Darwin, then she would take the train on to Melbourne. He would miss her each part of her journey.

Captain Sylvester was greeted by a salute of the sentry guard as he stepped back into the fusty library-like air of SCAP GHQ, all paper and ink. His shirt was already damp as he strode along corridors to his office. Officer Beirne caught his eye as he arrived as his door, carrying an armful of correspondence. He loaded the hook of the captain's arm with envelopes and letters, to the captain's frown. Officer Beirne reminded the captain there were two waiting in custody who were lined up for questioning that day. "Yes, Kokussen and Narishima." Officer Beirne looked surprised and the captain raised an eyebrow in response. "I've only been away three days, Beirne," "Ahhh, how was leave?" asked the young officer smiling, a twinkle in his eye. "Mind your own business," replied the captain with a grin. "Come on in," he added as he dropped the letters in the last available space on his desk and found his seat. The captain pushed the mail to one side, pulling the thick manila folder containing his investigation into the *Suez Maru* case from its home in the locked drawer. The captain found the notes he had made the previous week regarding questioning of Hidenori

Kokussen and Shunichiro Narishima, both had been seamen on the *Suez Maru*. "Did they come in together?" asked the captain. Officer Beirne shook his head, "No, Narishima was picked up yesterday. He was detained overnight and Kokussen walked in this morning waving his summons." "Good, then they haven't spoken, they haven't seen each other?" "No, Narishima is still in the cells and Kokussen is in room three," replied Officer Beirne. "Fine, I'll deal with Kokussen first since he is ready, Narishima can stay down there a bit longer, it'll be easier to crack him later." The officer nodded and they moved to the door, the captain tucking the manila folder under his arm.

Kokussen was sitting bolt upright. 'Too upright' thought the captain as he walked round the table and sat. 'Perhaps I should have let *him* cook longer and seen Narishima first, if Kokussen is going to take some boiling,' he thought. He sighed, placing the manila folder in front of him. He opened it and leafed through its pages, leaving Kokussen to wonder who would speak first. Kondo for once, had arrived on time and settled to his role quietly. He sat motionless awaiting the captain's first move. Kondo knew this approach and sensed the captain must think Kokussen would be hard work. The captain turned page after page, re-reading what he had already committed to memory. He was waiting, to test Kokussen. Whoever spoke first would lose the infinitesimal upper hand, and the captain knew for sure who would speak first. Kokussen sat, arms folded, his chin jutting as he moved only his eyes. The captain turned back a page interestedly, as if he had noticed something unexpected, and sure enough Kokussen blurted, "What do you want of me, why was I sent this summons?" The captain smiled imperceptibly, his mouth flat. "You were summoned to explain to me what you remember of November 1943." Kokussen's eyes did not move, he stared hard at the captain, then broke his stunned silence, "November 1943? What of it?" he shrugged. "You were aboard the SS Suez Maru were you not in November 1943?" Kokussen paled, his eyes darting back and forth. "Well, yes I was, I was a seaman..." he trailed off as the captain pushed sheets of paper towards him firmly repeating, via Kondo, "You will outline all you time aboard the Suez Maru, paying particular attention

to the events of November 1943, do you understand?"
Kokussen looked from Kondo to the captain and regaining his smug
posture he took the paper and reached for the pencil. "Tell him to read
out loud as he writes, you copy it and translate Kondo," the captain
said turning to Kondo who nodded. "Yes, of course." "First, tell him
to read the penal provisions, tell him it stipulates that any omissions or
false or misleading statements concerning war crimes will subject him
to prosecution and punishment." Kondo related the words to Kokussen
who swallowed hard but retained his somewhat shrinking confident
expression. "Does he understand?" asked the captain. "Yes," replied
Kondo. "All right then, let's begin." The captain settled into his chair
rearranging his feet under the table and taking his pencil, awaiting
Kondo's translation of Kokussen's words.

"He doesn't remember the date but around 5th or
6th September he was summoned by the company and
assigned to the Suez Maru. He boarded the ship as
a machinist at Ujina. About three thousand troops
boarded there under army orders. They stopped en-
route for two days at Takao, then a convoy of four
ships sailed from Takao, including the Suez Maru,
Yubae Maru, Dainichi Maru and the Taian Maru.
The next mooring the Dainichi Maru and the Taian
Maru were sunk by torpedoes. The Suez Maru and
Yubae Maru returned to the scene to begin rescue
operations. The Suez Maru rescued and took aboard
about eight-hundred army personnel and headed for
Manila where the survivors disembarked." "Yes, that
is all very well, what about November, what happened
in November, I want the detail!" barked the captain
impatiently. He knew Kokussen was spinning out the story, saying each
word slowly, deliberately stalling. Clearly Kokussen knew the event the
captain wanted to hear about, and Kokussen's part in it, he was creating
thinking time. "Well..." Kokussen continued, a little flushed after
listening to Kondo's relay of the captain's demand. "We sailed from
Manila, I don't know the date, and arrived at Cebu,
I don't know the date. We waited there for further

orders but I don't know how long. Then we sailed, I don't know the date, for Halmahera, and then from Halmahera, I don't know the date, after waiting for further orders. We headed for Ambon, I don't know the date, and on arrival, I don't know the date, our troops and cargo were unloaded." The captain rolled his eyes. Kokussen's voice, lacking any useful information had become monotone, tapping out a rhythmic metronome which the captain found irritating but hypnotic. His eyes drifted to the window and he found himself wondering how far away his Anne was by now. The captain coughed quietly, shaking himself back to the room. He waved a hand in small circles telling Kokussen to move on, get on with the story. Kokussen smirked, continuing, "I think about five hundred and forty to fifty prisoners of war and about two hundred Japanese patients were taken on aboard the ship, and about ten damaged airplanes were loaded on to the deck." The captain listened intently now, as Kokussen began, finally, to look slightly nervous. "We sailed from Ambon for Soerabaya and the ship was sunk by two torpedoes around 0900 hours on 29 November off the coast of Soerabaya. I did not know much about the ships course at that time because I was in the engine room. Well, it was hot in there-" "Damn the engine room, I'm not interested in the blasted engine room, what happened when the ship sank? What about survivors, what about casualties?" Kokussen grimaced, "Umm, well, when we disembarked a man from the engine room died from a leg wound, caused by metal shrapnel from the boiler exploding. Nothing unusual happened after that." The captain blew out his cheeks, readying to burst a tirade upon him to get the truth. Kokussen simply sat in his chair, his arms folded and a hint of a smirk at his lips. The captain released the air from his mouth and returned Kokussen's small grin. He suddenly knew exactly how to handle this suspect. "All right Kokussen, I think that's all for now." He turned to address Kondo, nodding towards the door, "Could you ask for an escort?" Kondo opened the door and a guard entered with quizzical expression. He had heard shouting and had started for the door, and now wondered what was needed. The captain addressed him, "Can you remove this suspect to the holding cells please. I have another witnesses to question" He turned to Kokussen, and Kondo translated, "I may get to you later today or tomorrow, if not probably by Thursday, but I'm sure we can resume by the end of the week." Kokussen's mouth dropped open and he began to protest. He startled as the guard's hand clamped his shoulder. Held tightly under his arm he was led out shouting wildly at the captain as he went. Once the guard and Kokussen had rounded the end of the corridor the captain turned to Kondo, whilst beckoning another guard. "I'll speak to Narishima now. Let's see if he's in a talkative frame of mind." The guard hurried over, "Can you bring up Narishima quickly, but first make sure he sees and hears Kokussen being taken down." Kondo looked down with a small smile. He was sure the captain would easily get the truth from both Kokussen and Narishima. He had never really doubted it.

Narishima was a small, weedy looking man, all twitches and tics. He was brought from his cell as Kokussen arrived shouting and begging that now he would talk and wouldn't need to go to a cell. Narishima's eyes widened. His short dark hair bristled and he gripped his chest in alarm as he was led by the elbow to the interrogation room. Narishima now sat alone. He looked around the dimly lit room. It was long after noon and humid. Paint peeled high up on the walls. He spotted a spiderweb laced with dangling victims. Bundled up insects as if tucked in cocoons awaiting the next life, awaiting reincarnation into something more beautiful. Narishima looked away on hearing the door open. The captain was speaking with Kondo as they walked into the room and arranged their papers and folders on each table. Narishima watched, looking from man to man, his face full of questions and twitches. The captain finished tidying his notes and looked at Narishima. He startled as the captain spoke, then startled again as the words were relayed from Kondo's corner of the room into his own language. "Do you, Shunichiro Narishima, swear that you have read the penalties you may receive for refusing information or for making false or misleading statements concerning war crimes?" The captain had slid a sheet of paper towards him as he began speaking, containing details of the penalties, written in Japanese. Narishima scanned the words looking increasingly alarmed. He nodded as he looked to Kondo and then back to the captain, "Yes, yes I swear." "Very well then," replied the captain, "I want you to write a statement about your duties in the Casualty Clearing Unit on Ambon and its relation to Army Headquarters. I want to know what you know of the sinking of the Suez Maru and the fate of the PoWs she carried, and I want names of anyone else involved or responsible. Do you understand?" Narishima paused a moment as Kondo finished the captain's words and looked back to the captain "Yes, yes I will tell you everything I know," he stammered. The captain nodded, reaching for sheets of paper and a pencil, sliding them towards Narishima. He nodded to Kondo indicating he wanted it translated aloud as usual. The captain then leant back, to listen. Narishima took the pencil and spoke before he touched the paper with its point. He repeated each word as he wrote, not once looking up. "The Casualty Clearing Unit at Ambon was to evacuate to a designated place, upon orders from the Army Medical Department, all patients in military hospitals who could not be given adequate medical treatment in the locality. There were four or five medical officers, and Captain Shinoha who was in charge and about thirty NCOs and privates. The number of men dispatched on evacuation duty was dependant upon the number of patients, it was roughly one medical officer to ten casualties. On the Suez Maru was Probationary Medical Officer Eto and it was he who selected the men to escort the patients. Therefore, I don't know the names of these men. At that time PoWs were occasionally transported aboard the same ship on which patients were transported. I knew nothing about the PoWs nor was my attention drawn to them, but I heard later about them from Probationary Officer Eto. It was the responsibility of the escorting Medical Officer to report, on returning to the Casualty Clearing Unit and at the beginning we used to gather round to hear in detail the things that happened en route. However as these evacuations increased they lost news value and we stopped listening. Then, when Officer Eto returned from the Suez Maru he did not say very much, perhaps he was instructed to say nothing. When I asked him 'How was it?' he said, 'All right' and refused to say anything further. Sometime later I forget why it came up, but he said, 'It's too bad about the prisoners of war!' So, I asked him, 'What has happened to the prisoners of war?' He said, 'There were prisoners of war aboard the Suez Maru in the custody of some unit. When the Suez Maru met disaster, the minesweeper wouldn't rescue any of them.' He seemed unable to continue for a while, but then he said, 'Those shipwrecked prisoners of war were shot by the navy'. So, I learned of the scene he had witnessed, but I regret I cannot recall any further details." The captain looked to Narishima's small eyes darting round the room, he felt something like pity for him. He had been a Medical Officer, trying to offer first aid and treatment to his countrymen. He said softly, "Do you have any information on the current whereabouts of Medical Officer Eto?" "Well, Eto was quite young at the time maybe twenty-three or twenty-four. He said he was a graduate of the Seoul Medical College and I heard he was a native of Osaka, but I recall he didn't have much of an Osaka accent. I don't recall his first name, but as he is a doctor his first name and address should be in the directory of the National Medical Association, if he is still alive. Perhaps by looking through the list of Seoul Medical College graduates. Also he was a Sumo captain with a magnificent physique, that may also help you find him." The captain nodded, "All right, you need to sign here and then you can leave. I shouldn't think I'll need to speak to you again, all right?" Narishima looked grateful, then looked to his statement, signing it where indicated by the captain's pointed finger. As Narishima was escorted away, the captain stretched his arms above his head. Covering his mouth with his hand he suppressed an exhausted yawn. He caught Kondo's eye. "I think I'll need some tea before I see Kokussen. I'll tell them to bring him up in half an hour, give him time to consider his options, all right?" Kondo nodded and the captain muttered to himself, "I will need to trace this Eto, this *Sumo* Champion Medical Officer."

Half an hour later Kokussen was brought up as dusk began to fade the sharp outlines of the buildings outside the window and the warm glow from within cast yellow shadows onto the street. Kokussen sat in the same room he occupied several hours earlier but his demeanour was now completely different. He was sweating, slightly grubby and his eyes were darkened from tiredness and self-pity. He was fidgeting, inhaling and exhaling loudly, and rubbing his damp hands together. It seemed an age to him before anyone entered, and when the captain finally arrived with Kondo, Kokussen could not help but be relieved. The captain sat heavily and came straight to the point, without waiting for Kondo to tidy his papers away, leaving him struggling to catch up. The captain pointed his index finger at Kokussen's face, "I want to know exactly what happened on 29 November 1943. Where you were, what you saw, what you said and what you did, I want every last detail down to what you ate for breakfast!" Kokussen eyed the captain nervously but nodded as the words filtered into his own tongue. He nodded after each sentence, agreeing to each part. He began to outline his actions on that day. "About 0900 hours on 29 November '43 I was lying in my cabin reading the ships news when I was startled by a commotion on deck. When I went up I saw a torpedo heading for the ship on the port side. So I dashed back towards the cabin for my life preserver. Just as I was entering the room there was a terrific explosion. The ship shook and I was

215

thrown off my feet and onto the deck. I thought my feet were injured but in a frantic effort to get my life preserver I just got up. Then there was another explosion and the ship began to list to starboard, so I rushed back into my cabin, picked up my life preserver and put on only my work-shirt. I went up on deck and hurried to the lifeboat. Men were already in the lifeboat when I got there so I jumped in hurriedly. There were only Japanese soldiers and ship's crew members in the boat I boarded. Before long the stern of the ship began to sink and our boat was lowered, we all tried to get away from the vessel. The oars couldn't be used because the boat was too crowded so we paddled with our hands and somehow we managed to get about 100 ken away from the ship. The men floating around sighted our boat and came up to it and clung to the ropes on the sides. We watched the ship with anxious eyes and it sank from the stern and just when the aft deck touched the water it stood upright and gradually sank until it disappeared into the sea. At that time, somehow I felt sad and when I looked at the men around me they were also staring blankly at the spot where the ship had sunk. As I recall about twenty-five minutes elapsed from the time the Suez was hit until it sank. There were people clinging to pieces of wreckage and wood which floated to the surface, and some were on six foot life-rafts. Others were hanging onto the ropes at the sides of the boat. It seemed to me that there was no distinction between friend and foe and everyone was just waiting to see what would happen next. I do not know exactly what time it was but twelve or thirteen aircraft came towards us and we felt uneasy again. I do not know whether or not the aircraft spotted us, but they went away as we watched and everyone seemed relieved. In the meantime, a sub-chaser came towards our boat and we were happy because we were going to be rescued. The sub-chaser came closer and just when it was alongside us the lifeboat capsized and I was thrown into the water. When I came up to the surface the sub-chaser was about 238 yards away so I called out but I could not be heard. I found an oar and clung to it, and after paddling in the water for about two more hours a small boat with four sailors aboard came by and picked me up. There was nobody else around me so I was the only one who was rescued and taken to the sub-chaser. I began to shiver after I boarded so I lay down in the shade of the turret. I must have been tired from the ordeal I experienced in the morning because I dozed off. I do not know how many hours had passed, but I was suddenly awakened by the sound of rifle fire. I stood up to see what it was about and I saw the Prisoners of war being shot at with the rifles from the gunwale. That was the first time I saw people being killed and it made me feel sick, so I curled myself up in the shade of the turret and closed my eyes and plugged my ears with my fingers. I think about two hours passed before the firing ceased."

The captain interjected, "How many PoWs did you see in the water? How many were killed?" Kokussen responded quickly, "There were about five hundred and fifty PoWs aboard and about half of them went down with the ship so more than two hundred or so must have escaped. I was rather far away, someone told me we circled at a radius of about four miles. From where I was I could see maybe forty or fifty PoWs. Later I heard someone say, 'There probably isn't a PoW living because we made a thorough search and killed them all'. When I heard this, I felt sick as if it were

my own affair. I could not sleep because it was so
dreadful and I could not forget it. Later I went
to the galley for a meal and a soldier said all of
them had been killed. After that the ship headed
for Jogjakarta and we arrived about 1900 hours. We
were taken to a warehouse and received clothing
and daily necessities." The captain listened carefully, noting
numbers and times in his manila folder nodding grimly. It all fitted
with the other accounts he had heard. When Kokussen finished he
looked to the captain as Kondo translated his final subdued words. "He
says he's sorry that he didn't speak earlier. His family had told him not
to say anything, but he says he really he didn't have anything to do with
it except witness parts of it and could he please leave now?" The captain
frowned but nodded to Kondo to show him the door. The captain
called to Kokussen as he stepped through the doorway "Don't go far
though, Kokussen." He nodded as he was escorted away.

Captain Sylvester had returned to work on the case for only one
day but it felt it like a lifetime. The weekend with his wife disappeared
as if only a matter of moments. He returned his attention to Kondo,
rubbing his eyes with his palms, "All right let's call it a day. I need to
trace this Medical Officer Eto, and tomorrow I have Maeda and Nukui
to question so better get some decent sleep."

"I thought you had questioned Maeda," said Kondo, his face puzzled.
Captain Sylvester frowned, "This is *second class deckhand* Maeda, not
Rear Admiral Maeda!" They exchanged glances and both let out a single
shout of laughter. Less to do with the name confusion, more in an
unconscious release of emotional pressure.

- 6 JULY 1949 -

Joji Nukui was a prim little man. Like a twitching old parrot he sat
knees together as if hatching a prehistoric egg under his bony bottom
on the sagging chair in the SCAP GHQ interrogation room. His
pinched face and beady eyes surveyed the room as he scratched at the
side of his nose absently. His feet, flat on the floor under the table,

rolled heel to toe as if rocking to some silent music heard only by him. He stopped abruptly, cocking an ear and listening as voices outside indicated someone's arrival. He straightened in the chair, still and bird-like staring with sideways stare at the closed door. The doorknob turned and muffled voices increased in volume and clarity through the crack in the door jamb. "Yes, very well, perhaps an hour. Keep him in the interrogation room or in a cell, whichever you prefer." The drawn-out Australian accented of Captain Sylvester's words floated to Nukui's ears but he did not understand the language. The doorknob released with a rattle and the door was pushed open by a small Japanese man carrying a stack of papers, a small cloth bag on top held in place by his chin. Kondo moved past Nukui, sitting at his usual desk as the captain thanked unseen persons outside and entered, the manila folder tucked as always underarm. He sat, withdrawing a pencil from his top shirt pocket and placing his cap on the table. He drew the manila folder to him with a low grunt. Kondo opened his cloth bag quietly, pulling a single pencil from it and drawing it closed, nodding his readiness to the captain. The captain pulled a paper with Japanese text on it from the manila folder and slid it across the table with a forefinger. "These are the penalties for refusing to give information or for making false or misleading statements concerning a war crime. Please read it, we shall begin your affidavit with this statement." Nukui looked at the paper and nodded seriously. His eyes bulged at the consequences he read as he listened to Kondo's translation of the captain's words. His mouth flattened to a thin line and turning to Kondo he nodded in final agreement. "You were purser aboard the Suez Maru and were present on the sinking of that ship on 29 November 1943. You witnessed the aftermath of the sinking, correct?" began the captain, Nukui nodded and the captain heard his reply through Kondo, "Yes I was, and I know what you would have me explain. I will write a statement of the facts of that day as I remember them." Captain Sylvester nodded his familiar request to Kondo, who repeated the English translation of Nukui's statement as he prepared it.

"I had boarded the Suez Maru as a purser around April 1942. In the afternoon of 25 November 1943, I heard from First-Mate Watanabe that patients with serious and also minor injuries were to be taken aboard. I was told about five hundred PoWs and two hundred Japanese soldiers and some civilian employees. Two aircraft were to be taken on board also. About 0900 hours on the 26th I went to the Intendance Department to make arrangements for procuring food for the embarking forces. This was quickly completed when I was told the PoWs did not need to be supplied with food as they were taking their own supplies on board and one week's supply would be provided for the Japanese. It was also the end of the month so it was necessary to pay wages to the crew so I also went to a bank to exchange some Japanese military currency. When I returned at about 1600 hours the aircraft had already been loaded onto the deck and troops were being put aboard. A medical officer in charge of the Japanese patients and a first lieutenant, who was in charge of the PoWs were discussing the assignment of compartments. Since it was considered unsanitary to accommodate all the PoWs in one place. Arrangements were made to place them in the third and fourth holds as a matter of convenience as these were provided with temporary galleys. The Japanese soldiers and civilians were to be placed in the first and second holds. The shifting was carried out and completed about 1700 hours. Since this was all many years ago, I don't remember how many persons exactly were on board or the time of departure but I remember it was about eighty crew, forty gun-crew members, fifteen lookouts, about five hundred PoWs and two hundred or so Japanese. We departed about 2000 hours that day, under the escort of Minesweeper W12, headed for Soerabaya. Later that evening I inspected the sleeping quarters of the Japanese patients and saw all was as it should be and that life jackets were supplied in sufficient numbers in the corner of each hold. After breakfast on the 27th, I advised the Chief Steward to supply adequate drinking water for the Japanese patients and in the evening that day I saw a PoW being given one or two doses of medicine from a medical officer and return to his quarters. When I heard the following day, the 28th, that a PoW had died I suspected it was the person who had received the medicine. When I went to hold three, I saw the body and the other PoWs, who all looked very sad. I saw the body being covered with a coarse cloth and some of the PoWs who were not sick carried him up and he was buried at sea at around 1000 hours." The captain interjected. "You believe only one PoW died en route, before the sinking?" "I said I only saw one PoW buried at sea, that was the day before the sinking." The captain raised a single sceptical eyebrow "Very well, continue," Nukui looked blankly from side to side trying to recall his place in his story. Finding his thread he continued writing, reading aloud as he wrote. "On the 29th November, after breakfast at about 0900 hours while we were cruising in the Flores Sea, I heard the cry, torpedo!" Nukui gesticulated suddenly, pointing out to an imaginary sea beyond the room, starling the captain and Kondo. "All right settle down, just continue without jumping about." "Sorry, well, I rushed out of the cabin, I had been chatting to the third mate in his cabin, and I ordered the Chief Steward to check immediately to see if everything was all right with the personnel and to prepare the galley crew to abandon ship. I then went to my cabin and gather important documents to put them in order. When I finally went to the captain's cabin with the documents in a bag, the order to abandon ship had apparently already been issued. On deck some persons were jumping overboard with life-rafts and boards, and lifeboats were being lowered by the crew members. Immediately I took out, with the captain, the ships funds from the captain's safe, and put them in my bag with the documents. I threw the bag into a lifeboat which was being lowered. The captain was calling out again and again, to rescue the patients in a serious condition. I ran back to my cabin to gather other important documents and began to burn them, then the ship listed rapidly and I dashed out of the cabin. I could not see any other crew or Japanese soldiers, but I saw about twenty PoWs frantically trying to abandon ship. In the distance were three crowded lifeboats, it looked as though several small and large rafts had been made up in the water and they were also crowded. The sea was littered with drifting debris and human beings as far as the eye could see, it was difficult to estimate just how many persons were in the water. Soon after I jumped overboard with a life jacket and swam out. I was so excited at the time that I was unaware of the people around me, and I was mindful of the safekeeping of the important documents and the ships funds. I saw many PoWs taking rest on life-boards. I rested for a while on a board and when I finally struggled to a boat I was so exhausted that I didn't recognise the face of the man who pulled me aboard. The boat was so crowded that it looked as if it would capsize at any moment. I was unconscious when I was rescued but I later found out that it was Kokussen who rescued me. I don't know how long I was unconscious for, but when I came to the minesweeper was about to begin rescue work. The boat was on the verge of sinking and many persons including three or four PoWs were clinging to the lifelines. When our boat finally approached the minesweeper the people who were holding the lifelines probably sensed danger and let go without being told. At that moment our boat collided with the minesweeper and capsized throwing everyone into the water. I regained consciousness at the shouting of 'Look out! Look out!' from the minesweeper and climbed immediately on top of the capsized boat. I was thrown a rope and was finally rescued by the minesweeper. Some crew members had of course been injured and they were crying in pain on the deck. I first saluted the busy minesweeper captain and took roll call. People were being rescued one after another. Our captain still remained to be rescued. The important documents and the ships funds could not be found as they apparently had been lost in the water when our lifeboat capsized. I thought about the future food supply for the crew. Losing the crew and passenger roster gave me more trouble than anything else. I thought it strange that the PoWs were not being rescued when the Japanese soldiers were, so I asked a man who looked like a petty officer what was going to happen to them. He replied that they were going to be rescued last. Boats gradually emptied as the rescue of the Japanese crew and soldiers neared completion. The PoWs boarded these boats and assembled nearby. There were some PoWs on life-rafts and boards. No doubt they were waiting with the idea that they would be rescued at the end. I believe there were about one hundred and fifty persons in the three boats, as each boat held about fifty men. There were about seventy or eighty persons on life-rafts and boards. I thought at that time that the remaining PoWs who had been in hold four had died instantly with the direct torpedo hit and had gone down with the ship. My estimate of our crew lost showed nine were missing. There were three patients in a serious condition and many other minor cases. While I was watching treatment being given to a patient in the dispensary, I heard a burst of machine-gun fire. I rushed out on deck thinking that we must be being attacked again. A lifeboat was already destroyed and there was a body in the water wearing a life jacket. There was another burst of machine-gun fire. The prisoners of war fell like insects in an infested place sprayed with boiling water. Some of them waved their hands and seemed to be saying something. I heard people moaning in pain when I returned to the dispensary. As a Japanese patient was carefully bandaged I heard more bursts of machine-gun fire, which did not stop for some time." The captain held up a hand, saying, "Did you not ask anyone what was happening and why? Did it not occur to you that this was not fighting, that this was murder?" Nukui looked to the captain, his eyes full of the terrible visions replaying in his head. "Yes, yes, I did. Such merciless action made me think that war was indeed horrible. Later, when they stopped firing I asked a seaman about it, he said they had all been shot and killed." The captain shook his head, "Very well, you may continue to tell me what happened then, and whether you were aware of a report being made?" Nukui nodded enthusiastically, "Well, then we resumed course for Java and I asked why the PoWs had been shot and was told something like 'Because there was an insufficient supply of food'. The minesweeper entered the port of Jakarta on the 1st December without further trouble. Daily necessities and shoes were issued to the crew and we went to quarters on two trucks. The injured went to hospital. On 2nd December the captain, the engineer officer and the chief mate went to HQ to obtain ships funds and to make a report. I went to the army hospital to visit patients and arranged clothing for the crew. I then went to Soerabaya to have those missing confirmed as killed in action after which I returned to Jakarta. Then I boarded the Midori Maru at the end of December and went to Singapore, and to Japan in January 1944. I swear by my conscience that I have told the truth concerning this matter and have added nothing and have concealed nothing." "All right then, wait here while your statement is typed then you can sign it with witnesses and then you can leave for now. Do you understand?" Nukui's eyes bulged with sadness and not for the first time the captain wondered for whom the sorrow was felt. "Yes, thank you," Nukui replied, returning to his bird-like posture perched on the chair, twitching to the window then the door at their receding backs as they departed.

Captain Sylvester walked purposefully along the corridor, Nukui's statement wafting in his hand. He found Officer Beirne, "I need this typing. I am questioning Saburo Maeda now, so when it's ready come for me and I will come back to witness the signatures, then he can leave..." Officer Beirne nodded and opened his mouth to speak but the captain continued "... also I don't want to question any more blasted second class deckhands for now. Get their details and I'll see them all next week. I have questioned enough low level crew, they saw what happened but few were involved or actually responsible, I need to question those higher up the command chain!" Officer Beirne responded, "Erm, well, we have Morimasu Kikuchi tomorrow, he was a fireman on the *Suez Maru*–," The captain rolled his eyes, exclaiming, "Exactly! Of *course* they need to give statements, in case they have other names or heard orders regarding the PoWs, but it's those *giving* the orders I want to see." Officer Beirne nodded and again attempted to speak but was cut short by the captain, "I want to see this Medical Officer Eto, has he been found yet? Also, is anyone looking for Yatsuka the gunnery officer? ... And what news on the PoW commander, Iketani? I need him found!" Officer Beirne paused, then replied, "Ahh well, we have Kikuchi, who I mentioned, as well as Ichiro Ehara, sorry, he was another fireman on the *Suez Maru*." The captain rolled his eyes again and opened his mouth to complain but Officer Beirne interjected quickly, "–but more importantly we have the minesweeper captain, one Osamu Kawano. He's been traced and being detained today, they will have him here later, or early tomorrow." The captain's eyes widened and he broke into taut grin "Well done! *That* is better news, –finally!" He sighed, turning to leave, but swung back to Officer Beirne "Don't forget about Iketani will you though, and Eto and Yatsuka and... well, yes, you have the list!" The captain limped gently away down the corridor stopping outside the interrogation room. Lifting his chin he pulled at his collar with two fingers, then tugged his shirt taut, nudged the knot of his tie between finger and thumb and entered the room.

Peering into the dim room Captain Sylvester saw Saburo Maeda's large frame slung in the chair like a squatting toad. He rounded him, noticing his expressionless features swallowed in plump cheeks. His lips puckered almost ready to kiss, except for the vacant eyes and blank stare. Maeda rolled his fat cheeks on the chair, straightening, and nodded politely to the captain. The captain opened his mouth to address Maeda but instead replied to a rap at the door, "Yes?" Kondo peeped sheepishly around the door, opening it fully and entering quietly on seeing the captain's flat expression. He flustered across to the far desk dropping papers and pencils, which he tried to pick up, only succeeding in dropping more papers. The captain rubbed his temple with his index finger, his eyebrows raised to his hairline, Kondo 'ahemed'. Maeda let out a chuckle, both the captain and Kondo turned to him and he abruptly stopped, his mouth returning to its puckered position. Kondo sat without further fuss, nodding to the captain apologetically, who returned to face Maeda. "These are the penalties for refusing to give information or for making false or misleading statements concerning a war crime..." The captain detailed the procedure. Kondo would translate Maeda's statement as he wrote. As Maeda began, his eyes shone with recollection. "I was on duty on 29 November,

when the ship was about to go down, I was eighteen
years old at that time. I was near the bridge when
the torpedoes hit at about 0900 hours. On the
bridge at that time were the first-mate,
quartermaster, the chief carpenter's mate and
myself. I was on watch at the port side. About 0920
hours the first-mate took a bearing and went into
the chart room. I was feeling bored and tried to
start talking to the chief carpenter's mate who
was watching the sea on the port side. His face
suddenly changed and he shouted in a loud voice
something that I did not understand, as he continued
to shout loudly and point to the sea I became
curious and looked over the side. I saw a white
foaming streak coming directly toward our ship as
the ship began to turn right. I was alarmed and
dashed to the steering station, and I saw the wheel
was turned hard to starboard, so I said 'No, no, to
the left!' I grabbed the wheel to turn it to port.
The quartermaster then grabbed the wheel and turned
it hard to port, but it was too late. Just then the
first-mate dashed out of the chartroom and blew
the whistle. The captain also came up the ladder on
the port side and looking at the torpedo he said,
'It missed us! It missed us!'. But not long after
the captain said that there was a tremendous
concussion and all the glass fittings on the bridge
were literally blown to pieces, leaving not even a
single one intact." The captain leant forward, speaking slowly,
"It doesn't matter about the fittings, did you see
the PoWs? Where were they at this time?" Maeda looked
back and forth between Kondo and the captain, his lower lip hung
open wetly, his eyes moistening, "Yes, yes, I saw there were
about six hundred Americans at the point where the
torpedo stuck the ship, in holds three and four."
"What makes you say they were American?" "Well, they

spoke like that, it sounded like American, but I suppose I don't know." "They were mainly British and some Dutch prisoners of war." The captain corrected. "Oh, I didn't know." "Very well, continue then." "Well, the ship was hit by two torpedoes I think, the poop deck was damaged at hold four. I dashed to get a life preserver which were kept between the third and fourth lifeboats, then I ran to my compartment in the bow, carrying my life preserver and got some cigarettes and photographs. When I returned to the deck lifeboats one and two were being lowered. Number three lifeboat hadn't yet been lowered. Lifeboat four was lost rescuing survivors of the Taian Maru when it was sunk by torpedoes. Also, we hadn't lowered lifeboat three because the sea had by now nearly reached it. I was watching the sea when the first-mate called to me to go with him to lower lifeboat three. So three of us went to the boat and lowered it. The first-mate told me to get in the boat and I asked him to get in first but he said he was not leaving, so I got in the boat. In five minutes, the lifeboat was filled to capacity by crew and Japanese soldiers so the chief engineer gave an order for all able-bodied men to leave the lifeboat, so I borrowed a life preserver as I must have left mine somewhere and jumped into the sea. There was a rope attached to the lifeboat so we tied this to a floating hatch cover and five or six of us clung to it. About three Americans, I mean PoWs swam to the hatch cover and also clung to it." The captain again interjected, "Were they the only PoWs you saw? Did you not see any aboard or leaving the ship?" "Well, it looked to me as we lowered the lifeboat that the torpedo had exploded in hold four. The cover and parts of the hatch were blown away. I did not see any PoWs alive in there, at that time. It seemed that they had all abandoned ship immediately after the ship had been hit by torpedo. Yes, the life preservers were all kept in hold four and all the PoWs had life preservers-" The captain held up a palm to halt Maeda, "-wait a moment, please clarify. If the PoWs in hold four did not survive, and the life preservers were also in hold four, how can surviving PoWs have been wearing life preservers?" The captain's eyebrows raised sceptically as he awaited a reply, he drummed the table in irritation. "Well, yes, because, well..." Maeda stammered, the captain stopped him with a wave, "I think you had better try that again." Maeda's face reddened, "I think perhaps the PoWs did not have life preservers. The crew and soldiers had the life preservers." Maeda looked at his hands, wringing in his lap. "That sounds more accurate, does it not?" replied the captain flatly. "Very well then, finish what you have to tell me and do not embellish." Maeda straightened in his chair, flustered, "Well, the minesweeper was circling at this time, stopping to rescue survivors. As one of the lifeboats approached the ship from the front it struck the stern and capsized, forcing those survivors to swim. I floated for about four hours, climbing to the hatch while the minesweeper rescued Japanese survivors, making sure to collect all Japanese. They even asked us if there were more. Once I was rescued I realised I was exhausted and fell asleep on the deck of the minesweeper. I think it was about an hour later I was startled by a sudden burst of gunfire. I jumped to my feet and saw that our ship was in the midst of the PoWs and was firing at them. This was the first time in my life that I ever witnessed the killing of human beings. I was nauseated and hid behind the depth charges on the deck, but I could hear the sound of gunfire for some time. I think it

was machine-guns and rifles. When the firing
stopped I came out of hiding and looked over to the
water, I don't think there was a single man alive
in the sea. Those PoWs that had life preservers
floated in them even after their death. Then the
minesweeper moved away and we picked up speed to
Jakarta, because there were magnetic mines in
Soerabaya harbour. I was unable to sleep because I
was on the open deck and there was a squall that
night, and in the morning I received a salted rice
ball. I don't know anything else about the PoWs or
the sinking." Maeda looked into his lap, his rounded shoulders
wrapped in on himself, a curled-up ball of a man, trying to hide again
against the depth charges. "All right, I will go over your
statement now, it will be typed then you will sign
it. You have some time until then to consider if
you should add anything." The captain pushed the chair away
with the back of his legs as he stood. He gathered his papers and turned
to leave, Kondo following silently. Maeda sat alone again, sweating in
the stifling room, his eyes mournfully watched a fly drift round the
ceiling as they closed the door behind them.

- 7 JULY 1949 -

The following day Captain Jack Sylvester opened the door of the
interrogation room with a clatter and stalked toward his chair, his brow
deeply furrowed. Morimasu Kikuchi jumped in alarm and attempted
to stand. Kikuchi stumbled, accidentally knocking over the table. A jug
of water and a glass went flying through the air accompanied by sheets
of blank paper which floated to the floor landing in the puddle of
spreading water. Kikuchi's mouth opened and closed and his eyebrows
waggled excitedly as he searched for an apology for the instant chaos and
mess he'd created. He was a rotund and scruffy figure, shirt unbuttoned
nearly to his navel, the buttons had popped because his stomach refused
to be contained. His face shone like a child's and his lopsided, somewhat

vacant expression indicated he possessed little malice and seemingly less intelligence. The captain lifted the table, holding up a palm to halt Kikuchi as he attempted to help, "It's all right, I will rearrange it. Please, just sit down won't you." Kikuchi looked puzzled and the captain, realising Kondo was again late, gestured to the chair Kikuchi had vacated, pointing in formal warning. "Ahhh," said Kikuchi as he ambled to the chair and sat with a thump. The captain righted the table as Kondo arrived. Kondo stopped in surprise, then stooped to help clear the wet papers from the floor. The captain and Kondo lifted either side of the table, returning it to the middle of the room. The captain gestured to Kikuchi to bring his chair up to the table. Kikuchi looked about blankly, a smile formed lopsidedly. The captain sighed. "Kondo, tell him to sit up to the table and we will begin, if everyone is finished that is." He was impatient to move on. After questioning Kikuchi, another fireman, Ehara was to be questioned. And most importantly to the captain, Minesweeper W12's captain, Kawano awaited him, having been brought in the previous evening. Captain Sylvester had decided to see Kawano last to give time for reflection. The captain sat, and taking several sheets of paper from the manila folder he made a neat pile in front of him. He offered a sheet to Kikuchi and absently tapping his pencil on the table he nodded to Kikuchi to read the statement on the consequences of making false statements. Kikuchi looked blankly from the sheet to Kondo and back to the captain. The captain raised his brow, realising Kikuchi could not read. He instructed Kondo to read the consequences to him. Kikuchi's eyes saddened, he looked from man to man as the captain spoke and Kondo continued, directing him to explain how he came to be on the *Suez Maru* when it sank in late November 1943. Kikuchi slowly realised why he had been summoned. His wet eyes began to visibly recall the events. He looked down, his fat bottom lip quivering. The captain made pencil notes as Kondo translated and Kikuchi began to stumble through his account. "I, I was on Ambon at the end of November 1943. And yes, I was on the Suez Maru, which was anchored at the port. An enemy plane attacked us on 25 November." Kikuchi's voice was deep and low, and the captain heard fear in it. "The day after we loaded one or two damaged planes and about two hundred and fifty patients and five hundred PoWs. We left for Soerabaya about 1600 hours. I was a fireman on duty on that ship. Ahh the attack was on the 29th, about 0920 hours, we were hit twice. I had just come up from the hatch, and was wearing only my loincloth, so I went back down to put on clothes. Then I jumped into the sea. There were some PoWs hanging onto a buoy. While I was swimming I made a raft from floating wood, trying it up with rope and I clung to it with some others. I think there were about twenty of us, the rest were widely scattered. I thought of getting into a lifeboat but it was filled with people so I stayed holding onto the raft. There were PoWs holding onto ropes and barrels. Then I saw some airplanes far in the distance, I was afraid they were enemy planes and was relieved when I was told they were friendly. I was rescued at about 1600 hours and was greatly relieved when I was given wine. They had called to us, for only Japanese to come aboard. Then I fell ill, I think with a sudden reoccurrence of malaria, because I was trembling and shaking and I fainted. When I heard the sound of firing from the deck of the minesweeper I went to look. I saw about ten bodies floating in the water and five or six in a boat. I heard people moaning all the time. Then the minesweeper proceeded to Jakarta and a squall continued for two days, and err we ahh, we arrived on the first of December."

The captain blinked at Kikuchi "Is that all? What about the PoWs? How many of them were in the sea? What about the firing? Who carried it out? What types of guns were used? How many were used? How long did it carry on for? Were you told about the shooting before it happened?" he asked, becoming more exasperated. Kikuchi blinked hard, "Well, in the sea with me were four

or five PoWs. They were on the raft with me, that I
had made. I think there were about one hundred and
fifty PoWs in the water when I was rescued. I don't
know who was firing, but I think they used machine-
guns and rifles. I don't know how many. But no, I
did not hear anything about the shooting before it
happened." Kikuchi looked to his wide hands fidgeting in his lap.
The captain opened his mouth to speak as Kikuchi looked up, his eyes
glassy and full of tears. He stared the captain directly in the eye and
blinking hard, his lip trembling with emotion, he blubberingly tried to
speak "When I looked... back to the raft after I was
rescued I saw two or three PoWs waving their hands...
When the firing stopped I saw those PoWs lying on
my raft. They raised their arms several times... I
think they had been shot." He paused, wiping his face with
the back of a large hand, before taking a quivering breath, "There
were no other survivors besides them. There were
bodies floating everywhere." Tears fell freely down Kikuchi's
round face as he sobbed. He smeared them across his cheeks again with
the back of his hand. He pulled in his bottom lip forming a trembling
rounded frown. His nose ran like a child's and he sniffed loudly. After
a moment he swallowed hard and looked up, staring pitifully at the
captain with big wet eyes, while his plump body continued to shudder
with emotion. The captain returned his stare, nodding sympathetically.
"Here is a boy in the wrong place at the wrong time." He muttered to
Kondo. "All right, that will do, you can sign the statement later on. I'll
arrange an escort for you to the canteen, you can have a drink and wash
your face and I'll come back in a while for your signature?" Kikuchi
nodded nervously his eyes filling again. He turned to Kondo, "Sir, I
can't write my name, I-I-I can't write at all." The captain looked up
from stacking his papers and nodded sympathetically. "That's all right,
you can leave a thumbprint in ink. All right?" "Yes sir, thank you,"
blubbered Kikuchi. The captain and Kondo stood to leave and Kikuchi
rose carefully to his feet, extending his hand. The captain was taken
aback but believed Kikuchi had nothing to hide and held no guilt. He
had merely witnessed the terrifying event. He took his hand, shook it

once and let go. Kikuchi sat alone quietly for a moment then holding his head in his hands he began to sob, like a child.

Captain Sylvester stood at the door of the next room along the corridor, giving instructions to the guard outside for Kikuchi's handling. A secretary passed and he called out to her, asking for water to be taken to Kikuchi. She nodded, and continued down the corridor. The captain paused at the door, taking a long breath before entering. He sat opposite the occupant of the room without looking at him, instead he scanned through his papers. When he looked up and across at Ichiro Ehara, he started. He was almost a twin to Kikuchi. He was thinner, but had the same baby-like eyes and childlike expression which caught the captain's sympathy momentarily. The captain blinked, and asked him to confirm his name, looking across to Kondo as he translated the question. Faltering, and clearing his throat of his first squeak, he replied, "M-my n-name is Ichiro Ehara, sir." The captain shook his head once and smiled briefly, "Well, all right, let us start. These are the penalties for giving a false statement. Now, I want to know what was your role aboard the Suez Maru, when it sank on 29 November 1943?" Ehara paused, looking baffled until the words translated into Japanese reached him. On hearing his own language he began his nervous reply. "I joined the Kuribayashi Merchant Ship Company Ltd in January 1943. In that July I was ordered to board the Suez Maru at Hiroshima as a fireman." "All right, what happened then?" Asked the captain briefly looking up from his notes. "Well, we left port and sailed in convoy to Formosa, then later we docked at Ambon. Whilst anchored at Ambon we were attacked by an aircraft. Then we began loading the ship, we took on board two aircraft fuselages and some aircraft parts, two to three hundred Japanese soldiers boarded and went into holds one and two, then five to six hundred what I thought were American soldiers came aboard. They looked physically very weak, and I realised they were PoWs. These PoWs were put into holds three and four.

We left Ambon the following day." Ehara paused, looking to the captain nervously, "It's all right, continue," "Well, I had just finished breakfast and was talking to someone in the galley when I heard someone shout 'Torpedo, torpedo!' I ran onto deck immediately. I was near the passageway to the officers cabins and saw the torpedoes approaching the ship on the port side. I was startled. The torpedo hit near holds three and four. I was stunned by the explosion and stood dazed for a while. When I came to my senses I rushed to get my life preserver from the galley and put it on. Everyone was throwing life-rafts into the sea and jumping overboard, so I also jumped. Then a life-raft floated by and I got on it and a soldier also got on. The ship began to sink gradually then it stood upright and sank completely. I drifted for some time, looking for my friends. I saw people occasionally, as well as boards and flotsam, drifting. It stretched over a few miles. Then the minesweeper arrived and lowered lifeboats. I thought we were to be rescued, but the first lifeboat capsized and was useless. I had head and leg injuries and I just waited, then a navy boat rescued me. I was put on the minesweeper at about 2pm. The crew quarters were filled with wounded and I was treated by a medical officer. I heard someone say that he wanted to rescue the PoWs, and only a short time later I heard the sound of rapid gun fire. I did not go to see, I was very tired and in pain and so I fell asleep. The day after, the minesweeper fired its heavy guns and I was startled. Someone said it was just a test firing. We docked at Batavia and I went to the hospital and my wounds were treated. I was in hospital for about a week. Then I went to Singapore and remained at the barracks. Eventually I returned to Japan on the Shinshu. I heard later that nearly all of the PoWs were killed, only two or three might have survived." Kondo finished the rough translation and offered the pages to the captain, who glanced at the text before sliding the last page to Ehara. The captain offered an ink pen, Ehara looked blankly at it, then held out his open palms. He opened his mouth to speak as the captain read his expression. "You can't write your name either can you? All right, you can make a thumbprint." The captain lifted a thumb, showing Ehara where he should dab the page. Ehara pressed his digit to an ink-pad then squashed his fat thumb onto the bottom of his statement, as the captain peeled the paper away. Ehara watched the result keenly. "I will come back later for you to sign a typed copy, but for now you may take a meal in the canteen. It's been a long day for you hasn't it? I'll arrange someone to take you, all right?" Ehara nodded at both Kondo and the captain, and thinking it was over he got to his feet. The captain put a hand on his shoulder, "No, wait here, someone will come for you." Ehara sat down, nodding at the captain in confusion. Kondo and the captain stepped out into the corridor, and the captain gave orders for Ehara to a guard. As they walked away down the corridor Kondo and the captain exchanged knowing glances. The captain had seen it before. Some suspects were simply observers, caught up in bigger events. In things they wished they had not witnessed. There was always the innocent hidden amongst the guilty.

The sky was threateningly overcast as Captain Sylvester dropped exhausted into his chair in his breathless office. He spread his hands over the manila folder. Scarcely a month before it was a single slip of paper, just one creased, folded letter. Now its fattening bulk strained the spine. He inspected a small tear which had begun at the top edge, fluffing the card and softening its sharp edges. His investigation had spread like a rash across his desk and up a large pin-board on the wall behind his desk. Just scraps of paper and notes, but like a spider slowly building a web, they were connected, the strings tightened and the suspects were drawn ever closer. He opened the manila folder and pressed it flat against the desk top, gently smoothing creases from the top page with the flat of his palm. Licking a thumb he turned the page over, scanning the neat typed copy and absently pulling a cigarette from a packet tucked in his shirt pocket. He balanced it in the corner of his mouth. Stroking his trouser pockets he searched for matches, and tapping a rectangular shape he found there he fished out a small box. He muttered the words from the page, making his unlit cigarette bob in his lips. He paused for a moment and his eyes widened, he shook his head briefly as he lit the match. The red bead burst into life in a flash but the captain did not move the flame to the cigarette. He continued reading, muttering to himself. He was lost. And so completely engrossed he didn't hear a rap at the door. He jolted as a louder knock shattered his concentration and the match burnt to his fingers. He dropped the match, shaking his singed fingers as he shouted, "Enter!" more irritably than he had meant to. Officer Beirne peered around the door, the captain's face uncrumpled and he motioned for him to enter and sit. The captain threw the charcoaled match into an ashtray as Officer Beirne looked round the room from pile to teetering pile of paperwork, trying to locate a chair in the chaos. Having not found a seat he elected to stand, but the captain did not notice. "What is it?" he asked, returning to his papers, the unlit cigarette still wobbling in the corner of his mouth. Officer Beirne spoke quickly, "It's Kawano, the minesweeper captain, he wants to speak with you." "Yes, I know who Kawano is, what does he want?" he asked not unkindly. "Of course sir, well, he didn't say. We have him in an interrogation room now." The captain stood. He looked at Officer Beirne and rubbed his temple, "Right, all right then. Prepare the papers for signatures from Kikuchi and Ehara and I'll go and hear what Kawano wants. Find Kondo won't you?" He bundled the papers back into the manila folder, tied a string about it and stalked from the room, scooping his cap from a tower of papers as he passed. "Right then," said Officer Beirne belatedly, following the captain at a trot. The captain couldn't imagine the questioning of Kawano would be finished quickly. "I think I had better keep him until tomorrow," he murmured to himself as he headed down to the last interrogation room along the corridor. There, waited Osamu Kawano, the captain of the minesweeper and by all accounts Captain Sylvester had received thus far, the man who had ordered the shooting of hundreds the *Suez Maru* PoWs. The captain's previous sympathies for Kikuchi and Ehara slid away as he grasped the door knob and prepared his opening question in his mind. "Osamu Kawano, you are to read the penal provisions which stipulate that any omissions, false or misleading statements concerning war crimes will be subject to prosecution and punishment, do you understand this?" The captain looked unflinchingly into the dark unblinking eyes of Kawano as he spread out his papers, making neat piles and passing the creased sheet of Japanese text to his suspect. His hand remained outstretched to receive the paper once it had been read. His jaw muscles flexed as he waited. He had expected Kawano to be taller, to have presence. As captain, as one who took command, someone who ordered an action that no one should have agreed with, but simply by his position they were obliged to comply, Captain Sylvester found him lacking. He was surprised by Kawano's smallness, his insignificant stature, his rotund stomach and receding hairline. Kawano was squat, as broad as he was short. But his rounded features displayed no hint of evil character within. He looked perfectly ordinary. His face though fattened, was worn and tired. His cheeks hung over his jawline like a bulldog and his reddened eyes sagged as if he hadn't slept well in a long time. He sat at the table with his chubby wrists lightly resting on the edge. The toes of his shoes only just touched the floor. The captain already had enough evidence to arrest Kawano based on the sworn statements of others, but he wanted to hear *his* statement before putting the formal charges to him. Interrogating Kawano the following day would give both time for reflection, and the captain knew he would get more from Kawano before revealing the extent of his own suspicions. Kawano's glassy eyes looked up from the sheet of Japanese. His face had hardly moved but the captain saw the inner monologue of denial forming within. "Well?" "Yes, of course," Kawano replied smoothly. "Very well, we will start with your statement," the captain announced formally as he pulled blank sheets from the manila folder. As usual he lay a pencil on top and pushed them across the table, offering Kawano take them. The captain returned to his notes, studying a sheet on top of one of the piles of papers, frowning as if unsure of dates and subject matter. 'Let Kawano think he has something of an advantage,' he thought. It was well-used tactic of his. It served as a facade, as if the captain didn't really know what he was doing, and wasn't fully aware of the facts. He acted as if he was simply asking a few un-researched questions, just a few wild stabs in the dark. Of course the captain knew each answer already, and knew of Kawano's guilty actions. But for his trial he would need to squeeze Kawano dry, draining him of every drop of memory of the events aboard the minesweeper that day. "All right, I want you to give me a statement about the events of 29 November 1943, when your ship, the er, the Minesweeper W12, was escorting a transport ship the, er..." he bent the corner of the page as if checking, "er... the Suez Maru, when it was torpedoed and sank. Everything you can remember about the event and anything else you recall. All right?" Kawano eyed the captain suspiciously, then shrugged. He sniffed loudly, wiping his pudgy nose with the back of his hand. "Of course, I remember the day well," he began offhandedly, pinching the pencil in his grubby fingers and licking the lead. The captain and Kondo exchanged glances. "Kondo here will translate, I'd like you to read aloud as you write." Kawano shrugged in acquiescence, looking at Kondo. "All right," he replied leaning over the paper, beginning to draw the complex lines and swirls of written Japanese. He began speaking and the captain nodded at Kondo to copy it down in English, as he grasped his pencil to take his own notes. "I ahh, think it was around November 1943 that I received orders to escort an army transport, the Suez Maru, from Ambon port. After we left Ambon I ordered the transport to sail close to shore and our ship kept a look out on the seaward side of the vessel. The night before the transport was torpedoed a look out crew member reported the presence of a surfaced submarine. We separated from the transport that night and our ship searched for the submarine, but we were unable to locate it. I worried about the transport as time passed and believing it was sailing the scheduled course we followed the route that night attempting to catch up with it. We overtook the Suez Maru the following morning. I also ordered the crew to keep a close look out while we headed to Batavia. I think it was around 0900 hours when I saw from the bridge a torpedo attack on the transport which then was sailing on the port side of our ship. I think three torpedoes were fired. I remember the Suez Maru immediately began to sink by the aft where it was hit, and the bow of the ship stood upright and sank. Thereupon our ship changed course and rushed towards the wake of the torpedoes and searched the area with an anti-submarine detector. Although we were not able to locate the submarine, depth charges were discharged anyway. As the search for the submarine continued the transport sank into the water and only men and other floating objects were seen on the surface. Time passed as we continued searching for the submarine. It began to rain and we were hit by a squall. Furthermore I realised that dusk was setting in." The captain nodded encouragingly, "I see, yes and what of the survivors, the men in the water?" "We had been ordered, ahh, by the army, to kill prisoners of war by shooting under such circumstances. I thought it would become difficult to search for personnel as evening drew near, so I had the Japanese personnel on the surface picked up by two lifeboats and one launch, while I continued to search for the submarine. In view of the ahh, the army orders and lack of accommodation board the rescue vessel I ordered my subordinate to kill the remaining un-rescued prisoners of war by shooting them." Irritated, Captain Sylvester shifted in his chair, breaking Kawano's train of thought causing him to look up. "Who gave you that order? Was it your superior?" the captain interjected flatly, trying to sound unmoved. "No, no it was an Army Officer. I think a First Lieutenant. He was the transport commander in transit. Ahh, the orders I mentioned just now, well, I meant it was a statement by this army officer. He said that in the army such extreme measures were taken in cases of emergency. But I had no such orders from the navy." "You didn't stop to think that what you were doing was committing a war crime? Didn't stop to question army orders, after all you weren't under their orders were you, and you hadn't been ordered by the navy had you?" Kawano mumbled... "Well, yes, I did hesitate for a moment, but confronted with this emergency I did agree with the army officer, and so I ordered my subordinates to carry it out. As I was in full charge, I did not discuss the matter with my subordinates. It was done solely on my own judgement." The captain said, "So you were responsible? Not the army? It was army orders wasn't it? Don't you think this transport commander bore some responsibility? After all it was he who gave you the order wasn't it?" Kawano shook his head adamantly, his rounded cheeks swaying, eyes closed. "No, no other person should be held responsible for it because I am solely responsible for the order." "Hmm," the captain exhaled, "please, continue."

"Well, as evening came and there was no one to be seen floating on the surface I abandoned the search. I then sent a report by wireless to my superior's office and left the scene of the disaster. The search for the submarine was not carried on any further on account of a shortage of fuel and the time of arrival in port. I also had to consider the distance to Batavia. The number of Japanese taken on board ship was estimated to be about two hundred, judging from the crowded conditions on deck where one could hardly walk around." Kawano snorted as if this amused him. The captain narrowed his eyes lifting his chin slightly. Kawano stopped short. The captain cleared his throat, "How many prisoners or war would you say you shot? How long did the shooting continue? What time did you leave the area?" he asked flatly, fixing Kawano with a stare. Kawano responded hesitantly, before regaining his confidence. "Ahhh, well the number of PoWs un-rescued and shot by my order was estimated to be from one hundred to one hundred and fifty. However this is only a rough estimate as I cannot remember the exact figures, I was at the wheel. We shot people in the water for about an hour, or two, commencing at around 1500 hours. We left the area at around 1700 hours as it was dark because of a squall. I am sure that there were no living persons in the water." Captain Sylvester finished noting down the last few words as they drifted across the room, translated by Kondo, and put his pencil down carefully. He gently placed his elbows on the table putting his hands together as if in prayer, touching his chin with his fingertips. He stared hard at Kawano. Kawano grinned back and nodded, then looked quizzically to Kondo and back to Captain Sylvester. The captain leant across the table and with flat palm slapped Kawano hard across his left cheek. Kawano's face wobbled slowly as he returned upright from his seated stagger. He bit his lip as he defiantly tried to meet the captain's gaze, eyes still arrogant and face flushing. The captain withdrew his hand quietly. He rested his hands on the table calmly but his eyes were full of fire. Kondo had paused half standing, his hands gripping the sides of his table. As the captain recoiled, Kondo sat, hardly blinking. Kawano had returned the captain's stare for a moment then could not. His eyes fell and he looked at his feet as he scraped the floor with his toes. The room was eerily silent as the echo of the slap seemed to reverberate for a long time, as if even the room was shocked. The muted ringing was broken by the captain's strong voice. "Osamu Kawano, do you have anything else to add?" he asked firmly. Kawano, his cheek reddening and his flabby jaw somewhat gritted, stared hard at the captain. When he spoke, his voice emerged as a squeak at first and he had to clear his throat. "Just that... ahem, just that, it was I, and

I alone who gave orders to carry out the butchery of human lives. I hereby state definitely that no other persons should be held responsible for the act. My mission was completed when the personnel disembarked on arrival at Batavia. I did make a report of this incident to Navy HQ, the 21 Base Force Headquarters. But, it was I alone. No one else." The captain rose quickly from his chair, pushing it back with a squeal of wooden leg on tile, "We will see in due course about that point." He strode to the door, peering outside and beckoning two guards. He indicated they should stand either side of Kawano then resumed his position opposite, standing in front of his own chair. Pulling his cap firmly on his head the captain addressed Kawano in a clear, measured tone. Kondo stood and repeated the captain's statement. "Osamu Kawano, you are under arrest for war crimes committed on 29 November 1943. Namely in the first, the murder of unarmed prisoners of war of not less than one hundred and fifty persons, possibly up to two hundred and eighty persons, to whom you had a duty to rescue and protect. Other charges regarding neglect, mistreatment, falsification of war records and concealment of a war crime will undoubtedly follow in due course. You do not have to say anything, anything you do say will be taken down and used in evidence. Do you understand?" Kawano opened his mouth then closed it, as the guards lifted him by the underarm. "Do you understand?" the captain insisted. Kawano's face flushed, his emotions changed from compliant and trite, as he imagined his future unfolding in a noose, and he screamed unintelligibly at the captain. Kondo did not translate immediately. The captain interjected, repeating. "Do you understand?" Kawano spat in English. "Yes." The captain nodded to the guards and Kawano was shuffled out of the room, wriggling like a fat worm on a hook.

Captain Sylvester paced down the corridor in the opposite direction to the receding Kawano still shouting and fruitlessly struggling. The captain spoke quietly with Officer Beirne who walked with him to his office. There, he arranged for Kawano to be held overnight at SCAP GHQ. He wanted to question him in more detail the following day. Kawano was then to be transferred to Sugamo prison, to await trial for up to two hundred and eighty war crimes. Officer Beirne followed the captain into his office. The captain rubbed his temples and spread his hands out on his desk. He breathed in deeply then asked about his requests. "We urgently need to trace the PoW transport commander, this Masaji Iketani. We must expand the search." He pressed that he was likely to be as complicit and guilty as Kawano. Officer Beirne nodded and left as the captain sat back in his chair. He took a cigarette from a crumpled packet on his desk, pushing it between his dry lips and began the long search for matches in the organised chaos of his desk.

- 8 JULY 1949 -

The captain jumped from his chair, reaching out to shake the hand of each of the three officers who had risen to their feet in his office. He thanked them, and they nodded agreeably to him. He continued to smile and nod gratefully as they each shook his hand in turn before turning as they left his office. Once alone the captain flopped into his chair, his eyebrows high on his forehead as he let out a long exhale. He allowed himself just a hint of relieved smile. A knock at his door cleared his smile away as he called out to enter. Officer Beirne looked round the door and the captain relaxed, waving for him to come in and sit. It had been an immeasurably long day already and it was not even noon. They had questioned two further civilian crew of the *Suez Maru* that morning. The accounts were almost identical and Officer Beirne had had the rough transitions typed, which he now proffered in his outstretched hand. The captain searched his desk for something while Officer Beirne waited, the papers in his hand wafting in the welcome breeze drifting through the open window. Captain Sylvester opened drawers, stuffed with lined notepaper and pencils by the dozen, he lifted corners of document piles and looked underneath, puzzled. He patted his shirt pockets then, staring hard at his desk he noticed a crumpled packet of cigarettes sitting directly in front of him. He seized the packet waving it towards the officer, a question on his lips. Officer Beirne looked on quizzically as the captain shook his head, "Never mind." He tapped the bottom of the packet expertly on the desk causing a crooked cigarette to half jump out of the packet. He drew the cigarette out with his lips enclosing it as he began a new search for matches. Officer Beirne, unable to watch another fruitless search, laid the papers on the desk and offered the captain a matchbook. He took it with a grateful incline of his head, lighting the end of his cigarette in a cloud of blue mist. He exhaled a long stream of smoke which curled and drifted to the ceiling to be caught in the wafts of the slow-moving ceiling fan. He turned back to officer Beirne, nodding at the translated papers in front of him. The captain studied the two sheets, one in each hand as his cigarette smoked to itself in an ashtray already filled with half-smoked cigarettes. Officer Beirne attempted a question, "Who were the three officers who left as I arrived?" "Hmm?" muttered the captain, engrossed, "Oh them? Well, yes, they were, well, let's just say I probably should not have walloped Kawano, but thankfully it'll go no further." He glanced over the papers to Officer Beirne and reddened. Officer Beirne knew the captain was not violent and certainly Kawano had deserved worse. He supposed he *would* get what he deserved, when he faced his trial. He would certainly be found guilty, the evidence was overwhelming. It was an open and shut case but it would still take the captain time to gather the rest of his suspects.

The captain returned to the papers in each hand, "So, Shinichi Minoda the second class engineer and Masasaburo Hirashima the first assistant engineer, were both civilian crew on the *Suez Maru*." The captain confirmed. Officer Beirne nodded, "Yes sir." The captain looked from page to page and frowned, "I suppose they would be similar. They're in the same place on the same ship. It's the same incident, and it does support the series of events we know already." The captain leant forward, placing the sheets side by side on his desk, reading from one then the other, outlining events of that day between them. "Well, Minoda says it was 20th November, at Ambon that they picked up Japanese soldiers and sick patients, and about four hundred PoWs. He says they sailed for Soerabaya on 23rd November changing course on the way. Hirashima says it was 26th November that about five to six hundred PoW and Japanese troops came aboard the *Suez Maru* at Ambon harbour. He says they sailed the same day. Minoda says was the morning of the third day, and that at about 0800 hours he had breakfast and went back to bed then he felt an odd jar. He went back to the mess and was told the ship had been torpedoed. He says there were a lot of people on deck and they said that the stern was blown away. The second torpedo was around hold four which opened a large hole in the hull of the ship. Hirashima says it was 0900 hours when a torpedo suddenly made a direct hit. He said he was shaken by the concussion and went to the engine room to see if anyone was hurt. He called down to see who was there, but there was no one. He said the engines had already stopped and he climbed back up to the deck. Minoda says he also rushed to the engine room, passing hold two, where people, obviously these Japanese soldiers, were putting on life jackets. Some had already jumped overboard wearing them. He said he was told by them that the ship could not remain afloat and so went to his quarters in the bow. After gathering personal items he went back to hold two for a life jacket. Then he heard the captain ordering them to abandon ship. Meanwhile Hirashima arrived on deck and also heard the captain give the abandon ship order. He said he saw members of the crew, Japanese troops and prisoners of war, all wearing life jackets and swimming across a wide area on the sea. By this time the aft deck was level with the sea, so he went to his quarters to get his life jacket. He says he passed the bridge when back on deck and actually saw the captain's face. He says the stern sank lower and he went to the bow of the ship. He said he picked up a piece of board from the deck, went down a rope ladder and jumped in the sea. He swam about fifty feet away and looked back to the ship, which sank from the stern. He says this all took place in twenty minutes or so. Minoda says that he had been told to get life buoys, and he jumped into the water with the Chief Engineer and about three others, near the rope ladder. He says they couldn't find the wooden and bamboo buoys once in the water and so they clung to floating objects. They were about thirty or forty feet from the ship, holds three and four were submerged and the ship sank quickly by the stern. He said he thought there were about three hundred Japanese and PoWs in the sea but later thought there were many more. He says they built rafts with boards and a hatch cover and the fifty or sixty men in his group all clung to or rode on top of it. He says there were five or six PoWs in this group. Hirashima also says they built rafts, gathering pieces of board that drifted by, tying them together with rope. He says he alternately lay on, and fell off the raft and drifted in the current. Then, the minesweeper came to his rescue. It first picked up sick and wounded. Those not injured continued to swim until the boat came. He was eventually lifted from the water and taken aboard the minesweeper. He said this was about 1600 hours. He looked at the sea and saw shadows of the PoWs clinging to life preservers and rafts. Minoda was rescued after drifting for four or five hours. He says the PoWs clung to floating boards, bamboo rafts, canvas floats and some wore life preservers. He remembers that he saw some rescuing others who were drowning. He thinks he was rescued after 1500 hours. He recalls PoWs still clinging to life-rafts, just as they had been, and the sailors said they would be rescued last. Hirashima says once aboard the minesweeper as he was cold and wet, he went down to the engine room where he dried his clothes. He said when he went back on deck he saw the PoWs on life-rafts being swept with fire from rifles and machine-guns. He doesn't remember how many were killed but maybe about one hundred and sixty PoWs, but he doesn't know. When Minoda went aboard the minesweeper he says there was suddenly the sound of machine-guns, so he went up on deck and saw some of the men from the boat that had rescued him and they said the PoWs were being shot. The PoWs had apparently been making preparations to endure a long period of drifting at sea, using the life-rafts they'd made. Some of the PoWs jumped into the sea when they saw what was happening and others had their hands folded together. He also thought about one hundred and fifty were shot. Hirashima finished by saying the minesweeper continued on its way and after about two days entered Batavia, about 1900 hours on 1st December. He says he thinks all the PoWs were killed, maybe two hundred who jumped from the *Suez Maru*. Minoda ended by saying he returned to Japan on 10 January 1944, and worked for a shipping company until the end of the war. He said whenever serving on government vessels he always got off before they sailed for foreign lands since witnessing that tragic scene. He says since the *Suez Maru*, he began to hate war." The captain let the papers drop from his hands to the desk and he looked to the window. Officer Beirne quietly got up. He walked across to the window and asked if the captain would like a cup of tea. He replied "Have we nothing stronger?" Officer Beirne smiled weakly, leaving to fetch tea. The captain looked back to the statements he'd read, now lying silent on his desk. His gaze moved beyond, to the ashtray, where his cigarette had burnt out. He had only drawn one breath.

Captain Sylvester replaced the teacup in its saucer, folded over the cover of the manila folder and tying thick string tightly around it, he tucked it under his arm. He pulled his cap down over his forehead and moved to the door. Kondo was leaning against the wall in the corridor and seeing the captain, he haphazardly gathered himself and ambled after him. Swinging open the door to the interrogation room, the captain paced to the far side of the table as Tamaki Shirakawa turned to watch him pass. He hardly blinked as the captain sat down, and the manila folder hit the table between them. "So, I have your amended statement, I have read it. Now I am going to ask you some questions." Shirakawa nodded nervously. The captain looked thoughtfully down his long set of typed questions, and the blank spaces underneath where he would write Shirakawa's replies. He spread papers on the desk and took a deep breath. Shirakawa startled even though he knew the captain was about to speak. He noted something had changed. Captain Sylvester's brows were knotted and his eyes flashed as he cleared his throat. "You are Tamaki Shirakawa, formerly master of the SS Suez Maru?" "Yes," Shirakawa sank. He realised the upper hand had left him, if he'd ever had it. "I am going to ask you some questions. You are not obliged to answer but anything you do say will be taken down and may be used in evidence." Shirakawa looked to Kondo and back to the captain. He opened his mouth to speak but the captain continued, "Did you witness the loading of the Suez Maru immediately prior to sailing?" Shirakawa looked uncertain but the firm tone and the captain's stern glare made him reply quickly. "Erm, no, I did not." The captain made a note and moved to the next question, fired as bullet fast. "Who was responsible for the supervision of the loading?" The captain demanded answers to his rounds of questions quickly, and Shirakawa fell into a rhythm of rapid reply. "Chief Mate Watanabe was responsible for loading. But negotiations regarding the type of cargo were carried out by the purser." "Before the loading commenced did you know the type of cargo that was to be loaded?" "I was informed the day before of the cargo." Kondo's eyes followed back and forth, as the questions, translations and responses flowed thick and fast in the air, "How were you informed?" "Ahh, I was informed verbally by Lieutenant Nishikawa, of the Shipping Command." "What did you learn of the type of cargo to be carried?" "I was then told by Nishikawa that Japanese servicemen, prisoners of war and damaged planes were to be carried as cargo." The captain asked the next question as Shirakawa's previous answer still rang in the air. "How many Japanese servicemen, prisoners of war and damaged planes were to be carried as cargo?" "About two hundred Japanese servicemen, about four to five hundred prisoners of war and two damaged planes." "Do you remember the actual numbers?" "I do not remember." "How surprising. Well, how many of the Japanese were sick or wounded?" "I do not remember the number." The captain rolled his eyes, "Well, approximately how many?" "I do not remember hearing the number." The captain thumped the desk, "Well, tell me were any PoWs wounded or sick?" "I heard later that some of them were wounded and sick." Shirakawa responded meekly. "Were you actually there? Were you the captain or not? You should know how many prisoners of war were casualties!" Shirakawa shuffled his feet, "Ah, I now remember that I did hear from Nishikawa that a number of casualties would be carried, but I am unable to remember whether he said all passengers, including PoWs or that only some of them were casualties. I am not sure but I believe the Purser, Joji Nukui, may have been with me at that time."

The captain noted the name and rank, Joji Nukui, purser. He nodded and moved on. "Do you remember whether Nishikawa mentioned stretcher cases among the casualties?" "I do not remember." "When you heard that sick and wounded were to be transported, did you ask why a hospital ship was not used?" "I did not ask or know the reason, but I supposed it was because of a shortage of ships, especially hospital ships." "Including personnel carried, did you take on any cargo in addition to the damaged planes?" "Yes," nodded Shirakawa. "What other cargo did you carry?" "I do not remember." The captain looked at Shirakawa incredulously. He spoke slowly, hands open palmed as he demanded a response. "You remember that additional cargo was carried but cannot remember what it was? Explain this?" The captain turned to Kondo, "We have an 'I don't remember' defence here!" Shirakawa looked from man to man. "I remember that a quantity of private goods was also carried, but it was not shown on the bill of loading." The captain nodded, glaring at Shirakawa. "What was the approximate tonnage of these goods?" He asked looking at his notes, "I did not hear the tonnage." "Have you any idea, was it more or less than a ton?" "Less than a ton." Responded Shirakawa quickly. "Less than a ton..." The captain repeated, briefly satisfied having finally received a reply, despite knowing it was probably untrue. "All right, in addition to two damaged aeroplanes what cargo was shown on the Bill of Loading?" "Only the two damaged aeroplanes were shown the Bill of Loading." The captain shook his head and changed tack. "Hmm, did you realise that by carrying sick and wounded on your ship that their lives were being risked unnecessarily?" Shirakawa looked uncertain, he wondered where this new line might take him. Warily he replied "Ahhh, yes." "Did you make any protest about carrying casualties?" "No." The captain raised a questioning eyebrow, "Wouldn't it have been possible to place red cross markings on the ship? To make arrangements to leave the aeroplanes to be carried by another vessel?" Shirakawa was matter of fact, "It was impossible to make arrangements to leave the planes behind." "Why?" "At that time the Suez Maru was the only ship available to transport goods between Ambon and Java," Shirakawa shrugged, but the captain pressed, "At the time did you realise the grave responsibilities you faced?" "Yes, I did realise." "Then why didn't you protest to the proper authorities?" "Because it was the army's order." The captain's patience thinned, he retorted in exasperation. "But you were the master, the captain of your ship! You could surely have made at least a token protest?" "I just complained." The captain seized the thread accidentally offered, staring hard at Shirakawa. "Ah! And, to whom did you complain?" "To Nishikawa." "I see, and what was the form of your complaint?" "I not only complained to Nishikawa, but to everybody but not in the form of a protest." "What did you say to Nishikawa?" "I said my ship had no special equipment to handle casualties, nor were there enough lifeboats." The captain narrowed his eyes, "What did you mean when you said, 'Everybody else'?" "I meant everybody else, the personnel of the shipping command, they were in the same room as Nishikawa." "Do you mean that after complaining to Nishikawa you approached individually everyone else in the Shipping Command and said to each of them what you previously said to Nishikawa?" "No, not in that meaning." The captain rolled his eyes and slapped the table. Shirakawa jumped. He expected the captain had meant the slap for him. "Explain yourself." A little stunned, Shirakawa stammered, "I-I-I mean I spoke in a loud voice, audible to everyone in the room, and repeated my complaint two or three times." "When you spoke to Nishikawa what did he reply? Quote as nearly as possible his exact words." The captain pointed a warning finger at Shirakawa. "I do not know whether Nishikawa replied to my complaint or not," "Did anyone in the office say anything or show any interest in your complaint?" "No one else said anything." The captain briefly re-read the notes he had jotted down, then returned to questioning, "You said, 'I do not know if Nishikawa replied to my complaint or not' That implies that he did reply, What do you mean?" "My phrase was a mistake, I meant no one said anything." The captain leant back against his chair and shifted papers about in the manila folder.

Shirakawa glanced to Kondo and back to the captain, who paused to take a long look at Shirakawa then launched into a new line of questions. "The Japanese passengers were quartered in holds one and two, while the prisoners of war were in holds three and four, is that correct?" "Yes," "In each hold was only one level used or more than one?" "Only one," "Did this apply to the four holds?" "Yes," "So, how many levels were in each hold?" "One," "What was the floor space of each hold?" "Approximate square footage of each was hold one, about 1,800 square feet, hold two was 2,000 square feet, hold three about 2,000 square feet and hold four was 1,600 square feet." "Were any special arrangements made for the comfort of the sick and wounded Japanese servicemen?" "No." "Were any special arrangements made for the comfort of the prisoner of war casualties?" "No, but I believe they had their own cook." "Did they? And where did the PoWs do their cooking?" "On the port side, upper deck." The captain paused for a moment. His eye followed down his long list of questions and notes as he ticked each off. Shirakawa was grateful for the moment break and reached for a glass of water as the captain began again. "Did you see any of the passengers taken aboard the ship at Ambon?" "No, I did not." "Did you ask about lavatory arrangements?" "No." "But, what arrangements were made?" "No special arrangements were made," "None? Then how could the PoWs relieve themselves?" "Lavatories were in the rear starboard upper deck." The captain frowned and made a note. He rubbed his chin and chose another tack. "Before the ship sailed, did you carry out an inspection of the vessel?" "No, I did not, I left the matter to the purser." "Between the time the ship left port and the time of her sinking, how many inspections of the vessel did you carry out?" "Not one, I left the matter to the Purser." "Do shipping regulations require the master to carry out personal inspections of the vessel under his command?" "It is required of the ship's master to check whether everything carried on board is kept in good workable order." The captain knew Shirakawa was avoiding answering and pressed again, his voice louder and harder, "Answer my question. Do Japanese shipping regulations require the master to carry out personal inspections?" Shirakawa was clearly rattled by the captain's dogged determination to discover such detail. He scratched at his nose, blinking at the floor before replying. "Ahh, I believe there are no regulations by which a ship's master is required to carry our personal inspections." The captain raised his eyebrows, "Really?" he said in a low voice. He stood and paced behind Shirakawa, papers in hand. "Did you learn either at the time of loading or later that a number of PoWs were taken on board on stretchers?" "No, I did not learn." "After leaving Ambon did you receive or request reports regarding the health and well-being of the passengers carried on board?" "I enquired whether anything was wrong." "How many times did you enquire?" "I do not recall." "Did you enquire daily?" "No, I do not remember, I believe I enquired or heard reports daily, but

I am not sure of this point." "Who did you enquire of, or receive reports from?" "The purser." "Do you remember that any complaints were received?" "No." The captain circled back to his chair and sat down again. He stared hard at Shirakawa for some moments before reluctantly peeling his eyes back to his papers. He knew Shirakawa was being evasive. He was reluctant and cagey, and whilst that would not stand as proof of guilt in court, the captain sensed Shirakawa had *much* more to do with the incident that he had revealed. The captain was determined to get to the core of Shirakawa's responsibility. He decided on a shock question, to measure the response from Shirakawa, demanding an immediate answer. "Did any passengers die between the time you left Ambon and just prior to the explosion?" Shirakawa's face remained fixed, he did not seem moved by the point. "Yes." "How many?" "Two men." "Who were they?" "Prisoners of war." "What did they die from?" "From sickness." The captain rolled his eyes, he was frustrated at having to pull each and every thread. "Obviously! What type of sickness?" "I do not remember." "Are you quite sure that only two people died prior to the time the vessel was struck by torpedoes?" "Yes."

The captain sighed inaudibly and moved onto his next round of questions. "Were PoWs permitted on deck during the day?" "Yes, upon requests made by the escort unit," "For what purpose were PoWs permitted on deck?" "For their health." The captain looked to Kondo and back to Shirakawa, clearly the irony was utterly lost on him. The captain repeated the words as a question, "For their health?" Shirakawa nodded, still unable to connect any problematic meaning to his answer. The captain shook his head slightly and moved on, "How many PoWs were permitted on deck at any one time?" "I do not remember," "Approximately how many?" "I was on the bridge and unable to see the deck." The captain bristled, "On the contrary, I believe the bridge would give you an almost uninterrupted view of the greater part of the upper decks, therefore you should know the approximate number of PoWs permitted on deck at any one time." The captain spoke evenly, his eyes narrowed as he awaited Shirakawa's response. "Most of the time there were between twenty and thirty PoWs on deck." The captain nodded, he knew the answer given was only to satisfy the question and not an accurate number. But, he knew Shirakawa could easily corner himself by doing so. "State the time between which the PoWs were permitted on deck each day." "About from 0700 hours until 1900 hours," "Was this the case on the day of the sinking?" "Yes, but I don't remember how many were on deck that day." "Of course you don't," the captain interjected "—no need to translate that Kondo."

The captain turned his question sheet over and drummed his pencil on the table, before selecting his next point. "To go back to the time of sailing from Ambon, what arrangements were made and what lifesaving devices existed to safeguard the lives of the crew and passengers in the event of the vessel sinking?" "I was unable to make any particular arrangements regarding the safety of the personnel on board. I gave orders that the crew members were to check all existing facilities." "State in detail what lifesaving devices were carried on board the ship at the time of sailing from Ambon." "Three lifeboats, about seven to eight hundred lifejackets, nine craft buoys, two were carried beside each hatch cover on the deck, and the other was reserved for the master and was carried on the upper bridge. Besides these, there were also about thirty to forty life-planks." The captain raised his eyebrows in surprise at the fullness of Shirakawa's answer. "What was the emergency capacity of each type of craft, lifeboats and buoys?" "Of the three lifeboats, two had a capacity of about sixty, the other about fifty. About twenty could cling to each craft buoy while only one man could be supported or two men cling to the round buoys. About four or five men could cling to each life-plank." The captain noted the details of each item, nodding in incredulity to hear such complete information for once. "Nothing wrong with *his* memory," he muttered to no one. "After leaving Ambon was any instruction given to passengers in lifeboat drill? "No." "Were passengers told where they were to assemble or what to do in the event of danger, or the vessel sinking?" "Yes." "What were they told to do?" "They were told to assemble on the poop deck or high position as soon as possible after a warning was given." "Were prisoners of war given that instruction?" "Yes." The captain raised a sceptical eyebrow. "How do you know?" "Because I instructed the medical officer and the purser to pass this information on to them," "Did you receive a report that this was carried out?" "Yes." "Who reported to you that your instructions had been carried out?" "The medical officer and the purser." The captain frowned. Shirakawa's answers were again becoming monotone, vague and evasive. He was answering but such that his answers sounded concocted. The captain's latest question was still ringing in the air as Shirakawa had repeated 'the medical officer and the purser' in a singsong voice, as if the captain had already answered his own question. Captain Sylvester was not deterred, it merely drove him on all the more. His experience had found evasion usually concealed at least some guilt and he was determined to expose it. He decided to present Shirakawa with a few hints that he knew more of the events of that day than he was saying. He planned to 'accidentally' offer the name of one of the crew. He hoped it would unsettle Shirakawa. Then he would unseat him with quick follow up questions. The captain wanted to know more about when the PoWs were locked in the holds as had been stated in the official report of the time. 'For reasons of security, the PoWs were kept in locked holds,' the captain re-read from the December 1943 statement in the manila folder. The captain looked to Shirakawa, watching him closely as he asked. "What was the name of your medical officer?" "I am unable to remember." Answered Shirakawa as quickly as he had heard the question. "Hmm, it was Probationary Medical Officer Kasuaki Eto, was it not?" Shirakawa's head snapped to the captain. He was certainly rattled and he clearly knew the name. Shirakawa's eyes betrayed recognition and the captain scribbled a note. In fact, it did not matter greatly if Shirakawa knew the name, the importance was that Shirakawa had been wrong-footed and the captain had also indicated to Shirakawa that he knew much more. The captain silently waited as Shirakawa stumbled to answer, finally spluttering. "I, I do not remember." The captain nodded mildly and moved on, "Were the hatches battened down at night?" Shirakawa was surprised by the sudden turn and stammered, "Ahh, no, no, but they were covered so as not to reveal any light." Shirakawa shifted in his seat, he rubbed his sweating hands on his knees and fidgeted in his lap nervously.

The captain looked back through his pages of notes and changed direction again, he wanted to finally get to the heart of the crime. What *was* Shirakawa's involvement in the PoWs' murders? He pierced Shirakawa with his eyes, "What was the time and date of the sinking of the Suez Maru?" "It was 0920 hours on 29 November 1943." "Immediately after the torpedoes struck the ship what did you do?" "I ordered Chief Mate Watanabe and Quartermaster Shimizu to investigate the damage and then report to me." Shirakawa watched the captain make a note. He wasn't able to decipher it, but it read 'Watanabe— chief mate, Shimizu— 1/4 master'. "At that time did you make any enquiry regarding the prisoners of war?" "No." "I see, and before abandoning ship did you make any enquiry of your subordinates regarding possible survivors who might still be on board?" "Yes, I did." "Of whom did you make enquires?" "Quartermaster Shimizu." The captain underlined the name in his notes and tapped his pencil on the desk, he asked, "Where is Shimizu now?" "He is dead." The captain bristled, having pursued a line of questioning he could not verify with a dead man. Exasperated but needing to complete the thread he asked, "What did you say to this Shimizu?" "I said search the whole ship for survivors and if any remain tell them to leave the ship immediately." "How long after the torpedoes struck did you give this order?" "About seventeen or eighteen minutes later." "By that time had most passengers and crew left the ship?" "Yes." "Then I take it that the only people left on the ship at that time with the exemption of your immediate subordinates, were wounded and dead – is that correct?" "Yes." The captain noted the reply, and asked, "Prior to giving the order to Shimizu to abandon the ship, had you given any instructions or orders for the removal of stretcher cases from the holds to the deck?" "I did not." "After the explosion and before leaving the ship, did you give any instructions or make enquiries of any of your subordinates regarding the fate of the prisoner of war in holds three and four?" "No, I did not." Shirakawa looked to the captain who grunted disapproval. The captain leant across the table, his hands braced either side as he shouted at Shirakawa, "You mean to say you did nothing at all for the PoWs trapped in the holds, and the sick and injured?" Shirakawa recoiled, spluttering. "Well, I-I-I did try to help the injured... ahh yes, yes I gave instructions to give priority to the sick and wounded, and I-I-I meant this to include the PoWs." The captain scoffed, and returned to his sheet, tracing a finger down the page to find his next point. He re-read the previous question and looked back to Shirakawa. "So, I take it that all prisoners who could, had already left the ship before you gave the order to Shimizu for them to leave?" "Yes." The captain looked sceptically at Shirakawa. "Then, the order you gave to Shimizu seems superfluous. Explain what you meant when you told him to search the ship for possible survivors and to tell them to leave the ship?" Shirakawa shook his head, his face flushed, "I do not think so." "You do not think your order was superfluous?" Shirakawa avoided the captain's eye, "Shimizu went to look, I did not know..." The captain frowned, "Very well, and on his return what did Shimizu report to you?" "He said, 'I searched the ship and am unable to find anyone'." "Did Shimizu report that any sick and wounded were left on board?" "No he didn't." "Did Shimizu include holds three and four in his search?" "I believe it was impossible for Shimizu to inspect holds three and four." "Why?" "Because both were already flooded." "At any time before the ship sank did you give any orders to make any enquires as to how many PoWs had been injured or killed in the explosion?" Shirakawa's face brightened. He was keen to divert the captain from his inaction and towards anything he might have done to help. "Oh, yes." "Oh? what did you do?" "I made enquiries regarding the number of possible casualties." "Of whom did you make these enquires?" "The chief mate and the purser," "What were the extent of your enquiries made to the purser and chief mate?" "I am unable to remember the exact words used-" he paused, and seeing the captain's expression he quickly elaborated, "-but I enquired to this effect, 'how many casualties among the passengers?' I do not remember clearly whether I mentioned PoWs." The captain raised a tired eyebrow. "Did you at any time following the explosions ascertain the number of casualties in holds three and four?" "No," "Why?" "It was impossible." "why?" "Because hold four flooded with water immediately following the explosions and the ship sank not long after that." "How long after the explosions did the ship sink?" "Twenty minutes." The captain leant back in his chair with a creak, and spoke slowly, "So, your order to Shimizu to tell the PoWs to abandon ship was after their holds were flooded and only a couple of minutes before the ship sank entirely?" Shirakawa looked to his feet as the captain waved a hand to Kondo to not bother recording the question, "That is a yes because it has already been stated. It was my observation only." The captain resumed, "When hold four was inspected for damage at first hit, why was no check made then of survivors?" "I forgot to order my subordinates to check the personnel as well." "Who checked hold three for damage?" "I ordered both Shimizu and Watanabe but did not specify the extent of the inspection. I do not know whether one or both inspected the hold." "Did you learn how many were killed in hold three?" "No, I didn't." "Were arrangements later made to remove casualties from hold three?" "I did not receive a report of casualties suffered by the occupants of hold three, nor of any arrangements to remove casualties from that hold."

The captain was beginning to feel tired and stuffy in the sweating room but could not pull at his shirt that clung to him like a damp rag. Shirakawa however tugged at his clothes where they stuck in wet patches. The captain neared the crux of his questioning – how much did Shirakawa *know* of the shooting and *what* did he witness. The captain pointed at Shirakawa with his pencil, "What was the greatest number of PoWs that you saw in the water at any one time after the sinking?" Shirakawa was wary as Kondo's translation drifted to him, calmly and evenly. "About One hundred and forty to fifty," "How many PoWs do you believe survived the sinking?" "ah, between about one hundred and forty and two hundred." "I believe that when the ship left Ambon she was carrying five-hundred and forty-eight prisoners of war. Based on your answers, about three-hundred and fifty prisoners of war must have been killed in the explosions. Do you believe that is correct?" "It is very difficult to give any sort of accurate number, partly because they were mixed up with the Japanese survivors." The captain stared hard at Shirakawa, "All right, what was the minimum number of PoWs who survived the sinking?" "The minimum was about one hundred and forty." The captain quickly wrote the number on his sheet, then without pausing asked, "How long after the sinking of the Suez Maru did Minesweeper W12 begin rescue operations?" Shirakawa felt the noose tightening about his neck and swatted at a fly there. "Ahh, I think about four and a half hours later." The captain glared at Shirakawa. "During the rescue operations did you see any prisoners of war pushed away from the rescue craft or struck in any way?" Shirakawa looked alarmed, "No." "Did your lifeboat hold the last of the Japanese to be rescued that day?" "No, it was the last of the lifeboats, but other Japanese had still to be rescued." "How many Japanese still remained to be rescued?" "About twenty or thirty." "Did you remain on the deck of the minesweeper until the last Japanese survivor was rescued?" "Yes." "Approximately how many PoWs did you then see in the water?" "between one hundred and forty and two hundred." "Are you quite sure that there were between one hundred and forty and two hundred PoWs in the water?" "Yes," "Did you then know that the master of the minesweeper did not intend to pick up the PoW survivors?" "Yes, I thought that none of the PoWs were to be rescued." "Why did you think that?" "Because I heard someone shout from the deck of the minesweeper that no PoWs were to be rescued." "Was that before or after you boarded the minesweeper?" "Before." "And after you boarded the minesweeper what did you do?" "After thanking the master of the minesweeper I checked the numbers rescued." "Then what did you do?" "I remained on deck watching the rescue of remaining Japanese survivors." "Where were you standing?" "Part of the time I was on the bridge and part of the time beside the funnel on the upper deck. I stood beside the funnel because I was shivering with cold." "Surely you would not shiver in a tropical climate?" "The water was very cold, but I may be mistaking the occasion." The captain's eyes widened, "You may have mistaken the occasion?" Shirakawa did not respond, and the captain pressed on. "Were you standing on the deck or the bridge when the last of the Japanese were rescued?" "I believe I was standing on the deck."

The captain inhaled a long, deep breath and plunged into his final line of questioning. "How long after the rescue of the last Japanese survivor did the massacre of the prisoners of war begin?" "About one hour later." "Are you quite sure it was as long as an hour later?" "Yes." "Did you take part in a conversation with master of the minesweeper regarding the murder of the prisoners of war?" "I am quite certain that I never heard, or ever participated in a conversation of this nature." The captain paused to inspect Shirakawa's face but he found himself uncertain whether the statement was truthful. Certainly Shirakawa was sweating and twitching like a guilty man, and his eyes were full of fear but the captain needed *proof* not an outright denial. He re-approached the final moments from a different angle. "Were you on deck when the machine-gunning of the PoWs commenced?" "Yes." The captain looked carefully at Shirakawa, eyebrows raised in surprise, "Why did you previously tell me that you were not on deck at that time?" "Because I was afraid if I told you the truth it would make a bad impression." "Were you not warned of the penalty of making false statements and advised to tell the truth?" "Yes." Shirakawa looked to the floor then up to the captain, "As master of the Suez Maru, were you not nominally responsible for the well-being and safety of each passenger carried on that ship, whether a Japanese national or a prisoner of war?" "Yes." "Then surely the master of the minesweeper conferred with you prior to the massacre?" "No, he did not!" Shirakawa exclaimed. "Why? He must surely have had to!" pushed the captain. Shirakawa was agitated. He sweated freely and his cheeks flushed in panic. "I have no idea what the master of the minesweeper thought. After the sinking of the Suez Maru everything came under the authority of the minesweepers master, except reporting of the sinking." The captain nodded thoughtfully as he paused to reassess his approach. "So, when you first went on board the minesweeper, did you protest or complain to the master of the minesweeper about his decision not to rescue the PoWs?" "No, I did not complain." "Why not?" "Because I thought such matters came solely under the authority of the navy. I could not have interfered with the navy." "When the massacre commenced, did you protest or complain to the master of the minesweeper?" "No, because I believed it was the master of the minesweepers affair." "Did you later complain of the murder of prisoners of war?" "No I did not." "Either at the time of the massacre or later did you question anyone or learn the reason for the action taken?" "No."

The captain made further notes on Shirakawa's answers. There was the possibility of charging Shirakawa with at least failing to protect, and of neglecting his duty of care to prisoners of war. He was also *at least* complicit in the act. Even if was impossible to prove direct shared responsibility. The captain considered his next questions and moved onto the actual act, asking, "What was the method used to kill the prisoners of war?" Shirakawa believed he had shown he did not order the act, and replied quite calmly, "Machine-gun fire." "How many machine-guns were used?" "One or two." "How many did you see and where were they located?" "I saw only two, one was located at the rear of the bridge on the port side of the bridge deck, and the other was also on the port side of the bridge, forward of the other." "Do you know whether other guns were used?" "No." "Was the master of the minesweeper on deck during the whole of the executions?" "He was on deck most of the time." "Where was he the rest of the time? Did he leave you in control of the situation when he left?" Shirakawa yelped in alarm, "No! He did not!" "Who was in charge when the master left the deck?" "Actually I now remember he was on deck during the whole of the time." The captain shook his head as he made note of the obvious lie. He believed Shirakawa had confirmed his guilt, his involvement, and it would be made clear at his trial. Changing answers instantly to avoid a line of questioning was as clear an indicator as one could ask for. "So, where were you standing?" "I was on the bridge." "Were you on the bridge during the whole of the massacre?" "Yes." "How long did the massacre last?" "Between one hour, and one and a half hours." "How many prisoners of war were killed during the massacre?" "Between one hundred and forty to fifty but it could have been as many as two hundred." "And what happened to the lifeboats after the Japanese survivors boarded the minesweeper?" "All lifeboats were cast adrift." "Did you see prisoners of war climb aboard the lifeboats?" "Yes." "How many PoWs did you see aboard each lifeboat?" "One was occupied by about fifty men and another by about thirty to forty men. I was unable to see the other lifeboat." "Where was the other lifeboat?" "I do not remember what became of the other lifeboat." "Were the remaining PoWs clinging to life-rafts and life-planks?" "Yes." "Approximately how many PoWs were clinging to each of the nine life-rafts?" "The numbers ranged from three or four to fifteen, but two or three were without PoWs clinging to them." "Were any PoWs floating in the sea supported by life jackets only?" "Yes, I remember seeing four or five swimming in the sea supported by only life jackets." "Prior to the sinking of the Suez Maru were prisoners of war issued with individual life jackets?" "No," "Where were the life jackets stored?" "In the holds with the PoWs." "Are you sure of that?"

"Ahhh, no, I am not sure.." Shirakawa trailed off. His eyes glazed as he looked anywhere but at the captain. The captain checked his notes and deciding he had completed his questioning for the time being, snapped Shirakawa back with a final demand, "So, you will sign a statement which will cover the points on which you have been questioned today?" "Yes, I will..." Shirakawa replied, looking pitiful and tired. He rubbed his eyes. The captain felt no sympathy. Undoubtedly Shirakawa was guilty of at least some part in the war crime. Perhaps he would be cleared of the actual acts of murder but he bore guilt and had plenty of blood on his hands. The captain addressed Shirakawa stiffly. "That is all for now, a statement will be made ready for you to sign. You may remain here for a moment. Someone will take you to a cell and bring you food. We will see what is to happen after that."

The captain returned to his office and hunched in his chair, writing and muttering to himself as Officer Beirne knocked and entered. He disturbed a column of grey smoke rising from an ashtray as he sat. He noticed the captain as usual had not smoked the cigarette. The ghost of its shape lay in perfect ash form along the edge of the ashtray like a sleeping Pompeiian, as the last of its smoke trailed eerily to the ceiling. "It's a serious business Beirne, a damn serious business. Each prisoner of war represents a murder, a single war crime. If Yoshio Kashiki is accurate in his figures that there were as many as two hundred and eighty PoWs shot and killed. That is two hundred and eighty life sentences for those responsible, and you know what that would mean. I must question them all and bring them all to trial." Officer Beirne nodded, "It was a horrible crime, sir, even by the war crimes we've seen. This really is a terrible case." The captain's face creased, his brow furrowed in sadness. The stress of the job lined his young face and his eyes reddened with exhaustion and emotion. Officer Beirne offered to fetch tea but the captain replied, "No, Kawano is being moved up from the cells now, I'm just finishing my questions." The captain made a note and stopped, tapping the pencil thoughtfully on the page. "You know, we still haven't heard anything about this Masaji Iketani, the PoW transport commander. It's clear to me that it's this Iketani who conferred with Kawano about the massacre and decided between them to do it. Oh, Shirakawa must have had a hand in it. I mean they were *his* passengers, they couldn't do it without at least consulting him. We need to arrest him too. And there's the gunnery crew who carried out the actual shooting. In fact, any survivor on board the Minesweeper W12, and her crew, who did not offer assistance to the PoWs is guilty in my view. That is, bloody all of them." The captain looked to the window angrily. Then his face relaxed and he sighed. "That said, I do appreciate some of the crew were just young fellas who had nothing to do with the PoWs. Those firemen who hardly came up on deck. They just jumped in the sea. They were horrified by the massacre. I don't think they hold any responsibility. But, this case is particularly difficult isn't it? Not only are there *no* PoW survivors to corroborate, but half the enemy witnesses are dead or missing, or untraceable! To make matters worse this was nearly two years before the war even ended. It's almost six damned years ago now, Beirne. those still alive are scattered all across the country, and beyond!" The captain shook his head, Officer Beirne nodded sympathetic agreement. He offered his consolation, "Yes it's a difficult case, but you already have one of the main suspects arrested. You *will* get the rest of them. I'm sure of it." The captain's face relaxed at the supportive words. He thumped the desk determinedly. He opened his mouth to speak again, but was interrupted by a knock. He nodded and turned instead to the door shouting in an angrier tone than he intended, "Yes, what is it?" A junior officer looked in, "Kawano is in a room and ready, erm, if you are, sir." "Yes, I am coming now." Captain Sylvester turned to Officer Beirne, pointing defiantly, "I *will* get the rest, but we need names from Kawano." He fixed his cap over his dark hair with a tug, collecting the thick manila folder under his arm. He smiled briefly, "Come on, I need you to find Kondo. Tell him hurry to the interrogation room!" he said, sweeping from his office.

The handcuffs were released from Kawano's wrists and he sauntered into the interrogation room. He looked small as he rubbed at the red marks left by the cuffs. Complaining bitterly to the guard that they had been too tight, he sat heavily in the nearest chair. He offered up a blushing wrist to the guard for inspection, who leaned forward raising a disinterested sarcastic eyebrow, then turned on his heel to take up sentry outside the door. Kawano was irritable and alone. He folded his arms obstinately as he waited, all bulging eyes and sneering mouth, until the door finally re-opened. The captain's face in contrast, was stern but calm as he sat opposite, pulling the chair under the table and motioning to Kondo who had followed him, to prepare. The captain slid the paper with Japanese text outlining the consequences of failing to offer the facts, across the table, and read the statement in English for Kondo to translate. "You must swear to tell the truth according to the dictates of your conscience, you shall conceal nothing nor will you add to the facts. Do you understand?" "Yes," spat Kawano bitterly after a pause. He faced the captain but his eyes were unfocussed. He hardly moved during the entire questioning. The captain recognised that a guilty man sat before him. "I am going to ask you some questions. You are not obliged to answer but anything you do say will be taken down and may be used in evidence. Do you understand?" The captain glanced to Kondo awaiting confirmation, and receiving a curt nod he returned to his questions and began. Kawano replied to each in rapid monotone. "You are Osamu Kawano, formerly master of the Minesweeper W12, is that so?" "Yes." "Besides the number W12 did your vessel have a name?" "No name." "What squadron or unit did your vessel belong to?" "21 Special Naval Base Unit." "Where was the H.Q. of that unit located at that time?" "Soerabaya." The clipped replies indicated to the captain that each piece of information would have to be prised out by painful individual probing. There would be no free flow, no spilling of information here. He pressed on, "Who was the commanding officer of 21 Special Naval Base Unit?" "I am unable to recall his name." The captain looked unimpressed. "Really? Well, was the commander at that time Rear Admiral Masatsuga Hoshino?" "I do not remember." The captain decided to change tack abruptly, to try and get things moving. The gritty detail could be dug out later. "After the torpedoes struck the Suez Maru did you send a wireless message to your H.Q. in Soerabaya?" "Yes." The captain sighed, rolling his eyes, "Yes? Well, how long

after?" "A few minutes after, it was sent in code."
"Code? I see, good, and what did you say in that
message?" "I sent a prepared code message which
the recipient would understand to mean that the
transport had been struck by enemy torpedoes."
Kawano emphasised the word enemy. The captain did not flinch, he
ignored the bait. "And did you receive any reply to that
message?" "No." "Did you inform your H.Q. by wireless
of your intended action?" "No, I did not."

"How many prisoners of war do you believe escaped
from the sinking Suez Maru?" The captain looked closely
at Kawano for even a flicker of remorse, but found none. "When I
left Ambon I did not know how many persons were
carried by the Suez Maru, and as I was at that time
a long way from the scene I am unable to estimate
the numbers." "Hmm," the captain tapped the pencil on the desk, in
subconscious irritation. "When you say you were a long way
off, how far do you mean?" "Approximately 1500 feet
distant from the Suez Maru." "About a quarter of a
mile?" "Yes." The captain turned over a sheet of his notes, reading
something on the back of the page, "Hmm yes... and when did
you first decide not to rescue any of the PoWs?"
"After I heard from the army officer." "And what
did you hear from the army officer?" "He said that
in the army when a transport carrying PoWs was
sunk and rescue was difficult, that they should
be shot." "What was the name of that army officer?"
"I do not know his name." "Do you not? Hmm, was
it Transport Commander Iketani?" "I do not know."
The captain saw recognition on Kawano's face. He was certain it was
Iketani who had passed the order to Kawano, but Iketani had not been
found, and could not yet confirm his suspicions. Nevertheless the
captain wanted to rattle Kawano with a name. "Where and when
did you speak with the army officer and learn of
the order permitting the execution of prisoners
of war?" "I was on the bridge of Minesweeper W12."

"Was this on the same day as the sinking of the Suez Maru?" "Yes." "Approximately how long after the rescue operations began was it that you spoke with this army officer?" "Immediately after the rescue commenced." "This was before the rescue of the master of the Suez Maru?" "I do not know when the master of the Suez Maru was rescued." "I understand he was in the last of the Suez Maru lifeboats. Was it before that time when you spoke with the army officer?" "I do not remember." "Had you ever seen a copy of the order to which the army officer referred?" "Never." The captain frowned and asked, almost sarcastically, "Was the navy at that time subject to army orders?" Kawano bristled, but remained motionless and unmoved. "From an operational point of view the navy did not follow the orders of the army, but in this case members of the army were concerned and had been rescued. So, I deferred to their opinions, and besides that the Suez Maru was an army transport." Captain Sylvester found himself incredulous at Kawano's version of events. That this naval captain would not discuss his plans with the captain of the lost ship, not even mention it, and deferred instead to a lieutenant seemed unbelievable, and tragic.

"Did you not raise the brutality and inhumanity of this decision to shoot the surviving prisoners of war?" "Yes. But for the army request I would have rescued them." Captain Sylvester's eyes widened. "So, there *was* room for them, then?" He shook his head at Kondo not to translate the thought, and continued. "Did you request the army officer's opinion, or did he make the suggestion that the PoW should be executed?" "I asked the army officer for his opinion." "Who else was present during your conversation with the army officer?" "No one else was in the vicinity." "Did you later verbally or in writing make a full report of your actions to your superiors regarding the method of disposal of the PoWs?" "I reported the matter orally but not in writing." "To whom did you make this report?" "The Batavia branch of the 21 Special Naval base Unit." "What is the name of the person to whom you reported?" "I am unable to remember." The captain frowned, "Was anyone with you at the time, or have you any means of proving such a report was made by you?" "No, excepting for signals sent from the ship to Batavia and Soerabaya." "Did the wireless messages sent by you refer only to the sinking or did they include a report on the method of disposal of the PoWs?" "Those messages included everything." "Tell me as nearly as you can now remember the wording of those messages." The captain leant forward in his chair, staring hard at Kawano, who replied, "I cannot recollect the full text of those messages." "Then tell me as much as you can remember." "The first wireless message was sent to 2 South Seas Expeditionary Fleet Headquarters in Ambon, 21 Special Naval base Unit Soerabaya and the Special Naval base Unit Celebes. It stated the location of the minesweeper and the time the Suez Maru was torpedoed. Some time after sending these messages aeroplanes flew over our location. They had come from Celebes. The message contained a report of the sinking of the Suez Maru. I forget what else it contained." "I shall ask you again, did you make any reference to the method of disposal of PoWs in either message?" "No."

Captain Sylvester rubbed his temple. His eyes scanned the long list of un-asked questions and he exhaled quietly. Such horror compounded by such arrogance and such a lack of remorse. He picked up his thread and continued. "My earlier question was, did you later verbally or in writing make a full report of your actions to your superiors regarding the method of disposal of the PoWs?" "I reported the full circumstances, but I am unable to remember the full context of this report." "So, was the report made verbally or in writing?" "Verbally." "Did you state the full reasons for the massacre of PoWs?" "Yes, I did." "... And what reasons did you give for the massacre?" "I said I had ordered their deaths on advice received from an army officer." The captain rolled his eyes. "We are going round in circles here," he muttered to himself. He moved onto the number of PoWs killed. "What do you estimate was the greatest number of PoWs you saw in the sea at any one time?" "About one hundred and fifty." "Could it have been greater than one hundred and fifty?" "I do not think there were more than one hundred and fifty." "Could it have been less than one hundred and fifty?" "Yes." "What was the minimum number?" "Not less than one hundred." "Do you know that the number of PoWs carried on the transport Suez Maru was five hundred and forty-eight, and according to your figures almost four hundred PoWs must have gone down with the ship?" "I believe that was possible." "Why?" "Because, I know that the PoWs were carried in the stern and that was where the vessel was hit by the torpedoes." The captain exhaled. It had been a long day and he was annoyed with Kawano's short, trite answers. Despite being tired he remained sharp and focused. He rolled his shoulders back and leant into his next attack. He wanted the truth, in full and in writing. Firing rapid questions at Kawano, he noted replies and fired the next. Without chance to pause Kawano might unwittingly tell the truth. "How long did the massacre last?" "One and a half hours." "What type of weapons were used to kill the prisoners?" "Machine-guns and rifles." "How many of each type were used?" "One machine-gun and about five rifles." "Who was in charge of the execution party?" "The gunnery officer." "What is his name?" "I am unable to remember his name. I gave the order to my second in command, an executive officer and he conveyed it to the gunnery officer." "What was the name of your executive officer?" "First

Lieutenant Daiso Yatsuka. At first he objected but nevertheless he obeyed my orders." "Before the execution commenced did you discuss the matter with the master of the Suez Maru?" "At that time I was not aware of his presence on board." "When did you first become aware of this presence on board your ship?" "It was much later, I think it was shortly after leaving for Batavia, when all the personnel aboard were checked." "Did the master of the Suez Maru or anyone else object or complain about the massacre either before, or after it took place?" "No." "Did you instruct Shirakawa, the master of the minesweeper, not to make any mention in his report of the sinking of the Suez Maru of disposal of the PoWs?" "I did not. I have nothing to do with the army or their reports." "Did you instruct anyone else at any time not to mention the massacre?" "Absolutely not!" "The former captain of the Suez Maru, Shirakawa has stated that you told him he was not to include anything about the massacre in his report of the sinking of the Suez Maru." "Shirakawa must be mistaken." The captain heard a hint of irritation in Kawano's voice and pressed. "Do you know Army Lieutenant Masaji Iketani?" "No, I have never heard of him." The captain shook his head, muttering to himself. 'Never heard of him? I should imagine he haunts you. You both signed the same fabricated report.' He frowned at Kondo indicating he should not translate, and composed himself before speaking again, "Iketani was, I believe the transport commander of the Suez Maru. You don't remember him?" "I do not remember him." "Well, I have here a copy of Iketani's report of the sinking of the Suez Maru here, in which he states that- 'After receiving two torpedoes in the stern in the vicinity of holds three and four, where the PoWs were kept, the ship sank in about four minutes. It seems that all PoWs went down with the ship.' This report suggests that no truthful account of the massacre was made. Did you arrange or know that such a report would be made?" "No." "You signed the report!" The captain waved a piece of paper in the air and Kawano looked away, shaking his head slightly. This was an open and shut case as far as the captain was concerned. He slapped the report onto the table and pressed for final details from Kawano. "Approximately how long after the last PoW had been killed did you set sail for Batavia?" "Between thirty minutes and an hour." "Did any prisoners of war remain alive when you left the scene?" "No surviving PoW were alive as far as I could ascertain." "What was the reason for remaining in the area after the killing of the last PoWs?" "In order to ascertain that all PoWs had been killed and at the same time I was still trying to locate the submarine." "Why did you wish to make quite sure that all prisoners of war had been killed? Was it an endeavour to cover up your crime?" "Of course." The captain shook his head and closed his eyes briefly. "All right, no further questions for now. Osamu Kawano, you are to be detained." The captain leant forward, checked his wristwatch and wrote in his manila folder, 'Interrogation terminated at 1845 hours'. He looked back to Kawano who was as expressionless as when they'd begun. He smirked slightly and leaned back in his chair, lifting his palms from the table and placing them in his lap. The captain looked away then quickly back as he noticed two disappearing damp handprints left by Kawano's palms on the table. They both saw the marks and knew they exposed Kawano's fear. They exchanged glances, the captain merely raised an eyebrow and Kawano knew the captain had outwitted him completely. The captain turned and asked Kondo to call the escort. The guard replaced Kawano's handcuffs and led him away. The captain watched his large frame in the doorway, expecting him to turn and speak but he shuffled from the room, without even a glance over his shoulder.

"It's clearly a watertight case on Kawano," he said to Officer Beirne who now walked alongside him to the captain's office. It was late on Friday evening and a long empty weekend loomed ahead. Monday would bring new suspects to question. The captain confirmed with

Officer Beirne as he sat, "It's the *Suez Maru's* Medical Officer, Eto on Monday isn't it?" "Yes sir," came the reply. "I want to hear his statement, compare it alongside Kawano's testimony. I think it will undoubtedly further implicate Kawano." Officer Beirne nodded kindly, his eyes full of sympathy for the burden of the case. The captain sat at his desk, lost in thought. Officer Beirne sat quietly for a moment, then offered to fetch tea and the captain nodded dully. When he returned the captain was asleep at his desk. The fat manila folder lay open and his nose was pressed into his inside elbow which rested on the untidy papers. A burning cigarette smoked quietly to itself in an ashtray.

- 11 July 1949 -

Monday morning dawned clear and fresh, but damp. The blossoms were long gone from the trees, but lingering petals swirled in soggy clumps around dirty puddles as Captain Sylvester arrived at SCAP GHQ, deep in distraction, he noticed neither the rain nor the blossoms. His young face was increasingly lined and his brow seemed to remain in permanent scowl. His skin felt taut as his body thinned. He rubbed his eyes as he left the bright sunlight of the street, moving into the darkened hallways and offices of the building. He nodded and helloed here and there as he made his way to his office, his limp increasingly prominent in the damp air as he reached for his door handle. He eased himself into his chair and rubbed his aching right thigh. His list of ailments grew with his time served with the 2nd Australian War Crimes Section and he longed for all the horror to be finished with. He glanced around at the sparsely furnished room, populated only by endless papers and documents covering dozens of previous investigations. None now more important to him than the case in hand. He wanted to go home, to Anne, but he wanted the job done first and done properly. He opened the wide drawer in the middle of his desk, and pushing papers and assorted stationery to one side he pulled a small silver framed photograph from the depths. He looked fondly at the picture and allowed himself a moment to close his eyes and think of her, of home and Moonee Ponds, Melbourne, where he grew up. He was such a long way from home. He sighed. Lost in his moment of home he did not hear the knock that preceded Officer Beirne's head peering around the door. Officer Beirne smiled as the captain started. He pushed the picture back into the depths of the drawer and coughed to cover his momentary embarrassment. "Hiramatsu has been brought in," said Officer Beirne, "Who?" replied the captain. "He was in charge of the Dock Operations at Ambon." "All right. Let's see him now, Medical Officer Eto has also been brought in today. I've much to ask him, so let's get Hiramatsu out of the way." The captain gathered the fat manila folder and stalked around the desk. Officer Beirne looked back to the desk wondering what the captain had pushed into his drawer.

Hiramatsu was a small man with a wide flat face, 'like a pancake' thought the captain as he sat opposite and addressed him, while Kondo translated. "I am Captain Sylvester of the Australian War Crimes Section, and this is Isao Kondo, interpreter." "Hello," replied Hiramatsu pleasantly. "I want to ask you about your time as commander, in charge of Dock Operations at Ambon, in November 1943." Hiramatsu nodded faintly. There was no concern on his face, and the captain pressed on. "Is your name Yoshio Hiramatsu?" "Yes." "And what work do you do now?" "I am Managing Director at the Nikon Boiler Manufacturing Company." "I see, and what do you remember, of your service history in 1943, and what do you know of the sinking of the Suez Maru?" Hiramatsu's expression remained unchanged. "Well, I was based at Ambon with the 2nd South Seas expeditionary fleet until the transfer of the fleet to Soerabaya. I was in charge of the docks operating area and had prior knowledge of the expected arrival and departure of all naval shipping. However, during the months of October, November and December my duties took me to Borneo, Celebes and Ambon. Also, I believe it was during the latter part of November that I was hospitalised ahh with dengue fever." The captain paused in his note taking and raised his eyebrows, turning to Kondo. "I see, and did you have anyone to deputise in your absence? If so, what were their names?" "Whenever I was absent, Commander Iwo Mimagawa, the S.O. Operations or Senior Staff Officer Tamura, took over all urgent matters." The captain felt this could be a waste of time, but pushed the subject anyway, to see if there were anything to explore. "And what did you know of the sinking of the Suez Maru?" "I did not hear of the sinking of the Suez Maru, either officially or unofficially. If anything was known of this incident then I believe Iwo Mimagawa and Tamura would know." The captain nodded. "Is there anything further you can add to this statement?" Hiramatsu looked blank, but somewhat innocent to the captain. He glanced to Kondo, eyebrows raised in perplexed question. The captain closed his folder. "That will do for now. Please wait here and I will return with a statement for you to sign."

The captain paced away down the corridor with Kondo, manila folder underarm and papers wafting in his hand, "I'm not sure that added anything to the investigation. I suppose I got two more names, who now need to be added to the never-ending list of damned un-traceables." Kondo nodded as the captain passed the papers to a secretary for typing. Behind them, Officer Beirne stopped with a shuffle of his boots at the door. He scanned the room and seeing the captain he spoke, "Kasuaki Eto, the medical officer on board the *Suez Maru* is ready," The captain nodded, "Thanks, I will be along in a few minutes." Officer Beirne turned to leave, as the captain spoke again. "I also have two more witnesses here who need tracing." He thumbed the manila folder bulging in his grip, pulling out a piece of paper and offering it to Officer Beirne. "One Iwo Mimagawa and somebody Tamura, I don't have a first name but they were both of 2nd South Seas Expeditionary Fleet, rank of Commander for Iwo Mimagawa, and Tamura was a senior staff officer." Officer Beirne studied the paper and nodded helpfully, before turning to leave. The captain finished arranging the typing of Hiramatsu's statement, and headed back down the corridor. He paused outside the interrogation room, nodding to the guard on duty there. It was a well-worn pattern, the captain needed to stop and put on his questioning face before entering.

Kasuaki Eto was stretched up on tiptoe at the small window, peering out, as the captain arrived. The captain stopped in surprise as he observed Eto, who sheepishly lowered himself onto his heels and stepped back, quietly mumbling. "He says he was just looking," offered Kondo in translation, as the captain moved slowly to the table. "Please," he said, a hand offering the empty chair to Eto, who meandered across the room awkwardly. His face was long for such a rotund figure, all high cheekbones and arched eyebrows. His body seemed almost spherical with protruding arms and legs. The captain watched him carefully. He remembered Eto had apparently been an athletic *Sumo* captain, now he filled the room with his bulk. Eto sat heavily as the captain began to speak. Kondo kept up the translation as Eto looked back and forth following Kondo's words and the captain's expression as if nervously watching a worrying tennis match. "I want you to write a statement regarding your time as Medical Officer aboard the Suez Maru, paying particular attention to your care of the PoWs, their condition and any assistance you gave. I want numbers of patients, numbers of PoWs you saw and I want to know every last detail from embarkation to the sinking of the ship and after." The captain turned to Kondo, "Does he understand?" Eto nodded energetically at Kondo, who pointed to the captain. Eto turned repeating his nod to the captain. "Very well. I want you to write it down, reading aloud as you go. Kondo here will translate. I shall be making notes and will question you later. Do you understand?" "Yes." "Very well, then proceed." Eto clasped his hands together, his eyes shining like little black sparks. He began as if he was telling an exciting story round a campfire. "Well, it was around the end of November that I received orders from Sasahara, Commander of the 40th Casualty Clearing Platoon to take about two hundred and fifty patients from the 15th Southern Army Hospital in Ambon to Soerabaya Hospital, with an escort of about twenty staff. I immediately began preparations. We understood from intelligence reports that the sea around Java was extremely dangerous so I made doubly sure we had enough equipment." "What equipment?" Asked the captain, "We had as many ropes, ladders, bamboo and life preservers as possible. Life preservers were attached to medical supplies, which were distributed throughout the ship. Patients were to be subject to escort personnel. Ambulatory and escort patients were mixed with stretcher patients to facilitate rescue. As probationary medical officer I travelled by truck to the port at Ambon. The ship was the freighter Suez Maru. The transport commander was not there when the patients arrived from the 3rd Southern Army Hospital. I was told the patients were to be in the forward part of the ship and went to inspect the hold. I then met the Transport Commander, who was First Lieutenant Iketani of the PoW camp. He said there were four to five hundred PoWs in the aft part of the ship." The captain held up a hand to interject, "Did you see the PoWs? What was their condition and what was their accommodation like?" "I recall that their hold was divided into two decks and used as passenger compartments. There were about twenty guards from the PoW Internment Camp, but I don't know if they were medical personnel. I told Commander Iketani to contact me on all medical problems, promising to do my utmost in such matters and then waited for departure." The captain frowned, "Please answer my question, what was the condition of the PoWs? Did you offer any medical assistance or treatment to them?" "I did. I directed the personnel of the PoW camp under First Lieutenant Iketani, to administer medical treatment to the PoWs. We used the PoW supplies first then shortages were supplemented by the Casualty Clearing Unit. I think there were about thirty stretcher patients and fifty escorted PoW patients. I went to their compartment five or six times to examine the PoW patients. I treated patients who suddenly developed temperatures or palpitations. Sudden illnesses were usually high fevers due to malaria, and expression of the chest due to a weakness of the heart from beriberi. I believe most of the PoW patients had tropical ulcers and external wounds. There were some severe cases of beriberi, and as a whole they appeared to be suffering from malnutrition. I don't remember if any died during the voyage, that is, before the disaster." The captain held up his hand again while finishing writing a note, and holding the pencil ready on the next line in his notebook, he asked without looking up, "And what of the food on board for the PoWs?" "Well, sustenance on the ship was not very good, I complained to the purser but he said nothing could be done." "Yes, yes, what of the PoWs' food?" "Food served to the PoWs was prepared and cooked separately and I heard that the PoWs were served better than the Japanese." The captain raised a sceptical eyebrow, and looked under his brow to Eto, "Did you witness the food served to the PoWs?" "No, I did not." The captain's eyebrows lowered, "Hmm, I am certain it was not better," he muttered. "All right, tell me now about the disaster, as you put it. What happened?" "Well, I saw with my own eyes that gruesome scene and heard with my own ears the agonising screams which I will never be able to forget." The Captain nodded, "Yes, I'm sure, tell me what happened as you remember it."

Eto's eyes dulled, his eagerness evaporated as his mouth dried. He tried to continue, but emitted only a hoarse squeak. He apologised and licking his lips he tried again. "When I heard the warning of enemy submarine I put life jackets onto the stretcher patients. I believe the same preparations were made in the PoW compartment under the direction of First Lieutenant Iketani. About 0900 hours we were hit.

I was treating a patient and the sudden explosion and concussion was so strong that I staggered and the tweezers in my hand flew into the air. I ordered the ambulatory patients to prepare to abandon ship. As they were getting ready I wondered if the ship was safe because no order had come to abandon ship. At that moment there was another explosion and a concussion which shook the ship. So, I went up to the bridge to see prisoner transport commander, First Lieutenant Iketani but I couldn't find him. The ship's captain and another First Lieutenant whose name I can't remember, were giving orders to abandon ship. People began to jump into the sea, and patients tried to help the stretcher cases. Both hits were in the PoW compartments. It was believed that most of them were killed instantly. The compartments quickly filled with water and I think most didn't have a chance to get out. It was a horrible scene and there were PoWs clinging to the sinking ship, some jumping and some swimming in the sea. In the fore-castle people were frantically helping each other and evacuating the ship and I rushed to the bridge but I saw the captain and medical officer had already abandoned ship. I came down and jumped overboard. I swam about two hundred and forty yards and was clinging to a piece of wood when I turned around and saw the ship stand up at a ninety-degree angle and sink as though she was being sucked into the sea. She sank about fifteen minutes after the first explosion." The captain stopped writing and lowered his eyes. No matter how many times he heard the terrible sinking described, it struck a blow to his heart anew. He felt the tragedy and loss, and it moved him deeply. "The pointless waste," he said to himself as he rubbed his temple.

He exhaled and picking up the pencil he looked back at Eto quizzically. "All right, let us continue. Can you tell me how many PoWs you saw in the water? And what happened next?" "Well, I think about three to four hundred PoWs went down with the ship because I think around one hundred and fifty to two hundred of them jumped to safety in the water." "Safety?!" exclaimed the captain. He stopped short and cleared his throat, "Ahem, continue." "Well, the transport commander, crew and patients as well as PoWs were all dispersed. I saw some PoWs on a raft. I called out to the crew and my men but we were so far apart they seemed like specks in between the waves and they couldn't hear me. I did manage to reach a few patients but I soon began to feel drowsy. Then something struck me." "So, how long was it before you were rescued and what did you hear of the PoWs' rescue?" "It was about four hours later, I was picked up with some of the patients. Once on board the minesweeper, I left an NCO to take roll call and went to help in sick bay. The casualties poured in steadily." The captain frowned, "So you did not see the PoWs in the water at all?" Eto shook his head, "Well, actually for a brief spell I went on deck to see how the surviving patients were doing and most looked relieved and happy but some were anxious and calling out for their friends in the water. So, I looked out at the water and saw about three hundred PoWs and Japanese still awaiting rescue. So, I went to look for the captain and the transport commander, but someone told me another patient had come into sick bay so I went back to sick bay to operate. While I was still treating patients I heard a noise from the deck that sounded like machine-gun or rifle fire. I thought it might be an air raid so I continued to operate. By the time I finished the operation and went up on deck the firing had finished. It must have gone on for about three hours. It was a ghastly scene. The

PoWs were shot with naval machine-guns and rifles by naval personnel, about seventeen of them. I saw about twenty PoWs shot, but there must have been many more prisoners killed." The captain stared hard, pointing his pencil at Eto, "Did you ask anyone the reason for such action?" "Yes, I asked one of the navy crew. He said they were carrying out orders." The captain shook his head. He found himself incredulous each time he heard it. "How many fatalities in total?" "I think there were ten of the ship's crew killed in the sinking, ten killed from the PoW Camp Guard and about-" "I meant how many PoWs do you estimate were shot?" "Yes, ahh sorry, I think about two hundred prisoners were killed." "I see, what happened then?" "Well, my hands were full with casualties on the voyage to Batavia. I saw the captain that evening and ate supper with him but we did not talk. I merely bowed. The survivors on deck were all talking about how shaken they were about the torpedoes and the sinking, and their friends who had died. But of course they also talked of the PoWs. They said that they sat up rigidly on their rafts with their chests out. Some prayed, others tried to hide under the lifeboats, they all died courageously. All of them had expressions of sadness." "Yes, ahem, I see." The captain was again moved. He cleared his throat and rubbed at his Adam's apple in order to continue. His chest was tightened equally by sadness as anger. "All right then. A few final questions. In your opinion do you believe there was sufficient space to rescue the PoWs? And do you believe there was enough food if they had been rescued?" The captain studied Eto's face intently. "Well, the deck of the minesweeper was filled with survivors, but if the PoWs had taken turns sitting, it would have been possible to rescue fifty to seventy persons at least. If they had been rescued, I believe they would not have starved because we had two meals the following day although they were meagre rations." The captain leaned back in his chair, his heart full of the tragedy. "All right, well, ahem, do you have anything to add?" "No, that is everything I remember of that day." "All right then, Kasuaki Eto, that is enough for now. Your statement will be typed and you will sign it shortly." The captain pulled himself to his feet holding the edges of the table. The burden of the case grew each day, with each statement and each new testimony. Eto passed his dozen pieces of paper across to the captain who slid them into the manila folder. Eto's writing was neat but angular. The spindly characters looked like hundreds of squashed spiders flattened as they ran across the page. The captain closed the manila folder and slipped it underarm and left the room. Kondo followed.

- 12 JULY 1949 -

Tuesday morning brought rain as the captain hurried, dripping and shaking an umbrella into the SCAP GHQ building lobby. His progress along the corridor to his office was punctuated with the usual salutes and his requests for strong tea. He asked Officer Beirne for a report on rounding up his 'wanted list'. He was given his correspondence, wads of envelopes, mostly opened and a few sagging files of documents. He gathered them all in the crook of one arm, pulling them close to his chest and pushing another wad under his other arm. He lopsidedly strode down the corridor as someone called out. He turned as a secretary waved an envelope. Laden with files and folders, she slid it atop his other post. He dropped the lot on his desk, carefully so as not to spill the mug of tea that had appeared. He opened the window letting in a welcome but soggy breeze. He had not slept well, his eyes bulged, reddening as he rubbed them with the heels of his palms. He ran his fingers through his dark hair as he eyed the pile of letters and files awaiting his attention. The forgotten last envelope he had been given caught his eye, sitting on the pile. He noticed a typed name and address on the reverse. He took a loud slurp of tea as he pulled the envelope toward him with his fingertips. Pulling out a wrinkled piece of paper he read a neatly typed letter from someone called Hide Kohno. 'Who the *hell* is *Hide Kohno*?' He said to himself scanning to the bottom of the letter. It was simply signed with that name. His eyes travelled back to the top of the page and he began reading. 'I apologise for bothering you with this but there is no other way.' Puzzled, the captain frowned as he read on.

On July 7th, all of a sudden, my elder brother Osamu Kawano, who had been living a peaceful life in the his country town, so very calmly and peacefully as a prefectural government official, was called up to the Legal Section of GHQ, SCAP, and after a brief inquiry was sent to Sugamo Prison the next day.

I understand he might have been concerned with a case indefensible, and I suppose in that he should assume his responsibility. But I believe that a war crime in the sense of the term involves anti-humanism, and in that case I believe I can advocate for my elder brother who seems to have been a humanitarian in his daily life.

I would like to plead for my elder brother and explain his character, personality, disposition, feeling and faith and career and so forth. I hope you can allow me to be a Special Pleader in any war criminal tribunal, with your special consideration.

Sincerely yours,
Hide Kohno.

The captain tossed the letter onto his desk in disgust. His eyes widened in disbelief. He shook his head and opened his mouth to swear at no one but was stopped by a knock at the door. Officer Beirne entered and seeing the captain's creased and furrowed brow raised his eyebrows in question. The captain did not answer, responding only with a low grumble and a dart of his eyes to the discarded letter. Officer Beirne passed the captain a folded slip of paper, and with just a glimmer of a smile he backed out of the room. The captain took the paper Officer Beirne had left, his eyes zipping back and forth across the words like a typewriter in overdrive. Quickly he jumped up, almost knocking over his piles of letters and the cooling tea. He thumped his fist on the desk as he moved round it, dropping the note he dashed from the room. The door slammed behind him as the note fluttered to the desk, landing amongst the unopened correspondence scattered there. It read,

```
--RESTRICTED--
Traced 1st Lt Masaji Iketani.
Suez Maru PoW Transport Commander.
Changed name to Masaji Koshio.
Estimate arrival at SCAP GHQ- 14 July.
```

- 13 JULY 1949 -

The following day the captain paced his office, as a secretary typed questions he dictated. The office had been largely cleared of visible paperwork as she had filed and organised the room. Only documents pertaining to the *Suez Maru* case remained, which spread haphazardly across his desk. He spoke in almost a whisper. "After these notes for Iketani are copied, I want to start the Case Summary Report. The prima facie, ready for trial." She paused, stopping the clickety-clack of the typewriter to nod in acknowledgement. "All right then, there are no more questions needed for tomorrow. Please make up a second copy." She pulled the sheet from the typewriter and placed it unturned on a stack, then turned the whole pile over. "It will be a long interrogation tomorrow," she said looking at the thick wad. "Yes, yes it will." He replied distractedly, then he looked up. "There's a lot to get through, and a lot to answer for." She rose to a knock at the door and nodded to take her leave. Officer Beirne held the door to let her pass. He placed a cup of tea on his desk and nodded to the captain, "Takeshi Fujimoto is in an interrogation room and ready, sir."

Takeshi Fujimoto paced the interrogation room agitatedly. He wrung his sweating hands behind his back and immediately began speaking as the captain arrived. The captain listened for a moment then held up a hand, quietening Fujimoto. The captain stared, taking Fujimoto in as he moved around the room to stand opposite. He placed the tea he'd brought on the table, and lay the manila folder next to it. Calmly looking through his notes he glanced at Fujimoto from time to time, making him shift in his seat nervously. The captain wasn't trying to sweat a statement from him. He was in fact waiting again, for Kondo. Fujimoto was a tall man but somewhat stooped and rounded shouldered, with hangdog expression. His eyelids drooped sleepily and his fat bottom lip formed a pout. The captain began to get up to look for Kondo as the door opened and he bustled in. He dashed across to the small table and sat panting, trying to quieten his breathing and failing completely. He glanced to the captain and grimaced an apology. Captain Sylvester said nothing, but turned slowly back to Takeshi Fujimoto. "You are Takeshi Fujimoto, former Boiler Officer on Minesweeper W12, which escorted the Suez Maru in late November 1943?" Fujimoto looked to Kondo, "Ummm, yes," he said, his eyes wide. He instantly knew what this was about. He knew all too well. He had almost been waiting for someone to ask him about it for six long years. Fujimoto sat quietly, his face twitching as he heard the gunfire erupt as clearly in his ears as it had that day. He blinked hard and listened to the captain. "I want you to write a statement regarding everything you remember from the time of sailing from Ambon to the sinking of the Suez Maru and everything afterwards. Do you understand?" "Yes," Fujimoto began drawing Japanese script in neat lines down the page as Kondo translated to the captain. "I was a member of the crew of Minesweeper W12 in late November as we escorted the Suez Maru from Ambon to Soerabaya. I was serving in the dual capacity of boiler officer and second assistant division officer. The first two days went by without incident but at about

2100 or 2200 hours on the night of the second day a submarine appeared. Orders were issued to man the battle stations and a few moments later depth charges were dropped. The rest of the night passed quietly. The next day I was on duty from 0800 hours to noon in the engine room. Just after 0900 hours I went above to the upper deck. Steam had begun to leak from a pipe in number one boiler room the night before and a petty officer was repairing it. I went to see how the repairs were coming along, it was just finished as I came up on deck. We stayed there talking for about ten minutes. At about 0930 hours, there were two successive explosions aft and as I was on duty I rushed towards the engine room. Someone said the Suez Maru had been hit and looking at her I saw that she was sinking with her bow at about a 45° angle. This was only two or three minutes after the explosions. I heard the order to man battle stations and hurried into the engine room. At about 1000 hours I went to the upper deck to take a look at things." The captain nodded and Fujimoto licked his lips and continued. "The minesweeper was then making a large circle around the scene of the sinking. The surface of the sea was covered with pieces of wood, boards, boats etcetera, and with Japanese and PoWs shouting for help. Some Japanese were crying. Since I was on duty I went back down to the engine room. About 1010 hours we slowed and I went back to the upper deck and saw that two cutters had been put over the side and were picking up survivors. They were commanded by petty officers. Around 1130 hours I was relieved from my post and went to the top deck where I saw about one hundred persons being saved. Others were still in the water calling for help and clinging to bits of wood or boats from the Suez Maru. There

must have been about two hundred Japanese and two
to three hundred PoW holding onto planks and pieces
of wood. I then went to my cabin to rest. About
1500 hours I heard a commotion on deck and went up
to investigate. The deck was so full of survivors
that one could hardly find room to walk. They were
all Japanese." Fujimoto squirmed in the chair, his face grimacing.
He ran a hand through his lank hair with a bony hand. He clearly
saw himself on deck again. Pointing here and there he described the
unfolding events, cupping his hands over his ears as he spoke to shield
himself from the awful sounds. "About two minutes after my
arrival I heard the sound of rifles and machine-
gun fire from somewhere overhead and forward. I
moved to a spot over the boiler room on the upper
deck and looking down to where a PoW was clinging
to a life preserver, I saw blood spurt from the
back of his head as he was shot from close by. I
was profoundly shocked and hurried at once to my
cabin to regain my poise. I had never before seen
a man killed, even in combat. Around 1600 hours I
could still hear sporadic firing. Making my way
gingerly back to the top deck I heard the rescued
Japanese who were rather excited say, 'Shoot every
PoW in sight!' I saw about two hundred men dead in
the water and returned to my cabin. I could still
hear the sound of guns firing. It stopped about
1630 hours and I went back to the top deck. I saw
about two hundred to two hundred and fifty bodies
floating. I could not see any survivors. Our ship
began to move gradually away from the scene. In the
ward room later, I ate with a first lieutenant. He
was the transport commander and was saying that
there had only been about three hundred PoW aboard
the Suez Maru." Fujimoto let his head fall between his shoulders,
as he sniffed loudly. The captain paused, then spoke softly, urging him
to continue. Fujimoto looked around the floor as if he were standing

on deck and scanning the terrible scene on the sea. He brushed his eyes with the back of his hand and spoke again, his voice creaking. "We headed for Soerabaya but changed course and went to Batavia as magnetic mines had been dropped in Soerabaya harbour. We were short of fuel so were worried whether we would get to Batavia." The captain leant forward rubbing the usual pain in his temple, "And do you believe the minesweeper was full to capacity. Would there have been room for PoWs to be rescued?" Fujimoto blinked. "Well, the top deck was full of survivors, we had to step on them as we went about our duties. But if everyone had stood there would have been room for many more. Perhaps a hundred or more as well in the crew quarters and cabins. But I don't know how this would have affected the ships stability." "Yes, hmm. Well, then you clearly did arrive at Batavia." "Yes we arrived with about five tons of fuel to spare." Fujimoto finished with visible relief, as the captain shook his head wearily. "All right, well now, do you now swear by your conscience that this statement is the truth, the whole truth and nothing but the truth?" "Yes, I do." "Very well then. Add that affirmation to the end of your statement. You will wait here while it is prepared and then you will sign it with witnesses. Do you understand?" "Yes." Fujimoto's face slackened, as if he had spent his long welled up burden. Now emptied, he listlessly flopped in the chair as the captain and Kondo began to leave. Fujimoto turned and glanced to the window as it began to rain, slapping and pattering the glass pitifully, as the sky turned a dark gunmetal grey.

- 14 JULY 1949 -

Masaru Kai awaited the captain in one of the small interrogation rooms as each suspect before had done, with sweating palms, shuffling of feet and unconscious twitching of the face. Kai was no different as Captain Sylvester arrived with Kondo on his heel. As he looked Kai over, the captain thought him a mature man, his saddened eyes were capped by tufted eyebrows, peppered grey. He was well dressed, fit and healthy looking, despite greying at his temples. His palms lay open in his lap and although he looked with concern at the captain, he did not have the unashamed look of the guilty. The captain had previously been caught off guard, so decided to start with a gentle tone. "You are Masaru Kai, formerly a lieutenant and chief engineer aboard the Minesweeper W12? You were aboard when it escorted the Suez Maru, when that ship was torpedoed and sank, on 29 November 1943?" Recognition and equally, relief flooded Kai's face. He nodded, his face creasing with sorrow. "Yes, yes I was," he almost sobbed. The captain, puzzled, asked, "Why are you upset?" Kai replied emphatically. "It was a terrible event, it has saddened me more than anything else I saw during that war. You can ask me anything about it. I will tell you what I remember." "Well," started the captain, "First, I want you to outline your time as crew aboard and go into as much detail as you can about the transport of the PoWs, their treatment and the sinking of the ship Suez Maru, and then give me the names of any crew, navy and army personnel you can recall." "Of course. Yes, I will try."

The captain passed blank papers to Kai, explaining through Kondo that he was to write his statement, and that Kondo would translate. Kai began confidently at first. "I was assigned to the Minesweeper W12 and boarded in late October 1942. ⸰I was Warrant Officer then, and I took charge of supplies aboard ship. On the dates you refer to, er, in late November 1943, we docked at Ambon harbour, as an escort to an army transport, Suez Maru. Fuel and fresh water were put aboard and we sailed late on 25 November. Later, I heard that the Suez Maru had on board army personnel and prisoners of war, but I don't know how many. We kept a lookout for airplanes and submarines, sometimes preceding the Suez Maru, sometimes following. We kept close to islands to cover us from submarine attacks and discovery from the air. We kept a constant lookout, using radar and sound locators. When I looked to the Suez Maru deck I saw it was full of persons who were cooling off, but I couldn't tell from that distance if they were PoWs or army. Black smoke was constantly issuing from the funnel of the Suez Maru as it sailed and I felt apprehensive each time I saw it as it would easily be detected by airplanes or submarines. Nothing happened for two days then at about 2300 hours there was a squall. The sky was very dark and lightning flashed. During one of these lightning flashes we observed a submarine about thirty degrees on the port side, about 3,000 feet away. We commenced battle stations. The Suez Maru proceeded ahead while we turned to attack the submarine. It had submerged by time we arrived at the spot. It was said that it couldn't be located and they turned on the searchlights. I thought the situation at this time was very dangerous. We had been discovered and were being followed by a submarine and so I felt very uneasy. I think the submarine was on its way to intercept us when we sighted it. We searched or it for about two hours then headed back to the Suez Maru, when we couldn't locate it. I remember that the attack occurred at about 0900 hours the following morning. I was on the rear deck when I heard the call to battle stations and the emergency bell ringing from the bridge. Then, there was an impact to the ship. I looked to the Suez Maru and it had been hit by a torpedo. The rear half could not be seen due to spray and smoke from the explosion. When the smoke cleared it seemed the rear part of the ship was broken and the ship was listing quite badly, with the bow pointing upwards. When I last saw the Suez Maru it seemed to me that the stern of the ship was torn and missing where it had been hit and there was a considerable list to the stern. The red portion of the bow below the waterline was visible. I think this was about one minute after the torpedo hit the ship. The upper deck was crowded and I saw people jumping into the water. I then went to take up my battle station in the engine room. We were ordered to increase speed to sixteen knots and attack the submarine. We launched a depth charge attack five or six minutes after the Suez Maru was hit and we dropped a series of five or six of them. We moved around, speeding up and slowing, and listening with echo ranging for about two hours before we were ordered to commence rescue operations. We cut the engines and lowered cutters from the deck. I heard about the use of the rescue cutters, it seemed that two were from the minesweeper and one from the Suez Maru were used. The engines were cut and we spent about an hour and a half rescuing survivors. Then I was ordered to proceed at slow speed, which we did for about thirty minutes, when suddenly from the upper deck I heard the firing of a machine-gun and about fifteen small arms. They were firing at intervals and it went on for so long that I told one of the firemen to go up to see what was happening and report back to me. When he came back he said they were firing on the PoWs and killing them. I was puzzled over this. The firing carried on for over an hour, then became less and less then stopped completely. Then, full speed was ordered and we proceeded to Batavia. I went up on deck but we were a long way from where the Suez

Maru had gone down so all I could see was pieces
of wood and patches of oil. I looked around at the
survivors on the deck and they were all Japanese.
There were about six-hundred of them, but not a
single PoW had been rescued."

The captain had listened quietly, not wishing to interrupt. There
was no doubt of the events of that day. It could never be denied. The
independent accounts resembled each other so closely, down to minute
detail that the truth had clearly been told. Each statement contained the
same horrors. The captain, despite his years of war crime investigations
still found the facts of the case deeply sickening and disturbing. He
found it hard to believe that no one had questioned it. And that no
one had spoken of it since. He turned to Kai, "Didn't you ask
anyone why it happened?" Kai shrugged apologetically,
"Someone told me that there wasn't room for the
PoWs and that they were killed on the orders of
the army transport commander. I heard that some
of the PoWs went down with the ship but the rest
were killed." The captain stared hard at Kai, offering him the
time to expand his reply, "I felt that this was a most
pitiful and regrettable occurrence. I believe it
was irresponsible for the army commander to have
ordered such action due to the sinking of the ship.
Furthermore, because the army and the navy are
not the same in their chain of command, I believe
that the captain of the minesweeper was extremely
imprudent in immediately carrying out the orders
of the army transport commander. I believe that
this incident was caused by a lack of cooperation
in transportation on the part of the minesweeper.
Even though space was limited I believe there
were many ways of meeting the situation, such as
temporarily leaving them on an island, or the ship
could have accommodated about fifty at a time." The
captain halted Kai's increasingly emotional monologue with the palm
of his hand. He tapped his papers with his pencil, and asked "How

`do you know that the transport commander gave the`
`order? Did you hear him? Do you know who actually`
`carried it out?"` Kai considered for a moment. `"No, I did`
`not hear the order given, but judging from the`
`chain of command I imagine the captain issued`
`the actual order to the gunnery officer, who was`
`Lieutenant Yatsuka. He would have then issued the`
`order to commence firing. The gunnery department`
`members and maybe some petty officers would have`
`carried it out."` The captain wrote down the name, 'Yatsuka'
and nodded impatiently, underlining the name several times. `"Very`
`well... That will be all for now. Your statement`
`will be ready for you to sign shortly. You can`
`wait here."` The captain gathered his notes, half listening as Kondo
finished his translation to Kai. As he rose to leave, Kai reached out
grabbing at the captain's sleeve, holding his forearm in a gentle grip.
"I am really very sorry for what happened. I was sorry then, and am
sorry now. It was very wrong, I have dreamt about it so many times...
if the army transport commander hadn't mentioned the order the navy
captain wouldn't have done it. I believe you need to speak to the army
transport commander, and soon." The captain raised an eyebrow, "It
will be sooner than you think." He said softly, lifting Kai's hand from
his arm and moving from the room.

Captain Sylvester rubbed his reddened eyes with thumb and
forefinger of one hand, pinching the bridge of his nose with each
movement. He stood inches from the door of an interrogation room,
the manila folder tucked under his other arm and Kondo at his side.
He was exhausted, but still sharp and ready to question his suspect. He
cleared his throat and pulled at the door handle. Former PoW Transport
Commander, First Lieutenant Masaji Iketani looked up, squinting
through his round spectacles. He had been sitting hands clenched,
eyes screwed shut, and on hearing the door jar he jumped. He was
a small pinched looking man. His face was sallow, his sunken cheeks
marked and pitted, and his dark hair stuck out in greasy clumps around
his skull. His eyes, barely open stared through his glasses around his
squashed nose. Captain Sylvester walked slowly across the room. He

had waited a long time to see this Iketani. As he pulled out the chair opposite the metal leg scraped painfully on the floor. Iketani winced. The captain placed his cap flat on the table and gestured to Kondo to promptly sit. The captain's face did not flinch from his stern frown as he descended to his chair, dropping the manila folder onto the table. Papers spilled out causing a row of freshly sharpened pencils to roll towards the edge of the table. The captain slapped a hand down on them, stopping them in their tracks. He rearranged the pencils and pulled the knees of his trousers straight as he sat. He was waiting for a knock at the door, which arrived just as he looked expectantly to it. A secretary quietly entered and sat opposite Kondo with her typewriter, poised to record the questioning. The captain looked back squarely at Iketani who looked down to the floor without moving his head. He appeared to be a man in turmoil, preoccupied with some inner battle. He started as the captain finally spoke. "`Are you Masaji Koshio, of Shizuoka-ken, Haibara-gun, Yoshida-che, Kando Number 239, and were you formerly known as Masaji Iketani?`" The captain looked across to Kondo who repeated the sentence in Japanese to Iketani, who in turn appeared more troubled with each passing word. The captain watched him intently, unblinking. Iketani replied to Kondo, "はい" who turned to the captain repeating, "`Yes.`" The captain ticked the end of question one as the secretary typed the dialogue, and continued, "`...and were you formerly a First Lieutenant in the Imperial Japanese Army and the PoW Transport Commander on board the Suez Maru when that vessel was sunk by an Allied submarine on 29 November 1943?`" Captain Sylvester lifted his chin to observe Iketani's expression, clenching his teeth, the muscles of his jaw bulging and flattening alternately. He bent his head to the left and heard a releasing click in his neck and his expression relaxed a little. Iketani shrank into his chair, his pinched face paled, as he answered a whispered, "`Yes.`" The captain picked up one of the pencils, pointing with it and looking squarely at Iketani, "`Why did you change your name?`" Iketani coughed then replied, "`Ahh, because I married into a family without sons and adopted my wife's family name.`" "Hmm," muttered the captain. He suspected Iketani had changed his name to avoid being traced after the war, he knew the crimes he had committed and wanted to become anonymous. There was little doubt in the captain's mind after hearing the testimonies, that Iketani was a major culprit in the atrocity. The captain considered it unlikely during his entire war that Iketani had not committed other war crimes. Those potential victims unlikely now to ever testify. 'He thought he'd got away with it,' thought the captain as he planned his first approach. He wanted every scrap of information from Iketani and began with his own statement of facts. "I have sworn statements from dozens of individuals, including the crew of the Suez Maru and the minesweeper, as well as some Japanese patients aboard. They name you as the instigator of a war crime, namely the killing of PoWs in the sea." Iketani recoiled, his head sank between his shoulders, the captain ignored his physical retreat and carried on. "I have arrested Captain Kawano of minesweeper W12, with whom you conferred about the massacre, before relaying an order that the PoWs were to be shot. Kawano is now held in Sugamo Prison, awaiting trial. You are to be arrested for your part in the crime itself and the subsequent covering up of your crime. You would do well to outline here your version of events, leaving nothing out and adding nothing." The captain paused, watching Iketani's face as the translated words reached him. "I want you to now write a statement regarding everything that happened from the time you left Ambon to the sinking and afterwards, to the time you arrived at Batavia aboard the Minesweeper W12, when you lodged a report on 3 December. Do you understand?" Iketani froze, his mouth agape. He stared blankly at the captain. His jaw moved a little, but no noise was emitted. He was jolted into replying by the captain's voice impatiently asking, "Well?" "Yes, yes, I will write a statement," Iketani said through chattering teeth. "Very well, it will be translated as you write, then I shall question you." The captain took blank paper from the manila folder and rolled a pencil towards

Iketani who took it, his fingers shaking in small twitching movements. The captain noticed the nervousness and nodded to himself. His firm approach had had the desired effect. Iketani took the wobbling pencil to the paper and began to draw small stuttering lines, reading aloud as he wrote. Kondo relayed the translation to the captain, and the secretary typed the rough translation, tapping quickly at the keys.

"Ahh, it was about April 1943, at sub-camp number three of the Java internment camps that I received orders to be assigned to the 7th Air Division with the object of establishing airfields on Ambon, Ceram and Haruku. Ahem, I repeatedly expressed the opinion that the order was ill-advised because those places had no accommodation for the four thousand prisoners and the amount of provisions needed would be unobtainable." The captain rolled his eyes, he recognised the self-serving preamble for what it was. He motioned for Iketani to get on with it with a winding motion of his hand. Iketani coughed and sat up straight. "My objections were in vain and the order was issued. We were forced to make preparations at Soerabaya and gathered a force of PoWs captured in Java. About one thousand from Batavia and about three thousand from Soerabaya. In mid-April we arrived at the destinations. We sent one thousand British PoWs to Liang, two thousand British and Dutch PoWs to Haruku and one thousand Dutch PoWs to Ceram. As I expected, a large number of prisoners became sick because of having to work in the rain to build their barracks. At that time it was the rainy season. The sick prisoners recovered slowly, but they did not recover sufficiently to work. The army surgeon and other officers and I repeatedly suggested to the unit commander, Major Sanso Anami, that a plan should be drawn up to send prisoners back to Java as soon as possible. He doggedly refused to listen. We urged him again and again and eventually he agreed." The captain noted the name, 'Major Sanso Anami'. He tapped his pencil on the table, the name seemed familiar but he couldn't immediately place it. He nodded at Iketani to move on. Aware he was simply pushing his own defence before even beginning to describe actual events. "Well, the first plan to return one thousand prisoners was drawn up accordingly. These prisoners were taken from the groups at Ceram, Haruku and Liang. All the places were a long way from the port of Ambon so, the sick prisoners were taken there in small ships. I think it was around 25 November 1943. I was to accompany the sick prisoners to the port, as I had to contact the main camp at Java and the freight depot in Soerabaya regarding financial matters. At the port I found that although two ships were originally scheduled only one would be able to sail. The other had been involved in an, ahh, an accident. But the Suez Maru was undamaged and was scheduled to accommodate five hundred Japanese patients from the Ambon Army Hospital. So the original plan to transport one thousand sick prisoners was abruptly changed. Instead 548 British and Dutch PoWs were placed aboard the ship." Captain Sylvester listened as the words drifted from Kondo's mouth across the room. Again he felt as if he was hearing the story for the first time. He felt deeply pained by his inability to reach out into the past and do anything to help those innocent Allied men. Despite all he had investigated previously, he felt deeply saddened and wrung dry each time this story unfolded. As if each time he could stop it before it ever happened. As if there could be any possibility of a different conclusion. But that could never be, those men were all gone. They had been gone some six years. He struggled with the unchanging knowledge that he could not prevent, nor undo it. He could only listen, investigate, and charge those responsible. He felt it was the least he could offer to those men trapped in the hold, sinking and drowning, and those clinging to lifeboats for hours, drifting in the endless heat of the sun and cold of the sea, only to find their brave survival was for nought. He pulled himself back into the present, looking across to Iketani, "So, how was it you came to sail on the Suez Maru?" The captain said at last. "Well, I received an order saying, 'Paymaster Second Lieutenant Iketani is ordered to return to the Java Main Camp with the five hundred and forty-eight PoWs, assisted by a sanitation NCO and ten Korean workers'. I thought that I was going to escort only the PoWs but, besides them there were about five hundred Japanese patients from various units. As I was the senior officer of the group the shipping unit ordered me to be the transport commander and I accepted the order, ahh unwillingly." The captain looked at Iketani blankly, "Five hundred Japanese patients? Are you sure of that number?" Iketani nodded unconvincingly. The captain decided it was not important for now, and spun a finger in the air for Iketani to continue. "Well, since I was the last one to board the ship, I witnessed the loading of prisoners aboard the ship. Holds one and two were already occupied by Japanese patients, so the sick PoWs were accommodated in holds three and four. There were ten to twenty persons brought aboard on stretchers. As the sea in the vicinity was very dangerous at that time I asked Unit Commander Sanso Anami, 'If this ship is attacked by torpedoes from enemy submarines and then sinks, what measures should be taken? And what should be done if the minesweeper escort ship doesn't have the capacity to accommodate everyone?'" The captain frowned, "That was a very specific question to ask, considering that was exactly what did happen." He stared expectantly at Iketani. "Well, the unit commander was clear about it, he said, 'You may shoot them.' Unit Commander Sanso Anami harboured a great deal of animosity towards the PoWs..." Iketani pressed his point, nodding enthusiastically, his eyes shining wildly. "... this can be seen in the fact that he did not quickly agree

to our advice previously given, to send the sick
PoWs back to Java immediately." The captain waved a hand
for Iketani to settle down, and continue his statement. Iketani coughed
and moved on, "Well, then our small transport and the
minesweeper left the port of Ambon. The next few
days passed without incident, but on the evening of
the 28th the minesweeper disappeared, apparently
having sighted a submarine, so we felt helpless. I
issued an alert order to prepare all the passengers
for any emergency, and posted a sentry at the PoWs'
hatches so they could be given instructions in
the case of emergency. I also checked that the
rafts and life jackets were sufficient." The captain
said nothing. He believed very little of Iketani's actions or intentions in
his testimony thus far.

"On the morning of 29th we saw the minesweeper
far to the rear and saw it steaming towards our
transport at full speed. We assumed we were now out
of danger. By the time I finished my breakfast and
went up onto the bridge the minesweeper was seen
emitting black smoke and sailing in front of us.
Then suddenly a shout of 'Torpedo' was heard from
the lookout. It was probably about 0920 hours.
Looking in the direction of the stern I clearly
saw two white traces of torpedoes. The transport
was apparently trying to dodge the torpedoes by
making a big turn at full speed. I waited for a
moment to see if we would be missed and prayed.
There was suddenly an explosion at the stern
and we were thrown around by the concussion. We
suffered two direct hits." He cleared his throat again, "I
immediately sent an NCO and a Korean employee to
assess the situation. The torpedoes scored direct
hits on hold four and on the ships lower hull.
The messengers returned and reported sentries were
missing. They fell into the ship's hatches due to

the concussions. The majority of the PoWs in hold three were coming out with their life jackets on. There were very few PoWs moving in hold four, so I assumed there were a considerable number of PoW victims because it received a direct hit. Those in hold three were instructed to help those in hold four. Since the ship was in a bad condition, I asked the captain whether the ship could continue and he said, 'Since the shaft is broken and the engines have ceased and the engine room is flooded, it will be utterly impossible to continue'. There was then confusion at the stern of the ship as it was sinking and, er, because the PoWs were ill. I ordered the Koreans to throw all the rafts into the sea. Then everyone must have abandoned ship. The PoWs jumped into the sea until there were no longer any aboard, and all the Japanese passengers seemed to have left. Because the list of the sinking ship became steep, I jumped into the sea with the senior crew who had remained until the end. I swam away from the ship and it sank stern first. It only took about fifteen minutes. Men were all around clinging to rafts and wreckage. I saw about two hundred to two hundred and fifty PoWs floating in the sea. I think I was in the sea for about three hours but it must have been longer because it was nearly dusk when the minesweeper picked me up. I spoke to Captain Kawano, the master of the minesweeper and we agreed that we were both feeling hostile towards the unseen submarine which had torpedoed the transport. Rescue work continued until shortly after I was taken out of the water, the boat was already nearly full." Captain Sylvester frowned. "So, you were feeling hostile towards the Allied submarine, so you decided to take it out on the PoWs?" The captain said flatly, then held up a hand so Kondo did not translate to Iketani, who looked blankly back and forth. "Never mind, tell him to just finish stating what he remembers happened next." "Well, then the captain confronted me with a problem on which I was to give a decision. He said, 'Having accommodated all the Japanese, the boat is very full, in order to prevent the boat from capsizing we cannot accommodate anymore persons'. I had no alternative but to nod in acquiescence. He also said, 'It is dangerous to leave PoWs drifting in the sea, because I fear they will be rescued by the enemy submarine'." Iketani shifted uncomfortably, blushing, "Go on," instructed Captain Sylvester. "Ahem, yes well, he said, 'I would like to kill them with a machine-gun, but do you think it should be done?' I stared at the surface of the sea and I saw there were about two hundred and fifty PoWs floating there. I then quoted the orders issued by Lieutenant-Colonel Anami at the time of departure from Ambon. Then, the captain of the minesweeper issued an order to an officer standing nearby." Captain Sylvester stared at Iketani in disgust. He opened his mouth to speak but closed it, noting down a question for later instead, as he somehow contained his anger. He wanted to push this Iketani out through the window. Instead he spoke through gritted teeth, "Finish what you have to say." "Well, ahh, soon after a whistle blew and there was much commotion aboard the boat. It seems there was a machine-gun at the bow of the boat and about twenty sailors appeared with rifles. I could no longer bear the atmosphere and crouched down on the bridge and pressed my eyes shut to avoid looking at the surface of the sea. It was about twenty minutes after my conversation with the captain. The sea was strangely silent due to deceleration of the boat until the piercing sounds of the machines guns cut across the surface of the sea."

Iketani's eyes flashed wildly. His mouth watered and spittle formed at his lips as he excitedly described the event. "The noise of rifle fire was intermingled with machine-gun fire and our boat made four or five rounds of the surrounding sea. I heard the voice of an officer on the boat who was pointing out the positions of PoWs floating on the sea, while he scanned the surface with binoculars. It soon became dark and it seemed all the prisoners had been killed and we finally turned and headed west after destroying the remaining lifeboats by ramming them with the bow of our boat. I was feeling gloomy and I ate the food given to me as I crouched in the corner of the officers cabin." "Gloomy!" muttered the captain incredulously. He shook his head, "Well, what of the rest of the voyage? What reports were made?" The captain had already read the report. He was now keen to hear Iketani's excuses for concealing the truth. "Well, at Batavia I made a detailed report to the Commander of the main camp, Major General Saito. I relayed the orders of Lieutenant-Colonel Anami. Major General Saito said to me that was probably the only method at that time. I do not know what his opinions were but he did not seem to want to become involved in the matter. He said I should discuss the matter with the officer in charge of PoW, Army Captain Hiroshi Suzuki, and make sure there are no oversights. So I related my report to Army Captain Suzuki and he thought the matter over for a while and told me to wait a day. He later brought me a draft which he told me to print my name and affix my signature on it. I did so and then I read it, but I found the text was contrary to the facts." "You signed it, THEN you read it?" asked the captain, disbelieving the rambling tale. "Well, then I asked if it was all right to leave the draft as it was, even if the text was wrong, and he said it was all right. I was only a supply officer, not used to writing reports so I did as I was told." "You were not! You were a First Lieutenant and Commander of the PoWs' transport! Not some lowly supply officer!" exclaimed the captain. He nearly stood but stopped himself. He sighed heavily, "All right, is that all? What did you do with the report?" Iketani shrugged, "I took a copy to the captain of Minesweeper W12 which was then anchored at Tandjong Priok. He read it and said, 'I approve of your report. You can handle the matter as suits your position." "Your position, - exactly!" The captain shouted, then waved to Kondo not to translate. Kondo abruptly stopped short. "All right, that is it for today," the captain turned to Kondo. "Call the guard, Iketani is going down to the cells. I'll cross examine more tomorrow." Iketani's face fell as two guards took him underarm, almost lifting him from his seat and escorted him away.

- 15 July 1949 -

The captain leant heavily on the table in the interrogation room as he read through his questions. He listened to Masaji Iketani's measured breathing opposite and he looked up at the sallow pinched face. Iketani leaned back in his chair, folding his arms and blinking in response. In the army it would have been called 'dumb insolence'. The captain's eyes narrowed as he returned to his pages. He rifled through the manila folder causing an edge of Yoshio Kashiki's letter to slip, revealing a neat triangle of cursive writing. The captain pulled the letter out between thumb and forefinger and a sentence caught his eye. The beginning of it all, the familiar words jumped at him,

I don't mean by this to inform the murderers to you, but I wish I could let the families of the Allied-Forces prisoners know the facts and mourn them.

Captain Sylvester blinked at the letter, absorbed by the rounded rows of words running across the paper. He pushed it back under other documents with his thumb. He needed to get to the root of this. He had been waiting so long for Iketani to be found, now he had him he wanted to question every detail of his statement. He knew he would reveal the lies and half-truths of the previous day. The captain looked at Iketani's unconcerned expression and dearly wanted to lift him from the chair and smack his smug face across the room. Instead he sighed. He would adopt a softer line of questions, at least to begin with. Interspersed with point-blank questions to expose the facts. He had found it startled suspects, knocked them off guard which often caused them to reveal truths. He hoped Iketani would be off-balanced, responding before he had gathered his defence of lies. Tapping his chin with the end of the pencil, the captain considered his first statement. At last the captain addressed Iketani, "I am going to ask you some questions. You are not obliged to answer but anything you do say will be taken down and may be used in evidence. Do you understand?" Captain Sylvester paused nodding to Kondo to repeat in Japanese. Iketani nodded at each word, and the captain stared, his jaw fixed. Iketani shifted in his seat and looked to Kondo quizzically. Kondo looked down to avoid eye contact or any suggestion of sympathy. Iketani looked back to the captain who still awaited a reply. "Yes, he understands,' said Kondo finally after a muttered word from Iketani. The captain slipped a pack of cigarettes from his top pocket and sliding one out between his pursed lips he looked to Iketani gesturing with a raised eyebrow, offering a cigarette.. Iketani reached forward and took one cautiously. The captain lit a match and leaned across offering it to Iketani. He brought his cigarette close and puffed out a cloud of blue smoke. The captain then lit his own. "So, where was this camp on Ambon from which the five hundred and forty-eight prisoners of war were held, prior to embarkation on the Suez Maru?" Iketani relaxed and puffed on the cigarette, holding it between finger and thumb like a cigar, he smiled at the captain, "They were taken from various camps... in Ceram and ahh on Ambon." Captain Sylvester continued, "Yes, I know that, but where were those camps?" The captain leant closer in, "Ahhh well, the British PoWs were from Liang, in the North east of Ambon Island, the Dutch prisoners of war were from Amahai, on the South coast of Ceram. I remember there were both British and Dutch from Haruku Island." Iketani sat back, but the captain pressed, "So, before they were on Ambon and Ceram, where were the PoWs held? Where were they captured? Do you know?" "They had all been captured in Java and were held in the Soerabaya and Batavia Prisoner of War camps I think." "Hmm," Captain Sylvester mused briefly, "and when were they transferred to Ambon and Ceram?" Iketani tried to appear in control, speaking firmly with a fragile confidence, his chin raised, "Sometime in April 1943." Captain Sylvester rounded, "And can you confirm for the record, why they were transferred?" Each knew why it had happened, but the captain needed to unpick the full knowledge Iketani held. How involved he was, and what he knew of day to day PoWs' treatment. It would then be impossible for him to suddenly deny having knowledge later on if he had confessed to being involved in minutiae up to that point. "Well? Why were they were transferred in April 1943?" Iketani broke as if he had heard the captain's thoughts. He stammered, "Yes, ah, it was to construct aerodromes in Liang, Amahai and also on Haruku." Iketani put out the cigarette in a small ashtray. It had dried his mouth, making him cough and splutter. He decided that he wanted to be seen more favourably, so he blurted more information quickly, causing Kondo to ask him to slow down. He was writing and translating, and couldn't keep up. Once he finished making notes Kondo turned to Captain Sylvester repeating what Iketani had said. "There were a thousand held in Liang, another thousand in Amahai and another about two thousand held on Haruku." Captain Sylvester flicked through his notes, "Yes, I thought so, yes I know this. He said all this yesterday." Iketani looked back and forth from captain to Kondo, then suddenly asked Kondo for water. Kondo looked away. Iketani looked back to Captain Sylvester who raised an eyebrow in question. Iketani mimed lifting a glass to his mouth and the captain nodded to Kondo to get water. Kondo splashed the liquid into a small glass and set it down in front of Iketani, who sipped quietly whilst watching Captain Sylvester over the rim of the glass.

The captain continued, "All right, so, what was the name of the Camp Commander where the PoWs were held, on Ambon?" "Ahh, ahh he was Lieutenant-Colonel Anami, I think his first name was Sanso but I don't know." The captain noted the name again, then moved on, firing questions at Iketani. "How many prisoners of war do you estimate were killed by machine-gun in the water?" Iketani put down the water and spoke through his fingers that dabbed at his mouth, "Perhaps about two hundred and fifty." The captain nodded in irritation, "So, why did you later make a false report to the Japanese authorities?" Quickly Iketani responded, "Because I was told to do so by the commander of the main camp, the H.Q. of the Java PoW camps." The captain looked down to his papers as he asked, "And, what was his name?" "I don't know." The captain rolled his eyes, "All right, what was his rank?" "He was a full colonel," replied Iketani flatly, "... and his title?" "He was commander of all Java PoW camps." Captain Sylvester inclined his head in acknowledgement, "Hmm, I think that's Saito," he murmured to himself. "All right, now. Was it before or after leaving the minesweeper that you discussed with Kawano that you would conceal the method of disposal of the PoWs?" "Before." "So, you planned to conceal the crime with Kawano? What was said?" Iketani squirmed and sat on his hands. He bit his trembling lip, looking to Captain Sylvester he replied, "Well, I-I-I suggested that a report be made along the lines of the one finally submitted as a Confirmation Sheet." "And, when was this?" "It was after I reported to the Commander of the PoW Java camps." The captain leant in, "And what did Kawano say?" "Well, he said, please do as you think proper." "So Kawano clearly intended to make a false report also?" "Yes... we both did." Iketani said finally. The captain leant back, rubbing the short bristles on his chin, folding his arms as he asked, "Did you mention the order from Anami to Saito?" Iketani nodded in recognition, "Yes, he said it could not be helped." "What did he mean by that...? That the order did not exist or that it did not apply?" "Well, I think he meant that the order did not exist." Captain Sylvester made fast scribbling notes on Iketani's replies, becoming more frustrated with each. 'What a pointless waste, what an avoidable waste!' He muttered. "All right. Finally can you confirm who Seichi Saito was?" "Ahh, yes. He was the major general in charge of the PoW Camps in the whole of Java and Ambon areas. I ahh, I made a mistake earlier when I referred to him as a full colonel." "Hmm, I see, and was he the officer to whom you reported when you landed at Batavia?" "Yes, he was." The captain finished a note and folded the sheet over. He collected the pages as he closed the manila folder. Iketani leant back, relieved the questioning was over, as the captain moved forward again, "I assume you are prepared to write a full and detailed statement?" Iketani bristled, but replied, "Yes, I will, but I have already practically covered everything about which I can write." The captain narrowed his eyes, "Yes, but I should like a little more detail." Iketani nodded meekly.

Later, in his office, as the captain re-read Iketani's statement and his own notes, he scanned ahead to check the name Iketani had offered,— 'Sanso Anami'. The captain called for Officer Beirne, to request information on the whereabouts of Anami. "It's not in doubt that Iketani told Kawano of this order. Whether it was actually an *official* order, whether Iketani relayed Anami's order or concocted it, encouraged perhaps by Kawano, is as yet unclear. Until we speak with this Anami we won't know for sure." He said to Officer Beirne, who nodded thoughtfully. "Either way it is surprising Kawano took an order from the army, given that he had command of his own naval vessel. He could easily have chosen to assert his authority and dismiss an army order. I'm sure whatever Anami says about it that he, and both Kawano and Iketani are equally responsible." Officer Beirne nodded, "Well, until we trace the Gunnery Officer, Yatsuka, and those who actually carried out the orders, that is." Captain Sylvester looked up abruptly, "Yes, quite so. There are many perpetrators in this case."

- 25 JULY 1949 -

Officer Beirne escorted Hiroshi Suzuki down the corridor to an interrogation room, just after nine on a humid Monday morning. Captain Jack Sylvester marched briskly along with Kondo, approaching from the opposite end of the corridor. They met outside the room with a salute from Officer Beirne to the captain, which he returned. Suzuki was shown into the room and offered a chair into which he lowered himself cautiously. His eyes scanned the dim room, taking in the closed window, the pale bulb illuminating the central table and smaller table in the corner, at which Kondo settled himself. The captain spoke briefly with Officer Beirne, before turning back into the room and closing the door with a soft click. The captain moved round the table slowly, pulling the back of the chair out with a scrawp, Suzuki winced. The captain began speaking as he pulled the chair forward under him, sitting with his last word. "You are Hiroshi Suzuki, a former captain in the Imperial Japanese Army, based in Java under the command of Seichi Saito, the PoW camp commander for all Java area, is this correct?" Hiroshi Suzuki looked astonished at the captain's knowledge of him as he listened wide eyed to Kondo relaying the question into Japanese. He nodded blankly, lifting his chin, "Yes, I was." "Very well, I should like you to think back to November 1943. I want to hear what you remember about the sinking of the Suez Maru, and the minesweeper that docked at Batavia, without the PoWs aboard, and your actions and involvement in the report that was lodged thereafter." Suzuki nodded again, then shook himself he began eagerly, his eyes brightening, "Yes, I know all about that. I remember there was a telegraphic message from

Lieutenant Colonel Anami, Commandant of the Ambon Prisoner of War Internment Camp, to Major General Saito." "Yes, what did he say?" The captain spoke patiently, "Well, it was to the effect that he was evacuating about five hundred PoWs." "I see, go on." "Well, I remember because it was unusual..." Suzuki squinted, his head on one side, as he reflected, "... there was a telephone call from Batavia Anchorage H.Q. saying they requested reception and accommodation because prisoners of war are arriving from Ambon." Suzuki took a deep breath, he had almost forgotten to breathe in his excitement to retell his part in the story. He panted for a moment, his eyes alight before continuing. "It was after hours, so I reported it to my superior, Lieutenant Colonel Matsunaga, as well as senior camp staff. I requested the motor transport unit to despatch ten vehicles to Batavia harbour for the PoWs. Then I immediately got in an automobile and went to the harbour myself." "And what did you find at the harbour?" Asked the captain, quietly. "Well, when I arrived at the quay, wounded soldiers were disembarking, some were on stretchers and some were on the shoulders of others. One after another they came from this naval vessel. I walked along the quay towards where I thought the PoW ship would be and there I met First Lieutenant Iketani." The captain suddenly stopped writing his notes, and looked to Suzuki in surprise, "Iketani?" The captain paused, waiting for Suzuki's response. He did not want to appear too interested in case it alarmed him. Suzuki nodded slowly without suspicion. "Yes, well, what did he say to you?" "Well, I was shocked to learn from him that all the prisoners of war had perished. He said they went down with the ship." "That is all he said?" the captain eyes flashed. He wanted to know every word that Iketani had said. It could prove pivotal in the case. Iketani's leaky testimony juxtaposed with someone who actually spoke to him at that moment, Suzuki could unwittingly expose the truth, *and* Iketani's lies.

The captain stared hard, "You must remember what was said. Try to tell me as exactly as possible, the words used," Suzuki's brow creased, he suddenly looked concerned that he was saying too much. The captain saw his hesitation and reminded him, "You do know the penalties for failing to tell the truth, and falsifying a statement concerning war crimes, don't you?" "War crimes!" exclaimed Suzuki, almost squealing. The captain's face relaxed, he spoke mildly "I am not accusing you, Suzuki. I merely want you to remember and tell me what was said. I am simply saying you don't want to obstruct a war crime investigation, do you?" "No, no. Actually, I-I-I do remember more of what was said. Let me think ahh, well, I saw Iketani and I said to him 'What's happened to the prisoners of war?' I said. 'I've arranged vehicles and I have come for them. Iketani said, 'The ship was attacked and torpedoed and all the PoWs perished,' he said, 'Two or three guards died and those seriously injured are now going into that ambulance over there.' I said, 'Is that so? Well, I will cancel the motor vehicle dispatch then. Please wait here for a moment and I'll take you to the camp myself, in my automobile'." Suzuki looked expectantly at the captain. "Is that all that was said?" asked the captain, sceptically, "No, we also spoke more in the automobile. I said, 'It must have been terrible, you have also lost your spectacles'. I asked him, 'How did the disaster happen?' Iketani replied, 'The troops lost all the equipment and everything else'. He said he was 'thrown overboard and remained in the water for about seven hours'. He said, 'At dawn the ship received a first torpedo hit in the aft hold and suffered a great shock. This was followed immediately by a second hit and he jumped overboard'. He believed the majority of the PoWs being in the aft hold died directly from the explosion there. And since the ship sank in no time, stern first, he believed that almost all of them went down with the ship." Suzuki lowered his voice and stared into the middle distance. "Then he said, 'Of course, the prisoners of war that came to the surface later were shot by the navy with machine-guns and rifles'." The captain watched Suzuki, who had eagerly repeated all he remembered of his conversation with Iketani. The captain made another note and moved to other questions. "All right, well, what happened later, at the main camp?" "Well, First Lieutenant Iketani went to the quarters of the main camp commander, Saito, to report the situation and I telephoned my superior Lieutenant Colonel Matsunaga. I told him that all the PoWs had died, and I told him that First Lieutenant Iketani had gone to report to Camp Commander Saito. Then, I returned to my quarters." Suzuki finished, his eyes shining brightly as he remembered it all. "I see, and did you hear any more about it from Camp Commander Saito?" "Well, yes. About two days later I was called to the office of my superior, Matsunaga. He said, 'On the assumption that all the PoWs went down with the ship at the time of sinking, I want you to get information on the date, location and circumstances surrounding the torpedo attacks from First Lieutenant Iketani and assist in drafting the confirmation affidavit'. So I drafted a plan, using a map and I submitted it directly to Lieutenant Colonel Matsunaga." Suzuki blinked at Captain Sylvester, "All right, then what did you do?" "Well, I made about one hundred copies and after receiving the seal of First Lieutenant Iketani I forwarded some of the copies to the Tokyo Prisoner of War Information Bureau and filed the rest in camp files." "Hmm." The captain tapped the end of his pencil on the table, drumming a slow beat that echoed around the small room. Suzuki looked to Kondo and back to the captain who asked, "What did you know of Lieutenant-General Anami's order to shoot the prisoners?" Suzuki eyebrows leapt to his forehead in alarm. "Me? I-I knew nothing. I know nothing of any order from Lieutenant General Anami. Also, also..." he continued, a finger in the air, "...no such orders were issued by my superiors, or by Camp Commander Saito. In fact, we had instructions from higher up to treat the PoWs fairly and humanely. I was told that the PoWs from Ambon had suffered a great deal and that most of them were in ill-health when they were shot by the navy." "Yes, yes I know about that. All right, what of your opinions on this action?" asked the captain. Suzuki looked uncomfortable. "Yes, well, I felt that it was, ahh... regrettable," replied Suzuki, lowering his eyes. "Hmm I see. Regrettable?" repeated the captain. "All right, that will be all for now. I will have your statement drawn up, someone will escort you to a waiting room." Suzuki nodded gratefully. The captain rose. As he passed Suzuki he suddenly reached out to catch at his sleeve. "It *was* regrettable. I do think that!" "Yes, I have noted that" replied the captain, peeling Suzuki's fingers from his arm.

- 26 JULY 1949 -

A month had passed since Captain Sylvester first questioned him, but Major General Seiichi Saito now strode into the interrogation room and sat as confidently and as resolute as before. He looked relaxed as he smoked a cigarette, blowing the smoke out in rings. Captain Sylvester spoke flatly. "You may again acquaint yourself with the punishments for giving false or misleading information to a war crime investigation." As he moved the document outlining these penalties in Japanese across the table Saito stared blankly ahead, without looking down to the paper. The captain pressed on, "I now have reports from those

you spoke with, those you ordered to conceal the
killing of prisoners of war. You do know that war
criminals have been hung for much less than this,
do you not?" Saito's beady eyes flickered to the captain and back
to the far wall where he had fixed his gaze. The cigarette burnt in his
fingers. The captain continued undeterred. "I have the report
you made on 3 December 1943, stating the PoWs went
down with the ship. I have a confirmation sheet
you later sent to the Chief of the PoW Information
Bureau. I also have testimonies and affidavits
from crew and passengers aboard both the Suez Maru
and Minesweeper W12. They concur that the PoWs
were shot. Also, I have statements from the Suez
Maru Captain, Shirakawa, and the W12 Minesweeper's
Captain, Kawano, as well as PoW transport Commander,
Iketani, regarding your involvement in concealing
the war crime. So how about it? Shall we re-visit
your statement and this time you tell me everything
about your involvement?" Saito shifted in his seat. His eyes
darted to the captain and back to the wall, then back to the captain
where they lingered. He slowly put out the cigarette as its embers
reached his skin. The captain's eyes glanced to the confirmation sheet
written by Saito, dated December 12, 1943. He ran a finger down the
sheet as its words swam in front of him.

    ...prisoners of war mentioned in the
named list are all patients and weak persons
who could not endure work were on their
way from Ambon Island to Java on board the
transport Ship Suez Maru...

The captain turned the page and eyed the list of names of the
prisoners of war lost on the *Suez Maru*. There were dozens to a page. He
turned the page. Name after name. All young men. His brow furrowed.
"Nothing weak about these fellas," he muttered to himself as he turned
another page, his eye tracing the many names. "All just ordinary fellas..."
It seemed so impersonal to see them as just a long line of names, like
a long line of men in the water. Each a name, a man, with hopes and

aspirations. Harry, Walter, Joseph, James, Arthur, Albert, John, Jack. Captain Jack Sylvester stopped. The name Jack caught his eye and he scanned back to the line. He frowned. 'Three years younger than me, just a young man,' he thought. 'Could so easily have been me.' A shiver trickled down the captain's spine, hairs stood straight on the back of his neck as goosebumps rose along his arms. Throughout his investigation he hadn't had time to look through the list properly. These were British and Dutch men. As such he wouldn't have known them personally as an Australian officer posted elsewhere. But these names, the never-ending list of men, of sons, husbands and brothers, made them so very personal, to someone. Anger rose in him again and the captain flushed. He turned back to Saito. "Five hundred and forty-eight PoWs on abroad the Suez Maru, some two hundred and fifty survivors killed in the water, and you helped cover up this war crime. You know the shooting of each man is a single war crime in its own right, and carries a sentence." He looked Saito squarely in the eye. Saito stood abruptly, pushing the chair backwards with a screech. Before Saito could speak the captain barked at him. "Sit down! You will give me a revised formal statement. Every last thing you know, now!" The captain's flash of anger abated, and he watched as Saito flopped down into the chair, hanging his head momentarily. When he looked up, his expression was worried, and his lip trembled slightly. Saito began to speak and the captain nodded to Kondo to translate and take notes. "I-I, received orders that one thousand PoWs were to be dispatched to Ambon Island for airfield construction, er, as I recall this was spring 1943. The groups left Soerabaya on transports with guards, several officers and N.C.O's under the command of Lieutenant-Colonel Anami. The outbreak of sickness among the PoWs increased as time elapsed on the island and since medical care was impossible it was recommended that these PoWs be returned on the ships available to their units in Java and given medical treatment. On 25 November about five hundred PoWs and approximately two hundred Japanese soldiers were put on board the Suez Maru. On 29 November she was torpedoed and sunk by an American submarine. Thereby bringing disaster to all the prisoners on board." The captain halted him with raised hand, "Yes, I know this, what of your later report?" Saito cleared his throat again, "Well, First Lieutenant Iketani was transferred to the escort ship and returned to Batavia and the following day he presented himself at the main internment camp. He reported the facts to Captain Suzuki. Iketani said that the ship was attacked and sunk and there were some deaths among the guards. He said approximately one half of the prisoners of war were lost in the sinking and the rest who had survived were shot by the navy while they were adrift. Orders for these steps to be taken, under such circumstances, had previously been issued by Lieutenant-Colonel Anami to Iketani. I reprimanded Iketani for the improper action he had elected to take and I conferred with the senior staff. I stressed that such inhuman acts were not right. I recommended that this sort of information be excluded from the telegraphic report which should state merely that all the PoWs had gone down with their ship. The matter could then be settled through the confirmation of death report. Thus, it was decided to absolve PoW Transport Commander Iketani of any personal responsibility. The telegraphic message was drafted and the report written judiciously according to my suggestions. Also, the scene of this incident was not within the jurisdiction of the internment Camp Commandant, Anami. Therefore I could not issue any further orders nor did I have authority over the incident." The captain lifted his chin, "-and if you had the authority, what was your view of the incident?" Saito coughed into his fist. "well, I regret that I did not warn Lieutenant-Colonel Anami beforehand that his idea was a great mistake. Also, I always insisted that my subordinates exercised fairness and kind treatment to PoWs. It seems that Anami told Iketani that it was permissible to dispose of PoWs if such action were unavoidable, such as in an emergency. I believe that this bold statement was made by Anami, in his capacity as unit commander even though his rank was low and it was not his true belief. I refer of course, to Anami's old warrior-like nature and the possibility that he personally shouldered the responsibility in the matter." "Hmm, I do not see how murdering unarmed PoWs struggling in the sea, is warrior-like," said the captain shaking his head. He knew Saito was twisting, wriggling on the hook by suggesting Anami was simply idealistic. He'd heard it all before, the *Greater East Asia Co-Prosperity Sphere* and all the ideological lies that had accompanied it. He made note of Saito's remarks but knew it would be shown to be no excuse. He turned to Saito, who seemed smaller in his nervousness and the implications of his actions. The captain sat straight and stated, "Your statement will be typed. Please wait here, then you can sign it. You will be escorted to a room where you can wait." Saito stood to leave, and the captain held out a palm to halt him, "Just wait here, for now." Saito sat again, as the captain gathered his papers and left with Kondo.

- 27 JULY 1949 -

Captain Sylvester was at his desk, rubbing his tired reddened eyes with his palms. His hands dropped to his desk and, his eyes closed, he listened to the world outside the window. He inclined his ear to the rustling of trees, occasional motorcar honk and the excited twitter of birds. He heard the distant low murmur of chatter out on the street, a few strangled voices not in his own language. Opening his eyes, he caught a glint of light on the picture frame enclosing the photograph of his wife. He had placed it on the corner of the desk to face him. He wished he were home in Australia with her now. He leant back into his chair and lifting his elbows to the ceiling he rubbed his aching neck. He yawned, a huge gaping-mouthed yawn that did little to lessen his tiredness. He shook off his lethargy and looked down to the manila folder and his notes, his endless notes. He was writing his final report. Putting forward the case to bring suspects to trial. There were still a few pieces missing, and a few people yet to speak to. He picked up his pencil as a knock at his door stopped his train of thought. He called out "Enter," without looking up. His philosophy was, 'If they're important enough to be greeted, they don't knock'. He heard the familiar 'ahem' of Kondo and looked up puzzled. "Ahh, I come to say it is ten to one, and you ask me to come for one pm, so I am here." The captain looked at his watch for a brief moment then said suddenly, "Yes, I did, come on." He grabbed his cap and stuffed the manila folder under his arm. They moved along the corridor quickly. The captain held open the door to the interrogation room, as Officer Beirne approached. "They're bringing him up now, sir," he reported, saluting. "Very good," replied the captain, moving into the shadowy room. The captain leafed through the manila folder pulling out a few blank sheets, which he placed in front of the empty chair opposite. Kondo arranged his own papers and pencils on his desk. The door creaked, and Minesweeper W12's Gunnery Officer Daiso Yatsuka was escorted into the room. He followed the captain's eyes that offered the empty chair, and he sat gingerly. Daiso Yatsuka was a smart-looking man, neat and clipped. His tidy hair was short at the sides and combed neatly to one side. His hands were clean, soft and smooth like a child's. He criss-crossed his fingers, balancing his intertwined hands on edge of the table, and looked expectantly to the captain. The captain took an immediate dislike to him. 'Self-assured and nonchalant,' he thought, but wondered if Yatsuka might be the key to unlocking the final details of the case. He sighed as he began. "You are Daiso Yatsuka, former gunnery officer aboard Minesweeper W12, when it escorted the Suez Maru in late November 1943, is that correct?" As his words echoed across the room, translated into Japanese, Yatsuka visibly deflated as if he'd been burst with a pin. He tried to gather himself. Coughing, he replied, "Ahh, yes, I was," cautiously to Kondo, who nodded toward the captain, reminding Yatsuka to whom he should address his replies. The captain continued, "I must warn you about making false or misleading statements regarding an investigation into war crimes, there are severe penalties and punishments." The captain slid the slightly dogeared sheet of Japanese text across the table toward Yatsuka, who glanced at it then looked back to the captain in alarm. The captain frowned and nodded, confirming the seriousness of the situation. Yatsuka coughed before he spoke, his palms spread wide. "Well, it was so long ago I don't think I can remember much about it." The captain looked sceptical, "Really, is that so?" "Well, I-I-I cant imagine what you, what you want, with, er, with me..." he trailed off, looking to Kondo for sympathy and finding none. Kondo frowned and looked away. The captain unpacked more papers from the manila folder, piling the documents on the table. Yatsuka recognised statements in Japanese text. He could read the odd word. He realised that there was no use being evasive. The captain clearly already had the events and evidence in detail. He sagged, "I can remember some..." The captain responded in slight mock-surprise, "Can you? That is good. Shall we begin then?" The captain's pencil was poised at the top of a clean sheet to make his notes, as Yatsuka began to write out his statement, chewing his lip thoughtfully. Kondo cleared his throat to translate. "Yes, I was on Minesweeper W12 when we escorted the Suez Maru. We left Ambon I think on 25 November bound for Soerabaya. We discovered that an enemy submarine had made contact with us on the evening of 28th I think, somewhere south of Celebes Island. We let the Suez Maru sail ahead and we tried to locate the submarine to attack it, but we lost contact because of the dark night and a squall. We gave up the attack before dawn and chased the Suez Maru. When we caught up with her it was late, and we continued our voyage. I was on watch the following day, at about 0920 hours and saw the wake of a torpedo about 2,500 feet aft on the port side. We immediately dropped depth charges but two torpedoes struck the aft hold and the Suez Maru in about twenty minutes began to sink from the stern. It seemed for a while that she would stay afloat but the water gradually increased and the vessel sank." Yatsuka's eyes dropped to the floor, but the captain had no intention of letting him have a moment, and pushed on. "What did you see of the Suez Maru? Did you see PoWs abandoning ship?" Yatsuka stared face to face with the captain, shaking his head, "Well, no, I was in charge of the anti-submarine attack and was dropping depths charges so I could only glance in that direction occasionally." The captain rolled his eyes, "I see, and what did you see when you 'glanced' there?" He pressed, firmly pushing his question. "Well, after the ship sank, I saw survivors through binoculars. They were gathered on two boats and a raft made from lumber and board." The captain sniffed deeply. The sense of unfolding unchangeable tragedy rounding in his mind. All poised to happen again. He ignored the weight in his chest. "And did you report the sinking at that time?" "Yes, I continued the anti-submarine attack, and I despatched a report to 21 Base Force Commander and 24 Base Commander." Yatsuka sat back as if finished. The captain, exasperated asked, "Well? What did you say?" Yatsuka tapped at the table with his fingertips, as if sending the Morse himself. "The gist of it was, ahh, 'Suez Maru torpedoed. Sunk by enemy submarine. 300 nautical miles east north east of Kangean Island. At 0920 hours on 29th. We are now attacking enemy submarine'. That was about it."

"Very well, continue," allowed the captain, Yatsuka nodded into the air, looking into the distance, "I saw a reconnaissance plane come over from Soerabaya, about 1300 hours but it left about 1500 hours. We continued the submarine attack and then our echo-ranging picked up the enemy submarine in the waters underneath the area where the survivors were floating, so it was impossible to make a depth charge attack there." The captain pointed with his pencil, "You don't think that might have been the sinking Suez Maru that you picked up? Did you sink the Allied submarine?" Yatsuka thought for a moment, but did not respond to the first question. The captain pointed again with his pencil indicating Yatsuka must answer. "I do not know if we sank the enemy submarine or not. So, we called off the attack and started rescuing the victims. The captain said to us, 'We are engaged in action against the enemy and we may be attacked again so we must rescue the survivors in a hurry. There is a limit to the number of persons we can accommodate so we will rescue our men first. While the cutters are engaged in rescue work we will circle the area and keep a lookout. When the cutters are full, we will pull alongside and transfer the people. Keep a sharp watch out'. So we began to rescue survivors." Yatsuka cupped his hands round his mouth, "I called out 'Pick up the Japanese first'. We carried on like this until around 1700 hours. Then all the Japanese were saved." The captain exhaled deeply, "Hmm, and what then of the prisoners of war?" "Well, there were a lot of them. In the water, clinging to boats, rafts and pieces of wood." Yatsuka's eyes drifted into the distance. "They looked tired... there must have been at least a hundred." "Yes, all right. So, what happened then?" "Well, an engineer officer came up and gave a report to the captain that we were low on fuel due to the submarine attack and chasing it the day before. They said we needed to go to Batavia because Soerabaya was mined, and we needed to set off immediately or we would run out of fuel." The captain considered Yatsuka's words. "I see, go on." "Well, I looked around for the captain of the

Suez Maru and then took him to see the captain of the minesweeper on the bridge." "Were you present for that conversation?" "Yes, I was." "Well? What was said?" "Well, I said, 'Captain Kawano, I have brought Captain Shirakawa of the Suez Maru transport vessel,' then Captain Kawano said to Captain Shirakawa, 'I realise the trouble you have gone through, were you hurt?' Captain Shirakawa answered, 'Thank you very much, but I did not receive a scratch'. Captain Kawano asked 'What is the condition of your crew?' Captain Shirakawa replied, 'About five of them are missing.' Captain Kawano said, 'That is too bad'." Captain Sylvester nodded, and Yatsuka continued. "Captain Kawano said to Captain Shirakawa, 'Who is your transport commander? Could you take me to him?' Captain Shirakawa said, 'It is First Lieutenant Iketani, and I will take you to him'. The captain and I then climbed down from the bridge and went to the foredeck where I met First Lieutenant Iketani. I took him to the bridge to meet Captain Kawano. Then they discussed the situation." Captain Sylvester looked to Kondo who held up a finger and blushed as he scurried to finish writing. He looked up nodding that he had caught up. "All right, what did Iketani and Kawano discuss?" Yatsuka fidgeted in his chair, rubbing his smooth chin with his soft hands. His eyes gleamed in the dull light as he continued, "I introduced Iketani to Kawano and he said, 'I appreciate what you have gone through, are you hurt at all?' Iketani said, 'I haven't got a scratch.'" Captain Sylvester frowned. "Iketani repeated the same words as Shirakawa?" he interrupted, turning to Kondo for clarification, who said, "It's similar, I think Shirakawa meant more like 'I was lucky to be uninjured' and Iketani meant 'he escaped'." "Hmm," mused Captain Sylvester as he nodded at Yatsuka to continue. "Well, then Kawano asked Iketani 'What is the condition of the Japanese passengers?' Iketani said, 'I can't be sure, there are sixteen missing but almost everyone seems to have been brought on board'. Kawano asked what part of the ship the PoWs were in, and Iketani said, 'They were in the aft hold, so it would seem that over half of them went down with the ship because that is where the torpedo hit'. Then Kawano asked, 'How are we going to dispose of the PoWs? Have you received any order from higher authorities?'" Captain Sylvester held up a hand, "You mean to say that Captain Kawano just suddenly asked how to 'dispose' of PoWs?" Kondo interjected, "It might mean sort of, what are we going to do with the PoWs." "I see, all right then continue." Yatsuka looked back and forth not understanding the exchange, then continued at the captain's nod. "Iketani said I have orders instructing us to shoot them if the ship were sunk. I request that proper disposal is made by the escort ship. So Kawano said, 'Is that so? Then, we shall shoot them' and Iketani replied, 'I will leave it up to you captain'." Captain Sylvester again held up a hand, "And you said nothing at all?" "No, I did, I said, 'Captain! This is not right to kill PoWs by shooting. I think it would be all right to leave them alone since the boats are afloat. Let us start immediately' but Kawano said to me, 'It is the expressed wish of the army. Also the enemy submarine is bound to emerge after we leave and rescue the survivors. The information about Japanese forces will become known to the enemy and will affect operations adversely. We must not let PoWs fall into enemy hands. If we cannot accommodate all of them, death is the only answer. Shooting them is unavoidable'." "Unavoidable?" repeated the captain incredulously, "—did you try to dissuade him?" "No, his mind was made up, he ordered me to shoot them." The captain bristled, "What was your view at that time?" Yatsuka shrugged, "I thought they were futile murders, but that was the situation. We were also facing the enemy submarine," replied Yatsuka calmly. "Ah, the submarine. You wouldn't want it to be known would you?" Yatsuka looked to his feet. "Very well, what happened then?" "Well, I thought that after I was given this order I should carry it out speedily and called the warrant officer to the bridge." "What was his name?" interjected the captain, pencil poised. "Miyaughi, or it may have been Noromaga, I can't remember." The captain made a note. "I ordered him to take charge of the rifle unit and deploy twelve men on both sides of the foredeck, and shoot the prisoners of war." The captain, unblinking looked Yatsuka squarely in the eye, without speaking. Yatsuka averted his eyes from the captain's gaze and continued. "I also ordered the commanding officer of the rifle unit and the lookouts to make sure there were no mistakes on the targets, because about twenty of our men were still missing." "Where was the captain and where were you during the shooting?" asked the captain flatly. "Well, the captain assumed command from the bridge and I was on the foredeck. I supervised the shooting." "How did you supervise?" pressed the captain. "The navy officers carried binoculars as a rule, especially during action with the enemy, and I of course was carrying my seven-power binoculars." The captain finished writing a note and put his pencil down. "Now, I want to know exactly what your command authority was. Did you personally command the rifle and machine-gun units?" "No, I commanded artillery action taken by the main battery, but I did not command the machine-gun or rifle units. I believe it was Warrant Officer Miyaughi who was in command of the rifle units at that time." "What was his first name?" "Miyaughi? His full name was Toshinori Miyaughi." The captain wrote the name on a separate sheet, headlined '*Suspects To Trace & Interrogate.*' He leant toward Yatsuka gritting his teeth and continued, "What were the names of the members of the rifle unit?" Yatsuka became agitated and fidgeted incessantly. His hands rolled over each other and his brow beaded with sweat. "I-I-I cannot remember the names of the members of the rifle unit but if you ask Toshinori Miyaughi he will recall I am sure. Also, Ensign Tenekichi Morowaga or Petty Officer Keshio Kawashiro. They were members of the crew at that time. You will be able to learn their names." "Hmm, are you sure you are not giving me names of dead Japanese?" the captain asked. "No! These officers were released before I entered the hospital at Soerabaya. I am pretty sure that Morowaga and Miyaughi were alive and on board at that time." "Are you quite certain? Are you positive?" asked the captain firmly. "No, I am not positive," confirmed Yatsuka recoiling. "Hmm. Well, after you ordered the rifle and machine-gun units to deploy, what happened?" Yatsuka again looked to his feet and spoke into his shirt. "After preparations for firing were completed the captain had the ship cruise at a slow speed within fifty feet of the PoWs. The port side of the ship facing the PoWs. He had the firing begin at 1715 hours. At first the PoWs were lying down since they were tired and hardly paid any attention. However, when they heard the sound of firing and their comrades fell to the left and right they tried to protect themselves by hiding behind anything that would shelter them. The water in the vicinity was coloured by the blood and the scene was so distressing it made one covers one's eyes. The lookout, probably it was Petty Officer Toshino, who was posted at the twelve-power binoculars on the bridge said that he could see a Japanese, so I took up his place and saw a completely naked person with closely cropped black hair lying on a board. When Captain Shirakawa of the Suez Maru was called and he looked at the scene he said it was a crew member and asked Captain Kawano to save him. We ceased firing and taking the ship close to the man we pulled him aboard. We saw that the torpedo explosion had taken the flesh off his back and he was nearly dead."

Yatsuka stopped speaking and looked to the captain. The captain gave him nothing, he merely nodded to resume. "Well, after returning to our positions, we approached the scene of our last firing and again started shooting at the PoWs in the water on the port side of our ship, whist watching for the submarine. There were..." Yatsuka faltered, the captain frowned, "Go on...There were?" "There were..." He sighed and stopped again, swallowing hard. "... some brave prisoners of war who, knowing they were going to be shot, stood up on the boards and presented themselves as targets for our bullets." The captain's face broke into a fierce scowl. He stared at Yatsuka in utter disgust. Yatsuka could not bear his gaze and looked away, but the captain barked angrily "Finish what you have to say. Now!" Yatsuka sniffed in self-pity and continued, "Well, there was nothing to hide behind as it was an open sea. Gradually the PoWs floating there decreased as they were hit one by one and sank." The captain reached across the table as if to grab at him, but Yatsuka recoiled shrieking, "It was an inhuman thing to do, I know! To kill unresisting men, but it was war and we had to do it!" The captain scowled unsympathetically, his clenched fists banging the table. "Is that what I should tell the families of those men? Is that what you said at the time?" "Yes, yes, I said to Engineer Officer Tamaka, who was standing beside me. I said, even if it is this way, it is a distasteful thing, isn't it? And he said it is pitiful isn't it. But I thought, if it was a means of winning the war it had to be carried out at any cost." The captain shook his head angrily, shouting, "How could that be a means of winning the war? Did you not consider it was a war crime?" "Well, I don't know, I was under orders. I had to do it." The captain sat back, his face reddened in frustration. In his mind it was the umpteenth time he was unable to do anything to save them. It was a moment before he spoke. "Well, what happened after that then?" Yatsuka's voice was a low murmur. "We continued firing until the lookout, I think it was Toshino, using the twelve-power binoculars on the bridge, reported that all the PoWs were dead. Suddenly one of those we had taken aboard suddenly shouted 'Torpedo'. We looked in the direction he was pointing, and saw a white object which looked like a water spray. On closer inspection it was not a torpedo but an object floating on the water. We checked that there were no survivors and the two hours of killing ended about 1900 hours and our ship left for Batavia." The captain's eyes narrowed in disgust, as he searched for words to conclude the questioning. He knew what to say, only the sentences seemed unable to fall from his mouth. His eyes searched Yatsuka's face for any emotion besides self-pity. The captain paused as the echo of gunfire receded from his mind.

The captain hadn't noticed how dry his mouth had become as he'd listened. His voice was hoarse as he began to speak. He coughed and continued croakily whilst reaching for a glass of water. "So the report you made at Batavia, was to whom?" Yatsuka was composed and spoke clearly. "We arrived at Batavia at 1700 hours on the 30th I think, and then transferred the men to their army units. It was the next day that the transport commander brought our captain a copy of a report dealing with the army's transport of men aboard the Suez Maru. They talked, but I don't know what the discussion was about, but I know they noted in the report that all the PoWs had died in the torpedo attack." "Hmm I see. All right, that is all for now," announced the captain, his mouth a flat, hard line. "Your statement will be prepared for you to sign, which will be witnessed. However, I would like to go back over the names of those involved that we have talked of and I would like a little more information." Yatsuka looked about in alarm, "I have already told you all the names I know." "Yes, we will go through them now." Replied the captain firmly. Yatsuka sat up straight in the chair as the captain ran a finger down the names compiled during questioning. Abruptly Yatsuka spoke, he was now sweating freely. "Ahh, I do know of others you should investigate and question..." The captain paused, without moving his head he lifted his eyes to Yatsuka, "Oh?" Yatsuka looked secretively to Kondo and back to the captain, "I do know more names," "Go on..." "I think you should investigate Sekita. He was the officer in charge of compiling combat reports, and although his predecessor Kuroda is dead, such laborious work could not have been done by Kuroda alone. You should speak to Maeda. I believe Kawano reported the shooting to him after arriving at Batavia. It was Kawano's duty to visit him and report, Maeda must have heard of the murders." "Tadashi Maeda?" asked the captain. "Yes," confirmed Yatsuka. "Anyone else?" asked the captain, his eyebrows raised. "Yes, ask Hirose, he is a civilian but he visited the minesweeper during our stay in Batavia. He must have heard of the murders as well. Officer Watanabe of the minesweeper must have read the combat report. He must have read that part of the log. He must also know." The captain noted the names, his pencil underlining surnames and noting that they were to be traced ASAP. "This information is useful, however, it cannot help you. You have been involved in a most heinous war crime. You will not be granted leniency for offering this information. Do you understand?" Yatsuka's mouth opened and closed, and the captain nodded as Yatsuka's motivation was clearly revealed. He had clearly hoped to gain something from revealing the names. "In a moment someone will someone will escort you while your statement is prepared." Yatsuka was still attempting to speak, his mouth making no noise as he was led out of the room.

Back in his office the captain checked through Yatsuka's statement against his list, for familiar names, including those volunteered at the end of the interrogation. He added them to a longer list of suspects yet to be traced and questioned. He glanced through his open door, calling out to Officer Beirne as he saw him passing. "Ahh, Beirne, I need these suspects finding, for immediate interrogation." Officer Beirne turned on his back foot and swung round into the captain's office. "Of course, sir." The captain offered the sheet of paper scrawled with his slanting writing. "Most urgent is this one I think, ahh Sekita. And I want Maeda back in again. I also urgently need a certified copy of Minesweeper W12's log entries for the period, er, 24 November to say, 24 December 1943, or whatever you can get." Officer Beirne nodded. He turned but the captain remembered another request, and spoke again. "... yes and I need an update on Sanso Anami, has he been traced yet?" Officer Beirne shook his head slowly, whilst reading the new list, then looked up. "No, sorry sir. There's nothing on him." "Did you check Sugamo? Perhaps he's already in custody. Also check the Singapore investigations, he may have appeared there already." "Yes, of course sir." Officer Beirne nodded and turned again, heading back down the corridor as the captain retreated into his papers.

- 10 AUGUST 1949 -

There had been not a drop of rain for over a week yet the sky bulged with threatening dampness. The heat was suffocating and humid. Moisture stuck clothes to his body and sweat sat on the brow and spine of Captain Jack Sylvester, it had nowhere else to go. The air surrounding him, pressing onto him, was full to capacity. He frowned at the circling fan in the ceiling of his office. The revolving blades whirred energetically but there was little movement of air for the effort. Opening the small window brought a breath of wind, but it was as warm as the air within. "Better than nothing," muttered the captain to himself. Piled on his desk amid his papers was the day's mail. Letters and packets which he sifted through with one hand whilst reaching for his cup of tea with the other. He slit open a fat envelope stamped 'Japanese Government' and pulled out a wad of sheets. His eye travelled to the subject line, 'Request for questioning, Anami, Sanso'. He put down the tea, unsipped. He grasped the letter with both hands. His eyes rushed about the page, stopping suddenly. "Damn it!" he shouted as he read the confirmation he did not want to see.

Legal Section Check List
Confirmed, the subject referred to as
Sanso Anami.
Was executed in Singapore, 12 September 1946,
enclosed is the certificate of death.

Captain Sylvester turned the corner of the page and scanned the certificate with a resigned sigh. 'Re- Former Lt. Col. ANAMI, Sanso. I hereby certify that the above person was executed as a war criminal in Singapore...' "Damn, damn, damn!" he said again, thumping the edge of his desk. "Dead men tell no lies, *and* no truths," he muttered. He knew both Iketani and Kawano rested their statements upon simply following the orders of this dead individual. Now, there would be no corroboration. It seemed highly unlikely they hadn't been aware their former superior was dead, and a convicted war criminal. He placed the letter in his tray, sliding its empty envelope into his wastepaper basket, before reaching for the next parcel. It was a thickly wadded military package, heavy and creased. It tore easily as he ripped open one end. A buff-coloured, stamped folder slid out on to his desk. It was marked, Confidential and underneath, Trial of Japanese War Crimes, Singapore. He gingerly opened the cover with thumb and forefinger, as if afraid of what he might find inside. Captain Sylvester read the report of Anami's trial. His eyes skipped across the front page of the report as he muttered the case number, "...235/886,"

He ran a finger down the names of the accused, looking for Anami. He missed the name at first glance, then looked again finding it at the top of the list. He read on, his eyes alighting here and there.

```
1. Lt. Col. ANAMI Sanso,
2. Captain UEDA Tadae,
3. Sergeant Major MORI Masao,
4. Guard KAWAYAMA Yoshikichi
... of the Imperial Japanese Army...
Place and Date of Trial, Singapore, 3-26 July, 1946.
```

He flicked through the report's pages, reading the list of charges he found familiar. The first charge dealt with the transport of PoWs. He skipped the second, as it related to Haruku and moved to the third charge.

First charge: Committing a war crime in that they at Soerabaya, Java, and at Sea, in the month of April 1943, when concerned in the transport of a draft of British and Dutch Prisoners of War to Haruku, Liang (Ambon) and Amahai (Ceram) Islands, were, in violation of the laws and usages of war, together concerned in the ill-treatment of the said Prisoners of War.

Third charge: Committing a war crime in that they at Ambon Island, between 1st May 1943 and 31st October 1944, the Accused 1 as Commandant Prisoners of War Camp Group, the Accused 2, as Medical Officer Prisoners of War Camp Group and the other accused named, as members of the Ambon prisoners of war camp-staff, being responsible for the well-being of British and Dutch Prisoners of War interned in the said Camp, were, in violation of the laws and usages of war together concerned in the inhumane treatment of the said Prisoners of War

resulting in the deaths of some and in physical
sufferings to others.

Other charges against the accused related to other islands and the
captain's eye wandered down the charges of inhuman acts. He was
about to stop reading when he noticed the sixth charge.

<u>Sixth Charge:</u> Committing a war crime in that
they on a voyage from Ambon Island to Java
in or about the month of September 1944,
when concerned in the transport of a draft
of British and Dutch Prisoners of War by the
Maros Maru, renamed Haruyoshi Maru, were,
in violation of the laws and usages of war,
together concerned in the ill-treatment of the
said Prisoners of War, resulting in the deaths
of some and in physical sufferings to others.

The captain sighed sadly. His thoughts reflected on the numerous
cases he'd investigated and the terrible stories of prisoner transports.
Voyages to and from hell. "What was the point?" he asked himself
sadly. He turned the pages over to the last and read a section titled,
'Findings and Sentences'. Again his eyes travelled the page in
search of Anami, eventually finding him atop the list. 1, Anami:
Guilty all charges, sentence: Death by hanging.
Captain Sylvester slowly closed the report, placing it in his tray.

The heading on the next letter read 'Japanese Government.'
The captain flicked the page over wondering if it were a duplicate
but the subject line read, 'Request for Information,
Minesweeper W12 Log Book.' "Aha! At last!" he shouted to
no one. His eyes scanned the document, flitting up and down, reading fast.
'...required log cannot be found...
Minesweeper No.W12 was torpedoed... April
1945... it is presumed the log was lost

with the minesweeper... impossible to
investigate... all the officers of the
minesweeper were lost when she was sunk...
no documents found at Soerabaya after
termination of hostilities.'

The captain dropped the letter onto his desk and groaned. He bent
the corner of the page forward, reading over its shoulder to the printed
sheet below.

'Japanese Naval and Merchant Shipping
Losses During World War II by All Causes,
Feb. 1947'. The document listed the Suez Maru — Nov 29,
1943, Assessment: Sunk. Further down the captain read,
Minesweeper W12, April 6, 1945. Assessment:
Sunk. He signed the bottom of the page to indicate he had read it and
flicked back to the first page. He noted that the succeeding Officer of
Minesweeper W12 was Lieutenant Watanabe. He had been repatriated
to Japan in 1946. "He needs tracing, now!" the captain muttered to
himself. He looked to the rest of the letters curiously. They were all
stamped 'Japanese Government'. Cutting them open he piled
the papers on one side of his desk and began to plough through them.
They were the result of endless requests for information about his case.
He had asked for the Minesweeper W12's log, and for details of the
Suez Maru. They had all been finally been answered. The next letter
was a reply to his request of 24 June, seeking a list of surviving crew of
the *Suez Maru*. This had arrived via information from the Kuribayashi
Steamship Company. He scanned the list.

1st Assistant Engineer S. Hirashima now
Chief Engineer Sanriku Maru.
Deck Storeroom Attendant Nagasaki now
Coxswain Kaminaga Maru.
Fireman I. Ehara now Fireman on Sakura Maru.

He stopped, peering closely at the familiar names. He frowned
and continued.

Machinist S. Minoda, now machinist on
Sanriku Maru
Machinist H. Kunimisa, now on reserve.

```
Fireman M. Kikuchi now on reserve.
Fireman K. Kojima now Machinist on
Seria Maru.
Seaman S. Maeda now Coxswain on Shinko Maru.
Purser T. Nukui - now retired.
Captain T. Shirakawa - now retired.
```

The captain underlined the names of those he had not yet questioned and placed the sheet on top of the growing pile in his tray.

Captain Sylvester took the next reply and scanning the typewritten text he recognised it was an untitled account of the sinking of the *Suez Maru*, dated 17 December 1943. At first glance it seemed to cover the same information obtained from every witness already questioned. His eyes darted about picking up familiar words and phrases of the sinking, then he stopped. He eyes had come to rest on a phrase that made him bristle with irritation. He returned to the top of the page and began reading from the beginning.

```
Army Transport Suez Maru, attached to the
Shipping Command.
Torpedoed 29 Nov. 1943, 0920 hours. Sunk en
route to Soerabaya escorted by Minesweeper
W12, departed Ambon 25 Nov. 43, the ship
changed course on 25th upon being notified
by Minesweeper W12 that Soerabaya harbour was
mined and to alter course to Batavia.
```

The captain made a note of the date as Captain Kawano as well as Fujimoto and Gunnery Officer Yatsuka all spoke of fuel shortage due to the change in course to Batavia as if it was a last minute detour and that it was part of their reasoning why they could not rescue PoW survivors. The captain tapped at the desk with his pencil. A low growl rumbled from him as he read the rest of the page.

```
At 0920 hours on the 29th two torpedo wakes
were sighted and before the helm could be
fully turned at full speed they found their
mark on the port stern. An immediate survey
found that the poop deck had collapsed and as
well as holds three and four, which had been
```

```
completely flooded. Thus all efforts were
directed towards lowering lifeboats...
```

The captain eyed the document suspiciously as if it were itself a suspect sitting in the chair opposite and lying directly to his face. "Lying bastards!" The captain said to himself, "They mean to say that immediately both three and four holds collapsed and flooded. That there were *no* PoW survivors!" He shook his head angrily, his eyes scanning the rest of the page.

```
...after the ship had been abandoned a thorough
search was made for survivors but none were found.
```

"None were found! Damned liars!" the captain shouted, thumping his desk and causing the assorted papers to jump.

```
A short time later the ship sank rapidly
from the stern and at about 0940 hours the
bow rose from the water and the ship sank
stern first. It was a cloudy day, a light
south-westerly wind was blowing and the waves
were gentle.
```

The captain threw the paper to his desk "Oh, by all means discuss the weather!" he barked sarcastically, knowing it was simply a reporting protocol. He was angry for the blatant omissions and clear cover up. He snatched up the paper again and finished the document with a grunt.

```
...the minesweeper dropped depth charges
for about three hours and then returned to
the vicinity of the sinking circling round
rescuing survivors.
```

"They just stated none were found! That there weren't any survivors! Of course meant their own!" shouted the captain to himself in exasperation.

```
...a very thorough search was made however
no more survivors could be located and the
search was discontinued at about 1900 hours
and we resumed our journey to Batavia.
```

The captain puffed his cheeks and blew out hard, shaking his head "What a load of old—" his words were drowned by a knock at his door and the captain returned to the present, "Yes?" he called angrily. Officer

Beirne pushed his head round the door. "I was asked to see if you were all right? Only, there was a lot of shouting and..." The captain nodded, waving at him to enter. "Yes, quite all right, but since you're here Beirne, I need an urgent trace for one Teiichi Mitoshi, Commander of Java Branch, 3rd Shipping Transport Command in '43." The captain tossed the paper towards Officer Beirne, "Here read this, tell me what you make of it. Falsifying war records, and concealment of a war crime, I believe." The officer took the sheet and looked past it to the captain, "Any others traced yet? Hirose, Watanabe, Miyaughi, Morowaga, Kawashiro?" "Not yet sir, but we will find them." Officer Beirne nodded to the captain, continuing, "Also, when you are ready, Koji Sekita is ready for questioning. He's in the room now. When you are ready, sir." "Yes, I'm ready, get a hold of Kondo will you?" snapped the captain as he got up, angrily reaching for his tea and taking a stone cold sip.

The captain opened the door to the interrogation room and Koji Sekita sat up keenly. The captain measured his steps across the room, lowering himself into his chair while examining Sekita closely. Twitchy and avoiding eye contact, he rubbed his hands together, and tugged at his ear as he smoothed his hair. The captain noticed all the signs of nervousness, and suspected at least knowledge, if not guilt. The captain began immediately, Kondo translating quickly, sensing the captain's urgency "You are Koji Sekita, presently working for Nippon Yusoki Co, and formerly a Lieutenant-Commander in the Imperial Japanese Navy, based at 21 SNB Unit, Batavia during late November, 1943, when the ship Minesweeper W12 arrived carrying survivors of the Suez Maru, which sank on 29 November, is that correct?" Sekita didn't flinch but stared at his hands wrapped around each other and tightened his grip, knuckles whitening, "Yes, I was at Batavia, yes I heard of the sinking of the Suez Maru." The captain rubbed his chin thoughtfully, "I see, and what do you know of the massacre of Allied prisoners of war in the sea from that ship?" Sekita startled, his eyes wild, "Ah, ah, I heard of the sinking of the Suez Maru, but I never heard of a massacre of PoWs!" "I see, what do

you know of Captain Kawano, of Minesweeper W12?"
"Well, I met with Kawano several times, but he
never told me about a massacre. I don't think he
told me anything about the Suez Maru at all." "I
see, so how did you hear about the sinking of the
Suez Maru?" "Well, I-I-I was attached to the Naval
Harbour Masters Office at the time of the sinking
and transferred to the Base Force HQ in March of
the next year, ahh, 1944. Maybe it was there that
I heard of the sinking..." "I see, so you never saw
the combat report from the Minesweeper and did
not receive a report on the sinking of the Suez
Maru?" "No, I do not recall that." Sekita bit his lip to stop
it from trembling. The captain glared, causing Sekita to look away.
"So..." the captain said flicking a page back and forth, as if checking
a detail. "... as Lieutenant-Commander you regularly
received reports from incoming transports. You
helped compile combat reports and loss of vessel
reports. Is that not correct?" Sekita rubbed sweat from his
palms under the table and scratched his neck uncomfortably. "Well,
yes I did receive reports and assist gathering
information-" The captain jumped in, "-so you are telling
me that amongst your duties you also assisted in
writing these reports?" "Well, yes-" "-but you never
heard of the Suez Maru, only in passing. Some time
later, and you don't know about the shooting of
the PoWs?" "Well, I-I-I that is to say, that..." The
captain again interjected, barking at Sekita, "You saw the battle
report and you saw the report of the sinking, didn't
you?" "No, I-I didn't see anything. I was not in
command. It was Kuroda that was in charge of these
matters..." The captain leant forward, placing his palms together
patiently. "You were not in charge? Would you like to
explain the chain of command that a battle report
would travel? I also want the chain of command for
receiving wireless reports, as not less than three

were sent..." he paused, flicking through his papers again. "Yes, three wireless messages were sent on the sinking and during the ensuing battle with the submerged submarine." Sekita looked apprehensive as the captain pushed blank sheets of paper to him with a pencil, "Do you know the penalties for giving false information to a war crime investigation?" Sekita's eyes narrowed as the captain pulled the sheet of Japanese text from the manila folder, "Here," he said sliding the sheet across the table. Sekita read it, twitching nervously. He pulled one of the blank sheet towards him, and drew a flow diagram of names and titles. Long arrows criss-crossed the page as the captain looked on. Sekita twitched back and forth looking to the page and the captain nervously, then he explained. "The Warship sends a runner," he said, tracing a line with the word runner written along it, "to the Document Exchange then it comes down to the officer in charge of General Affairs, then-" The captain cut him short, "I need names..." "Well ahh, this was Takahashi, I think. Then, it goes to the chief supply officer, ahh which was Shoraburo then to the Senior staff Officer, ahh Shinohara, and also to 2nd SEF who kept a copy and they sent one on to the Navy Ministry. Ahh... Shinohara would send it on to SO Engineer which I think was Shoji and on to the secretary which was Kuroda, but he is dead. And he would send it on to the commander of 21 SNBU, who would also send a copy back to the chief supply officer." "Hmm" said the captain examining the messy diagram, "...and you helped Kuroda?" " No, I did not. Well, not often..." The captain frowned. "Did the master of the Minesweeper Kawano keep a copy of the combat report?" Sekita considered the question for a moment, screwing his eyes shut and probing his memory. 'Hmm maybe a moment of truth' thought the captain. "Ahh, well if Kawano carried the combat report with him, he must have handed it to the general affairs officer or the chief supply officer. None of the staff officers accepted any official document directly." The captain rubbed at his chin, his questioning was not yielding all the information he was looking for. Nonetheless, he noted down the names. It would help identify whether further charges of falsifying war records and concealing war crimes could be brought. Finding those responsible beyond Saito, Iketani and Kawano and Yatsuka would be a longer task. The captain exhaled and returned his attention to Sekita, "What was your impression of Kawano?" Sekita stiffened. He straightened his back as if Kawano were in the room and Sekita were readying to salute. He lifted his chin admiringly, "He was reputed among the 21 SNBU officers for being scrupulous and faithful to orders. However busy he never complained. He was the eldest of all the masters of minesweepers under 21 SNBU. In those days there were few minesweepers." The captain curled his lip at Sekita's reverential tone. He considered briefly whether to tell Sekita that Kawano was currently sitting in Sugamo Prison awaiting trial for at least two hundred and fifty murderous war crimes. He found it irritating to hear Sekita bleating on as if Kawano were some honourable leader instead of the cowardly cold-blooded murderer he knew him to be. The captain stood abruptly, turning to Kondo, "We have all we need for today." He straightened his tie and gathered his papers as Sekita looked on. They left the room and the captain gave the sentry orders to wait with Sekita.

- 17 AUGUST 1949 -

"So, you are currently an advisor to the Nitro-Nissan company?" the captain asked Seiichi Maeda as he began to interview him for the third time. Maeda sweated profusely in the cramped interrogation room of the SCAP GHQ building. He nodded, eyes blazing and his chin raised defiantly. He was deeply displeased at being called in again. The captain had noted Maeda's attitude and he planned to use it to his advantage, pulling every thread to leave him bare and exposed. "I should like a little more detail from you, starting with a brief outline of your service history." Maeda nodded, replying curtly, "I was a Naval Captain based in Batavia from late September 1942, working as Liaison officer. I was promoted to the rank of Rear Admiral in May 1945. Then, I was repatriated to Japan in May 1947." The captain's face did not change, he replied smoothly. "That is too brief, I think you can expand on that." "Very well," said Maeda disappointed to not have irritated the captain, "I was appointed to the dual post of liaison and staff officer by the Naval Ministry, and was stationed at Soerabaya and Manila for a few months then I was placed under the command of the 2nd South Sea Expeditionary Fleet Headquarters, in Batavia." "And your role was...?" asked the captain evenly, not raising his eyes from his notes. Maeda realised he was not in charge of the room, he sighed resignedly, "My chief duty in Batavia was liaison with the army concerning military administration. In May 1944, I travelled to Makassar. Whilst there I heard that a while before, an army transport carrying a great number of PoWs had been torpedoed and sunk. I heard that almost all of the PoWs were dead. Having been questioned by you I now believe that the transport they were referring to was the Suez Maru. I also want to say that since I was last here, I have contacted a former subordinate, Captain Norio Kajitani, who was one of my assistants in Batavia. He said he could not remember anything about the execution of surviving PoWs from a sunken transport. But it's possible he didn't hear of this because he was relieved of his duties at Batavia in December 1943. I also contacted another former subordinate in charge of general affairs section, ahh, Makete Ishikawa. I asked him if he had any knowledge of the incident to meet me at Tokyo Station at 0800 hours this morning. He did not show up." Captain Sylvester looked up at Maeda in surprise, "Hmm, I see," he replied, noting down the names. "And what of Kawano? Do you think he did send a report of the incident?" "Well, it's likely that Kawano did forward his combat report through my office, but it could be forwarded without being seen by anyone as it would have been a sealed document." "Hmm" said the captain again. "Is there anything further you would like to add?" "Well, I would certainly suggest that you interrogate the senior staff officers, staff officer engineers and the commander of the 21st Special Naval Base Force concerning the combat report." "Very well, I will consider it in due course. You may leave after your statement is prepared and you have signed it in front of me." The captain folded the cover of the manila folder over, trapping the papers and documents inside. Kondo walked alongside him all the way down the corridor, but the captain did not notice, his mind was alight with questions and theories. He slipped quietly into his office, unconcerned with anything but tying all the loose strands of his investigation together.

- 30 AUGUST 1949 -

The captain's office door was closed, only the hesitant sound of a clicking typewriter revealed occupants within. Officers and staff blurred up and down the corridor outside as they hurriedly attended to business and their own concerns. Within his muted, still office Captain Sylvester was oblivious to the bustling world beyond. His hands spread over masses of papers covering his desk as he dictated his investigation progress report to a secretary. She pulled a sheet out through the platen roller and laid it next to the typewriter. She patted it flat with the palm of her hand before rolling a fresh sheet through. The first page was typed with a single word, CONFIDENTIAL. She typed the next page falteringly, as the captain's speech lingered here and there. The repetitive clack-clack of the typewriter hammered, alternately punctuating and leaving silent spaces in the air.

Report detailing Progress of the
Investigation in the SS Suez Maru Case - Fate
of 414 English and 133 Dutch PoW.

(1.) Investigation of the subject incident was
begun following receipt of a letter of 4 June,
written by Yoshio Kashiki, a former member of
the Japanese Army and at present an invalid in
Tokyo National Hospital.

(i) Kashiki says, "I was one of 200 Japanese
hospital patient en-route to Soerabaya on 25
Nov '43. In addition there were about 550 sick
British and Dutch soldiers on board. The ship
also carried 3 or 4 damaged airplanes on deck.
We left Ambon escorted by a destroyer."

(ii) Around 0930 hours on 29 November the Suez
Maru was torpedoed and sank immediately. In spite
of the fact that the persons aboard, other than
the PoW Commander and crew, were all patients,
all the lifeboats were occupied by the crew. We
were saved after three hours of drifting, and not
one of the Allied PoWs were saved at that time.

(iii) On board the destroyer the fate of the
PoW was sealed by a few words such as 'Let's
dispose of them' exchanged between a person
who seemed to be the commander of the destroyer
and the commander in charge of the PoW. Shortly
afterwards, about 17 or 18 non rated seamen,
each armed with a rifle, lined up on the forward
deck and shot and killed the 270 or so men who
were screaming for help. After killing every
single one of them the ship left the area in the
evening, and headed for Java.

(iv) I have written this in the hope that the souls of the dead men (PoW) will rest in peace. I am a convalescent forsaken by my one and only elder brother and would be placed in an embarrassing position if my name became known in connection with this case. I ask that my real name be never made known.

(2.) Following receipt of the above mentioned letter, verification of the sinking of the Suez Maru was obtained from the following publication: Japanese Naval and Merchant Shipping Loses during World War II by all Causes, (page 47) prepared by the United States Joint Army Navy Committee, February 1947.

(i) At the time of receipt of the communication of Kashiki. One Saito, a former civilian interpreter with 2 SSEF, was being interrogated by their Section in connection with War Crimes in Soerabaya, Java. He was questioned regarding his probable knowledge of the sinking of the Suez Maru as he was at that time in Soerabaya. He admitted hearing of the sinking while visiting the H.Q. 2SSEF. His knowledge (hearsay) was incorporated into his statement and consists of a number of scraps of information. In brief, Saito heard that the Suez Maru, a large commercial ship drafted as a transport and hospital ship was bombed and sunk near Soembawa Island in the Java sea while en route to Japan. She was carrying 400-500 Japanese sick and wounded servicemen, and 300 or 400 Allied PoW, in addition to a number of aeroplanes.

(ii) The following day Fumio Nomaguchi
a former Lt-Comd and Adjutant to the 2SSEF
was called and questioned in connection with
the incident. He admitted to hearing about
the sinking of a Japanese transport in Nov
'43, but claimed he was unable to recall her
name. He did not hear the type of cargo or
passengers carried. Nomaguchi named Commander
Yoshio Hiramatsu SO Engineers then with 2 SSEF
as a possible source of information. Yoshio
Hiramatsu was called and interrogated but
he denied all knowledge of the incident. No
statement was taken.

(iii) It was learned through Liaison Div.
Legal Sec. CHQ, SCAP, that the Suez Maru had
belonged to the Kuribayashi Steamship Company,
whose offices are in the Marunouchi Building
in Tokyo. Thereafter a report of the sinking
of the Suez Maru was requested. This report
has been received and a certified translation
obtained. The first part of this report gives
names and present locations of ten former
members of the crew of the Suez Maru. The
remainder consists of a transcript of a report
made by Teiichi Miyoshi, Commander of the Java
branch of the 3 Shipping Transport Command.

(iv) It reads as follows—

17 December 1943

'Army Transport Suez Maru, attached to the
Shipping Command. Torpedoed 29 Nov. 1943, 0920
hours. Sunk en route to Soerabaya escorted by
Minesweeper No. W12, departed Ambon 25 Nov. 43,

344

the ship changed course on 25th upon being
notified by M/S No.W12 that Soerabaya harbour
was mined and to alter course to Batavia.
At 0920 on the 29th two torpedo wakes were
sighted and before the helm could be fully
turned at full speed they found their mark
on the port stern. An immediate survey found
that the poop deck had collapsed and as well
as hold compartments three and four, which had
been flooded. Thus all efforts were directed
towards lowering lifeboats. After the ship had
been abandoned a thorough search was made for
survivors but none were found. A short time
later the ship sank rapidly from the stern and
at about 0940 hours the bow rose from the water
and the ship sank stern first. It was a cloudy
day, a light south-westerly wind was blowing
and the waves were gentle.'

(v) On 28 June 49, a report on Japanese
police notepaper was received from Liaison
Division. This report gives the position of the
sinking, tonnage and route followed by the Suez
Maru at the time of her sinking. The passengers
carried were,
> (i) The 40 Casualty Clearing
> Platoon
> (ii) PoW Escort Detail
> (iii) PoW (Nationality unknown)
> (iv) the 42nd Infantry regiment
> (v) The 44 Field Anti Aircraft
> Artillery Battalion.

(3.) The following twenty-two named were
interrogated and sworn statements obtained.
Confirming the facts of the massacre of between

100-280 PoWs by machine-gun fire from the deck
of Minesweeper W12 after the rescue of Japanese
survivors, following the sinking of the Suez
Maru by Allied action on 29 Nov. 1943.

SUEZ MARU
1) Shirakawa, Tamaki - Civilian, Ships Master.
2) Minoda, Shinichi - Crew member.
3) Hirashima, Masasaburo - 1st Asst Engineer.
4) Kikuchi Morimasu - Fireman.
5) Kokussen, Hidenori - Crew member.
6) Nukui, Joji - Purser.
7) Ehara, Ichiro - Fireman.
8) Maeda, Saburo - Seaman.
9) Narishima, Shunichiro - Crew member.
10) Nagasaki, Yoshimitsu - storeroom asst.
11) Eto, Kasuaki, -Probationary medical officer.
12) Iketani, Masaji, now Koshio, Masaji -
Former Army Lt. and PoW transport officer
(confession).

W12 Minesweeper
13) Kawano, Osamu, -Former Ships Master
(confession).
14) Kai, Masaru,-Former Lt and Chief Engineer.
15) Fujimoto, Takeshi,- Former ensign.
16) Yatsuka, Daiso, - Gunnery Officer.

OTHER
17) Nomaguchi, Fumio, Former Lt-Comd and
Adjutant of 2 SSE Fleet.(Evidence of doubtful
character).
18) Hiramatsu, Yoshio, - Former commander and
SO (Engineers) on the HQ of 2 SSE Fleet, Port
Officer at Soerabaya, (denied all knowledge of
the incident, no statement).

19) Saito, Seiichi -
- Former Major-General of 16th Army,
  commander of all PoW camps in the
  Java, Ambon, Ceram areas.
20) Suzuki, Hiroshi, - former captain
- 16th Army PoW camp staff, Batavia.
21) Sekita, Koji -
- Lieutenant Commander, Navy 21 Special Naval
Base Unit, Batavia.
22) Maeda, Tadashi, -
- Rear Admiral, Imperial Japanese Navy.
  (3 statements taken).

(i) In his statement Kawano confessed to
ordering the execution of the surviving
prisoners of war. He said the decision was only
made after being told by Iketani of a verbal
order he (Iketani) had received from Col. Anami
(deceased) prior to leaving Ambon. He further
stated that on arrival at Batavia he reported
the true facts of the massacre, and the reasons
for the action, to Maj-Gen Saito Seiichi,
commander of all PoW camps in the Java, Ambon
and Ceram Areas. He was then told to report
to a Captain Hiroshi Suzuki, to whom he also
told the true facts. Later Suzuki made out
an incorrect draft report which he, Iketani,
signed, which was finally submitted to the
Japanese authorities in Tokyo. A copy of this
report is currently in the possession of this
Section. Iketani handed a copy of his report to
Kawano two or three days after the Minesweeper
arrived in Tandjong Priok Harbour, Batavia.

(4.) Sometime in June or July of 1943 about
4,000 PoW were transferred from Java to Ambon,

Haruku and Ceram. Of these, approximately 1,000
British PoW were sent to Liang on Ambon, about
2,000 British and Dutch were sent to Haruku
on Haruku Island, and approx. 1,000 Dutch
were sent to Amahai on Ceram Island. These
PoW were to construct airfields for the 7th
Air Division. About 1,000 of them became sick
and were to be returned to Java on board two
vessels, but only one vessel was available.
This was the Suez Maru, on which 548 PoWs were
sent.

(5.) Suzuki Hiroshi supports Saito's and
Iketani's statement and says, 'A couple of days
after the minesweepers arrival in Tandjong
Priok harbour I was called into the high class
officers room. 1st Lt. Iketani was with me. I
was ordered by Lt-Col Matsunaga to hear from
1st Lt Iketani, the time, place, conditions of
the torpedo attack and under the supposition
that all the PoW went down with the ship,
to help him draw up the certification of
confirmation of death. I later presented the
completed document to Matsunaga in accordance
with his orders.

(6.) Also interrogated was Daiso Yatsuka, the
W12 Minesweepers Gunnery Officer. He stated
that he was under Kawano's supervision and
orders. He will give names and ranks of the
actual executioners. He states that Kawano
decided to execute the surviving PoWs,
after consultation with the transportation
commander, 1st Lt Iketani. Iketani told Kawano
in Yatsuka's presence that his orders were to
execute all PoWs in the event of the transport

being sunk. The shooting commenced at 1715
hours and continued until 1900 hours on 29th
Nov. 1943.

(7.) Yatsuka alleges that the shooting of
the PoW was duly recorded in the Minesweeper
W12 log and that later a true account of the
massacre was made in a Naval report to 21 SNBU
and forwarded through Rear-Adm Tadashi Maeda,
in Batavia. The day following the arrival of
Minesweeper W12 in Tandjong Priok, 1st Lt.
Iketani returned to the Minesweeper and handed
a copy of his report to Kawano, this was later
attached to the Naval report.

The captain took a deep breath and looked to the secretary to check
she had caught up. She finished typing and he nodded to her, "This part
is especially important," he said, running his pencil down his notes. He
spoke slowly and clearly to ensure each word was captured. She had barely
looked up but now glanced back and forth to confirm what she heard as
the captain nodded for her to complete the report. He did not want
this section overlooked, so asked her to underline the entire paragraph.

(8.) It is considered that there
is sufficient evidence to constitute a
prima facie case against Osamu Kawano,
Masaji Iketani, Daiso Yatsuka, and other
subordinate officers and crew members of
the Minesweeper W12, whose identity is as
yet unknown, but some if not all of whom
could be identified and apprehended as a
result of further investigation, and to
bring these participants to trial.

(9.) Sufficient Evidence is now held that
Lt-Comd Sanso Anami, who allegedly gave the

order to Iketani, was tried in Singapore in
Sept 1946, and was hanged as a result of the
court finding. Therefore, whether or not Anami
in fact gave or passed on the alleged order to
execute PoWs will in all probability never be
proved.

(10.) (i) Seiichi Saito, can be tried as
an accessory after the fact, because in his
statement he supports fully the story told by
Iketani who states he reported to Saito that
about 200-280 PoW were executed by machine-gun
fire from Minesweeper W12 after rescue of the
surviving Japanese.

(ii) Saito says he reported the facts
to Major-General Harada, Numakichi, (dec'd),
who suggested a false report be made to the
effect that, as many sick and wounded PoWs were
carried on board the Suez Maru, they had all
gone down with the ship. He thereafter returned
to his office and ordered Lt-Col Matsunaga,
Masatoshi, (now dec'd) to arrange that a false
report be made. This was done through Captain
Suzuki, Hiroshi.

(iii) Saito returned to Japan in December
1943 and according to him, reported the true
facts of the massacre to Major-General Hamada,
Hiroshi (now deceased - suicide), and Hamada
said it was not lawful but that he could
understand.

(iv) It is submitted that the evidence
already in hand indicates not only that Saito
and the commander of 21 Special Naval Base

Force and/or some of his staff officers failed
to take any disciplinary action against the
persons concerned, but also that they conspired
with the actual perpetrators to conceal the
crime.

(v) It was deemed necessary to arrest
Osamu Kawano in order to prevent him from
absconding. He was therefore arrested by this
section on 8 July 49, and is now held at Sugamo
Prison, Tokyo.

(11.) Hereunder is additional information
concerning two of the Japanese referred to in
this report-

(i) Anami, Sanso -convicted war
criminal, executed Singapore 12 Sept 46,

(ii) Hamada, Kumakicki -convicted war
criminal, executed Singapore 25 May 47.

The captain paced the room, his hands behind his back until he
reached the window where he held the frame. He stared out, unaware
of either the street noise below or the secretary asking, "Will that be all?
Sir? Is there more? ... Sir?" She tapped his arm lightly and the captain
spun around. He apologised for his pause, explaining that he had a
final section to record. He began, "There are a number of areas still to
investigate, so this will be, er, section 12, Undeveloped Leads..." He
returned to his chair, resting his chin on his knotted fingers, elbows
resting on his desk.

(12.) Undeveloped Leads

(i) The actual existence of an army order or authority permitting the atrocity.

(ii) Whether or not an order was given to Iketani by Lt-Col Anami, Sanso (deceased) to execute Prisoners of War.

(iii) Whether a true account of the incident was ever made to 21 Special Naval Base Unit by Kawano.

(iv) The identity of the actual executioners (should be a relatively easy matter).

(v) Responsibility for transporting sick and injured PoW on the SS Suez Maru instead of a hospital ship, (probably implicates 19th Army Ambon and 16th Army, Java).

(vi) The fate of the remaining 3,500 PoW who were distributed in camps on Ambon, Ceram and Haruku Islands, (Dutch investigated in part).

(vii) Responsibility of PWIB in Tokyo for disregarding international agreement in that the manner of the deaths of the PoWs was concealed.

The captain's face was flushed as he finished speaking. Every part of the case angered him. He leant forward, wiping sweat from his forehead with a handkerchief that he returned to his trouser pocket, stuffing the trailing end in with his thumb. He turned to the secretary, "Thank you, that will be all for now. I will check the text over and give you the report to copy shortly. There may be additions, but I'd like five copies tomorrow please." She smiled with tired eyes and nodded, taking the last sheet of paper from the typewriter and placing it face down on the pile. She turned the bundle of sheets over and handed them to the captain. "Thank you," he said as she slipped quietly from the room. The captain glanced at his watch and considered whether to call it a day. He looked to the mess of papers scattering his desk as the words in the title of his report caught his eye, drawing him back, 'Suez Maru Case - Fate of 414 English and 133 Dutch PoW.' He sighed, leaning into the chair and, with a scratch of his nose he started re-reading his report, from the beginning.

- 15 SEPTEMBER 1949 -

The captain stood with his back to his desk. His eyes darted across the large pin-board on his wall, almost completely covered with papers and notes, names and lists, all connecting the clues of the *Suez Maru* case. Paper corners fluttered gently in the cooling breeze drifting through the window. He held a letter in one hand, and a telegram in the other. Of the former he had read only the first few lines. The latter he had fully read and it was heavily creased. He had screwed it up, and thrown the crumpled ball angrily across the room. Only to retrieve, smooth it, and re-read it. "Damn, damn! Damn it all to hell!" he had shouted to no one. He turned, his gaze drifting across the piles of papers scattered across his desk, his eyes settling on his final investigation report. He fell heavily into his chair and with a long exhale read the short telegram again.

- - RESTRICTED - -

Re: War Crimes Trials - Suez Maru Case

Policy decision now taken that 30 September
must be maintained as terminal date for
Japanese War Crimes. Request you take action of
any accused now in arrest unless Australian and
SCAP authorities say otherwise.

--PRIORITY.--

The captain was incredulous, his face crumpled into pained disbelief. He looked again at the telegram then his eyes moved to the letter in his other hand. The familiar rounded handwriting took him back to that first letter by the same hand, which unbelievably had only been written just over three months earlier. He read the new letter again.

Dear Sir,

On 4 June I made a report to you about the mass machine-gun massacre of Allied prisoners of war, of mainly British and some Dutch soldiers. Has it been investigated yet? When that investigation is made contact the Tokyo Demobilisation Bureau and the captain of the minesweeper and the captain of the Suez Maru. I request a thorough investigation be made on the mass machine-gun murder, and an expression of condolence should be made to the spirits who lost their lives at that time. I am sorry I have not written earlier but I was taken into hospital as the condition of my health became very bad and much blood came out of my mouth (I am sorry I don't know the medical word for this), I am sorry for the delay and I send you here the letter from my doctor and I apologise again for the delay...

The captain flicked the corner of the letter over and scanned the capitalised handwritten words of Yoshio's doctor. 'Medical certificate... Yoshio Kashiki... raised much blood from the mouth... diagnosis: *Phthisis*... absolute rest necessary.' The captain mulled for a moment, muttering '*Tuberculosis*'. He tutted sympathetically, shaking his head before reading on.

... The responsibility of the mass killing rests on the captain of the escort ship and the leader of the prisoners of war escort. I believe these above two personnel on mutual agreement have murdered the prisoners. After this investigation is concluded I wish to publicise widely to the Japanese of these incidents in writings and never to repeat such atrocious acts. The

Japanese should know for themselves what atrocious, inhuman, brutality existed in the shadow of the Pacific War. They should be awakened to know that no matter how secretly an act was committed, that one day that act shall be made known to the public. We should build up Japan with strongness for justice, who love peace!

I await your reply. I will end now,

Yoshio Kashiki.

The captain could hardly bring himself to finish the letter. He had always tried to maintain a professional and somewhat removed approach to his investigations over the years, for self-preservation. But *this* case, *so* late in the day, and so *terrible*, cut him deeply. Disbelief merged with his sorrow. Despite it not being his own family and not in his general demeanour the captain bowed his head. His face creased and he wept silently into his hands. His mute office seemed to weep with him in its stillness. He grieved soundlessly, surrounded by the very documents and statements that would bring to trial the dozen or more accused in the case of the *Suez Maru* murders. Now, all for nought.

- 19 OCTOBER 1949 -

Emanuel Shinwell, Labour's Secretary of State for War paced in his London office. On his desk lay a one-page précis of a war crime case under investigation in the Far East. It awaited his attention and ultimately, his decision. He squinted at the report title. The single page had been edited down from the longer report prepared by Captain Jack Sylvester sent by the 2nd Australian War Crimes Section. Shinwell frowned at the sheet. The page contained basic information, but was it enough to make a decision whether to allow this case special permission to come to trial. It opened a series of questions for Shinwell. Questions he did not have time nor inclination to seek answers to. "Why has it taken four years for this case to be investigated?" he asked rhetorically of his secretary as he motioned for her to sit. He removed his round horn-rimmed spectacles and rubbed his small eyes. Running a hand through his thinning grey hair he leaned across his desk and picked up his pipe. Stuffing it with tobacco he muttered to his secretary to take his dictation. He wandered to his window and looked out at the darkening sky. "Letters to, ahh, Foreign Secretary Bevin, Lord Chancellor Earl Jowitt and Attorney General Sir Shawcross, if you please. Copy the same to each and enclose a copy of this report." He picked up the single sheet, wafting it in the air as the pipe waggled in the corner of his mouth. He dictated his letter, checking dates and names on the one-page report as he proceeded. All the while sending puffs of smoke into the air like a locomotive, as he moved around his desk. A hanging layer of grey mist accumulated in the dark wood panelled room. "Ahh, the usual, ahh addressing my Right Honourable colleague dah, dah, dah..." The secretary scribbled the letter down...

As you may know, the intergovernmental Far East Commission, which under its terms of reference deals with policy in regard to Japanese war criminals amongst other matters, decided in February last that there should be no more trials of war criminals (of the Nuremberg kind), and in April made a recommendation to Member Governments that *if possible,* investigations in connection with other war crimes should be completed before 30th June 1949, and all trials concluded if possible before 30th September 1949.

My attention has now been drawn to a new case, that of the *Suez Maru,* which our people in the Far East have sent forward for advice. As you will see from the attached précis, it is a very bad case. I am advised that it we decide to proceed with it, the best course of action would be to bring the trial *only* the three main instigators of the crime, Lieutenants Kawano and Iketani and Ensign Yatsuka, although there are *prima facie* grounds for proceeding against a number of subordinate officers and men not so far identified. I do not know why the case has taken so long to bring forward, but I understand that the investigation has been done by the Australians and that *our* people in the Far-East are not responsible for the delay.

The G.O.C. in C. FARELF, Lord Louis Mountbatten, Supreme Allied Commander South East Asia, has recommended that the case should be allowed to go to trial, and that the trial take place in Tokyo. The question is, however, whether or not there should be *any* further trials in view of the recommendation by the Far Eastern Commission and the fact that we are bound to put some term to trials of this kind. Either way, as I see it, we must be prepared to face criticism. If we started a new trial now, we would be open to attack for waiting more than four years after the end of the war to deal with a crime committed six years ago, and in the contrary event, the relatives of the murdered prisoners of war might well cause questions to be asked if they heard that those responsible would never be brought to justice.

On balance, *I* feel that there are very good grounds for regarding 30th September as the terminal date for Japanese trials. It is unfortunate that the first case to be ruled out should be a particularly bad one, but for all we know there may be others as bad and if we do not drop this, or any other bad case, I cannot see how we shall ever put an end to these trials. I should be glad to hear whether you agree with my view of the matter. I am writing in similar terms to, ahhh, add the others here if you please, and reference the report here.

Yours, and signed E. Shinwell etcetera..."

He rolled a hand in the air and the secretary glanced at Shinwell knowingly as she completed the shorthand letter. She looked expectantly to him. "Thank you, that will be all," he finished as she made a last note on the page before leaving the room. Shinwell moved back to the window, and looked out over the rippling Thames and the tall distinguished buildings of London as rain began to streak the glass, blurring the dark, smoky cityscape.

- 2 NOVEMBER 1949 -

Shinwell sat comfortably in a deep leather armchair, smoking his pipe in his office. Letters in reply to his lay opened and date stamped in a pile on his desk. He had sifted absently through them, reading quickly and scanning each for their agreement. He sat back satisfied that each minister had unhesitatingly agreed with him. He would now recommend they *do not* allow the case of the *Suez Maru* to proceed to trial. His fellow ministers reasons varied but he was grateful for their support regardless of their motives. Each saw the opportunity for personal embarrassment and criticism due to time elapsed in the *Suez Maru* case. Not one of these senior British cabinet ministers sought to ask the simple question, *why* had the case been investigated so long after the war crime? Lord Chancellor Earl Jowitt had expressed horror at the crime and concern that it had taken so long to bring forward. Shinwell glanced to his letter. "It is true that the case of the *SS Suez Maru* is a particularly nasty one and one which would arouse great feeling in this country as it concerned so many Allied men murdered in the sea..." Shinwell turned the page over and picked up the letter from Foreign Secretary Bevin. His eyes leapt about the page settling on a paragraph. He heard his lugubrious tone in his head, "... The issue of timing is not necessarily insurmountable, if it could be demonstrated that there was a reason why the Allies had been prevented from pursuing the case earlier. There must inevitably be a strong *moral* case for bringing war criminals of this kind to trial, despite the delay! It is most unfortunate that the first case to call into question the decision of the Far East Commission on war crime trials should be one as bad as that of the SS *Suez Maru,* but it would be preferable to support the decision of the Far East Commission and maintain the suggested terminal date for Japanese trials. I believe there would also be opposition from General Douglas MacArthur to any attempt to conduct such a trial in Tokyo, as suggested by Lord Mountbatten." Shinwell returned the letters to the pile and tucked them all into a folder marked TOP SECRET. He rubbed his chin as he puffed thoughtfully on his pipe.

- 8 November 1949 -

Captain Jack Sylvester could do no more. He had spent almost two months doggedly arguing his cause to his senior officers, for this last case to be tried. He awaited the final outcome of his heartfelt appeals. A last telegram had been sent that day, put forward by the Lieutenant Colonel in order to lend further weight to the push to bring the suspects to trial. Captain Sylvester hoped it would not be not in vain. They had asked for a formal acknowledgement of the case, and permission to investigate and arrest those responsible who were not already in custody. There was now a frustrating delay in receiving a response. No further documents had been sought and no further details had been asked for. Captain Sylvester found it curious, but rested in the knowledge that his rather lengthy and detailed report had outlined the facts clearly enough. But still, he could not understand the delay. He knew it should be a clear decision in light of the crime being such straightforward case. Resigned to waiting, all the captain could do was wait.

- 15 NOVEMBER 1949 -

Some six thousand miles from Tokyo in the smoky dusk of a chilly and damp Manchester evening, George raised a glass with his family in his snug sitting room, as he did every year on his brother birthday. Today, Jack would have been twenty-nine. As George wiped a wet drop that had forced itself from his eye, he managed to return his wife, Elizabeth's smile. George was immeasurably grateful to have survived the war. He had served across Britain almost throughout until he had been abruptly posted to India in 1944. It had been a cruel turn of fate, coming only a few months after learning of his younger brother's death at the hands of the Japanese. He had been sent to fight them through India and Burma. He was grateful to have survived, and knew he was lucky to have made it home. He felt Jack had been close by and with him through the jungle when his *Hadrian* glider had been shot down. He and three others had foraged for survival for weeks on end. George had imagined the kind face of his brother, and felt him standing nearby in the flowering humidity of the ripe jungle. They had encountered Japanese snipers tied into trees, it had been impossible to tell if they were dead, or alive and about to open fire.

George was grateful, every day, for the miracle of his survival despite the illnesses and ailments he had gathered. He was grateful to have the fresh chance of life, and of family. But inevitably he deeply missed his younger brother. He tried not to dwell on what might have happened to him. It was just that they had been told so little, practically nothing. The letter to their parents gave no answers yet raised so many questions. It simply stated it had happened, 'on a transport ship'. It explained nothing more. George, along with all the other families of those men aboard the *Suez Maru*, was oblivious to the facts of the sinking. He had no knowledge of the terrible war crime and the now unfolding chance to prosecute those responsible. A chance that was slipping away even as he raised his glass to his dear brother. George had never even heard the name *Suez Maru*, and did not know of Captain Sylvester. He had no idea that atonement for his brother hung in the balance that very day. And unbelievably, unforgivably, that it rested in the hands of his own country's cowardly Labour government.

-15 November 1949-

It was a wet Tuesday morning in London as Shinwell summoned his secretary into his office. He closed the heavy door behind her with a creak of the old oak. "Telegram if you please, take this down..." The secretary sat without a word, notebook in hand, pencil poised and ready. Shinwell scratched his cheek nervously with a forefinger. His brief deliberation after reading his peers support, had entirely made up his mind. But still, he had to word his self-preserving decision. He cleared his throat and rattled off his message to the secretary. "Restricted telegram to FARELF and SCAP GHQ, Tokyo. Regarding the War Crime Massacre at Sea of Allied PoWs of the SS *Suez Maru*. Further to their earlier request, they are advised that the War Office decision to terminate Japanese war crimes trials by 30 September *must* be maintained. FARELF is instructed to release any suspects unless required by other authorities. Ahh, I believe that one Osamu Kawano is the only suspect in custody, and so, ahh do they concur in his release? Ahh... mark as high priority, restricted." He frowned at his pipe, noticing it had gone out. "All right, thank you, ahh that will be all." The secretary nodded soberly, flipped her notebook closed and moved quietly through the door he held open. Shinwell knocked charred remains inside his pipe into a large ashtray, lowering himself into his comfortable leather armchair he reached for his tobacco pouch to refill his pipe.

- 29 NOVEMBER 1949 -

Captain Jack Sylvester waited impatiently in his office. He looked from window to the tapping pencil in his hand, as Officer Beirne knocked and entered. The captain looked expectantly to him, searching with probing eyes for a letter or telegram about his person. The officer showed his empty palms, shrugging apologetically. Captain Sylvester gestured for Officer Beirne to sit. It had been weeks and nothing had been heard. The captain had written a mass of letters to enquire about a decision, he sent endless telegrams and still had received no word. He chose to try to see it positively, "Perhaps it is taking a long time to go through all the documents I sent? And it will need a lot of discussion." He commented hopefully to Officer Beirne, grimacing lopsidedly. Officer Beirne managed a weak smile in return. It was not lost on Captain Sylvester that it was six years, to the day, that the *Suez Maru* had been torpedoed and surviving PoWs shot. His frustration was that it had only been five months since he had been informed of the crime. It was not long to entirely complete an investigation. But, he was now stalled and awaited permission to complete his work. To arrest and charge the remaining suspects. Despite the delay the captain had been somewhat pleased with his efforts to gather the evidence in such a short time. He was confident the case could not now be dismissed, "It's an open and shut case isn't it. What *is* the delay?" he blurted at Officer Beirne, who nodded in agreement. He tapped his desk with his pencil, opening his mouth to speak as a rap at the door startled both men and they exchanged glances. A secretary brought in a telegram. The captain noticed it had already been opened. Feverishly he unfolded the paper, his eyes greedily gathering up and absorbing the words. His face collapsed. His grin fell flat as he dropped the paper to his desk. Officer Beirne picked it up and read aloud.

RESTRICTED -War crime massacre at sea of Allied PoWs. Further our earlier request. Have been advised by FARELF that War Office decision to terminate Jap war crimes trials 30 Sept must be maintained. FARELF instructed to release any suspects unless required by Australian or US authorities. Osamu Kawano only suspect in custody. Do you concur in release? - Priority.- stop-.

He had spoken the last few words quietly and falteringly in disbelief. The captain exploded from his chair. "No, I damn well do not concur in his bloody release!" The captain snatched the paper from Officer Beirne. "I damn well concur that the other murderers should be arrested and we should proceed to trial! It is an open and shut case, for god's sake! As clear cut as any other, where we've convicted. This..." he waved the paper in the air angrily, "... this... is an absolute nonsense! A disgrace! A bloody disgrace!" Officer Beirne stood in stunned silence. There was nothing to say. The appeal was lost, perhaps never heard. The captain could not believe it, nor stomach it.

- 1 DECEMBER 1949 -

The captain sat alone at his desk, papers and documents no longer bulged from every available drawer and space. The pin-board behind his desk was bare and pockmarked with useless, pointless holes. There were only two neat piles of documents on his desk and a single drawer in his filing cabinet containing a thick manila folder— the *Suez Maru* case file, otherwise his office was echoingly empty and still. A mist of despondency hung in the room. He looked to his window, birds hopped on the sill, chirruping. They were blissfully unaware of the horrors of war, the brutality and inhumanity that had spread across the world like a plague. A moment of which had briefly distilled into this room. The captain rubbed at his bony temple. He felt old, worn out and battered. A single knock as his door pushed it open with a creak, revealing Officer Beirne carrying a telegram. "I'm sorry sir." He said offering the paper to the captain's outstretched hand. He read it aloud, his voice flat to begin, but growing increasingly angry.

> <u>Restricted</u>, War office decision to terminate Jap war crime trials 30 September must be maintained, stop. Instruction to release suspects, stop. Request this section to arrange such release, stop. Kawano Osamu only suspect in custody and NOT required by US or Netherlands authorities, stop. Do you concur in release? - <u>Priority</u>.-stop-.

The captain stormed from the room, hastening up the corridor lurching on his bad leg as he hurried, heading to his superior's office. He barged into a larger office startling the officer behind the desk. The captain swung the glass door closed behind him, apologising for the intrusion whilst waving the telegram in the air. Officer Beirne had followed and stood watching from the corridor, listening to the heated exchange. The captain thumped the desk mutely and the senior officer stood, barking in reply. The typing pool secretaries had stood up at their desks, gingerly peering at the commotion. A few snatches of sentences could be heard. "I do *NOT* concur!" shouted the captain. "Damn it, I know! But I am overruled!" came the equally angry reply. The senior officer moved to the door and called for a secretary. The secretaries looked to each other, all reluctant to be involved until a young woman was nudged. She quietly moved forward. A telegram was dictated and a release form completed. The captain refused to sign either. He stormed from the office and limped away down the corridor. "Damn it all to hell!" he shouted to an open-mouthed Officer Beirne as he passed. The secretary left the office carrying the two documents. Officer Beirne followed her, reading over her shoulder as she typed, her eyes full of apology.

CIPHER MESSAGE(.)

RESTRICTED:2 AUST WAR CRIMES SECTION (SCAP)(.)

<u>CONCUR</u> IN RELASE OF KAWANO, OSAMU(.)

```
Memorandum,
Request release of KAWANO Osamu, arrested 8
July 1949,
Subject is interned at Sugamo Prison.
Reasons for request of release: No longer required.
- Priority. -stop-.
```

- 16 DECEMBER 1949 -

Captain Jack Sylvester boarded the *De Havilland* bound for Singapore on the first leg of his journey home to Australia. He had gripped the rain-soaked handrail, limping his way up the blustery aeroplane steps as the engines had started. Casting a regretful glance backwards, his usually neat hair waving wildly, he sighed deeply and stepped into the plane. He smiled for a moment as he imagined his wife waiting at Melbourne. It would be a few days until his arrival, but she would be waiting. Now he was leaving Tokyo behind he could begin to count down the days and the hours. He allowed himself another small smile. He let it go almost immediately, his face dropping to a frown as he peered from the window. His emotions competed for attention in his chest as the plane began taxiing down the runway. He looked across Tokyo as his plane lifted into the sky, his fingers drumming the armrest in the absence of a pencil. Captain Jack Sylvester was in turmoil. He was disgusted and outraged by the decisions taken by his own, the Allies. To him it was unthinkable to have dropped the case. It was a clear straightforward prosecution. But, instead they had released those who had admitted the crime and their guilt even without the huge weight of evidence against them. What more could he have done? His heart was heavy with his own strangling unplaced guilt. He felt he had failed those men. Those who had sacrificed and given everything. They deserved better than this. Their families deserved to know what had happened. They deserved the peace of knowing their loved ones murders had not gone unpunished. But the families of those men were not even aware the crime had been committed. They knew nothing. It was all over before they could ever have known.

Captain Sylvester overnighted in Singapore before boarding a *Lockheed Constellation* for the tiring leg to Darwin. He watched through his small window as his route hugged first, the coast of Sumatra, then Java before heading over the Flores Sea, flying on over deeper waters. He looked out, scanning the greenery of the land as it merged into and disappeared beneath the dark sea. He blinked into the sunrise twinkling on the deep ocean, and thought of those poor souls adrift on this great expanse of blue as it turned crimson around them. No, there was nothing more he could have done. He knew he had done all he could. He lifted his chin. He *must* leave them behind. He *must* try to look ahead to the life before him, free of horror and sadness. He simply had to leave it all, and them, behind. He would be grateful now for his own family. He hoped for a long and happy life. He nodded to himself. 'I *will* leave you all now.' Captain Jack Sylvester whispered to them as he allowed himself to relax a little, settling into the seat as his plane arched into the sun.

In Captain Jack Sylvester's still, quiet office back in the SCAP GHQ building, in Tokyo, three officers gathered the remaining piles of documents and folders from the filing cabinet. One of the officers picked up a heavy manila folder from the desk, looking briefly at its title before adding it to the pile. They packed each neatly into thick card boxes, tying them securely with string. The boxes were stamped, sealed and marked, 'RESTRICTED'. These were stacked into large wooden crates and sealed again. The crates were wheeled out of the office, leaving it empty, bare and echoing with the click of the closing door. The crates were shipped to Australia along with the departing remnants of the Australian Army and its paperwork. Eventually, the crates were moved to a secure store, deep in the Australian National Archives where the contents lay still and undisturbed. Stored amongst many others, the papers brittled as their crates gathered dust for nearly sixty years.

- 29 NOVEMBER 1949 -

In Manchester, life had carried on as it had to, for everyone. George spent precious time with his growing family, all the while unaware of the *Suez Maru*. He didn't know anything of the war crime that took his brother or how close those responsible came to being tried as war criminals for their actions. George did not know that now and for all the days to come of their long lives, those responsible roamed free and at large. *They* lived their lives as freely as if they were innocent. George knew only the deep sorrow of his missing younger brother. The empty spaces unoccupied by him surrounded George and he missed his kind voice in his ear. That day George was up early for work, as a postman he was used to getting up with the sunrise. He enjoyed the quiet streets and time for silent thought as he cycled away from their small house on Smith Street to the Post Office depot at Gee Cross. The rain spattered softly into puddles between cobblestones and tapped on his coat as he pedalled. This day, on his journey home, he would take a detour. He had something to do, an appointment of sorts to keep. He had waved 'bye to his wife, Elizabeth and eldest son, Iain. The eight-year-old had stomped sleepily down the stairs, his toy aeroplane in hand, making loud nee-ow noises. George had laughed, lifting him the last few stairs to the ground and kissing his fluffy hair. Alastair, the youngest at three years old had waved shyly, hiding playfully behind his mother's skirts, his cheeks flushed and his floppy hair shading his dark, kind eyes, his father's eyes. George ruffled his hair with the palm of his hand, making them both giggle. Middle sister, Betty had looked down from an upstairs window, waving him off. She had waved her dolls hand to her dad as he looked up and smiled. His heart was full. George had pecked Elizabeth on the cheek and blew kisses to his children, he burst with pride in them all. He had turned, walking away up the street, pushing his bicycle rattlely along the cobbles. His smile had faded as he breathed deeply, letting out a long, sad sigh in the cold air. His thoughts were elsewhere. He felt deeply, immeasurably, grateful for all he had, but in any terms and at any time, loss is loss. He turned and looked over his shoulder, watching as his family disappeared in turn into the darkened shadows of their warm house to be readied for school, and a lump lodged in his throat. George threw a leg over his bicycle and, pushing hard on the pedal, he cycled away.

That evening as the sun slunk lower, George leant his bicycle against the wooden stile at the top of the path leading up Werneth Low. He clambered over and leant into the slope as he climbed the meandering hill overlooking his town of Hyde. At the top he stood in the shade of the war memorial, watching grey clouds roll silently across the sky. It felt sparkling cold as the sun glanced out from behind darkening clouds to cast long black shadows amongst beams of glittering sunlight. He watched tiny motes dancing in the sunlight as he felt about in his pocket and brought out a small silk poppy. The two layers of petals crisp red around the black bitumen centre. As he had many times before, he lay the flower amongst a few weathering poppies from the recent remembrance offerings, at the foot of the memorial. He took a step backward and bowed his head. The petals fluttered, moved gently by a light gust of breeze that preceded the beginning of rain. Splatters at first, quickly turning to slanting, industrial smelling Manchester rain. He was grateful to feel it patter on his face, despite the soaking cold. His mouth was bone dry as he reached inside his coat for a crumpled piece of notepaper. Written on it was a verse he had penned for his brother— when he'd first known, in 1944. He stood alone at the monolith that cold, wet November afternoon and, as rain streamed down his face, his cheeks whipped by the growing swirling wind, he read aloud. His voice was clear and calm. "My dearest Jack, silent thoughts, true and tender, just to show we still remember."

- CHAPTER FIVE -

すえず丸

- 8 OCTOBER 1943 -

The funnel of the *Suez Maru* spluttered black swirling smoke into the sky as the ship made erratic evasion manoeuvres. She was under attack. Torpedoes seemed to fire from all directions. Two ripped through the hull of the *Taian Maru* to her starboard, which quickly began sinking. The sea boiled around the *Suez Maru*, as the escort ship to port burst into the air. The *Dainichi Maru* to her rear received two direct torpedo hits, disappearing under the sea in a plume of litter and oil. The convoy of six ships had been transiting Luzon Strait as the attack exploded under and all around them. It had come from nowhere— the invisible lurking terror of American submarines. The *Taian Maru* and *Dainichi Maru* were gone and whilst the two remaining escort ships frantically searched for the submarine, the *Yubae Maru* and *Suez Maru* escaped, swerving wildly and steaming away. Then, the *Suez Maru* slowed, circling back to the scene of the sinkings to rescue some eight hundred survivors who bobbed amongst the flotsam. Captain Shirakawa ordered every available seaman to look-out posts as his ship took the terrified, bedraggled souls on to Manila, closely following the two escorts ploughing ahead. Waves crashed onto the deck of the *Suez Maru,* spraying the wild-eyed, soaked Japanese survivors huddled there. The ship lurched on, untouched and undamaged, only having lost one of her four lifeboats in the terrifying sea rescue. The *Suez Maru's* crew stood blinking and gasping on deck, as shaken as their trembling, rescued comrades.

- 17 NOVEMBER 1943 -

The *USS Bonefish* had sat in dry-dock at Fremantle, Western Australia for weeks. The captain, Lieutenant-Commander Thomas Hogan, of the Gato-class submarine had sent his weary crew on two weeks recreational leave after returning from their successful First War Patrol, while his submarine was overhauled. The crew had been exhausted but in high spirits after receiving a commendation for tonnage destroyed on their maiden patrol. They'd been ready for the chance of recuperation in the refuge of an Allied port. The *Bonefish* needed time for an overhaul on three of her four main engines and the auxiliary engines needed checking. The refit adjusted the hydraulic pump, and alterations were made to the torpedo tubes outer doors and shutters so they'd close more smoothly. But, she wasn't as banged up as her crew had felt after the long month trailing through the South China Sea searching for enemy shipping. They'd fought and survived five intense battles, sinking at final confirmed tally, at least nine enemy vessels. The crew had grown close as brothers through the challenging conditions, and most had served aboard for the previous six sweating months.

The *Bonefish* had swept down the ramp at the *Electric Boat Company* in Groton, Connecticut on 7th March and was commissioned on 31 May, when she took aboard Lieutenant-Commander Hogan who was promoted to captain the same day. Most of the current crew joined that day, including Lieutenant-Commander Guy O'Neill, Chief of the Boat Eugene Freaner, Junior Lieutenant Lawrence Amburgey, Junior Lieutenant Davis Dunn Jnr, and Junior Lieutenant Russell Johnston. Only some of the torpedo crew, including Torpedo-man Joseph Lynch and Torpedo-man's Mate Guy Harman had been aboard longer due to their lengthy torpedo training, officially taking up their posts on the 7th of March as the *Bonefish* launched. As the submarine had prepared for her First War Patrol, Lieutenant-Commander Fraser Knight, Chief Petty Officer Grant Moses, Engineer Ken Canfield came aboard, completing the sixty strong crew ahead of their long voyage to the South Pacific. The crew knitted together as the dark shape of the submarine slipped through the deep sea in pursuit of enemy tankers, convoys and shipping. They'd gathered as one, hearts in mouths as water droplets fell from the bulkhead onto papers. Their tense faces illuminated by the blinking revolving dot at the radar station and the flashing red, pulsing glow of battle stations. Silence accompanied the taut, breathless claustrophobia of the submarine. All were quiet and ready, their shirts damp with sweat, each forehead glistened as they wiped furrowed brows. The submarine had moved sleekly through the water, alert and listening, ready to torpedo the first target of their first mission. Now, safely back in Allied territory, their fears dissolved and memories of danger misted in high camaraderie and spirited overindulgence of the familiar sanctuary.

Late in the afternoon of the 17th, the crew returned, a little worse for wear, and set about making ready with the professionalism for which they had been commended. With repairs complete, the *Bonefish* set out on manoeuvres for day and night torpedo approaches, and general crew training. A few days later she returned to Fremantle to load ammunition, torpedoes and supplies, in readiness for her second mission. Packed to bursting, the men busy about their tasks, the mood anticipatory but buoyant, the submarine slipped out of Fremantle harbour in the bright, clear morning of the 22nd November. The *Bonefish* joined sister submarine *Le Triomphe* later that day and the two conducted night torpedo approaches and training dives until late evening. The *Bonefish* left *Le Triomphe* behind at 2300 hours, heading for her Second War Patrol. The patrol area would first be Borneo-Celebes by way of Exmouth Gulf. Captain Hogan directed Petty Officer Grant Moses to keep the written log, and, as the *Bonefish* moved away from the darting sharks of the coast and into deep blue ocean, the unknown awaited.

The prisoner of war camp at Liang now held more men crammed into the overcrowded sick hut than in any of the surrounding huts, as seven months of appalling treatment, malnourishment and disease weighed down every damaged man. Men spewed from the dilapidated structure, lying out on the narrow step in full burning sun, they curled in its shade and crouched, panting, under trees. All were reduced to skin and bone. Emaciated, ulcerated and exposed they lay, awaiting a final space in the sick hut for their final hours, or a miracle. Their still walking brothers fed them a share of what little there was. Those who could rise to shuffle to some other spot, were followed by incessant clouds of mosquitoes and flies. They watched mournfully as the morning's skeletal working party formed up in the clearing, those in the sick hut would have much preferred to be able to make the journey. Yet, there was little to distinguish the sick from the working. Ragged and spent, bowed and near broken, a few hundred men stumbled toward the camp gates, past the guard house. The same number again languished in the sick hut. More than one hundred and forty Liang Marchers had already gone to Boot Hill. The numbers at Liang camp had dwindled, then swelled with sorrowful-eyed replacements from the equally hellish Haruku island. With work on the airstrip more or less complete, the surviving men were sent to plant camouflage amongst the blazing coral. A pointlessly futile attempt to disguise the searing white scar cut along the islands coast, clearly visible from the air to Allied reconnaissance aeroplanes. The weary men unconsciously leaned on one another, swaying gently in the light breeze as they stumbled forward, shuffling for the two-hundredth time to the airstrip. Amongst the slow moving line, near the end of the procession, a bruised, round-shouldered man intently watched the bare feet of the man in front, following his gait, head bowed. As his head bowed, Jack's lightened hair flopped forward. His body, scarred and aching, shuffled onwards, indistinct from the other wretched men. The line bundled to a halt in the warming mist of the morning, before spreading out across the empty *Death Runway* they had built.

They moved like ghostly apparitions, as they gathered baskets and slowly knelt to fill them with flowers and greens to tuck into the sparse soil of the haunted runway. These were the 'healthy' men, the ones still sent out on working parties. Jack's body creaked as he reached for a basket with bony hands. His thin arms pulsed as he placed it on his shoulder. Unconsciously he followed his dulled senses to the verdant edges of the strip. There he knelt, amongst a thicket of saplings. He moved the soil around a small plant, brushing a fly from a leaf with painful hands. Once the basket was filled, he gathered himself and hefted it again to his shoulder, moving back to the sparkling white centre of the airstrip. There were fewer guards and soldiers now, they had dwindled as the workforce had lessened and weakened, they preferred the still shade of the camp. Jack blinked in the sun and closed his eyes momentarily, allowing the rays to permeate his eyelids, creating a flickering world punctuated only by his quiet breaths. The faint breeze ruffled his tattered sleeveless shirt, held together by a last button and more luck than stitching. He listened as a bird whooped, crying out to another. It chattered shrilly, unaware of the unfolded nightmare below, lost in its own avian concerns. Jack wiped his brow and looked to his basket. Lifting a delicate plant with soft rounded leaves and tiny orange and red trumpeted blooms in his cracked palm, he knelt in the glassy coral dust. He pushed a shallow hole in a patch of thin soil with his forefinger, moving the precious earth to the side with his thumb as he lay the tiny plant into its dry new home. He pressed the displaced soil around its small roots and patted it gently. "Settle in little plant, grow strong." He whispered gently to it. He worked on and the hours slid tortuously by. As he reached for the last plant in his umpteenth basket a man called out as he walked towards him, it was Bill. A kindly chap, he had often kept everyones spirits up singing tunes from home, although always out of soldiers' earshot. He was only a couple of inches more than Jack, but seemed taller with his energetic presence. He welcomed each fellow PoW as an old friend, with wide toothy grin and a crinkly cheeked, sparkle to his eyes that refused to dim, despite their circumstances. Bill placed a hand on Jack's shoulder. He looked up with unfocussed eyes, "*Makan*, time for rest," Bill said softly. Slowly, Jack unfolded to his feet and, leaving the basket to mark his place, followed his friend across the runway. The others, one after another straggled to form a small group of tired and hungry men in the shade of cocoanut trees at the edge of the airstrip. Jack sat, leaning heavily against a trunk, his wrists resting lightly on his bent knees, head bowed as Bill kindly brought him a mess tin in which squatted a small hard ball of rice in a shallow puddle of greyish water. Jack smiled gratefully, mouthing with chapped lips, "Thank you." They sat together chewing in reflective silence. The brief pause soon ended and they made their way back to the pulsing heat of the exposed airstrip. Jack knelt at his task as the afternoon slipped away, and the men again gathered to trudge back to camp.

In the gathering gloom of dusk, the men finished morsels of rice slop as a truck rumbled to a stop at the camp gate. Camp Commander Anami climbed down, straightening his jacket and looking about at the groups of men sitting here and there. He curled his lip, muttering angrily as he marched into the Japanese officers' hut. All about the camp, soldiers had scrabbled to attention, straightening caps and jumping to low reverential bows. The men watched proceedings warily, achingly gathering themselves to stand and back quietly from the clearing, moving into the shadows of their huts. No one wanted to be on hand to bear the brunt of whatever angered Anami, better to wait in the gloom. Jack had just taken the last mouthful of his six-mouthful meal and was considering sharing some water with someone, when shouting rose in the officers hut. The outburst quickly spilled onto the covered deck of the hut as Anami stepped out, barking and pointing at the bedraggled men who moved further back into darkness. The clearing filled with soldiers and guards, all listening intently to the shouting Anami as he motioned this way and that, swishing his baton through the air dangerously. Iketani scurried at his side, scribbling with a pencil into a small notebook in the palm of his hand. Anami turned to Iketani pointing, clearly issuing an order. Iketani began to speak, stopping immediately as Anami poked him hard in the shoulder with the baton. "You *will* be transport commander, and you *will* ensure their timely arrival. They have more work to do, much more!" Anami jabbed Iketani's shoulder with the baton on each word. He glared at Iketani then turned to leave. "B-b-but, sir, what if the transport is attacked? What of the PoWs?" Iketani flinched as Anami turned back to face him, his eyes flashing with anger. "You must not let them fall into enemy hands. I don't care what you do with them, but your emperor demands you obey. Kill them if you have to! Not one is to escape, do you understand?" Iketani looked beyond Anami, to the interested faces of the soldiers and guards who had gathered. He smirked and nodded resolutely, bowing and saluting to Anami's departing back. Jack heard a whisper from someone behind him, "What the hell's going on? What are they saying?" Jack responded with a silent concerned shrug. "Damned if I know, but it doesn't look good, does it?" "God only knows what they're saying," came whispered responses. Jack glanced around at the gathered men, searching their shadowed faces for answers. The barking had ceased as Anami, sweating and frowning furiously, left in his customary dust cloud, leaving soldiers and guards turning to look expectantly at Iketani. He stood under the gaze of all, soldiers, guards and men alike for a moment, then angrily pointing to two soldiers he marched back into the officers' hut, the soldiers following closely. The gathered PoWs listened to the constant jabbering for a long time until, unable to make any sense of what had occurred but knowing it was unlikely to involve any improvement in their situation, they moved quietly into their huts to lie down for the night. Hardly anyone slept.

Anami sat squatly in the front of the truck and swatted at a fly moving along his neck. He had chosen this. He hated the idea, it was like granting them freedom, but there *was* no alternative. As he stepped down from the truck outside his commandeered lodgings, he turned to the officer holding the door open, "Telegraph to Major General Saito, at Batavia," "Yes sir, what should I telegraph to him?" Anami stood stiffly for a moment and rubbed his chin. There was no use, it had to be arranged. "Telegraph Major General Saito to say I am evacuating five hundred prisoners immediately."

Captain Tamaki Shirakawa folded his sailing orders and stuffed them into a top shirt pocket that was damp after the days heat and climbed a ladder to the upper bridge of the *Suez Maru* to view preparations and the loading of his ship. He'd been ordered to Ambon a few days before and had waited all that day for further orders. From which he now learnt they were also to transport four to five hundred prisoners of war, and some two hundred wounded Japanese soldiers back to Soerabaya. This was along with two large aircraft fuselage, which were now proving cumbersome to lash to the deck. He watched his crew manhandling the first as it swung wildly about on its hoist. Shirakawa wished he could simply transport the soldiers and cargo. He had no time for these Allied prisoners of war who would be arriving soon. Nevertheless he grinned to himself, being as he was paid well for the short but dangerous journey. He turned to his Chief Mate, Watanabe. "We wouldn't have to transport all these prisoners on one ship if the enemy hadn't sunk the *Taian* and *Dainichi*. There were supposed to be two transports in this convoy." He looked at Watanabe, shaking his head angrily. Watanabe nodded, "–and the *Yubae* was damaged. We will be sitting ducks, now we're sailing with only one escort. These prisoners are more trouble than they're worth!" Quartermaster Shimizu joined them, panting, "The airplane fuselages are in place, we've tied them to the deck, they should stay there. There's nothing else to load until tomorrow when our patients arrive." He announced. "Yes, good, there are also prisoners. Enemy prisoners, coming aboard. We are taking them to Soerabaya," acknowledged Shirakawa with a raised eyebrow, unconsciously patting his pocket containing the orders. Watanabe and Shimizu exchanged glances. Shirakawa turned to watch his crew on deck and noticed they stood idly, flicking cigarette ends into the water. He was about to admonish them when he heard a low rumble. Instinctively Shirakawa ducked, hunching his shoulders, looking up while shielding his eyes with the palm of his hand, "Where are the lookouts?! Enemy aircraft! Man the gun!" he screamed. The crew scrabbled, watching an enemy aeroplane in panic, and rushing to fix and operate a machine-gun on the deck. The aeroplane dropped down and sprayed the sea with bullets in one swift crashing motion. There was no time to turn the gun. They leapt to the deck, bellies flat on the glossily painted metal. The crew on the quayside dropped to the ground and lay nervously prostrated, as the water around the ship leapt into the air in shocked fountains. The aeroplane swirled by with a roar, curling eddies in the ships smoke in its wake. Despite the low, close attack there was neither damage nor injuries, but Shirakawa and his crew were shaken. He shouted after the aeroplane as he looked around at the wide-eyed, blank faces of Shimizu and Watanabe. "Damn them!" He shouted as he stormed down the ladder and across the deck to his cabin. He had never felt more bitterness towards their enemy.

- 24 November 1943 -

The morning broke, hot and humid. Jack was awoken earlier than usual by movement all around him. He raised himself quickly to his bony elbows, squinting in the warm light of early sunrise. The guards were directed by a shouting Iketani as they dashed about frenetically. It appeared to Jack that they were packing parts of the camp up. It didn't look like the whole place was making ready, but clearly something serious was happening. Crates were stacked, supplies were piled near the clearing and generally the soldiers were abuzz. The men looked to each other with concern as the mornings ritual procession to roll call began. They shuffled along the hut, each craning to see what was happening in the clearing. They watched intently as soldiers set out a small table and two chairs. Iketani paced, reading from papers on a clipboard while a soldier, seated at the table flipped over pages of a large bound folio. At his shoulder stood Sergeant Major Yamamoto. Iketani chuntered endless instructions to the seated soldier who nodded quickly to each. Yamamoto scowled at the gathering men as they lined up. The usual guards and soldiers loitered about watching the men assemble. Jack felt uneasy, he looked sideways from soldier to guard, careful to avert his eyes, searching for some sense of what was happening. The men gathered in close ranks, looking about warily. Iketani broke the breathless silence, speaking loudly in faltering pre-prepared English. "Ah, we are very concerned some of you have fallen ill, and have caught some ahh, diseases. Your *generous* camp commander has arranged that you will be taken from the camp and taken for ahh, treatment. Some of you, ahh some are well. You will stay and finish work here. Sergeant Major Yamamoto will read out the names of those who are to be transported. You will collect items you ahh, need for your journey and assemble again after you have been ahh, fed your morning meal." He paused as the men looked to each other open mouthed, unsure what to make of it and unable to take in the full meaning and implications. Iketani cleared his throat and concluded. "Ahh, you will no doubt be grateful for the kind regard we have shown you and will obey instructions carefully." The men waited in stunned silence, looking to each other to confirm that they had indeed heard they were to leave. Those at the front did not move a muscle, but a low murmur began towards the back, as each man turned to the next to quietly exclaim. The rising sound was quickly extinguished with a shout from Yamamoto. "These are the men who must make ready." He paused, cleared his throat then began reading from the bound folio as the seated soldier ticked off each name spoken. "Abbott, Affleck, Agar, Alderson, Alton, Andrews, Argust..." The roll call drifted through the air endlessly as the men stood frozen in anticipatory hush. Awaiting the call of their own. Jack looked on as each man acknowledged hearing their name with a nod and a slight twitch of their shoulders. Each stayed still, unsure what to do about it. Jack realised it would be sometime before the 'F's' would be called, and began to daydream of the possibilities before stopping himself with a cold shudder. Leaving the camp did not mean the end of the war, or the end of captivity, did it? His mind remained unfocussed as words floated across the clearing, "... Fitch, Flavell, Foster, *Frith*, Frost..." Jack jolted. He felt as if he had surfaced from deep water. His ears cleared. He had heard his name! Someone gently slapped his back and he turned with a half-smile. Each felt the relief to be leaving and the sudden concern where they would be going to. Each man thought, 'God, I hope this is the end of the worst.'

Jack was not considered a patient as he was no longer in the sick hut but he weighed about seven stone, had a nasty leg ulcer and countless cuts and wounds that had not properly healed as nothing did. He had been a slight man before his captivity. He wondered briefly if he had been chosen for the transport because of his small frame, perhaps he looked worse if that were possible. He stopped himself, the Japanese of his experience did not take pity. Those chosen must have been at random. He pondered the vagaries of fate as he waited in the warming sun. With the remaining names eventually called the men made their way back to their huts to collect what little they had to take. Jack pushed his meagre belongings into his worn shorts pockets and pulled his thin shirt from its hiding place. He held it in one hand as he stuffed the small pocket, unable to grasp what was happening and what he was doing. *He was leaving!* His eyes bulged with tears, as he tried to remember he had only survived *for now*. There was a new unknown looming which could be *worse* than the here and now.

But, his mind swam with the thought of the food in the Java camp. It seemed luxurious now. He pulled on the remains of his threadbare shirt, with its single button, rubbed his nose on the remains of the tattered collar and cleared his throat. The hut was complete chaos as men salvaged hidden items stashed in the roof and under boards, and tucked between bamboo slats. Every face told the same story. Heart-bursting relief to leave, nervous trepidation of whether the destination would be worse, and the heavy burden of gut-wrenching pity and guilt for those who watched. They sat mournfully, heads in hands. Those whose names had not been called. Jack sat on the edge of the bamboo slat that had been his bed and his home for seven months and looked to the chaps nearby. "I am sorry," he said. They smiled and nodded, "Its all right, you'd better get going!" Jack moved to each man and held each hand. "Best of luck! Cheerio! God bless you!" Came the calls from the brave remaining men. Jack was overwhelmed by their courage and stoicism. He moved with the departing men out to the clearing where the first twenty or so were directed off to the sick hut. Jack realised he'd been engrossed, and now looked to the poor souls lying out in the sun, and set about to help. The sick patients were loaded onto stretchers and Jack, weakened as he was, grasped the poles with the strength of determination. He spoke to the semiconscious man swaying below, "You'll be all right, hold on now. We're getting out of this hell. You'll be all right, no one is leaving you. We go together, all right?" The man smiled weakly and gratefully as he was loaded onto a truck. Jack turned about and headed back to help bring another man out. The team of stretcher bearers worked for over an hour bringing man after man into the sunshine, watched by the Japanese soldiers who backed away. They did not want to get close to the rising diseases ferried from the sick hut. Jack lumbered past the guard hut at one end of a stretcher, and bowed his head, he hoped for the last time. He looked back briefly at the place that had so long been his hell, as the bamboo gates swung closed and the guards turned their backs. Eventually, the stretcher bearers were pulled up onto the trucks for the journey to the port. Iketani barked a last command to his subordinates, then reached up and pulled himself into the first truck's cab and they finally rumbled off. Jack wiped the sweat from his forehead with his bare arm as he watched the camp recede away down the unmade road. His stomach lurched as the sorry faces of those left behind disappeared, merging into the foliage which gave way to open grasses framed by cocoanut trees. He sat in the open-backed truck, holding the wooden slatting of the sidewall as he peered through the gaps. He watched his life disappear backwards. The journey over seven months ago but in reverse. Except that then, they had marched. Presently the sea appeared on his right, bright and sparkling in the sunlight, innocent to the sufferings on the island it surrounded. Jack felt he recognised each step he had fought to take some seven months previously. He looked around at the other men squashed in the truck as they bounced sickeningly toward the dock. Their eyes revealed they were all consumed by the same thoughts. Such pointless hardship could so easily have been avoided. The journey that took two days and a terrible toll then, took only a few hours now. Yet dusk was already growing by the time they arrived at the dockside.

As soon as the trucks halted the barking Japanese orders commenced. The truck still jolted from braking as Jack began to clamber down. His bare feet felt the ebbing warmth of the hard earth through his soles. He inhaled the pungent smells of oily coils of heavy rope and salty spray of the sea and his stomach lurched with hopeful possibilities. The dockside was not much changed from their arrival, except the ramshackle buildings were now overrun with Japanese officials, supplies and stores. A large ship was moored at the dock and another two were anchored out in the bay. Iketani quickly appeared, shouting orders at the soldiers who jostled the PoWs forward, toward the dark hulk of the ship, on up the gangway and onto the deck. There they were herded to a ladder descending into the aft hold. Jack watched the procession as he helped carry stretchers off the trucks, lining up the occupants in rows on the quayside. The light drained from the sky as he found himself moving slowly up onto the ship. He held the poles of a stretcher and was unable to see his footings. Both he and the stretcher occupant swayed precariously. Jack was grateful to climb on deck where he carefully laid out the semiconscious patient. He grasped his hand, speaking softly to him as a soldier pushed him hard with his boot, yapping and gesticulating to get up, hurry up. Jack stood and moved towards the mouth of the rearmost hold. At the top of the gaping hole he turned about and climbed down the ladder into the darkness. It felt almost like taking a deep breath and slipping underwater. The hold was stuffed full. Some three hundred men crouched in every available space, and nearly the same again were pressed into the hold in front. Jack squeezed himself into a small space on the upper platform, where the already packed men had tried to make a little room. He thanked them and wedged himself in, arms hugging his bony knees. Jack was no sooner sat when a bucket of sloppy rice was lowered into the gloom, containing what would be the only food for the three hundred hungry men of hold four.

Night fell in earnest and the quiet muffled talk on board was of their abrupt change in fate. The officers had pushed as far as they were able to make sure the sickest men were taken on the draft. Those selected hoped they would be returned to Java to recuperate. One of the Japanese guards had been overheard saying something about the transport and the words 'hospital in Java' had been deciphered. Jack listened but did not speak. The idea of hospital gleamed in his mind. He imagined clean, crisp white sheets, the drifting smell of antiseptic, someone carefully dressing his legs and food... what food he imagined! Images of the feasts he would have danced dreamlike through his thoughts. As night arrived in full pitch blackness Jack picked tiny hard pieces of rice from his teeth with his drying tongue and gazed at the emerging stars. Each arrived invisibly. He watched as if someone had simply turned them on, one moment they were not there. Then suddenly almost with a ping, each appeared. At first he counted them, four, five... then ten, twelve, twenty, thirty, until as he looked there were too many in the space where there were none moments before. He curled his fingers into a circle, making a telescope with his hand as he had as a child, and squinted through it to his dazzling panorama. At last the sky was littered with tiny pinpricks of light, blinking and sparkling in a dark sheet of almost touchable closeness. As Jack watched breathlessly the others continued to talk, their voices low and full of concern. "Are we moving?" someone asked in the darkness, "I can't hear the engine. We would hear it, and feel it, wouldn't we?" replied someone else. "Maybe this is just somewhere for the night?" Jack did not hear the rest of the conversation as drowsily he slipped into cramped foetal sleep perched high up in the dark hold, his hand still half-clenched in an 'O'.

- 25 November 1943 -

Chief Purser of the *Suez Maru* Joji Nukui huddled on deck in the midday sun conversing loudly with Chief Mate Watanabe. Nukui pointed a bony finger at the prisoners of war, who had been ordered from the holds at dawn and now formed a long straggling line down onto the quayside. He watched their arms swinging as they passed boxed supplies along the line. "*These* rations are for our wounded soldiers." Nukui exclaimed. "I have been told the PoWs have their own food," "Yes, ahh, yes I believe they do," replied Watanabe vaguely, he was more interested in whether wages had been obtained than food supplies for PoWs. He watched Nukui's face eagerly. "I also have money for the crew. Shall I give it to the captain or would you oversee it?" Watanabe shrugged and looked away, but took the leather pouch Nukui offered without hesitation. Nukui twitched, then made excuses and moved away as First-Lieutenant, now Transport Officer Masaji Iketani marched across the deck. Iketani stamped to a standstill and flung a salute to Watanabe, who studied Iketani curiously, lifting a hand to his temple hesitantly. "I understood there were supposed to be two ships. I have hundreds of PoWs here for work in Java and elsewhere. I have men transported over from Haruku for this draft and more waiting at camp." Iketani slid his round glasses up his sweaty nose with a finger. His face twitched with agitation, which went unnoticed by Watanabe who was inspecting the pouch keenly. He replied disinterestedly without looking up. "It can't be helped, there's a shortage of shipping. The enemy sinks vessels faster than we can deploy them." Iketani rolled his shoulders back attempting to assert his unfelt authority, "*I* am Transport Commander for this journey, and I *must* see what arrangements have been made. There were also to be two escorts I believe–" Watanabe bristled. Closing the bag he faced Iketani, who shrank a little. "No, there has been a change of orders. The other escort ship must go to Manila, but we'll still be escorted by a minesweeper." He waved his hand to the two ships anchored in the bay. Iketani's stomach sank. He swallowed hard but was unsure what he could reply. He opened his mouth but Watanabe had begun to move away clutching a bag he seemed keen to examine. Iketani looked down to the quayside, absently watching the PoWs struggling to carry and load supplies in the heat. A soldier prodded one of them hard with the butt of his rifle and the PoW stumbled. Iketani smirked. He lifted his eyes and his gaze floated back across to the minesweeper out in deeper water. It's snout pointed in the direction of the mouth of the bay as if looking on out to sea. Iketani shivered involuntarily. It appeared to him to lurk. It sat watching, ominously overshadowed by clouds rolling in. Iketani shuddered at the prospect of the dangerous transit to Soerabaya and silently hoped the escort minesweeper would protect him.

Aboard Minesweeper W12, Captain Osamu Kawano rubbed his small eyes, and looked back towards his cabin. He stretched and yawned. It had been a long morning already, preparing for the voyage to Java, or rather ordering his subordinates to make ready. He ambled to the bridge, taking a few salutes on the way and stood on the foredeck observing his crew. He turned to look across the bay to the transport ship, the *Suez Maru* as loading continued. He had watched the last few days as her crew scurried about, tying two aircraft fuselages on deck. The day before Kawano had then seen them stand back warily as a long line of thin men slowly made their way along the deck, disappearing down into the holds. Kawano had frowned and turned to his Gunnery Officer Daiso Yatsuka, who nodded and bowed reverentially, a question on his face. Kawano had pointed with an upwards nudge of his chin as he looked to the *Suez Maru*, "What's going on there?" he'd enquired. "I believe they are prisoners of war, sir." "No, not them! I know they're transporting prisoners. I mean the aeroplanes," Kawano snapped irritably. "Oh, ahh I don't know, sir..." Yatsuka began. Kawano ignored him and went on. "Well, they're going to get shot out of the water with *those* on deck. Looks like a warship transport doesn't it?" Yatsuka tried again, "Sir, I have plotted a course close to the islands. We should be able to avoid deeper open water until almost the dash across to Soerabaya." Kawano looked at him absently, "Hmm, all right. Well, let's hope it will be enough for *them*!" Yatsuka bowed and climbed down from the bridge foredeck. Kawano did not acknowledge the bow. He stood against the rail and pulled a cigarette from a packet, cupping his hands around the flame as he lit it. As the cloud of grey smoke from his cigarette drifted away, he looked down to the deck of his own ship, where his crew ambled about. He shook his head, looking warily back across to the *Suez Maru*.

On the deck of the *Suez Maru* Fireman Morimasu Kikuchi had come up and ambled to the rail on the gunwale. He stood beside engineers Ichiro Ehara and Shinichi Minoda who smoked cigarettes, chatting as they leant over the side. Kikuchi didn't like the smell of the smoke so he moved along a little, turning his back to the sea and leaning his elbows on the rail while he watched the line of PoWs loading the final supplies on deck. Some had tattered shorts and remains of shirts but most now wore only a loincloth to cover their modesty. Known as a 'Jap Happy', it seemed to make the soldiers laugh. Kikuchi smiled and nodded to himself without malice, as it was in fact his preferred article of clothing. In the heat of the engine room and humidity of these islands, he found the thin folded cloth the best attire. He stood watching, then frowned as he realised they weren't simply thin men. They were terribly ill and horribly emaciated. His mind struggled to understand what had happened to them. His eyes moved to the guards and soldiers escorting the prisoners. He now saw how they prodded and shoved at them, bashing any man who slowed or dropped his load. Kikuchi's brow creased and he rubbed his temple. He couldn't understand it, but he felt deeply sorry for them. He lowered his eyes and ambled back down to the engine room not wanting to see more. Ehara and Minoda called out to him but he waved a hand and disappeared below. They too now turned to watch. Some of the PoWs were re-boarding having completed the last of the loading. The crew hadn't paid much attention when the PoWs came aboard the previous night, and they'd been busy making preparations for most of that morning below decks, in the boiler room, kitchens and engine room. Now they watched. As the hollowed men came back aboard, gathering on the deck the crew stood back. Their eyes followed the spectres as they slipped down into the hold, like skeletons into a pit. Ehara shivered. These staring men frightened him. They stood mutely watching until the roar of a coal barge disturbed the still air and they turned away, grateful for the distraction.

On the quayside Medical Officer Kasuaki Eto waited. He had watched the PoWs complete the loading of cargo as well as they could in spite of their condition. Some were in no condition to help. He had counted about thirty stretchers on deck and many others were supported by their fellow PoWs. He stood back from the men as he recognised the symptoms of malaria, and the endless coughing of beriberi. He looked them up and down. They were all ill, somewhat wounded and stumbling on ulcerated legs. Eto held a handkerchief to his mouth as they passed, filthy and hollow-eyed, every man spindly, suffering as a whole from malnutrition. He turned to look as the sound of the barge he'd waited for motored up the bay, then slowed as it came alongside the *Suez Maru*. Eto stood back, shaking his head as coal-blackened men emerged like bent sticks of charcoal and formed up on the quayside. Dozens were supported or carried by similarly exhausted looking men, who gently laid them down on the ground. Eto sighed and shook his head. These were *not* the men he'd waited for. Nevertheless, he gestured to an assistant to help inspect the prisoners. Between them, without getting too close, they moved down the lines of wobbling men, occasionally prodding and nodding their heads. Each man lying on the ground Eto pointed to with a baton, gesturing to a waiting truck, its engine idling. The prone men were hoisted up like sacks of coal and carried onto the truck by their brothers, to be sent on to Liang camp. Eto had moved through about half the men, dispatching some two dozen onto the truck. The rest began to slowly climb the gangway to join others already squashed in the holds of the *Suez Maru*, as the sound of another motor barge turned every head to look across the water. Eto quickly dismissed the remaining men with a flick of his baton and dashed to meet the incoming barge. *Here* were his patients. The barge contained two hundred wounded Japanese soldiers. They disembarked in a disorganised cluster onto the dockside, limping, bandaged and nursing arms in slings. They were fully clothed in IJA uniform and were well-fed and healthy looking despite their maladies and injuries. Eto quickly demanded the PoWs move out of their way. The escorting soldiers from Liang barked at the men to move back. Eto then set about quickly triaging the incoming soldiers. With a care he had not shown the PoWs, he directed the walking wounded up the gangway where they were met with offers of food and drink and helped into the two spacious, uncrowded forward holds.

Yoshio Kashiki had lifted his thumping head slightly as his barge had putted to a slow chug. He craned his neck looking out to see his destination as the boat came alongside a dark transport ship. He watched closely as they moved along its flank and came to a stop, bow to its stern at a small quayside. Yoshio squinted as he felt the breeze, which ruffled cocoanut fronds and rattled jittery roof tiles on the collection of buildings alongside. He winced painfully as he rolled onto his side and swung his legs out from the bench he lay on, planting his feet on the deck. Yoshio stumbled and limped down the short gangplank along with some two hundred other Japanese servicemen, equally limping and wounded. They hopped with crutches, holding on others. Bloodied bandages peeled from a few temples, some arms were splinted and in slings, one or two coughed as they hobbled onto the quayside, then back up a gangway onto the *Suez Maru*. Some Japanese soldiers were taken aboard on stretchers, held at either end by quick marching Japanese medical orderlies. Almost every soldier had a cigarette hanging from his lip as the damaged parade shuffled past the ships civilian crew and an escort of Imperial Japanese Army soldiers. Yoshio intently watched his feet as his two-toed rubber boots wobbly ascended the gangway. He looked up to see how much farther, squinting as three or four figures on deck caught his eye. They wore rags and their thin bodies were sunburnt. They sagged as they pulled remaining cargo onto the deck hoisted from the quayside. Their eyes sunken and vacant, they don't seem to notice his stare. Yoshio glanced back open-mouthed, to ask the soldier behind who they were, when he noticed a gathering of similar pitiful men on the quayside. He was shocked. He must have just passed them without seeing. He had been engrossed. He was wounded, shrapnel here and there, bandaged and painful, but not life threatening. It had been the combination of his wounds and a bad case of malaria that had weakened him, enabling him to be sent for some weeks of hospital recuperation. Yoshio was grateful for the reprieve. He couldn't stand the war. He detested the fighting and the horror. He found the strain of not knowing whether each day would be his last, unbearable. He would have preferred it was all over, one way or another. He watched the men on deck and realised these men were prisoners of war. He had heard stories, the rumours, tens of thousands had surrendered. Now they were helping their enemy, working for them, the Japanese. But these were not the fit, fighting army of their enemy. These men were ghostly, worn down and deathly ill. Yoshio had paused on the gangplank, attracting the attention of his superiors. They shouted to hurry aboard, that they were departing soon. Yoshio continued up onto the deck, transfixed by these haunted men. He realised this was clearly the work, the inhumanity of his *own* army, his *own* country, and he felt ashamed. He moved along in line, passing six or seven of these sorry souls, some wearing ragged shirts and some only in loincloths. He passed a man with intense blue eyes, light floppy hair who wore a tattered shirt as he waited to move down to the quayside. Each transfixed the other with their gaze. Yoshio's one of shock and regret. The PoWs face was stern, determined, yet his eyes showed deep compassion. Yoshio looked away, full of sorrow for the predicament his country had clearly poured on these unfortunates. He made his way quietly along the deck, glancing into one of the holds to a sea of darkened faces turned upwards, staring out, like cattle squashed in trucks en route to the abattoir. He recoiled in horror, hurrying along the deck and down a metal-runged stairway to the mess. Jack had stopped, standing quite still on deck, his head lowered, eyes alert and watching as the Japanese soldier had limped past. He saw pity and kindness in his enemy's eyes, and found it hard to reconcile. He swallowed hard, his mouth parched as he moved back down to the quayside, gathering the ends of thin bamboo stretcher poles, hoisting up the last of the Haruku PoWs from the coal barge. Jack mounted the gangway for the last time and slowly made his swaying way back up to the *Suez Maru* deck. It had been dark the previous night and he had not noticed the ships name. Now he looked up as he retched dryly. He saw on the overbearing dark hull as he boarded, the name painted on the stern, すえず丸

Jack was permitted to stay on deck briefly with three others, to tend the stretchered men lying on the hatch covers. With effort Jack moved one man along a little, to shelter him under an aircraft fuselage loosely strapped to the deck. The man spoke, his voice weak and rattling, "That will make us a nice target won't it?" He lifted a bony hand pointing with his bent finger. Jack squinted, leaning under the shadowed belly of the wingless plane, and shuddered. "Don't worry, it'll be fine," he lied evenly, his stomach knotted with worry. Soldiers milling about the deck burst to life on hearing shouted orders. Jack didn't understand the language, but recognised well enough the call for alert readiness. He raised himself to his feet as a soldier pushed him with the butt of his rifle. Jack needed no persuading to avoid a bashing and stumbled back toward the nearest hold, at the stern. The soldier shouted angrily and pushed him forward, toward the amidship hold. Jack nodded quickly, moving to join the remaining men to go down into hold three. He stood, the last PoW on deck to descend. He watched his brothers ahead disappear into the dark void. Jack looked into the gloom and saw his fellow PoWs packed in the darkness, their expressions sorrowful, their eyes large in their stark gaunt faces. Each looked on as Jack descended the ladder. He stepped onto the uppermost platform, looking for a space to wedge into as soldiers shouted from above. He curled himself into a corner where he could still see the top edges of the trees framing the island on both sides.

Captain Shirakawa shouted orders which were repeated by those around him. The echoes prompted Iketani to begin shrieking commands at his subordinates to be about their tasks. They obliged, running to and fro. Jack listened to his wild ranting voice, interspersed with Iketani's bouts of coughing, and his nearly constant spitting on the deck. Clearly Iketani was ill, and it put him in an even more foul frame of mind than usual. Jack reminded himself, when no reminder was really needed, to keep a very low profile. Low conversations began in the hold as the men tried to settle themselves. They knew it would be a hellish voyage, at least as terrible as the outbound journey. But back then, they were not even half so ill as now. Jack listened as a group of Dutchmen discussed he knew not what, in quiet kindly tones. They turned to look at him and he nodded to them, envying their camaraderie. He hadn't seen anything of the men he knew best, Harold and Henry must be somewhere there but he hadn't seen much of them since their names had been called out at Liang. He had seen William taken off the ship with two dozen others to make room for the sick draft arriving from Haruku and none of the others he knew seemed anywhere nearby. William had reluctantly retreated down onto the dockside, his eyes downcast as he looked back at his brothers. He nodded in silent prayer for them as he climbed up onto a truck bound for Liang camp. In the darkening hold, Jack closed his eyes and listened. He turned the rumble of voices into a comfort he didn't feel and imagined himself home. Instantly, he recalled his street and saw the front door of his home vividly. He reached out a hand and pushed it open. Jack inhaled the domestic smells of clean house and warm baking and listened for familiar voices. He imagined once again hanging his hat and coat in the hallway. Dropping the weight of his coat on a hook he observed his reflection in the stand mirror. He rubbed his chin, and felt the bristles standing proud on his bony jaw. 'Would his mother still recognise him?' His thoughts drifted to Irene, 'would she recognise him?' He had neither seen nor heard a word from anyone for nearly two years. 'Would she still be waiting for him, at home? Would he get home?' He wondered if she was thinking of him. He sighed, he knew deep down he would have to let her go. She would not be able to wait so long without a word. Would she? He wished he could tell her where he was, and that he was thinking of her. He had always imagined England as it was when he'd left, cold and rainy despite his young summers of sunshine. He'd embarked in sleety winter and was trapped into seeing home in snow and rain. Just as he could not previously have imagined the fragrant humidity of Java and Ambon, he could not now conjure the intense feeling of cold in Manchester. To shiver and be chilled to the bone seemed an unimaginably lost world to him. He hugged his knees close to his chest and opened his eyes. It was no use imagining he was anywhere else today. The incessant chatter of Japanese and the stinking mess of the hold, merged with his thirst and hunger, were too powerful a reality to wish away.

Above, two crew deckhands moved the hatch partially over the hold opening as the ship shuddered. The rumbling from somewhere deep within signalled the terrible journey was beginning. The dusk of evening was taking hold as the *Suez Maru* set sail, following in the wake of the minesweeper. Jack saw wafting across the hold opening, dark smoke issuing from the funnels, signalling their departure to all near and far, and suddenly he felt alone and exposed. He craned to look back at the waving fronds of cocoanut trees and found he held up a hand to wave back. He had never been more grateful to leave a place, but had learnt the hard truth that one could never assume the destination would be any better. Jack watched the island recede as the two ships left the mouth of the inlet, chugging out into open water. Soon the ship criss-crossed to the shallows of the next island then moved into deeper water. Darkness fell as the bow crashed through inky seas. Waves splashed and foamed over the deck, spraying and soaking the men in the half open hatches below.

Out in deeper ocean, on an unknown intersecting course, the *USS Bonefish* slipped silently through the blue-black sea. Its great mass groaned metallically under the weight of water above, causing silvery deep-sea shoals to dart as one, and great giant octopi to leap from its path. Presently, the sleek submarine surfaced in the moonlight. Its periscopic eye blinked in the waves as its body rose, shedding water from its broad back. It slowed to a stop, watching and waiting.

- SUNDAY 28 NOVEMBER 1943 -

Aboard the *Suez Maru* a chaotic routine of sorts had been established between the civilian crew and embarked wounded Imperial Japanese Army soldiers, alongside the soldiers and guards escorting the prisoners of war. For Jack and the men pressed deep in the holds of the *Suez Maru*, the previous few days had slid together in an unending lurching, hunched darkness. Two men had passed on the twenty-sixth and another on the twenty-seventh. Their brothers in war had carefully laid their bodies out, wrapping them gently, before lifting hand over outstretched hand up onto the deck. They dropped the men into the sea, lingering to murmur words stolen by the wind, for as long as the Japanese soldiers would allow. Jack stood to at the gunwale, then retched as the ship turned heavily, sloshing though the dark sea. At dusk a bucket was lowered into the gloom, swinging this way and that until someone with enough strength caught it on the backswing, and took the weight. It contained a slop of rice, the smell of which would have turned any stomach, yet the men were used to the disgusting mixture and quietly shared a small portion out to each man. Jack retched dryly for want of a small drink. Most men lay weakly still, unable to reach out for their share. Those around them gently lifted their emaciated shoulders and helped them take a few mouthfuls. The recipients blinked grateful thanks. It was impossible to know how long the journey might last. Jack counted on his thin fingers to the man next to him, "What was it on the outbound journey? Five or maybe six days to Ambon wasn't it?" He coughed, rubbing his bony chest through his flapping shirt, still held by the last button. "It's been, what, four days, so we could dock tomorrow, couldn't we? That means hold on one more day doesn't it? After everything, we can do that can't we?" Someone called out flatly, "If we *are* going back to Java that is." Jack conceded, "Yes, if that's where we're going but where else could we be going? You heard the rumour, someone overheard Soerabaya is the destination." There came no reply. "It's better than the staying in Liang isn't it?" Jack finished quietly, to remind himself as much as anyone else. Murmurs of agreement echoed in the darkness as each man receded into his own thoughts.

Aboard Minesweeper W12, Captain Kawano glanced at his watch, and back at the map. Quartermaster Shimizu nodded agreement as he pointed to the outline of Soerabaya harbour on the chart. A report had been received of magnetic mines laid there by the enemy. Kawano frowned. He did not want distractions, nor costly delays. He did not like being at sea longer than he had to. This stretch of ocean was under constant enemy surveillance, and although he wouldn't say it aloud, he was deeply afraid. Shimizu ordered a new route plotted and Ensign Masuro Kai took the order through to the chart room. Kawano pulled a finger round his damp collar and looked warily to Shimizu, who nodded at Kawano's unspoken concerns. All day they had weaved in and out of islets, hugging the islands to guard against submarine attack. Now, as dusk grew the minesweeper slowed, letting the *Suez Maru* take the lead a little way ahead. The naval crew were on rotating lookout shifts, and under strict orders to keep a close watch on radar and listen carefully to their sound locator. There were three lookouts on the raised deck around the main bridge, scanning the sea with binoculars and another two on both the forward deck and rear gun post, maintaining a constant watch. Kawano was in the chart room inspecting the new course laid out in pencil across the map of blue. He watched thin grey lines being drawn across the paper as their position was plotted around the diversion. An officer relayed information for the log, "South of Celebes Islands, heading–" He was interrupted by a shriek from the foredeck of the bridge. Kawano strode out of the room as a lookout shouted wildly, still staring through his binoculars. "Sub, a sub! I am sure it was a submarine. There!" He raised a hand, pointing with his whole arm, "Over there!" Kawano snatched the binoculars, pressing them to his eyes. The sea blurred as his sight ran across it. The cross-haired range danced about on twinkling specks of light reflected off the waves. Kawano's eye caught something. He stopped. A shape of a long black submarine was surfacing to their rear. It was a way off and had only just surfaced. Kawano could just make out water still pouring from its deck as it settled above the waves. He shouted orders for the *Suez Maru* to continue on, the minesweeper would break away. Kawano called for battle stations. The minesweeper turned in the water looking to re-establish the submarine's position as she came about. Kawano ordered full speed as they scanned the sea for their enemy. The sky was darkening, threatening a squall. Reflections of heavy cloud rolled across the dark grey sea. The submarine had vanished. Kawano watched from the upper bridge, searching the sea. He demanded they find it, pursue and attack. The position and distance had been logged but they could not meet their target quickly enough. The minesweeper searched the area for two hours, watching and listening but it seemed the submarine had submerged and moved away. A ping was heard and excitedly two depth charges were dropped, but nothing came to the surface. Kawano realised they had completely lost track of it, as the squall began in earnest, pitching the ship and soaking those on deck. The minesweeper searched for another hour until the skies became too dark and the sea too wild. The ship then turned and put on full speed to catch up with the *Suez Maru*.

On board the *Suez Maru* the crew had watched the squall approaching as the minesweeper suddenly turned, heading toward the storm. They'd looked to each other, puzzled. Jack had just been given permission to come up on deck to use the 'box,' and he'd taken the chance for a moment of air. The sky darkened as he made his way along the rail. He'd watched their escort ship turn and disappear. He abluted nervously, standing swaying on deck and holding the rail with one hand. Twilight turned to moonlight, obscured by rolling dark clouds as the pitter patter of rain began. Jack looked about, the crew seemed increasingly tense. He turned back to the ocean of grey water surrounding the ship, uneasily realising they now sailed alone and vulnerable through the open sea.

The route had been set, drawn in neat grey lines on the chart, as the *Bonefish* moved forward entering Lombok Strait. Below deck all had been noise, oil, sweat and close humidity. The men hurried about, swimming along cramped decks attending to instruments, filing papers, recording notes on clip-boards and checking gauges and panels that filled the bulkheads of the American submarine. Orders were shouted along decks and into speaking tubes, points were measured on maps and angles checked. She transited with silent ease, slipping through the ocean as birds soar through the air. *Bonefish* entered the Flores Sea and surfaced briefly, like a whale coming up for a lungful of air before dipping away and down again in the gathering dusk and approaching squall. Captain Hogan felt calm as they'd surfaced. Lieutenant-Commander O'Neill and Chief of the Boat Freaner exchanged glances as the captain motioned to the watch. "Report?" "Surface radar detects a contact 17 miles out, maybe a minesweeper. Bearing 266°T. We are not detected." Captain Hogan nodded, "Very good. Officer Moses, note it in the log. Keep a track and prepare to dive." *Bonefish* slunk beneath the flat salt sea as the squall approached and gentle waves began to lap over her. She slipped below, dipping down silently as you would slowly dip a toe into a bath to test its temperature. There was hardly disturbance of the surface, the huge submarine disappeared with the smallest of ripples. A bird landed on the water where only a circle now echoed out from the conning tower that was last to disappear. The ripples were swallowed in the increasing roll of waves whipped up by the advancing squall as the bird, sensing danger flapped away.

- MONDAY 29 NOVEMBER 1943 -

- 0525 HOURS -

The *Bonefish* turned in the water, her periscope rotated to survey the direction of travel as Chief of the Boat Freaner spun around to watch Lieutenant Johnston, his face glued to the viewer. "No doubt about it, sir. Definite smoke on the horizon, sir." Freaner turned to Captain Hogan, who nodded, his face taut. Lieutenant Johnston on periscope spoke breathlessly, "Bearing oh six-eight degrees true. About 25,000 yards. Position, latitude 06-34.S, longitude 116-47.7.E." "Note it in the log," said Captain Hogan calmly, his hands behind his back. He narrowed his eyes, and reached for the periscope to confirm for himself. He pressed his face to the eyepiece, nosing the handles this way and that gripping them tightly. "Yes, confirmed," he muttered, turning to Lieutenant-Commander O'Neill and nodding. He handed the periscope back to Johnston, "Track it Lieutenant, don't lose sight of it," he said, then turned back to O'Neill, "Ready battle stations. Radar, close watch please." O'Neill nodded, repeating, "Readying battle stations, tracking," as he spun around. The quiet of the submarine bridge burst into action, as commands were repeated and information was announced aloud. "Target identified. Large AK, similar to *Nozima*. One escort, similar to SC53 type. Both ships making heavy black smoke." Radar showed blips on the rotating arm as it passed, the positions closing as the *Bonefish* moved to intercept. The red light of battle stations flashed their faces with an eerie glow as the crew stared hard at consoles, checking gauges and recording measurements and distance. In his corner cubby, Radioman Canfield pressed fat rounded headphones to his ears, listening intently to every click in the surrounding ocean. Petty Officer Moses scribbled observation notes which would later become the typed official log.

```
05.25. Sighted smoke on horizon
05.26. Battle stations for tracking, target
identified as large AK similar to Nozima (Janes
1941). Accompanied by one escort similar to
SC53 type. Both ships making heavy black smoke.
```

Captain Hogan nodded slowly, paused then spoke. "Submerge and commence approach."

- 0910 HOURS -

Minesweeper W12 pushed through the waves ahead of her protected transport ship. On the rear deck, Ensign Kai looked back toward the *Suez Maru*. He noticed the deck seemed filled with figures moving around in the early morning sunshine. He squinted, but could not make out who they were. His eye wandered along the ship to her funnel, billowing a long cloud of black smoke, and he shuddered. He looked beyond the ship to the open sea, and the trail of smog floating above the *Suez Maru* like breadcrumbs for a watching enemy. He shook his head, looking to the sky for aircraft. After the previous evening's encounter with the escaped submarine he felt exposed and vulnerable.

On the deck of the *Suez Maru* Captain Shirakawa rubbed his temples in circles with his thumbs, the sun was up and warmed his face as he strode towards the ladder to the lower deck. He stood at the rail and looked out over the sea and stretched. He had just finished a large breakfast and absently rubbed his belly as he took out a cigarette. First-Mate Watanabe quickly joined the captain and offered him a light, cupping his hands round the small flame to protect it from the sea breeze. Shirakawa looked across as three deckhands wandered lazily along the poop deck, stopping at the supply store. Quartermaster Shimizu had arranged for them to gather tools and paint for a few repair tasks. Storehouse-man Nakanishi, Deckhand Miyahiro and Deckhand Usami made their way to the storeroom, arguing quietly about who should do what. They continued muttering to one another as Miyahiro grudgingly entered the store and passed out an assortment of tools to Nakanishi and Usami. Captain Shirakawa looked beyond them to a few PoWs shuffling along the rail towards a latrine box hung over the side. One prisoner stopped as he emerged from the hold. He was barefoot, wearing tattered shorts and a thin ragged shirt, fastened with one button. The prisoner stood momentarily still, blinking in the sun then looked about curiously. Shirakawa watched as slowly the man began to move to the rail, reaching out a hand.

- 0915 HOURS -

In the belly of the *Bonefish*, Captain Hogan turned his head. He was waiting, his square features illuminated in the blinking red light as a drop of sweat beaded on his temple. "Make ready for battle stations..." He said at last, turning to the console. "Sound report?" Radioman Canfield cupped a hand around one of his headphones, the other he pushed away from his ear as he half-spun his chair to speak. "Target bearing oh nine zero degrees true, about 25,000 yards, sir." Captain Hogan nodded calmly, "Plot and speed?" Canfield spun back round, "Screw count, one-three-two rpm. Speed eight knots, sir." Captain Hogan paced the short distance along the command deck, then stopped and waited. O'Neill approached him, "Sir?" he ventured. Still the captain waited. Eventually Captain Hogan turned and nodded to sound for another update. "Echo ranging 16,000 yards, sir." Captain Hogan nodded. He looked directly at Freaner then turned back to O'Neill, his stare fixed, "Load forward torpedoes, tubes one through four," he said firmly.

Jack stood holding the *Suez Maru* rail waiting his turn at the box, he felt the sun warming his body as a light breeze ruffled his hair. He closed his eyes and imagined a freedom he wished he could grasp. He started as behind him someone coughed. He turned to see Iketani smoking a cigarette and watching the sea. Jack lowered his eyes and moved a little along the rail.

- 0917 HOURS -

Captain Hogan looked back to sound and radar, checking their status reports then moved back to the periscope for his own final confirmation. The grey outlines of the two ships merged with the sea sloshing around their hulls, as black smoke chugged from both their funnels. For a moment all was silent. The captain rubbed his temple. His men watched him breathlessly for the order they knew would be given any moment. In turn, Captain Hogan waited, for a final report from Torpedo-man Lynch. Down in the forward torpedo bay the crew sweated. They had loaded two torpedoes and were lifting a third to its tube with a grunts and shouts. Lynch and his first-mate, Harman hefted the fourth torpedo from its cradle and slid it into the loading tube. They made their checks, sealed the inner doors and opened the outer doors. Lynch spoke breathlessly into the mouthpiece, calling to his captain. "Loaded and ready sir." Captain Hogan listened through the speaker, then turned to sound. "Report?" "In position, sir. Latitude 06-22.S, longitude 116-35.E." Captain Hogan nodded, "Target report?" The final reply came, "Target on course two-six-seven degrees true, range 2600 yards, speed eight knots. *Bonefish* is at oh-three-zero true degrees. Torpedo track sixty port, thirty right gyro for the bow tubes, sir." Captain Hogan glanced at O'Neill, then looked back to the crew, speaking firmly and calmly, "Fire one. Fire two!" Lieutenant Johnston noted the times from the submarines internal clock, writing quickly as each firing was announced.

09.17.55 Fired #1 tube,
09.18.05 Fired #2 tube

Immediately, captain Hogan ordered the second volley of torpedoes, "Fire three. Fire four!" Johnston again scribbled the times in the log.

09.18.13 Fired #3 tube
09.18.23 Fired #4 tube

The bow tubes released gasps of air as the torpedoes slid from their mouths. The submarine paused, a leviathan metal whale in the dark depths, hanging motionless for a moment. Leaving comet trails through the water the first two projectiles moved forward in the silent sea. Two more torpedoes exploded from the sub, slicing the ocean like bullets in suspended motion. The four trails of bubbles created a wake projecting forward, placing their intended target dead ahead.

- 0920 HOURS -

The morning sunshine had dried the deck of the *Suez Maru* from an earlier rain shower as Deckhand Saburo Maeda sauntered to a stop just outside the bridge. He made a deep bow to First-Mate Watanabe and Quartermaster Shimizu who moved past him into the bridge, deep in discussion. Maeda watched through the glass as Watanabe took a bearing and went into the chart room. Shimizu began speaking to Captain Shirakawa, who then stepped out and climbed down to the lower bridge and lit a cigarette. Maeda realised they would not talk idly to a low-ranking deckhand and turned away. He moved along the upper bridge deck, stopping beside Deckhand Hino who was on lookout duty. Hino stared hard through his binoculars but peered sideways at Maeda as he spoke. Maeda offered a cigarette and continued talking as Hino's face crumpled into terror. Maeda looked blankly as Hino shrieked wildly, pointing out to sea. Maeda turned to look as Hino finally shouted, "Torpedo!" Maeda gasped, his mouth sagged open as Hino shrieked. "Hard to port!" The ship began a violent turn to the right. Panicked, Maeda shouted, "No!" and ran into the steering station. The wheel was spun to the right, "No! That's starboard!" Maeda shouted, "Port! To the left!" Quartermaster Shimizu had frozen, he simply looked on in fright. Suddenly, he lunged forward pulling the wheel to the left, hard to port. Watanabe dashed out of chart room and blew a whistle as Captain Shirakawa ran up the ladder, panting and pointing. "It's missed us! It's missed us!" he gasped, his eyes darting across the sea wildly. Shirakawa looked slowly to Shimizu as Watanabe shook his head and reached out to hold onto the window ledge. They stood for a moment wide-eyed and holding their breath. The tremendous concussion when it came blew every pane of glass to pieces in a second. The bridge exploded in a fountain of flying shards as the whole ship shuddered and each fell to their knees. Captain Shirakawa was first back on his feet as he leapt to the door, almost falling over the foredeck railing in his haste to survey the damage. He looked aft and stopped short. The entire stern of his ship was shrouded in a mist of sea-spray and smoke from the explosion. Turning seaward Shirakawa pointed lamely. His crew followed his gesture and all now saw *another* two foaming streaks heading directly for the stern. He opened his mouth to speak but no sound was emitted. He watched paralysed as the mist briefly cleared revealing the rapidly sinking stern. Seawater poured into the ship as a second concussion hit aft. Everyone held on as the impact smashed into the ship. Everything seemed to implode. The poop deck burst into a ball of fire. It lifted momentarily then collapsed in on itself. The first flames leaping from the hole were extinguished with a hiss, as the gaping maw was immersed in rapidly advancing seawater. Into this chasm fell Nakanishi, Miyahiro and Usami. Shirakawa watched in horror as the three deckhands he'd earlier seen wandering about, lazily organising their tools, disappeared into the abyss. He grasped the rail with both hands and turned to Shimizu and Watanabe, "Go and check the damage. Now!" his subordinates jumped down the ladder, their feet either side of the slide rail, and dashed across the slanting deck. Watanabe pushed aside PoWs who were climbing out of the hold three. Everywhere crew and Japanese soldiers threw buoys overboard and leapt into the sea. Men merged with enemies, the latter ignoring the former. Watanabe caught up with Shimizu and they quickly surveyed the stern of the ship. The deck had collapsed in on itself, the upper storehouse and aft water tank were gone, hold four was flooded and three was filling fast with seawater as desperate PoWs tried to climb out, helped by their fellow men. The ship lurched again as crates, barrels, cargo and men slid away down the deck into the gaping inferno and the sea.

Assistant engineer Hirashima had been on his way to the engine room and was violently shaken as another huge explosion rocked the ship and the engine stopped. He gathered himself, stopping in the doorway of the boiler room. He leant around the door frame, and called out through the smoke. No one answered. Hirashima shielded his eyes with a hand and pulled his shirt up to cover his mouth as he entered the room. As the smoke thinned he saw the fragmented boiler, "That must have been the huge explosion," he muttered to no one. Suddenly he felt water at his feet. He looked down to see seawater sloshing around his legs, rising fast. He backed out of the room and looked through the door to the adjacent engine room. Fireman Minoru Matsuzaki lay on the floor with horrible leg injuries, shrapnel from the exploding boiler Hirashima surmised. He helped Matsuzaki up and together they began to struggle towards the main deck.

Meanwhile, Seaman Hidenori Kokussen had been in quarters when the torpedoes hit. He'd had an enormous breakfast, returning for thirds as his crew-mates had laughed. "What?" he'd spluttered, food flying from his mouth as he filled his cheeks, "I'm hungry!" Not long after he'd felt overly full and had lain down on his bunk to digest and read ships news. He'd been laughing at something or other when he was thrown to the deck with the first torpedo impact. He tried to stand but found he couldn't. Looking to his feet he realised he'd sprained both ankles and probably broken a few toes. He tried to stand again as the ship lurched with another impact and he fell again with a squeal. Dazed, his ears ringing, he got to his painful feet and grabbing a shirt and life preserver he limped from the cabin. Others fled ahead of him and a few were still gathering belongings but Kokussen knew he had to get off the ship. He limped to the stairs, encountering Hirashima in the corridor struggling with Matsuzaki, who had draped an arm about Hirashima as he stumbled forward. Kokussen sighed impatiently and took Matsuzaki's other arm and together they climbed up to the main deck. Hirashima and Kokussen lay Matsuzaki down on the slanting deck as they heard the captain shouting the order to abandon ship. Kokussen dashed to investigate the lifeboats that were already being unfastened and their oars unstowed. Hirashima meanwhile turned to the sea and saw soldiers, crew, PoWs and an ocean of debris on the water. He spun round in fright to see the aft deck was already level with the water. At that moment, Watanabe and Shimizu were making their way back up the ship. Hirashima grasped at Watanabe's sleeve, frantically telling him of the devastation he'd seen below deck, that the boiler room was flooded. Watanabe nodded, releasing Hirashima's grip, finger by finger. With some effort and holding tightly onto the rail Watanabe and Shimizu climbed back up to the bridge to report the hopelessness of the doomed ship to the captain. Hirashima had nodded thanks as Kokussen returned and lifted the semi-concisous, injured Matsuzaki, half carrying him to a lifeboat quickly filling with soldiers. The sight prompted Hirashima to dash back to his quarters and grasping his life preserver he quickly tied it around him and ran back to look for a space on the lifeboat. He'd looked up as he dashed along the deck, and had seen Captain Shirakawa standing on the bridge. He bowed, but the captain was busy speaking with Shimizu, and Watanabe who nodded and bowed backing away from the bridge and climbing down to assist with the lifeboat operations. Hirashima heard a creaking groan and turned to see the stern dipping under water. In fright he scrambled up to the bow, then shinned down a rope ladder before he released his grip and dropped into the sea.

Low in the bow of the ship, deep in crew quarters, Storeman Nagasaki had been off duty when the first direct hit had knocked him out of his bunk. He lay prone on his belly on the floor, his eyes wide in fear as he felt the great metal ship vibrating through his body. He heard a groan and saw Engineer Minoda lying nearby. Minoda had also gone back to his bunk after breakfast. He now leapt from the floor and ran to the doorway. Nagasaki began shouting for anyone in quarters to follow him, as he ran with Minoda from the room and toward the deck. Minoda turned away at the bottom of the ladder. He watched Nagasaki go for a moment then ran down to the galley to warn the cooks and crew there. Nagasaki stopped short, shouting to Minoda to follow him but quickly gave up, panicking in realisation the ship was rapidly sinking. Nagasaki looked at the odd lurching angle of the ladder in fright, and quickly climbed the slanting rungs onto the main deck. He paused to catch his breath, watching the commotion wide-eyed. The lifeboats were hastily being lowered, and quickly filled with Japanese soldiers. Watanabe directed proceedings, shouting to the crew to pull at the ropes. "We are abandoning ship then?" Nagasaki called to no one listening. He looked up and saw Shirakawa on the bridge in frenetic conversation with Shimizu. Nagasaki turned and saw soldiers were throwing planks into the sea and dashed across to help. He threw two life-rafts overboard, and wondered if he could immediately jump in after them.

Meanwhile, Minoda ran to the galley. He had rounded a corner and crashed into Fireman Ehara. He had just finished breakfast and was idly talking in the corridor outside the galley, when they heard the scream, "Torpedo!" Ehara now ran past Minoda, climbing up on deck and arrived panting, near the officers' cabins. He stood dazed for a moment then ran toward his cabin for a life preserver, pushing past soldiers throwing planks and boards into the sea. Ehara grabbed a life preserver from a pile, put it on and leapt over the rail, free-falling into the packed sea. He landed awkwardly, his leg hitting a life-plank as he splashed under. He surfaced, crying out in pain. After passing the stricken Ehara in the corridor, Minoda had dashed into the galley to find Third-Mate Takahashi shouting in wild panic that the ship had been torpedoed. Someone said the stern was gone and the ship was sinking. Minoda retched in fear as the crew frantically leapt to the doorway to get out. Minoda shouted for calm, telling them they must get up to the main deck carefully. He stepped back as the throng jammed the doorway, then he turned and ran back to the ladder. He climbed up and out onto the deck, emerging near the forward holds. There, he saw Japanese soldiers swarming from hold two, fastening life preservers around themselves, pulling the cords tight around their waists and jumping wildly overboard. Minoda realised ship was sinking fast, and there was nothing to be done. He stood in the melee for a moment, frozen in fear then something inside him sparked and he ran up to his quarters in the bow. He searched in the mess of strewn about belongings for his own valued possessions which he kept packed in a tin. He stopped, hearing a quiet moan. Turning he saw Narishima lying on floor. He had also been relaxing in his bunk and reading at the first torpedo strike. He had fallen heavily, concussing himself as he landed awkwardly. Minoda helped him to his feet, "We must abandon ship, where is your life preserver?" He spoke urgently to Narishima's dull expression. Behind them Maeda dashed into the room. He stood panting in the doorway then rushed for his own life preserver. He yanked open a small trunk and fished about inside, pulling out a fistful of photographs and a squashed packet of cigarettes. Maeda turned, shouting wildly to Minoda, "Abandon ship! We are abandoning ship! Come on!" He didn't wait for a reply. Maeda turned and ran, clutching his few belongings and the precious life preserver. Minoda sat Narishima on a bunk unsteadily, and began searching for more life preservers. As he rummaged about, throwing things in the air, getting down on his knees, and pulling things from underneath the bunks, he suddenly found the small tin he'd been looking for. He held it in the air with glee as the ship lurched. Minoda grabbed at a bunk and hauled himself to his feet, quickly stowing the small tin in a pocket. He gazed about uncertain of his plan and spied two life preservers hanging on a wall. Grabbing them he screamed at Narishima to hurry, pulling him along as they ran wobbily back up onto the deck. There, soldiers were throwing rafts and various flotsam overboard. Minoda began to help as he heard someone shouting the superfluous order to abandon ship. Half the crew and soldiers were already in the water. Narishima sat slumped against the gunwale as Minoda tied a life preserver around him, then fixed his own over his head and pulled at the cords. He pulled Narishima to his feet and they stared at the stern of the ship. For the first time they fully saw their terrifying nightmare. The poop deck had been blown away and the ship listed horribly. Minoda gasped as he looked at a huge hole and the rushing seawater that filled it. He was terrified and dumb-stuck. Minoda turned as he vaguely heard Nagasaki shouting at them to take the buoys he held. Nagasaki's face came close to Minoda's as he shrieked, pushing a buoy at him, pointing to Narishima and to the sea. Dully, Minoda took it and pressed it into Narishima's hands, shouting into his ear as he pushed him overboard, "Don't let go!" Minoda grabbed another buoy and without looking back he followed him, clutching it tightly. As Minoda had jumped, he fell through the air frantically clutching the buoy. When he surfaced, he realised he'd lost it in the plunge and he panicked. He thrashed around wildly, sucking in seawater, convulsing and retching. Someone swam to him and slapped him hard. He lay back in the water, letting his feet float to the surface. He tried to control his breathing as the sea swashed around him.

Captain Tamaki Shirakawa had been afraid of the very nightmare that was unfolding, for the entire journey. He'd been a civilian captain for many years and was nervous when his ship had been commandeered for war service. Each journey he'd made felt like his last and although he enjoyed the money he was making, he longed to retire to his home town where his wifes family ran their small restaurant. He dreamed of simply strolling in the park and sleeping in his own bed beside his wife. He'd pulled on the cigarette as he stood on the lower bridge, calmly watching the sea and feeling the ebb and flow of the ship as it chugged through the sea. He felt tired and rubbed his eyes as the cigarette burned to a stub. The shriek of 'torpedo!' Had burst his fatigue as he fell to the floor, recovering quickly to order the rapid survey. Watanabe began reporting to Shirakawa before he'd even climbed back up to the bridge. "The poop deck is collapsed, the main mast is gone and hold four is flooded!" he shouted, panting. Shimizu followed behind breathlessly. "The engineroom is flooded and the boiler has exploded. Seawater is now coming into hold three." Shirakawa had blinked, all his fears collapsed in on him. His stomach retched itself into a knot as he felt blood drain from his face. It was no use. He stared at his senior crewmen, shaking his head. Shirakawa paused as Purser Nukui dashed up the ladder clutching a large bag under his arm. Shirakawa nodded to him and turned to his crew pointing to them in turn. "We will abandon ship. Watanabe, you oversee lifeboat operations. Shimizu, you have the bridge. Nukui, you come with me." No one moved. Shirakawa rounded, "Watanabe? The lifeboats. Now!" Watanabe frowned but turned back down the ladder and dashed to the nearest lifeboat. Nukui had only minutes earlier been standing in a doorway chatting idly to Third-Mate Takahashi in his quarters when they'd heard someone shout, "Torpedo! Torpedo!" Nukui had leapt up, then paused for a moment, ordering Takahashi to hurry to the galley, and tell the crew to prepare in case they had to abandon ship. Nukui rushed to his own cabin. Gathering documents into a bag he ran up to the bridge to find Captain Shirakawa. As Nukui ran along the deck he'd watched wide-eyed as soldiers and PoWs alike plunged wildly into the sea. He cringed in fright as life-rafts were thrown in after them. He saw a lifeboat being lowered but could not stop to get in as he wished to, he had important protocols to follow. He found the captain on the bridge talking animatedly with Shimizu and Watanabe. Captain Shirakawa had broken off when he saw Nukui and together they jogged to the captain's cabin. The captain nodded as Nukui showed him the contents of his bag. Then, taking all the ships funds from a small safe, he tucked the money into Nukui's bag. They nodded in unspoken agreement over what needed to be done. Then, Nukui left and ran onto the deck, searching for the lifeboat he'd seen and hoping it would have room for him. Watanabe had ordered the lifeboat crew to unfasten the boats properly and make ready as Nukui ran up and stopped beside him, panting. He nodded to Watanabe and threw a bag into the lifeboat. Watanabe held up his palm, "You have five minutes, no more!" Nukui nodded and dashed back to his cabin to gather more documents. He tipped the contents of a drawer into a bucket and began burning them, sweating in panic. Suddenly the ship lurched. The bucket and the loose contents of his cabin slid along the floor. Fire leapt up a blanket hanging off his bunk and quickly took hold. Nukui jumped up in alarm, his arms braced the doorway as he backed out of his cabin and ran.

Captain Shirakawa had left Nukui and returned to the bridge, relieving Shimizu, who turned to descend the ladder as PoW Transport Commander Masaji Iketani clambered up to the bridge. Breathless and coughing, Iketani spluttered at the captain, his speech racing, "Ship flooding! Everyone jumping overboard, we are sinking!" Iketani's panic startled Shirakawa. He stared curiously at him for a moment. "We *are* abandoning ship. Get a hold of yourself!" rebuked Shirakawa. But, Iketani's fear had infected him and immediately he turned, ordering Shimizu to hurry and throw a rope ladder down the bow of the ship. "I saw three deckhands fall into the ship!" spluttered Iketani, his eyes wild. Shirakawa turned back to Iketani, calmly. "Assist in throwing life-rafts overboard. Now! Do something. Don't just stand there. The ship will be gone in a matter of minutes, you must help or go overboard!" Shirakawa's patience had ended and he pushed Iketani out of the bridge. Iketani shook involuntarily as he wobbled down the sloping deck. The remaining crew were heaving heavy life-rafts into the sea as the stern bubbled with seawater as it went down. Iketani looked about frantically. He had no wish to leap overboard and be sucked under with the disappearing ship. Suddenly, he noticed a third lifeboat. It was almost level with the sea and two of the crew struggled to free it from its fastenings. Iketani dashed across, pushing past the few remaining PoWs who reached out for the rail. He tripped and fell haphazardly. His spectacles leapt from his face and slid across the deck. When he found them, the glass was completely smashed. Watanabe had been directing the lowering of lifeboats for some ten frantic minutes. He'd watched the first lowered, filled with Japanese soldiers and had shouted at them to get out. He ordered it should only take injured soldiers. At that moment Kokussen staggered up, half carrying Matsuzaki, whose eyes drifted about. Watanabe directed they both climb aboard. Iketani saw his chance. He turned, looking about for a wounded soldier to 'help'.

At first torpedo strike Fireman Morimasu Kikuchi had dashed up on deck wearing only his loincloth. He tried to get into one of the lifeboats but was told they were for patients only. He turned, the slow realisation of emergency pouring over him. He watched as buoys were thrown into the sea. Kikuchi dashed back to crew quarters and quickly dressed. He came back up on deck wearing an odd assortment of clothing, over which he'd roundly tied his life-preserver. He looked out to sea and simply ran at the gunwale, vaulting over with a one-handed spring, into the water. Now Maeda ran back on deck clutching his photographs and cigarettes. He had somehow lost the life-preserver in his scramble to get on deck. Someone had grabbed at it, and fearful of losing his photographs and unable to hold them all he let go of the life-preserver. Now he stood in the lurching chaos, looking this way and that, searching for another while panic rose in him. In fright he realised two lifeboats had already been lowered to sea level, which appeared to rise rapidly as the ship sank to meet the surface. He tried but could not get into either. Maeda stood watching, silently fearing the worst as Watanabe suddenly shouted him to help lower the remaining lifeboat. Seawater had now risen level with it. He sloshed to it, up to his knees in advancing water as the ship slipped lower, tucking his photographs into a breast pocket. Maeda was now joined by Hino, and together with Watanabe they pulled at the ropes, righting it as the water splashed its small hull. Watanabe tried to hold the boat steady, "Get in! Both of you! Now!" Hino gate-vaulted aboard as Maeda grasped the prow to lift himself up, and in. Maeda turned, as Watanabe backed away. "Sir, aren't you coming?" Watanabe shook his head, "Not yet," he said as he turned, racing back up the sloping deck toward the bridge. Hino and Maeda grabbed the ropes lowering themselves further down as nearby Japanese crew and soldiers piled in.

Chief Medical Officer Eto had been treating one of his Japanese patients when the first torpedo hit. His tweezers flew out of his hand and arched through the air. Bracing his shoulder he fell hard against the wall. He knew immediately what had happened and the consequences. Eto quickly instructed his orderlies to take the walking wounded up on deck and prepare to abandon ship. He looked back to the soldiers still awaiting treatment and began throwing bandages, medicines and assorted instruments into a deep leather bag as the ship reverberated with the shock of a second explosion. "Get all the patients on deck *now*, get them into the lifeboats! *Now!*" Eto shouted. He grabbed the bag, pushing past soldiers and ran up on deck, in search of a lifeboat. He stopped momentarily as he saw PoWs pulling each other out of hold three and struggling to the rail to drop overboard. Eto lowered his eyes and ran past. When Watanabe would not permit him to board either of the first two lifeboats Eto became frantic. He sat on the upper deck watching, awaiting his chance. Then suddenly, he saw Watanabe leave the third lifeboat and dash away towards the bow. Eto saw his chance. He jumped down and made his way to the last lifeboat. He clambered aboard, gritting his chin determinedly. "I'll see to these patients now." He said authoritatively, avoiding any eye contact as he pulled bandages from his bag, leaning in close to the nearest patient. Hashimoto, shook his head and gave in, nodding as Eto settled into his place. A young wounded soldier, Yoshio Kashiki asked if he could please board as the sea came up to meet the lifeboat. He looked sickly even without the bloody bandage wrapped round his head. Yoshio found his limping suddenly supported by PoW Transport Commander Iketani. Iketani had been wading around the sinking deck searching for a life preserver and had heard Hashimoto shouting for the able-bodied to get out of the boat. He then saw the wounded Yoshio making for the lifeboat and saw *his* chance. Iketani pulled himself aboard and turned, pulling at Yoshio's hand, "I'm with him, I am helping him. He's badly injured." Yoshio grunted as he fell aboard. The boat was now full and began drifting away from the sinking ship, as the doleful occupants looked to cach other. Iketani tried to make himself blend in, tucking his chin into his life preserver and avoiding any gazes, but Hashimoto noticed him settled in beside Yoshio. "Wounded only!" he shouted as the boat bobbed away. Maeda, sitting opposite Iketani, looked up guiltily. He assumed he was being spoken to and reached down into the bottom of boat and pulled a soggy life-preserver from the dirty puddle sloshing there. Maeda pulled it over his head, tying the long cords round his body twice and pushed himself backwards overboard. Iketani slunk further back as Maeda surfaced. He thrashed about in the cold seawater as his photographs slipped from his pocket and floated away. As the sepia faces began to submerge, he reached out for the bobbing pictures in the chaos. He stopped briefly as wide eyed and terrified PoWs holding on to a hatch-cover floated past. Everyone on board the lifeboat stretched out in Maeda's vacated space, Hashimoto tutted and moved away from Iketani.

On deck, Purser Nukui had noticed a few PoW still remained on deck after all the crew and soldiers had gone overboard. He looked to the sea. It was littered as far as the eye could see. Nukui shrugged his shoulders, pulled on a life jacket and jumped overboard with a small splash, as the ship was now nearly level with the water. He began to swim, and quickly became tired and breathless. He saw a raft and swam to it, resting an arm on it as it drifted. He looked to the others clinging to it, who had not spoken a word on his arrival, and saw they were all PoWs. They stared, hollow-eyed and nervously at Nukui, who stared back, equally nervously. He caught his breath and swam backwards, pushing himself away from the raft with his foot. He was grateful to see the raft float away, parting ways with him. The bobbing PoWs worried him, and he grimaced crookedly as they watched him drift away. He turned and spluttered as he tried to swim. Each floppy arm splashed uselessly at the water around his thick life preserver, his head lolling from side to side. He blinked in disbelief as a lifeboat full of familiar faces approached. It seemed to swim in and out of his vision as the world around him faded at the edges. He came to as someone pulled his heavy sagging body from the water and he fell against the bottom of the lifeboat. He looked up at the faces, who eagerly watched him, open mouthed and expectant. Someone touched his shoulder and he started. It was Kokussen, it was *he* who had pulled him from the sea. Nukui patted his arm gratefully, breathlessly mouthing his thanks. His eyes widened as Kokussen lifted up a stuffed bag. Nukui grinned. It was the bag of documents and ship's money, Kokussen had kept it safe. He had jumped into the lifeboat, as the *Suez Maru*'s stern began dropping away fast. The lifeboat overflowed with soldiers and crew as Watanabe had shouted to lower it. Kokussen had watched Nukui throw in the bag and had caught it. He'd peered inside and realised its importance and so had alternately clutched it to his chest or sat on it, making sure he kept it close throughout the ordeal. Kokussen now grabbed at the oars to get the lifeboat moving away from the steadily lifting bow of the ship as it creaked upwards. He struggled to release them but there was not enough room to put the oars out. Those who were conscious splashed at the water in panic, paddling with their hands to get away from the rising hull. Kokussen looked to the sea as they cleared the sinking ship. Struggling figures splashed about, trying to swim for the lifeboat as they screamed for help.

Nagasaki had stayed on deck near the forward holds until the bow rose so fast he struggled to remain standing upright. He realised there was no time left and ran, pulling the cords on his lifejacket tight. He realised he must jump now. As he stood at the very prow of the bow he heard a shout and turned to see Captain Shirakawa leap from the starboard side of the bow into the sea. Nagasaki then jumped. He surfaced quickly, turning to look up at the ship as Shimizu leapt from the disappearing bow. Shimizu was the last to leave the *Suez Maru* alive. Nagasaki swam to him and together they climbed onto a life-raft that had drifted toward them. They lay flat out on it, panting and dripping with their legs in the water, watching as some thirty PoWs, clinging to rafts and barrels bobbed by. Both enemies exchanged looks. Each realised they shared the same terrible situation and they simply drifted away from each other in the swell. In every direction the sea was awash with PoWs and Japanese all swimming for their lives.

Those soldiers crowded into lifeboats pulled their comrades aboard, tying out long ropes for others to hang onto. They loosened the fingers of any PoW daring to get hold of their lifeboat, pushing them away with hands and oars. The desperate scuffles and splashing around the lifeboats abruptly ceased as a terrific creaking groan split the air. Each head turned to watch the *Suez Maru's* final moments. The ships stern had sunk completely underwater and her bow pointed upwards. A sickening gurgle floated across the water, its sound amplified by the waves as the *Suez Maru* seemed to take a deep breath ahead of her impending plunge. The bow rolled back, pointing directly upwards as the ship stood perpendicularly for a moment. Then, she started her descent to the depths. Those witnessing the scene gasped as they heard underwater explosions, and saw fire flashing as the ship was devoured, swallowed in a bubbling maelstrom as air pockets contracted and released. The *Suez Maru* disappeared with a final groaning gurgle as she dropped down to the ocean floor. The sea washed over the surface where the ship disappeared. The waves licked higher and a south-westerly wind blew away traces of the ship, aside from the flotsam of men, soldiers and crew floating on the surface. All stared blankly at the empty space where the ship had been. It seemed as if no one could blink, nor breathe again, as the gurgling final sounds echoed in their ears. Exhausted and afraid they drifted on the blank endless stretch of blue ocean as the sun rose higher. Only twenty minutes had elapsed since the PoWs had been braced in nightmarish but buoyant holds, and the Japanese crew had been finishing breakfast and smoking cigarettes. The latter as relaxed as anyone could during the dangerous voyage. Now, it became a terrifying struggle for survival, for all.

Aboard the minesweeper, Captain Kawano had watched alternately through binoculars and blinking sunlight, in stunned anticipation as he watched the *Suez Maru* take two successive hits to her stern. He was unable to tear himself away from the scene before him as the ship ripped in half, collapsing in on herself and falling away with an anguished groan in twenty brief minutes. He viewed the attack first from the port gunwale where he had been vacantly staring ahead, occasionally looking back as the *Suez Maru* chugged beside and slightly to the rear of his minesweeper. He had glanced to her, and turned away as his brain belatedly registered two white slashes beyond the *Suez Maru*. His head snapped back in disbelief. He gawped open-mouthed as the ship tried to turn at full speed, first lurching inexplicably to starboard into the torpedos path, then a moment later turning a dangerous hard to port. The *Suez Maru* swayed, unable to turn in time as a massive explosion erupted at her rear. Kawano had shouted immediately for binoculars. He ordered a full speed circling pattern, and battle stations, as he snatched the binoculars offered by Ensign Kai and dashed to the bridge.

Ensign Kai, an engineer aboard Minesweeper W12, had watched from the rear deck as the *Suez Maru* burst with two successive explosions. He had dashed to his captain, offering his own binoculars as their minesweeper stood to battle stations. He in turn, took binoculars from Ensign Fujimoto, who had been on watch nearby. Kai could hardly take in the devastating view. The *Suez Maru*'s stern became obscured in a plume of spray and smoke. As the mist dissipated the rear of the ship was no longer visible as it began to sink. Kai squinted and looked again as the bow of the *Suez Maru* began to rise into the air. The hull of her red underbelly protruded from the water as tiny ant-like figures swarmed from the stricken ship. Takeshi Fujimoto had been in the minesweeper's boiler room, he'd been bored and had come up on deck to supervise a boiler pipe repair. Whilst standing idly talking he'd been asked to temporarily relieve a lookout. He'd heard the explosions and seen the devastation and had dashed to the boiler room on the order to battle stations. He ran along the deck, looking over as he headed below deck. He watched, shocked as the *Suez Maru* began sinking, her bow at a forty-five degree angle. Gunnery Officer Yatsuka was on watch on the starboard side of the minesweeper. He had run across to port on hearing a shout of, 'Torpedo'. He estimated the two traces were about 2500 feet out and closing on the *Suez Maru*. Captain Kawano had immediately ordered battle stations, and turning to Yatsuka, ordered the depth charges readied. Yatsuka dashed to the ladder, shouting below deck as they heard a massive explosion from the *Suez Maru*. He turned to see a plume of seawater and smoke in the air. Yatsuka ran to look over the side. He thought perhaps she might not sink until a second explosion jolted the whole ship, settling her by the stern as she began to slip down, bow protruding upwards. He quickly followed his captain back to the bridge as they monitored the sinking ship, and began to circle her. Then, Yatsuka watched the sea, his gaze drawn magnetically to the scene he could not pull away from. The *Suez Maru* pitched downwards, figures leaping, falling into the bubbling water around the sinking ship. Explosions, flashes of orange and red, and thick smoke blurred his view then receded to reveal the hulk of the ship disappearing rapidly under the sea. He could not hear anything except the movement and activity on his own ship, but frightened imagined sounds formed in his ears nonetheless. Creaking, screaming, the twisting of metal and desperate shouting. Yatsuka motioned to Kawano in alarm as oil began to spread out like a blossoming bloodstain on the ocean, filled with choking men. Their tiny slender bodies fell like stick figures into the inferno of water and debris, then flailed in the thick oil. Yatsuka turned his attention to his enemy and frantically called out to the lookouts. "Anything?" He received shaking heads, and 'no sirs' in reply from each of the dozen men lined up with binoculars. They were supposed to be searching for the submarine, but they too were drawn to the unfolding scene. Their binoculars drifted back to the sinking ship as Yatsuka screamed at them. "You want to be sunk as well?" Hastily they returned to scanning the sea. Yatsuka turned to Warrant Officer Miyaughi, who served as Yatsuka's assistant, "Prepare type two depth charges for immediate deployment." Miyaughi bowed, and left the bridge to direct unfastening the rows of fat depth charges, caged in racks at the stern. The type two charges were a new style Yatsuka had yet to test. They weighed nearly 250lbs and sank ten fathoms per second. They didn't rely on the old style pressure gauges, these contained a small compartment which allowed a cylinder to fill with water at a steady rate. When full, a piston moved and fired the charge. This meant the newer design exploded at a greater depth. Yatsuka sweated as he scanned backwards and forwards though his binocular sights, his vision resting here and there on floating debris, mistaking each for evidence of the sought after submarine. He dipped the binoculars, looking over the sights to check Miyaughi's progress, as the first depth charge swung out of its casing, dangling on the end of its hoisted chain. Yatsuka twitched. He turned to the signalman, Petty Officer Yoshino, "Record the times in the log." Yoshino nodded a bow, and began marking a spidery script into a heavy ledger, as Yatsuka repeated, "Zero nine twenty hours— began depth charges, type two. Ah battle speed." Yatsuka looked again to Miyaughi, who indicated readiness to drop the first charge, Yatsuka responded with a shriek, "Now! Attack!" Yoshino scribbled into the ledger.

0930 hours: first depth charge attack.

Meanwhile, Captain Kawano had summoned Ensign Kai to take a message to the radio operators. "Write this down." Breathlessly, he pointed to the notebook Kai carried in his top pocket, as he continued, "To, ah, 21 Base Commander and 24 Base Commander. *Suez Maru* torpedoed by enemy submarine. Sinking fast. Ahh position is three hundred miles East, North-East of Kangean Islands. Ahh time, nine twenty, the twenty-ninth. Now attacking enemy submarine." He waved his hand impatiently. "All right, go! Send it now!" In the depths of the minesweeper the Morse key clicked rapidly under Ensign Norohaga's quivering hand, as Kai stood over him, reading Kawano's message. They held on in the cramped room as the ship lurched in turns, dropping depth charges as it zigzagged in ever widening circles around the wrecked *Suez Maru*. As Minesweeper W12 came about, Yatsuka looked again to Miyaughi. Yatsuka held up his flat palm, his fingers and thumb outstretched signalling to drop a set of *five* charges. Miyaughi nodded, turning to the emptying rack of explosive barrels. They were quickly readied and Miyaughi looked for Yatsuka's command to go, which was given immediately with a drop of Yatsuka's hand. All aboard the minesweeper listened, waiting for signs of a direct hit on the submarine. Yatsuka scanned the sea for tell-tale oil and jetsam, as they circled around again. Nothing could be seen. Kawano stamped the floor in frustration. Yatsuka turned and nodded as Yoshino again wrote in the ledger.

```
0940   hours:   Second   depth   charge
attack,— Results  unknown.
```

The minesweeper widened its turn, as the crew on deck heard a roar from survivors in the sea. All eyes turned to watch anxiously as the *Suez Maru* disappeared under the gathering waves. Yoshino turned back to his ledger.

```
0940 hours: Suez Maru sank.
```

Kawano shook himself from the scene. He turned to Yatsuka and ordered, "Continue anti-submarine operations. Visual search and echo raging. All ahead, standard speed." "Yes, sir," bowed Yatsuka.

The crew of the *USS Bonefish* had listened silently and breathlessly as Sound-man Canfield clutched his earpiece and reported to Captain Hogan, "Sir, oh nine-nineteen hours, one torpedo hit heard... screws have stopped, sir." Johnston relayed the scene from the periscope viewfinder. "Confirmed. One torpedo hit under the mainmast. She's listing, sir. Settling by the stern now, there's an aircraft on deck, sir." "Identification?" Captain Hogan asked. "Looks like a *Zero*, sir." He nodded calmly as his crew looked to him for permission to respond to their success. He was about to congratulate his men, but stopped, frowning at Johnston's furrowed expression. "What is it?" "Sir, she's going under. Stern is under now, bow rising. Now at thirty degrees, still rising, sir." Captain Hogan turned to Petty Officer Moses, "Note the time in ship's log." He paused, adding, "She's sunk! Very well done, men!" His face broke into a wide beam as the crew of the *Bonefish* whooped on their captain's praise of their success and clear confirmation that the enemy target was rapidly sinking. Captain Hogan slapped O'Neill's back, who turned to Freaner and grinned. "Well done, well done all of you," smiled Captain Hogan. Moses wrote quickly into the green lined book, recording their victory.

```
09.19 One torpedo hit heard and seen under
mainmast.
  Target's screws stopped as she took a list and
settled immediately by the stern. One aircraft,
appeared to be a type 'ZERO' seen stowed on
forward well deck.
09.22 The target's stern was seen to be under
with the bow rising at about a 30 degree angle.
```

Their shouts reverberated around the control room as Johnston rubbed his eyes at the periscope and pushed his face back to the eyepiece, "Er, sir..." he started, "...the escort is changing course–" Captain Hogan's grin dropped. He turned to look the length of the bridge, calling, "All hands. Rig for dive!" O'Neill simultaneously reached across to a panel flicking a switch to sound the diving alarm. Johnston dashed to a station monitoring the submarines depth and pressure on various gauges, and sat unblinking at the panel. Canfield called out urgently, "Captain, depth charge! Distant," Captain Hogan nodded calmly. "All right, let's keep our heads men. Continuous reports please, Sound." "Yessir," Canfield replied, turning back to his station. Captain Hogan turned to O'Neill, looking for confirmation the submarine was ready to dive, they had no time to waste. O'Neill quickly repeated the reports he'd received, "Yes sir, rigged for dive, sir." Captain Hogan responded instantly, "Take her down!" Canfield called out again, "Target fully submerged, sir. Breaking up on descent, sir." "Acknowledged," replied Captain Hogan as Moses scribbled the alarming change in situation.

```
09.23 Escort put on speed and headed towards
us. Went to deep submergence. Received one
depth charge - distant. Sound could hear
typical ship breaking up noises in direction of
target.
```

Captain Hogan breathed out slowly, silently. He had almost been holding his breath as sweat dripped from the end of his nose. The crew did not move. No one made even a footfall for fear of accidentally making a loud noise. Everyone remained frozen in place, listening in near silence. Only Lieutenant Johnston whispered depth reports, "Fifty feet." Captain Hogan nodded. Everyone looked to the captain, hardly blinking until Johnston spoke again in hushed tones. "Depth, one hundred feet, sir." The *Bonefish* dropped down into the darkness, as Minesweeper W12 desperately searched for her. Suddenly Canfield called out, "Depth charges. Imminent!" "Brace!" ordered Captain Hogan. The men held on and stared at each other, waiting for the impact. Two shuddering explosions rattled the submarine. The enemy was getting nearer. Captain Hogan wiped his brow. "Open bulkhead flappers, start ventilation." He whispered to O'Neill, who gave the order down the tube to the forward engine room. He waited for their response, then confirmed to his captain, "Bulkhead flappers open, ventilation started, sir." Captain Hogan nodded in the still air. "Depth, two hundred, sir," came Johnston's report. The crew looked more uneasy. The submarine could take the depth. Their concern was the deadly depth charges. They were difficult to hear in the submarines own bubbling descent and would act like dynamite to a tin-foil boat. No one would stand a chance. "Depth, two-fifty feet, sir." Johnston turned in his seat to the captain. "Negative temperature gradient, sir." Captain Hogan's face hardly responded. A slight incline of his head, a barely perceptible nod only a tightly knit team could have read. Johnston saw the acknowledgment and turned back to his panel. The captain chose to wait. The submarine reverberated at high frequency, creating ripples in the captain's mug of tea, which sat on a navigation map. The men looked to the captain as they braced, and the pressure increased. "Steady, men!" he breathed. "Depth, three hundred feet, sir," Johnston repeated quietly. The submarine was entering her maximum depth limitations, and shuddered as the sleek-hull pushed deeper still. "Take her to three-fifty," responded Captain Hogan. The crew, still braced, hardly blinked as they watched the depth gauge. Johnston stared at its needle flickering incrementally down until at last he repeated, on a relieved exhale, "Depth, three-fifty feet, sir." Each man took a breath as their captain nodded, and ordered, "All stop. Ahead one-third." With audible relief in his voice, O'Neill gasped, eagerly repeating, "Answering all stop, ahead one-third, sir." Captain Hogan raised his eyebrows at O'Neill's tone, who briefly half-grinned. The two men knew each other so well, that each heard the other's unspoken caution and relief. Captain Hogan ordered, "Begin evasive manoeuvres. Let's get out of here!" O'Neill nodded wholehearted agreement as Canfield blurted, "Depth charges. Coming fast, sir!" Captain Hogan responded immediately, "Evasive manoeuvres, now! Brace for impact!" The breathless calm burst as five depth charges exploded in close proximity, rattling the submarine and shaking the occupants. Every man reached for something solid, swinging about from the bulkheads as all matter of items fell and clattered to the floor. They held on, eyes creased shut, cringing with the danger of imminent potential breach. Each man feared the sudden influx of gushing sea-water and each braced himself in the unseen grip of their enemy, lurking on the surface. The succession of charges burst one after another all around the boat, each seemed closer than the last. As the final explosion faded, each man gingerly let go of his handhold and the captain cleared his throat, "Thank you very much, Congressman May! All right, damage report!" O'Neill relayed the order, nodding to the junior lieutenants to obtain reports from all departments. Moses wiped his forehead with the back of his hand and tried to swallow, his dry Adam's apple bobbing as his pencil dashed across the page.

```
09.23-45 Two depth charges. Negative
temperature gradient found beginning at
250 feet. Went to 350, commenced evasive
manoeuvres.
09.26-27 Five depth charges - very close.
```

The crew reported in. All compartments were secure from fire, no damage had been found. Captain Hogan acknowledged each report with a nod. Near silently the screw turned, gently moving the submarine away from the danger area. Canfield pressed his headphones hard to his ears, to obtain every flicker of sound outside their metal hull. He turned as he recognised the shimmying rattle of heavy bombs dropping through the sea, "Sir! Two depth charges!" Captain Hogan responded immediately, "Put on speed, evasion manoeuvres!" The submarine rattled, her lights flickering off and back on again as two explosions burst nearby. They were close but not as close as the previous bombardment. The crew exhaled, they felt relieved as the sound receded. It had felt far too close. "Sir, I think they may have lost us, the escort screws are moving away. Yes, fainter now," Canfield reported as the *Bonefish* moved on. Captain Hogan nodded. "Are they still echo-ranging?" "Yes, sir." Canfield tilted his head, pressing the earpiece, "Depth charge, sir. Some distance away now." "Very good, note it in the log, 0945 hours." Captain Hogan had looked at his watch as he nodded to Moses, who replied, "Yes, sir." The captain moved away and began to speak to O'Neill as Canfield interrupted, "– Another one sir, depth charge! Further out again, sir." Captain Hogan moved quickly to the sound station, "Still echo-ranging?" Canfield pressed an ear to the headphone, "Yes, sir. Noise from the sinking ship is fading out. Nothing but echo ranging now sir." Captain Hogan motioned to O'Neill. "I think we should take a look. We're a good four thousand yards now." O'Neill nodded agreement, "Yes sir, let's see what's happening." Captain Hogan ordered, "Make ready for surfacing. Snorkel depth." "Yes, sir." O'Neill turned to the crew, "Secure the ventilation. Shut bulkhead flappers. Make ready for surfacing, snorkel depth." The crew set about preparing the submarine to slowly come to the surface, and presently all compartments reported ready. It was an hour and a half after firing their torpedoes when the *Bonefish* came to snorkel depth. Johnston pulled the periscope shaft down from the stowage well. He gripped the training handles tightly and immediately began reporting. "Escort bearing three hundred degrees true, range about four thousand yards." Canfield at sound added, "He's still echo ranging with long scale all around." He turned in his seat, "They're still looking for us, sir!" Captain Hogan smiled, nodding. "Note it in the log, Moses." The *Bonefish* continued slowly away from the scene until the minesweeper seemed almost on the horizon. Captain Hogan strode briefly about the deck as they progressed, then turned and nodded at O'Neill. "Continue tracking, keep watch. You have the bridge." "Yes, sir." It was almost one in the afternoon, some three and a half hours after the attack when the captain returned, asking for a position report. O'Neill responded, "Position, latitude 06-28.4 S., longitude 116-36.5 E." Johnston added, "We can still see the escorts smoke over the hill, sir." Captain Hogan furrowed his brow, asking no one in particular, "What are they still doing there? How long does it take to rescue a few survivors?" He stood for a moment trying to make sense of it when Johnston suddenly spoke, "Sir! *Pete* 'plane! Bearing two-seventy-nine degrees true, course about oh-fifty degrees true, range about five miles!" The captain took the periscope, "Yeh, it's a Jap recon float-plane all right! All hands, rig for dive! Take her to one-twenty-five feet." The submarine again dived, moving down through the water sleekly.

Captain Kawano was furious his depth charges had seemed to yield no result. A reconnaissance seaplane flew over to aid tracking of the submarine, but no trace of it could be found. The old *Mitsubishi* F1M had buzzed drowsily around the sky, radioing 'no contact' to the minesweeper. Kawano and Yatsuka had listened to its propeller yawning through the gathering clouds as the minesweeper eventually conceded and called off their search. "Ah, all ahead. Prepare for rescue operations, and lower the lifeboats." Kawano ordered dejectedly. He hated the enemy and worse, he hated defeat in front of his crew. Yatsuka nodded at the order and started for the door as Kawano caught his arm, "Rescue Japanese military and civilian personnel first. No prisoners!" Kawano spat. Yatsuka nodded, bowing as he left. The minesweeper circled back and came to a stop amongst a group of survivors bobbing in the water. Takeshi Fujimoto looked over the side, exchanging glances with Kai who peered from the gunwale. "There's hundreds of them!" "They're all prisoners, maybe three hundred of them!" "–and another few hundred of ours. Look!" Fujimoto watched the desperate faces rolling up and down in the sea and felt sorry for the PoWs shouting for help as they held on to tattered boards and straggling ropes. They looked exhausted. The ship moved away slowly to panicked shouts from the PoWs. The minesweeper then stopped at a group of Japanese patients half aboard and hanging from a battered lifeboat. Kai saw tears in their eyes and their emotional expressions as the minesweeper attempted to draw near.

Kokussen sat aboard one of the lifeboats bobbing in the sea. It had been a long wait in the sun. His superiors had shared out rations and water, and they'd tied shirts around their heads, securing them with their belts. He was grateful to have eaten a large breakfast. To have started out with a full belly as the day stretched away had certainly helped his strength. Kokussen thought he might be the first to be rescued as the minesweeper approached, but it turned and stopped at another group a little distance away. He watched, muttering "Lucky bastards." Then, he gradually noticed no one was going aboard. The minesweeper abruptly moved off and approached his lifeboat after all. As it neared it loomed over the small boat Kokussen began to panic and those on board began moving about, rocking the boat. "Stop!" He shouted, but it was too late. The minesweeper bumped the lifeboat with a crack, pushing it over. The occupants fell overboard as it capsized. Kokussen and the others surfaced. In panic he realised the bag of documents and money was lost. He dived down, looking around, but could see nothing but the blur of underwater bubbles. He spluttered as his air ran out and he quickly surfaced. Spitting out seawater he grabbed an oar and floated, shouting out for rescue as he drifted away from the minesweeper. The crew of the minesweeper threw down ropes and climbing nets, and the capsized soldiers swarmed up onto the safety of the ship. Kokussen felt a surge of energy and tried to thrash his way to the netting, but it was no use. He could not move quickly enough and amongst the melee of splashing rescues the minesweeper began to move away. He hadn't been seen. Kokussen held the oar tightly and wept to himself.

Some of the crew drifting in the currents had gathered boards and planks, tying them together to make rafts, aboard which they pulled soldiers as they encountered them. Kikuchi had helped make a large raft along with Hirashima. They'd gathered four or five Japanese crew together. They had also rescued some fifteen PoWs as they'd seen them in the water. Together they lay out in turns. Kikuchi had floated in the sea on the raft he'd made, drifting for hours on his tiny island. As the minesweeper approached he shouted out excitedly. The PoWs watched warily as the minesweeper slowed to a stop and netting was thrown down its side. Soldiers and crew scrambled gratefully aboard. Kikuchi flopped onto the deck and looked about, panting. The rescued crew gathering on deck seemed familiar to him and he suddenly recognised that only Japanese had been brought aboard. Kikuchi turned back to the sea, to the PoWs on the life-raft he'd made. They waved their arms, shouting words he didn't understand, but with a panic he recognised. Kikuchi turned to ask someone when they'd be rescued. The crew were too busy to speak to him, they jostled him as they dashed about and Kikuchi turned sadly back to the men on the raft. He'd grown quite fond of them. He'd watched as they'd put arms around each other helping lift a man, despite being exhausted themselves. As the hours had drifted by, they'd tried to sing a few songs. They'd talked quietly and cajoled any man who seemed to be drifting away. They'd kept up their spirits with a remarkable show of courage and brotherhood. Kikuchi had been quite taken by their spirit, grinning at them and nodding along to their songs. Kikuchi now stood with both hands on the gunwale as he began shaking uncontrollably. His knees buckled and he dropped to the deck. One of the crew saw him and offered him a cup of *sake*, which made his legs tremble all the more. He tried to speak, to ask about the prisoners in the water but hypothermia turned his jaw and mouth into a useless flapping orifice. The crewman put a hand under his armpit and helped him up. Kikuchi leant heavily on the crewman as he walked to the top of a stairwell leading below deck. Kikuchi's head lolled and he caught a glimpse of 'his' PoWs watching from the raft. His eyes filled with tears as the pair steadily climbed below. Kikuchi hardly noticed the twenty armed gun-crew passing them by, as they marched to the bow of the minesweeper.

Assistant engineer Hirashima had been plucked from the water and had briefly watched the PoWs gather together. They heaved themselves onto the life-rafts and into vacated lifeboats as the Japanese were pulled aboard. Hirashima shivered and turned away, he knew the best place would be the engine room to get warm and dry his clothes. Medical Officer Eto was one of the very few who came aboard the minesweeper bone dry. After his rescue he made his way to sick bay and began tending the constant stream of rescued Japanese coming aboard. He had just finished bandaging an arm, tying a neat knot as a ricocheting crack came from the deck. He turned to the orderlies, a puzzled expression on his face and started to the door as Ehara staggered to the doorframe. Ehara leaned heavily then slumped to the floor as Eto dashed to him, directing the orderlies to pick him up. Ehara lay, crumpled on the table as Eto cut away his trouser legs to inspect his injuries. As Eto worked, Ehara came to. They exchanged stricken glances as they heard a rapid thunder-cracking commotion above deck. Ehara passed out as Eto inclined his ear to listen, but he was unable to *see* what was happening. In the corner of the room sat Kikuchi. He now felt a little better and his trembling had stopped. He looked pointlessly up to the swaying ceiling light as he listened fearfully to the barrage of noise from above. He clambered to his feet and slipped from the room. Kikuchi made his way to the place he knew he'd feel like himself again. As he stepped into the engine room he was startled by a small voice in the gloom. Kikuchi turned and saw Hirashima, looking drawn and shaky. "Come on," Kikuchi said, "sick bay for you." Hirashima responded dully. "I couldn't find it." "You're in luck, I've just come from there."

Eto was still attending to Ehara as Kikuchi helped Hirashima into sick bay. Eto impatiently nodded to an orderly to see to Hirashima as a new cacophony erupted above. "What is *happening* up there?" asked Ehara. "I don't know," replied Kikuchi blankly. "Well, go and find out!" shouted Eto, "... and take him with you." He gestured at Hirashima. The orderly responded. "Yes, he only needed a drink. He's fine." Hirashima and Kikuchi looked at each other then headed back up on deck. The pair arrived at a lull in the commotion. Hirashima sat down under a ladder, waving his hand for Kikuchi leave him be, he again felt faint and nauseous. Kikuchi nodded as he looked about trying to make sense of the fearful faces of those huddled on the deck and the excited shouting of the navy crew at the gunwale. "What's happening?" he asked one of the crew. Warrant Officer Nakajima responded flatly, "Carrying out orders!" Nakajima pointed to the sea. Hesitantly Kikuchi moved to the rail and looked out. The minesweeper had slowed to rescue one of the crew of *Suez Maru*, Hidenori Kokussen. Kokussen had been found drifting alone, holding onto an oar and jabbering incoherently. As he was picked out of the water, a small group of PoWs nearby watched in terrified silence. Shaking with fear and suddenly unable to speak, Kokussen dropped to his knees on the deck. Kikuchi was about to speak to him as the commotion began again. Only now, he heard what it was, and saw the consequences. He stared in sickened horror as the PoWs were swept with gunfire. Kikuchi saw two men on a raft, lifting their arms. They had clearly been shot. He could not bear to look and ran from the deck, back to the familiar warmth of the engine room.

Almost two hours previously Yatsuka had looked down at the deck from the lower bridge, as it slowly filled with dripping, shaking Japanese soldiers and the civilian Japanese crew of the *Suez Maru*. He made his way down the ladder, pushing through the wet bodies, stepping over those sitting on the deck. He asked here and there, "Where is your captain?" Dazed and shivering crew pointed to a dark figure gripping the gunwale, staring out to sea at the continuing extraction of Japanese from the water. Captain Shirakawa's eyes sank in their sockets as he swayed in place, he was clearly a long way away. He startled wildly as Yatsuka touched his arm. "Captain, are you all right?" "I-I haven't a scratch on me," Shirakawa responded blankly. "Can you accompany me please, sir?" Shirakawa nodded dully, turning from the scene and following slowly. On the bridge Captain Kawano looked Shirakawa up and down, as they exchanged salutes. Shirakawa's salute wavered, his face flat and expressionless. Kawano began, "I realise you have had a difficult time of it. Are you hurt?" "No, I am not injured at all, somehow I seem to have managed to–" Kawano ignored the additional chat. "And how is your crew?" "Well, I think there are five missing. I am not sure yet." "I am sorry to hear that, but I suppose it's to be expected," Kawano's face did not reflect the concern of his words. Kawano stared hard at Shirakawa but neither spoke. Kawano looked to Yatsuka with raised brows. Yatsuka took the prompt and broke the short tense silence, turning to Shirakawa, "Who is your transport commander, in charge of the PoWs? Could you take me to him?" Shirakawa's face creased. He'd looked blankly at the floor since responding to Kawano and startled again on Yatsuka's question. Stammering through chattering teeth, he replied. "I-I-I will take you to f-find him." Yatsuka raised a stare at Kawano who shrugged and turned to look out at the vast expanse of sea, his eyes narrowing. Shirakawa shuffled down the ladder and looked about the foredeck for

PoW Transport Commander Iketani. He spotted him quickly, leaning over the gunwale pointing and shouting as the remaining Japanese soldiers and crew were identified and pulled from the water. "First Lieutenant Iketani, the captain would like to see you," Yatsuka said, tapping Iketani on the arm. Iketani seemed not to notice. He continued shrieking and gesticulating, pointing to another soldier in the sea. Yatsuka briefly looked to Shirakawa who blinked mildly. "Lieutenant? Commander?" Yatsuka tried again, more firmly. Iketani turned, his face wet with sea and sweat, "Ah, yes, of course." He followed Yatsuka back to the bridge, leaving Shirakawa to return to watching the sea blankly and absently. Yatsuka announced Iketani, "Captain, this is the Prisoner Transport Commander, First Lieutenant Iketani." Kawano looked over his shoulder, turning away from his lookout to face them. Iketani and Yatsuka paused, halfway through the doorway to the bridge. The door was wide open and outside, along the narrow passageway stumbled a dripping solider, a damp blanket around his shivering shoulders. The soldier stopped before the open door and dropped to his trembling knees. He fell back against the outer wall of the bridge and closed his eyes for a moment,— Yoshio Kashiki was utterly exhausted. He had been pulled back from the army field hospital after being wounded. Not seriously wounded, but he'd also taken ill with recurring malaria which had further weakened and sickened him. The medical officer had then added his name to the transport departing for better facilities at the army hospital on Java. Yoshio raised his shaking hands in front of him and watched his trembling fingers. He pulled the blanket tighter around his wet body and again closed his eyes for a moment. He started as a loud voice asked, "I appreciate what you have been through, but are you injured?" Yoshio opened his eyes and responded quietly, "I-I think I am..." he looked around, but there was no one there. Then he heard the reply to the question that was not for him, from inside the open door. "Yes, thankyou, I mean no, no, I am not injured." Iketani replied, unconsciously looking down at himself. Yoshio realised he was eavesdropping and attempted to stand, but paused on hearing another question. Kawano had ignored Iketani's hesitation. "What's the condition of the Japanese passengers?" Yoshio held his breath a little, cocked his head to one side and listened carefully. On the bridge, Iketani frowned,

"Well, we can't be sure of the figures yet, but I think there are still sixteen missing, but almost everyone has been brought aboard." "I see, and where were the PoWs held on your ship?" Iketani bristled, "They were in the aft holds. It seems more than half went down with the ship. The enemy torpedoes hit the ship to the stern." Kawano rubbed his rounded chin and rocked on his heels. "And what of those PoWs still in the water?" Iketani's brows knitted. Puzzled, he opened his mouth to ask a question, stopping as the realisation dawned that Kawano clearly did not intend to rescue them. Iketani shook his head as Kawano stared unblinking, his beady eyes fixed on Iketani. "And so," he said evenly, "how shall we dispose of them, then?" Iketani's face expressed no surprise, but his mouth opened as he looked out across the sea of debris. Kawano pressed him, leaning his face closer. "Have you any order from higher authorities?" Iketani twitched, his eyes firing. He dropped his voice low. Yoshio, outside the door, had to shuffle nearer to make out the words drifting from the open door. "Well, we have orders instructing us to-" he hesitated, "to, er, to shoot them if the ship were sunk." Kawano's mouth twitched. "I see, and so, what is it you want me to do about it?" he asked leadingly, turning away as if he were not especially interested. Iketani looked to Yatsuka who looked back to Kawano, somewhat alarmed. Iketani braced himself, pushing his shoulders back and lifting his chin. "Captain Kawano," Iketani said formally, "I request that proper disposal of the prisoners be made by your escort ship." Kawano turned, his face expressionless. "Is that so? Then, we shall shoot them!" Yoshio held his hand to his mouth to stifle a gasp of alarm. He backed up along the gantry, almost tripping over his trailing wet blanket. Horrified and afraid, he hurried down the ladder and hid amongst the other soldiers on deck. Kawano turned to Yatsuka as Iketani bowed, mumbling as he backed to the door, "Yes, I will leave it to you captain." Yatsuka waited until Iketani had reversed out of the room, and the door was finally closed before speaking. "Captain, you want me to shoot them? Wouldn't it be easier to just leave them here alone since there are few lifeboats afloat. They'll drown soon enough. We could just leave. Let's start immediately!" Yatsuka felt little compassion for the PoWs, but he couldn't stomach the effort involved in shooting hundreds of them. Not to mention the time it would take to carry out. Kawano rounded on Yatsuka. "It is the express wish of the Imperial Japanese Army!" he shouted. Kawano's face had reddened, spittle formed at his lips which flecked Yatsuka, who blinked. He stepped back as Kawano continued, "... and the enemy submarine is bound to emerge after we leave, and rescue survivors. We must not let the PoWs fall into enemy hands. Shooting them is unavoidable!" Kawano punched a fist into his cupped hand angrily. Yatsuka's face in turn had reddened, in misplaced shame. He bowed deeply, turning quickly and dashing from the bridge. On deck he called for Miyaughi, and ordered him to gather the gun crew. "Take charge of the rifle unit, deploy twelve on each side of the foredeck. We are going to shoot the prisoners." Miyaughi looked alarmed for a moment but saluted and hurried to gather his rifle crew. Yatsuka did not returned his gaze, but turned to face the sea. To watch. By five-fifteen, twenty Japanese rifle crew had lined the foredeck, standing to attention with loaded .99 infantry rifles. Four of the crew had carried two machine guns up to the lower bridge deck and set them ready, pointing toward the sea. Yatsuka nodded as the minesweeper's navy crew took up lookout positions with binoculars, watching the water and the groups of floating PoWs. Miyaughi checked his rifle crew, and reported to Yatsuka that all was ready. Yatsuka re-joined Kawano on the bridge, lifting his binoculars to watch. "Slow to fifty feet. Range on the targets." Kawano ordered.

Some six hours after diving, Captain Hogan gave the order to re-surface the submarine. The *Bonefish* had made steady progress away from the sinking of their target, the *Suez Maru*. Now, a squall gathered pace as she came to the surface in growing dusk. Johnston took to the periscope, reporting, "Escorts smoke *still* visible over the horizon astern, sir." Captain Hogan shook his head, perplexed. "What the *hell* are they *still* doing there?" He paced once up the bridge deck then shook the question from his mind as he re-focussed on the remainder of their second war patrol. "Plot a course. Proceed northward toward Makassar Straits." "Aye, captain," came the reply. The *Bonefish* moved slowly over the horizon, completely unaware of the tragic circumstances of their attack.

Jack had been thrown overboard the *Suez Maru* by the shuddering explosion of her boiler. The blast had ripped apart the engine room gouging a gaping hole in the hull, already split open at the stern from the two torpedo strikes. Jack had cried out involuntarily as he fell, his voice swallowed by the sea as he landed creating a deep splash. He'd surfaced a few moments later, spluttering and gasping for air as he looked about for something to grab onto. The memory of his underwater near-drowning unravelled in the chaos of the sea. The ship had been torpedoed in the early morning light, leaving hundreds of PoW survivors swimming and floating listlessly in the rolling sea for hours. They watched while the escort minesweeper rescued their Japanese captors. Two lifeboats, eventually vacated by the rescued Japanese, were slowly occupied by the weary men. They climbed aboard, pulling their brothers to safety. Much of the larger wreckage from the floating debris field was gathered and used over the course of the long day. The men lashed flotsam together, making loose rafts. They had all gathered together by the time the Japanese had been rescued, amassing in lifeboats, on rafts and as a long line of drifting men, stretching some distance across the waves. The straggling line of driftwood planks, bits of rafts and men bobbed in the heave of the merciless ocean as they took it in turns to lie on planks or a lifeboat to sit out of the water awhile. Their bodies never dried properly, they simply sat burning in the sun. Jack had drifted deliriously for hours after gathering into a group of about fifty but had begun to fade as was pulled from the water by his brothers. He now sat astride the bow of a lifeboat, his thin legs drying of the salt and oil slick that was the sea. One leg dangled lazily as if punting on a carefree summer's day, his foot breaking the surface as the swell dipped down and wet his toes. After the initial hours of chaos, fighting for survival and the loss of men who had barely clung on, the wearied men settled into uneasy, unblinking stretches of silence punctuated by quiet groans. Occasionally a man attempted to swim away. The others would call out, "Where are you going? There's nowhere to go." They would watch as the escapee moved from flotsam to flotsam, coughing and spluttering. Officers would shout for them to come back, but only the circling menace of the escort minesweeper would persuade them to return. There was simply *nothing* to be done, but stay together, and wait. So, in near silence they waited. The only sound was the changing of positions of those on driftwood rafts and the creak of the lifeboats.

The silences droned on for hours. The escort ship sat over them, moving this way and that, collecting their own. At first the PoWs thought they were to be rescued immediately. But those who swam to the ship were pushed away, shoved violently back down the rigging. The PoWs were easily identified, there was no chance the Japanese could mistake their thin bony bodies with hardly a rag covering them, with the fattened guards in their wet but untorn uniforms as they were pulled, arm over arm aboard the safety of the minesweeper.

With each slowly passing hour more men lay out in the sea. After surviving the shock of the exploding, sinking ship, the crashing waves and the terror of thrashing about in the water, many quietly passed away. Their empty stomachs had been distended with gulp upon gulp of wretched seawater they'd swallowed. They had been sick to their stomachs as they coughed and spluttered on. Now they were quiet. When roused to take a place they were rolled over and found to have gone. Their unblinking, drying eyes showed they could not have lasted a moment longer. Under the beating of the sun and its unblinking gaze, some ten more gasped their last. The swell gathered, tipping Jack's lifeboat forward atop a wave. He watched his brothers sadly roll a man into the sea as the lifeboat dipped down again. He licked his dry cracked lips, tasting seawater tinged with oil which sickened him, and he retched futilely. His tongue was swollen and dried with the salt. He felt suffocated by the injustice of it. It was exceptionally cruel that *these* men had survived it all. All the hardship of the camps, the ill treatment, illnesses and starvation, and sinking of their transport ship, only to breathe their last dried-out breaths under the burning sun, drifting listlessly upon the glazed ocean. They were so close to anticipated rescue, and from there they had only to last until landing at Java. Then, who knew what the future might hold thereafter. Perhaps better food and easier work, as he remembered it had been before leaving for Ambon. His thoughts rolled on. Perhaps it would not be long until the end of the war itself. Perhaps it would not be long before he might be returning home. He could not have known that neither he, nor any of his brothers would be returning home. The floating men had watched the Japanese on the deck of the escort ship. They peered over the gunwale, pointing and gesticulating, making decisions and planning the PoWs fate. Japanese survivors were long gone from the sea, yet still the men waited. A nervous discussion broke out amongst those on Jack's lifeboat. "Why are they taking so long?" "They'll have to let us aboard soon. Won't they?" "Unless they are leaving us here." "There's, what, at least two hundred and fifty of us, stretched across a mile of sea. How can they leave us all?" "Perhaps the submarine is still close and they're waiting for it to leave?" "Perhaps it will come for us, perhaps we will be in Allied hands by tea-time." "We can't float here for days on end." "They must hurry, the light is fading." Jack listened to all the voices, but felt too exhausted to respond. Their words drifted around his mind as he wondered, and waited.

Two dozen soldiers on the minesweeper carried long rolled packages along the deck. They dropped the canvas bundles, bending down to unwrap them carefully. Jack saw a few arrive at the rail but couldn't make out what they were doing, they were too far away. He couldn't see clearly, other than shadowy figures moving about. Still, Jack felt uneasy. A soldier on the fore-bridge looked briefly out to sea. He stared at the bobbing floating men, then looked away. He lifted one end of a heavy machine gun from its wrappings, as another soldier took its weight and began fixing it to its mounting. Jack craned his neck, squinting. What was it? He couldn't see what was happening, but knew *something* was in preparation. Around the front bow of the minesweeper, some twenty soldiers jog-marched, rifles at their shoulders. They took up positions all around the gunwale. Jack looked to the other men in alarm, and for confirmation of his nauseous suspicion. He rubbed his eyes as he tried to suppress a rising fear in the pit of his stomach. Jack looked to the men nearest the escort minesweeper, who looked wildly at each other. They began shouting and splashing the water in alarm. Someone shouted, "What the hell are you doing?" Jack stared from his raised position in the prow of the lifeboat. He clambered to his knees, rocking the small boat from side to side as the minesweeper turned and moved towards the men. "Wait..." Jack shouted, his palm in the air. A Japanese soldier looked directly at him. They were some twenty feet away when they lowered their rifles. The magazine roll was loaded onto the machine gun. "*What* are you *doing*?" Someone shouted. Jack watched mutely as if paralysed as they continued to prepare the machine gun.

The minesweeper completed its turn to their nearest end of the line of survivors. Jack and the men as one, gasped. They watched, mouths open in disbelief as the soldiers cocked the machine gun, aiming towards those men at the end of the line. At the same moment the soldiers on deck lowered their rifles. "Wait!" Jack protested, his hands outstretched as the first burst rang out.

Pandemonium ensued. The machine gun moved up and down the first ten to fifteen men, bullets spraying through the air. Each man fell into the sea in fountain of crimson. All down the line every man exploded into action. Jumping into the sea, leaping from lifeboats and rafts, trying wildly to swim away. Jack ducked, leaping to the bottom of the lifeboat, lying flat out in the puddle of dirty seawater accumulated there. Some of those men in his lifeboat had fallen. Some had jumped overboard. Five remained in the boat. They gathered, hiding under a hanging piece of tarpaulin as the rake of machine gun fire moved down their boat. Three more were killed outright. They slumped down beside Jack and lay still, their eyes casting a permanent gaze to the sky. Another man had fallen backwards overboard. Jack was unsure if he'd been hit or had jumped. He had heard the notes of the bullets as they had sounded on water, on the wood of their lifeboat and then on his brothers. He panted, covering his ears with his hands. He lay flat on his stomach in the bottom of the boat as bright red water swashed up and down. It soaked his belly, arms and legs and sloshed in his face. It took him a moment to realise what it was. Jack gagged, and immediately tried to stifle the sound with his hand, filling his mouth with bloody water that was not his own. He felt something touch his leg and jumped in shock. A man had survived in the boat with him but was unconscious. Jack dragged the man alongside his own body and pulled the tarpaulin over them both. The ship sounded further away and Jack chanced a look through a rip in the tarpaulin. The men were now stretched across a wider area. The long struggling line of men had dispersed erratically as the minesweeper had ploughed through the middle of them. The ship now turned and each side of the terrible looming bow, men plunged into the sea. In the chaos it was impossible to know who had been hit and who had leapt into the sea. Everywhere were floating men. Some moved weakly, most were silent and vacant eyed.

A man treading water and holding onto a ragged rope hanging over the lifeboat tried to move away and was quickly caught by close gunfire. His arms reached up then fell as he splayed out prone in the water, a tide of red washing from him. Men on the rafts raised their arms in protest. Shouting 'stop' as the guns turned to them and the sea boiled with their screams and their blood. A Japanese voice from the minesweeper screamed. "Don't leave anyone alive!" Another shouted, "Shoot every PoW in sight!" The men in the water could not understand the language, but heard the clear hatred and the venom. The line had dispersed into chaos, but Jack and the unconscious man lay still in the boat, Jack breathing heavily and listening intently. The men who had jumped into the sea, now tried to hide amongst flotsam and under debris. Two or three men tried to swim for it, but there was nowhere to swim for, and nowhere to hide. There was only frothing rolling sea, and nothing but horizon in every direction. As each man was spotted the sea erupted into spray around them from a hail of bullets. As the shots and engine noise receded again, Jack reached up and looked out. He could not believe his eyes. The enemy soldiers had made their way back down the line and began turning, to circle back for another run. The line was now a sea of groaning, twitching pained men and still lifeless forms. Jack sank back down into the lifeboat, his mind racing with impossible ideas of escape as he looked again through the tiny gap in the tarpaulin. Slowly the Japanese approached the lifeboat nearest to his. It still seemed to overflow with men trying to escape, slipping off the sides into the water. The minesweeper slowed as the soldiers lifted their rifles and took aim. Three PoWs at the front sat up in the boat. They shouted to the Japanese, challenging them. Their voices angry and defiant. One man climbed to his feet, bracing himself as he wobbled in the lurching boat. He threw his hands in the air and shouted out, "C'mon then you bastards. You cowards! You Japs, *this* is England, Come on!" he slapped at his chest with his palms, his eyes flashing like fire, his teeth bared. The soldiers paused, looking to each other for a split second. Then they shot him. The force knocked him sideways off his boat and he splashed headlong and lifeless into the sea. Jack and the other men roared with anger. Those nearby on rafts tried to stand, shouting out. "Cowards! Bastards!" Jack looked away to the far end of the line. He could hear singing, defiant and angry, "*Rule Britannia...*" Jack looked to the other man in his lifeboat and saw that he had gone, his unblinking eyes stared directly at him, and Jack felt a surge of fury. "Damn the Japs, damn them all," he muttered as he gathered himself unsteadily to his feet. There was no point asking anything of a cowardly enemy who valued the lives of courageous men so little. These maggots had punished each man in the blink of an eye, and thought nothing now of ending hundreds of brave lives. Even then, Jack looked around at the sea for a last chance, but there was simply no escape, and nowhere to fly to. He could not hold his breath, nor cover himself. In that split second he was resigned. As he stood up, he felt as though he stood alone. A solitary one-man island. A thin, burnt and bruised, worn out young body, standing alone on a bright white lifeboat, perched upon a never-ending sea of blue and red stretching into infinity in every direction.

As the Japanese minesweeper neared his floating island he felt angry resentment rising in him. He could not speak. Instead he raised his fist. They stared expressionlessly. He tugged at his ragged shirt, pulling off the final remaining button. He considered it curious what his mind chose to observe, as time slowed. He watched as the last button freed itself from his shirt. The tiny thread hung loose as the button gently, slowly spun through the air. He looked at his bony chest, his bashed, sunburned ribs, his reddened skin and bruised side where he'd fallen against the gunwale as the first torpedo had hit. He braced each foot against the sides of the lifeboat prow and shouted out in rage as he gripped his flapping shirt. He yanked it wide open as they approached. "Come on then, cowards! Take what is not yours! Damn you all to hell!" Jack closed his eyes and muttered a few soft words intended to somehow spirit themselves to his family, as he spun from his left side, falling backwards into the sea.

The minesweeper receded into the distance leaving a frothing wake. The throb of its engine faded to a hum then a quiet buzz, like an irritant fly circling before it disappeared. The hum mingled with the quiet groans of the last men of the *Suez Maru*, as they too ceased to speak. They floated in the gentle breeze in near silence, punctuated only by the rhythmic slosh of waves on the hull of the damaged, half-sunk lifeboat as it pitched, and the stretched creak of a rope hanging from its bow as it dipped into the sea, dripping water onto Jack's face. He pinched his eyes shut then blinked, as his head bumped the lifeboat dully. The drone of an airplane drifted out of his hearing, merging with the swash of waves against the boat. He let go of the rope and drifted out, starfish shaped on the sea, listening to the swish of water. He heard then only the soft muted crack of air bubbles in his submerged ears. With eyes closed he could for a fraction of a moment, imagine he was on the sea as a child. Dipped in the pale blue and laughing as the sun baked his pale skin and the quiet sway of the sea massaged his young bones. He saw the sky now, azure blue above him and felt no pain. Light receded from his vision. The men and bobbing lifeboats appeared distant and silent, as the departing ship slid over the horizon. He blinked once again against the brightness of the setting sun. He thought he saw a bird from nowhere, beautifully silhouetted against the shimmering sun. She flapped twice, silently and effortlessly, then once more as she drifted higher, disappearing into the haze of sky and burning sun. He thought he heard English birds singing, but couldn't now tell if he was dreaming.

Captain Kawano sniffed the air defiantly, then ordered a telegraph be sent to the commanders at 21 Base Force and 24 Base Force, dictating the message. "Ah, confirmed, at ah, 1900 hours on the 29th, we left the scene of the disaster after rescuing the survivors of the *Suez Maru*. We expect to reach Batavia at 1700 hours on the 30th." Petty Officer Yoshino half listened to Kawano's message as he copied notes from his ledger into the ships log.

```
1700 hours: Rescue of Japanese military and
  transport personnel completed.
1715 hours: Shooting of PoWs in the sea began
  after consulting transport commander.
1730 hours: A member of the transport crew
  is rescued.
1900 hours: Shooting of PoWs completed.
  Left scene disaster. Headed for Batavia.
  - ends -
```

- 1 December 1943, Batavia -

It was late in the day as a telephone rang out in the quiet office where Hiroshi Suzuki sat dozing, his crossed feet up on his desk. The voice on the other end sounded urgent, requesting immediate reception and accommodation for prisoners of war just arriving at the dock from Ambon. Suzuki nodded, repeating, "*Hai, hai, hai.*" He pressed a forefinger to the cradle to end the call, lifting it quickly to make a telephone call to Lieutenant Colonel Matsunaga. Suzuki requested an immediate motor transport unit of ten or more trucks to be despatched to the dock. He then grabbed his uniform jacket and rushed to the harbour in his chauffeured car. At the dock wounded Japanese were already being escorted off the navy minesweeper, some were being carried on stretchers. Suzuki walked along the quay looking for the prisoners and met First Lieutenant Iketani. Suzuki held out his palms, puzzled. "What's happened to the prisoners? I've arranged vehicles to come for them." Iketani twitched. "Ahh, the ship was attacked by torpedo. Ahh, all the prisoners of war perished. Three guards died too, and a few were seriously injured, they're going into that ambulance over there." He pointed with grubby finger and shrugged. Suzuki blinked, his mouth open. With effort he rearranged himself, "Well, if that's so, I'll telephone and cancel the motor transport dispatch. Please wait for a moment and I'll take you to the camp in my car." In darkening dusklight Suzuki walked back to Iketani who stared blankly at the minesweeper as he smoked a cigarette. He flicked it to the ground and pressed it with his boot as Suzuki approached. "This way, my car is over here," Suzuki gesticulated for Iketani to follow. Iketani did not speak as he walked slowly behind. He climbed awkwardly into the back of the car while Suzuki held the door open. It was cooler inside. The soft creak of the leather seat as Iketani slid across it made him think of the luxury of simply riding comfortably in a car, as flashes of the exploding ship and plunging seawater rose in his ears, amid screams of men in a swirling sea of red. He coughed politely as Suzuki joined him on the back seat and tapped the drivers shoulder to proceed. He turned to Iketani, "It must have been *terrible* for you. Oh, did you lose your glasses?" Iketani reflexively touched his temple where his glasses were not, but did not speak. Suzuki pressed, "What happened to you?" Iketani looked out of the window, staring at the small image of the receding minesweeper in the car wing-mirror. The bow stood tall against the dockside, where orderlies took the last of the soldiers onto trucks. The same tall bow flashed in Iketani's mind as it pushed through a thick carpet of innocent lifeless men in life preservers, lying out on rafts and huddled in lifeboats. "Yes, it was *awful*. The troops lost *all* their equipment and everything else. And *I* was thrown overboard and was in the sea for *seven* hours." Suzuki gasped, Iketani gazed across at him fleetingly but did not respond. His eyes were glazed as he continued, turning his head back to the window. "We were first hit at dawn, the stern collapsed and the whole ship shook. A second hit and the ship exploded and I jumped overboard. I think most prisoners died in the aft hold where the torpedo hit. It sank in no time, stern first. Almost all of them went down with the ship. A few prisoners who came to the surface later were, of course, shot by the navy." Iketani was matter of fact. Suzuki had listened open mouthed as Iketani's monotone voice had repeated his version of the sinking. All the while he looked fixedly out of the window. As he finished, he turned to Suzuki and grinned. "I need to be taken to Major General Saito. I will have to make a report." Suzuki shook himself from the shock. "Yes, of course," Suzuki prodded the shoulder of the driver again, giving new directions. "I will leave you at the camp. Take the car, I'll make arrangements for quarters for you." Iketani's face twitched. "Yes, ahh thank you. It shouldn't take long." They drove in silence until Suzuki got out at the camp and his car continued on, taking Iketani to Saito. Suzuki watched his car disappear as he stood in the road. The small expressionless face of Iketani stared from the rear window. Suzuki shook his head and walked slowly into the camp.

- FEBRUARY 1944 -

- 13 SPRING STREET -

It was cold that early February morning in Manchester and a light frost had made the cobbled street sparkle like Christmas morning. Children screamed as they slid along white patches of ice, rendering the veneer so frighteningly slippery, but such good fun. Their mothers called from half open doorways to get to school. The children, deliberately oblivious, continued their game. George Frith was up early, having become used to getting up with the sun. He'd arrived at his parents late the previous evening, the first day of a week's leave after completing four months technical training at RAF Blackpool, learning to fit airframes. Leading Aircraftman George Frith would soon take up his next posting, with RAF 16th Squadron in West Lancashire to ready *Spitfires* in preparation for Operation Overlord, D-Day. He was grateful for a brief break with his family and to be back with his wife Elizabeth and their two children. They had stayed on at Spring Street whilst George re-trained. His breath billowed in the frosty morning air as he walked back from the shop with an extra paper tucked under one arm. The little family counted themselves fortunate to be together. To have learned Jack was no longer 'missing in action' but had been taken 'prisoner of war,' was horribly worrying but infinitely better than their previous fears.

George stamped his feet, hanging his heavy RAF coat on the hook in the hall as his heart warmed to the sound of familiar voices throughout the house. The children were laughing with their mother upstairs, as she dressed them warmly for school. George heard his own mother, Florrie in the back room. He stopped at the door, to listen. The topic, as so often was of Jack. "I wonder how he is doing now?" murmured his father, John. He nudged the catching coals with the poker from his armchair nestled by the fire. "Well, it was good to get his letter. Jack said he is well. So we must only think of what we know, and *not* what we don't" said George coming into the room. Florrie could hardly say a word, she found it impossible to speak about Jack without sobbing. She embraced George briefly, pecking his still freezing cheek before bustling away to fill the teapot and fetch his breakfast. George turned to his father, trying to reassure him, at least, "It is good news that he's only been a held only a few months isn't it? When did they say it was?" George crossed the room to the fireplace, lifting the creased war office letter from the mantle and searching its contents for a date. "Well, they didn't say when he was taken captive, but it confirms he's *now* a prisoner of war. The letter is, May '43, so that's only..." George began counting the months on his fingers as John looked up at his eldest son and smiled. He didn't really want to know. "Where was he all the year before, though? What was he doing in '42?" George continued, frowning. He paused on hearing a stifled cough from his father. "He'll give them hell, won't he?" John said, his face folding into a pained grimace, "My god, I hope he's all right," he crumpled as George placed a hand on his shoulder. "He *will* dad. Jack will give them *hell.*" George was about to say something more but there was a knock at the door. He turned to answer it as his mother darted past. "Postman," she offered in haste. George and his father resumed their conversation and hardly noticed Florrie return quietly to the room. She walked slowly, turning a small brown envelope over and over in her hands. They stopped talking and stared as she dropped into a chair at the table and placed the buff-coloured rectangle in front of her. She stared hard at it, taking in the dark typed letters, and the significance of within. She did not want to read it. She closed her eyes and wished it would disappear. She opened her eyes and looked, it was addressed to her husband.

```
Mr. J.R. Frith,
13 Spring St,
Hyde,Manchester.
```

George moved to the table, the blood draining from his face. His father pulled at George's sleeve, moving him from his path and stood trembling next to his wife. John couldn't see well enough to read the letter, but still reached for the envelope as Florrie shook her head. She lifted it and gently turned it over. She slid a forefinger under the gummed flap and removed a folded, almost greaseproof-paper thin letter. With shaking hands she uncreased the page, glanced once at it and scrunched it into her palm, her mouth opening in anguish. Florrie grasped at the tablecloth pulling it towards her toppling the sugar bowl, teapot and milk that stood there. John reached for the upturned cups, turning to look to his wife. He heard a sound escape her lips as he reached for her instead, finding her slim wrist. He pulled her up toward him, crumpling the letter between them, crushed in their sobbing embrace. George gathered round his parents, wrapping his arms around them both. He removed the letter from his mother's hand and laid it on the table. Smoothing its creases he read seventy-six unbelievable words. It would be all they ever knew, all they would ever be told, of what had happened to their youngest son, their precious child.

```
Tel.RUGBY. 3354.        Reference CAS/P
                        R.A. (HAA) Records
                        St.Marie's Hall,
31. Jan. '44            Dunchurch Rd, Rugby.


            1794521 Gunner FRITH.J.

Dear Sir,

   I deeply regret to inform you that a report
has been received from the Japanese Government
that your Son has died as a result of the
sinking of a Japanese transport vessel on which
he, together with others was being transferred
from Java to another Prisoner of War camp,
location not stated, on the 29. November. 43.

   The official notification of death
is enclosed herewith.

   Please accept my deepest sympathy
for you in your sad loss.

                Yours faithfully,
                w O'Grady
                (W.D.O'Grady) Major,
                For Col i/c R.A.(HAA) records.
```

CHAPTER SIX

Before Yet After

- OCTOBER 2010 -

The sweating heat of Kanchanaburi was relieved slightly by the fast moving breeze as we motored down the swollen River Khwae Yai in a boat only just big enough for the three of us perched in it. The outboard hummed and the surfaced rippled in our wake as we approached an arched bridge spanning the river at Tha Makham. "I think this is that famous bridge from that film," I said. "That war film, *The Bridge on the River Kwai*." I must have been the only person not to have watched it, that staple of holiday television schedules. "Had the British fought here during the war? Had we held it against all odds? Was it like *Bridge at Remagen*? I couldn't recall." It seems unimaginable that I did not know. How could I not know, anything? We climbed gratefully out of the boat and visited the bridge. Walking along the track we followed the railway lines to their vanishing point, but still I didn't understand. I later discovered the depiction of PoWs in the film *The Bridge on the River Kwai* was nothing like the truth, but standing on the bridge that day I saw nothing to explain. Glancing around everyone else seemed to know. They were quiet and reflective as they stepped lightly along the tracks. Later that day the museum at Kanchanaburi explained. Walking shell-shocked through rooms of glass cabinets filled with decaying exhibits made by prisoners of the Japanese, I stared in disbelief. My eyes filled with tears. A battered spoon made from scrap metal, a rough bowl of scrap wood, a single lonely sole carved from scrap bark, sorrowful all of them. Unable to continue the museum visit, we moved outside and walked the neat rows of white teeth aligned like dominos in the clipped verdant grass of Kanchanaburi Commonwealth War Cemetery. Overwhelmingly, each named a life lost. My heart ached, and I knew then that I owed a debt to these men and deep down to one in particular. This was the last day before I knew. But was already so long after.

My paternal grandfather, George, had passed away in February 1982 a month after I turned ten years old. He had a brother I'd never met whose name I shared, Jack Frith. A name so familiar, but Jack Frith and Jacq Frith never met yet I vaguely remembered hearing stories of him. I'd recalled he had been a prisoner of war, but where? I thought he'd been a prisoner of the Japanese and was on some ship during the war. I searched my memory and definitely recalled something about a ship, but couldn't pull the thought into focus. Perhaps he'd been here on the Thai-Burma railway at some point? I'd looked at the cabinet displays and read the neat typed information, eyes pouring with sadness. Overwhelmed and feeling foolish for being overwhelmed we later walked the length of the Konyu Cutting at Hellfire Pass, unanswered questions weighing heavily in the sticky heat. I stood near the tree by the tracks and sobbed. I felt aware of an unseen someone standing alongside me. Almost as if someone I did not know who equally felt warmly familiar, was with me. It was not unnerving but I felt a strong pull to discover more about my older namesake. A few days later as I stared at the crashing waves of the Indian Ocean, I found him. With only a name, a service number and a date, there he was. Great uncle Jack became Gunner Jack Frith, Royal Artillery 77th H.A.A. Regiment, 239 Battery. The date of his passing confirmed in a short paragraph that he had been killed aboard the *Suez Maru*. I read the précis of the events of 29 November 1943, in disbelief and with much sadness. I then discovered Gunner Frith had been commemorated for his sacrifice at Kranji Memorial, Commonwealth War Grave Cemetery, Singapore.

The heat was marginally milder in Singapore. The rows and rows of those 'Known Only Unto God' stretched across the crisp neat lawns of the Kranji Memorial. Cicadas clicked in the humidity and the grass was wet from ticking sprinklers watering the thick foliage. The memorial roof soared above like a giant bird wing. Moving up the steps, the supporting columns under the vast wing were covered with inscriptions, and each inscription was a name. Running a hand along the white limestone, it had appeared smooth from a distance but felt rough under the palm. The close-fitting joints of each slab, incised with so many names, of men who could not be found, lost at sea or simply lost. Among the thousands of neat lines, each remembering a life, in the middle of column eighteen, was my name. His name. It read J FRITH. Six neatly carved letters to remember and describe twenty-three years of life, loves, hopes, imagination and energy. His determination, his talents, his ambitions and dreams for the future. Just six tiny letters were almost all that remained of a man who had suffered his last two years with grit and a steely bloody mindedness to survive. Until at last that was impossible. The six letters were *almost* all that remained, but not quite.

I walked past dewy, scented English grass along the crunchy gravel and stopped. I stepped onto a dark limestone pavement, on which sat a dark grey limestone cube, made from 414 dark grey limestone cobbles. As it began to rain, the drops splattered the stones and turned the cobblestones jet black. It's not well known but inside this huge limestone cube rests a small glass jar. In it is coral-white sand, four or five sun-dried cloves still clinging to their branch, and one green leaf, now dried and brittle. Collected from the island of Ambon, they represent the places Jack had been captive. The sand I collected from the beach where they washed, that ran alongside the airstrip Jack and the Liang men were forced to build. The cloves I picked up on the route the Liang marchers took in April 1943. And the leaf came from a tree on the site of Liang camp, onto which I'd tied a poppy, brought from England. The jar sits within the only memorial to the British men of the *Suez Maru* in the world. Built at the National Memorial Arboretum, Staffordshire, it was dedicated by the families of those lost, on the seventy-year anniversary of the sinking and subsequent unpunished war crime. We stood together under a break in the clouds on 29 November 2013, and I prepared myself to make the short dedication speech I'd written. Initially, I was unable to utter a single word. The weight what had been sacrificed by those we remembered descended upon me. It was as if Jack and all the lost men of the *Suez Maru* gathered round us, forming a second circle of translucent attendees around the circle of gathered families. That day each name was read aloud by their relatives to remember each man. The last post was played, the flag lowered and tears were shed as dozens of poppy crosses and wreaths were laid in remembrance. *Lest We Forget.*

It had been a long journey from the River Kwai to the National Memorial Arboretum by way of Java and the island of Ambon. The outline of this book was first written looking out over the Indian Ocean when I'd stayed in a wooden house with a tropical garden, during the trip to Kanchanaburi. I scribbled rapidly flowing thoughts and half-imagined Jack in his uniform standing amongst the wet palm fronds and flowering hibiscus. I've heard from people that knew him and of him, that Jack and I share more similarities than simply a name. It would appear we have the same belligerent attitude to principles. We're unafraid to demand wrongs are righted and determined to see things through to the end. I know I have a strong voice of my own, but it is my keenest hope that it might be *his* voice that is heard most clearly within this story.

Why do we become conspicuously aware of our own mortality as we age? Why do we feel the need to discover more about those who made us, those who came before? Those fading faces, sending their genes down through the generations, adding something of themselves to our character. Simple bare codes with no sense of the person, memories and thoughts long gone. The tiny strands do not carry human emotion yet it's these invisible threads weaving back through time that connect us. They gift more of ourselves than a bend of the nose or an instinctive talent to play piano. When I was young the adults in my family seemed old. I suspect most children feel that, however as I grew up many of mine were. I knew four grandparents, two great-grandparents and a good number of great aunts and uncles. Such was my upbringing that I had great respect for them, my elders. I loved them, and loved their stories.

My great grandmother Florence, born in 1894, and I made afternoon teas together and she would tell me of her travels to Oberammergau and Switzerland. My maternal grandfather Harry would tell stories of fighting with 'Monty' in North Africa, storming the beaches at Salerno and surrounding Monte Cassino, whilst leaving out the frightening details. My paternal, Scottish grandma Elizabeth made big cut-and-come-again cakes and I'd sit by the fire while she plaited my hair. Her skipping West Scots accent now only half-remembered. Her husband, my paternal grandfather was born in 1916 to working-class parents in Manchester. He grew up, surprisingly not as grandad, but George. Younger brother to Gladys and elder brother to Jack. It's often difficult for the newest generation to think of older relatives as once young. Staring hard at wartime photographs of him now I can hardly see my grandad, I see a young man I hadn't known. In contrast to grandad Harry, grandad George never mentioned his war to me. I know now that it was too painful. I remember he was quietly reserved, slim and gently spoken with kind eyes. He seemed to consider his words carefully and was thoughtful in his speaking. When I knew him, he sat in a straight-backed wooden chair with a small tray balanced on its curved arms. On which he carved and painted small wooden animals. I wish very much I'd known him better, but I was only just ten years old. Such regret grips the throat, I wish very much that I could sit with him, talk to him and to listen to his stories and ask him questions. I find that thirty-eight years later I have many questions.

Sometimes you remember something from childhood, just a wisp of a smell. A thought caught like an aroma on the breeze. The scent catches in your nose and you squint. You urge your mind to clear the cloudy scene, but you can't quite catch the memory itself. I searched my mind to find more moments we'd spent together, my grandad George and I. So many I remembered easily and vividly. Making swans with sunflower seeds at Easter-time. Setting the table for lunch in their back room, laying out jams and spoons and mismatched plates and cakes. But, it's the scent of cut grass that takes me to a precious moment held in the depths of my mind. There, I lay on their lawn in the last embers of summer. Cheeks in my palms I peered closely at a ring of toadstools, as he sat beside me on the warm grass. He told me how he'd carefully mown around them and that you had to be careful to not damage toadstools. I can hear myself asking why, and he'd said the faeries who lived underneath, needed them and they kept them dry. He'd asked me where they would live if he mowed them over? He had smiled and I must have tucked away in my mind the scent of cut grass. Sweet and fresh while the warm sun blinked sun-beamed halos in the dark shadows around us, as motes danced in the air. Years later, his words blurred with half-remembered magical stories of the *Cottingley Faeries* and I couldn't separate them. Now that I am grown and he has sadly gone, I almost believe they still live there, at the bottom of his garden in the fading light. And in the dusk and low lying mist they come out and dance around the rings of tall red and white toadstools.

- Japanese War Crimes -

In October 1971, Hirohito arrived in Britain for a three-day state visit. He was met with near silent crowds. Those lining the route simply watched the carriage carry the Queen and Hirohito to Buckingham Palace. At that evening's state banquet the Queen said, "We cannot pretend that the past did not exist, we cannot pretend that the relations between our two peoples have always been peaceful and friendly. However, it is precisely this experience which should make us all the more determined never to let it happen again." Hirohito made no reference to the past and offered no condolences in his reply. He remarked only upon the "joint efforts ... for the preservation of tranquillity in the world and the promotion of the welfare of mankind." Letters were published in newspapers at the time, written by far east veterans and former far east prisoners of war, with *clear* memories of their Japanese treatment. A former Far East prisoner of war placed a wreath at the Cenotaph in Whitehall inscribed 'with vivid memories of the treachery and inhumanity of the Japanese.' Lord Louis Mountbatten did not attend the state banquet at Buckingham Palace.

In London in May 1998, former Far East prisoners of war lined the Mall awaiting the procession of Akihito on his first state visit, having succeeded on Hirohito's death ten years previously. As the royal carriage, also carrying the Queen, came down the Mall, in a gesture of contempt veterans turned their backs and whistled the wartime anthem 'Colonel Bogey'. Later, outside Westminster Abbey, Akihito laid a wreath at the Tomb of the Unknown Soldier, whilst five hundred protesters repeated the gesture, turning their backs and humming 'Colonel Bogey' again. Addressing a state banquet at Buckingham Palace, attended by the Queen, Duke of Edinburgh, Queen Mother and eleven other senior royals, Akihito spoke of his 'sorrow and pain' over the 'suffering inflicted by his country during the war,' but did *not* apologise for the treatment of prisoners of war. He said vaguely that he could 'never forget' the 'many kinds' of suffering experienced by 'so many'. This referred to and included Japanese experiences during the war. Veterans at the time said Akihito had not gone far enough and demanded a 'real, meaningful apology.' The Glasgow newspaper *The Herald* published a story on the visit and the demonstrations of former prisoners of war. "Their gait may have been unsteady, but their memories were strong. Mostly, those memories consist of torture, humiliation, and starvation. They recall being forced to stand in the sun for days for refusing to bow to their captors. They remember their comrades shot for attempting to escape while they were made to dig and fill in the graves. They recall that their own lives were ruined because they were taken prisoner by the Japanese. They came back broken and many have not recovered. Yesterday, as the Queen and Akihito rode down the Mall in the Irish State coach with all the pomp and ceremony that surrounds a State visit. There was no forgiveness in the hearts of those who survived the Japanese torture camps. Nor was their any hint of apology from them for being disrespectful to the Queen by insulting her guest. They burned the Japanese flag, thrust red gloves into the air, symbolising the 'bloody hand of the Japanese' and turned their backs on Akihito and the Queen, as the coach escorted by the Household Cavalry, made its way down the Mall. Some PoWs gave a version of the Churchillian two-fingered salute. Many more booed as the procession of eight carriages passed them by. If there were cheers, they were drowned out by the catcalls."

A summary of Japanese 'apologies' since the end of the second world war incorporates statements spanning nearly seventy-five years. These statements generally adhere to a 1995 government agreed wording, sidestepping and misdirecting the key issue. Various statements given by the Japanese government regarding their war-time actions since 1945 have used the term 'remorse' although some neighbouring Asian counties were eventually offered 'apologies'. Japan did not single out their barbaric treatment of prisoners of war for their 'regret' until the 1990s. This single reference to prisoners of war, (probably only referring to the handful of American PoW's present at that speech) however, was a long way from a formal apology. Their statements serve as contradictions of intent and sincerity.

In terms of Allied responsibility for untried and unpunished war crimes, it should be recognised that Lord Louis Mountbatten, Commander-in-Chief, Far East Land Forces and Supreme Allied Commander South East Asia (FARELF) recommended on the *Suez Maru* that, "The case should be allowed to go to trial, and that the trial take place in Tokyo." Undoubtedly, the work of the Australian Captain, Jack Sylvester in investigating the case of the *Suez Maru* requires recognition. Captain Sylvester's investigation, unflinching interrogations and attention to detail are clearly visible in the methodical reports he compiled and questionings he carried out. It is a source of much frustration that his full report was not received by Labour's Secretary of State for War, Emanuel Shinwell when he was consulted. Surely the resulting decision must have been to proceed to trial. Shinwell must not be ignored as one of many erroneous links in a chain that included only the précis being sent, despite his not being in full possession of the lengthy detail of the case he *was* afforded the main facts of the murders and subsequent cover up,— he chose to ignore them. The facts he was presented with alone *should* have warranted further investigation on his part. At the very least Shinwell should have asked a single question to allay his concerns over the length of time since the crimes were committed— a major stumbling block and one of his reasons for denying justice to be served. Shinwell's part in not bringing those responsible to justice was a deliberate and poor decision, based upon his fear of criticism which ultimately determined that the *Suez Maru* atrocity not only went unpunished, but was then *concealed* from those who most surely should have been made aware — the families of those lost. Shinwell's response in questioning "whether or not there should be *any* further trials in view of the recommendation by the Far Eastern Commission and the fact that we are bound to put some term to trials of this kind," lacks a shred of empathy or understanding of what was at stake. His concerns centred on his fear of personal and political criticism. In his *own* words he worried that, "Either way, as I see it, we must be prepared to face criticism. If we started a new trial now, we would be open to attack for waiting more than four years after the end of the war to deal with a crime committed six years ago, and in the contrary event, the relatives of the murdered prisoners of war might well cause questions to be asked if they heard that those responsible would never be brought to justice." This last statement resonates profoundly— *that the relatives of the murdered prisoners of war might well cause questions to be asked if they heard that those responsible would never be brought to justice.* Shinwell's self-serving decision and deliberate blunder was that he not only *knew* that these British servicemen had been murdered, he also recognised the potential outrage by families of those killed and *their* criticism, but then *chose* to ignore the truth for fear of facing criticism himself, from political peers. As Labour's Secretary of State for War (October 1947-February 1950), it *was* in his power to authorise the request to proceed the trials of *confessed* war criminals, who were already named, or in custody. Whether he ignored the advice of Lord Mountbatten or not he *knew* it was right to proceed but he chose to guard himself from criticism instead. It is little wonder that Lord Mountbatten described Shinwell as 'the lowest form of Labour life'.

While his decision was yet unmade, Shinwell had suggested "If we decide to proceed...the best course of action would be to bring the trial *only* the three main instigators of the crime, Lieutenants Kawano and Iketani and Ensign Yatsuka, although there are *prima facie* grounds for proceeding against a number of subordinate officers and men, not so far identified." It is quite incredible that those responsible were not some unknowns. They were *named* suspects, *known* to the British government. The case had been investigated in detail and two were in custody, although Iketani had temporarily been released. Shinwell's passing the criticism buck was evidenced in his words, "I do not know why the case has taken so long to bring forward, but I understand that the investigation has been done by the Australians and that *our* people in the Far East are not responsible for the delay." Amongst the near constant stream of telegrams between London and Tokyo regarding war crime investigations, it seems negligent that his single question was not raised. Why was this case so late in coming forward? The simple response would have explained, 'because it is only three months since Yoshio Kashiki brought the atrocity to the attention of Allied authorities'. Shinwell presumably assumed the Australians had simply taken their time to investigate this case. He could equally have asked for more detail than given in the précis, if he felt there was insufficient information. Captain Sylvester's painstaking work and his full detailed report would surely convinced *all* but the most sceptical of self serving politicians to proceed.

It is poignant that despite the passing of nearly seventy-seven years since this war crime was committed, the families of the *Suez Maru* men lost *do* cause questions to be asked, as it *is* now known that those responsible were *never* brought to justice. It is little consolation that Jack's family, his parents, and his brother and sister especially, were spared the knowledge of the awful truth of 29 November 1943. The lack of explanation, save the initial letter caused decades of sadness amongst members of his family. The families of the *Suez Maru* men did not know a war crime had been committed, or that it had been throughly investigated. They did not know that prosecution of those responsible had teetered on a knife edge. The families were, moreover, completely unaware of the circumstances of their loved ones passing. Some may have even voted for the very political party which then ignored their moral duty to bring those suspects to justice. They also ignored their moral duty to offer the truth to those whom were most affected by it— not politicians fearing criticism, but the mothers and fathers who lost sons, siblings who lost brothers, wives who lost husbands, children who lost fathers. It is these acts of negligence for which they *should* have faced criticism. Since discovering the truth, rather than the *Suez Maru* case being forgotten, the families of those lost have grown in both number and determination to see justice done. We, as a group fund-raised and built a permanent memorial to the men of the *Suez Maru*. The *Suez Maru Memorial* of 414 cobblestones was designed by Jack Frith's nephew, Alastair R Frith, to represent each life lost and each family's remembrance. The memorial now sits in the centre a *Hellship Memorial Garden* which later grew around it.

In turning to remembrance that we consider the thousand men of Liang. The Thousand Liang Marchers who arrived on Ambon in late April 1943. Of their number only three hundred and ninety-seven survived. This represents a sixty percent mortality rate, about the highest discovered at Japanese Far East prisoner of war camps. By far the largest proportion of the thousand men who perished were the three hundred and forty-eight lost in the *Suez Maru* Atrocity. However, many Liang Marchers died on other Japanese hellships. Sixty-two were lost aboard the *Maros Maru*, one of the Liang men died alongside fourteen hundred other PoW's, and more than four thousand *Romushas* on the *Junyo Maru*. Two Liang marchers died on the *Kaishun Maru*, two on the *Tencho Maru*, six more on the *Taiwan Maru*, one on the *Sugi Maru*, and four men died on the *Kenzen Maru*. Many were never to leave Ambon. One hundred and forty-nine died at Liang and were buried at Boot Hill. A further two died at Ambon Town. These men stayed on the island and now rest at Ambon Commonwealth War Grave Cemetery. A few of the thousand died elsewhere, ten at Muna, seven more were lost in the sea near Muna. Two died at Wei Jami, one near Soerabaya and six more after returning to Java. *All* perished pointlessly and needlessly.

Of the fifty-thousand British military personnel taken captive by the Japanese almost a quarter died or were killed in captivity. Survivors and their families have spent years campaigning, on behalf of the twelve and a half thousand who died and those who barely survived, for an apology from the Japanese. The author also calls for a full meaningful apology from the Japanese emperor and Japanese prime minister. In addition, recognition is sought from the British government that the decision not to bring those responsible for the *Suez Maru* massacre to justice was not only cowardly but entirely immoral. For which a full apology is due— to the families of those men so utterly failed by their own government, when they had already given so much. This decision caused, and continues to cause, deep anguish for the families of those murdered men, which persists through the generations today. We remember that the crime was carried out and then concealed first, by the perpetrators of the cowardly act then, by the British Labour government of the time. Apologies cannot repair and time cannot unwind the past, but recognition of errors made and apologies for them would go some way to healing the ever-spreading wound of this war crime and its concealment. Families with first-hand memories of those lost aboard the Suez Maru on 29 November 1943 are dwindling. Only in August 2019, the last family to personally know Jack Frith, Carole Brough, his niece, sadly passed away. And yet, the determination of each affected generation grows stronger. It is now time the Japanese and British governments addressed this long overlooked war crime.

It is outrageous to consider the truth, that Osamu Kawano, Masaji Iketani, Daiso Yatsuka and his gun crew, Seiichi Saito, as an accessory after the fact and others, lived out their lives completely unpunished, as if innocent. It is significant that some of those responsible had previously been convicted of war crimes, such as Sanso Anami who had been tried, convicted as a war criminal and hung in 1946. Between them, Anami and Saito, commanders of the Moluccan and Java POW camps respectively, in overall charge of these concentration camps, committed their own Far-East holocaust against these forgotten and abandoned men. Yet, the Commander of all Java PoW camps went untried. Even now, perpetrators present at Nazi concentration camps are rightly sought, and where found complicit are tried and sentenced, despite advancing years. And even now, Japanese perpetrators may yet survive. It is possible that somewhere in Japan, perhaps siting idly, and elderly on their porches, waking with yawns and shuffling to morning ablutions, enjoying the comfort of visiting children and grandchildren, are some of those responsible. They have paid *no* price for their crimes. Surely it is a gross miscarriage of justice, an insult to those murdered by the Japanese, and painful for their families that there were *no* war crime hunters tracking down *Japanese* war criminals. It is never too late to seek justice by prosecution and apologies from states and governments. It is a national injustice that suspected war criminals in the Pacific theatre were not, and are not, pursued as *Nazi* war criminals are hunted. This grave injustice stems from a deeper miscarriage of justice in my opinion, that the Far East War Crime Trials were given an arbitrary 'end date'. This politically motivated and short-sighted decision was, and is, the very *opposite* of justice served.

To conclude, one of the restricted documents in the war crime file for the *Suez Maru* case, dated 19 August 1949 and addressed to HQ,

War Crimes Section in Singapore, states that the principal figure in the case, Osamu Kawano, was under arrest in Sugamo prison but that other arrests had not yet been made, pending further instructions and that, 'those suspects remained at large'. It is a more than regrettable fact that this is *still* the case nearly seventy-seven years later. Those responsible remained at large for the rest of their natural lives. However unlikely, some may yet survive in a country whose population is oft lauded for the gift of longevity. In 2018, a 96 year old suspected Nazi war criminal was arrested in the unending search for war criminals responsible for the European, Nazi Holocaust. Those who perished needless and desperate deaths in the Far East at the hands of the Japanese have been grossly under-served by justice, international law, war crime tribunals, governments and human rights courts, and neglected by their own country's legal indifference. It is small wonder they are considered a *forgotten army*. They are, however *never* forgotten by their families. As a great niece of one of the murdered prisoners of war aboard the Suez Maru I *do* cause 'questions to be asked, because I *know* that those responsible have *never* been brought to justice'.

29 November 2019.
Seventy-six years later.

-WERNETH LOW, 2019-

I stood with my dad, George's youngest son, Jack's nephew, at the war memorial upon the hill. It was cold and blustery, but we had been warmed a little by the short hike to the top. We stood together in the northern wind and placed a small poppy on the stones in front of the monolith. The wind stole our words as we quietly repeated—

SILENT THOUGHTS, TRUE AND TENDER,
JUST TO SHOW, WE STILL REMEMBER.

George Frith, 1944.

Either way, as I see it, we must be prepared to face criticism. If we started a new trial now, we would be open to attack for waiting more than four years after the end of the war to deal with a crime committed six years ago. And in the contrary event, the relatives of the murdered prisoners of war might well cause questions to be asked if they heard that those responsible would never be brought to justice.

Emanuel Shinwell MP,
Labour Secretary of State for War, 1949

- ACKNOWLEDGEMENTS -

First, my very grateful thanks to Allan Jones, son of Lewis Jones and author of *The Suez Maru Atrocity*, without whom it would not have been known, for a *second* time.

Thank you to Yoshio Kashiki, without whom it would not have been known *at all*.

My thanks to Australian Captain Jack Sylvester, whom I have not been able to trace family of, to offer thanks for his investigation of what *remains* one of the worst unpunished war crimes of WWII.

Thank you to William Mundy, for coconut tales on Ambon, *Ben Hur* stories and for *not* sailing on the *Suez Maru*.

Thanks to Lesley Clark, Chairman and Treasurer of the *Java Far East Prisoner of War Club 1942*, and my 'Java buddy' - for endless support.

Thanks to Joanne Hudson for support and encouragement.

My grateful thanks to Mr Steve Lloyd and Mr Darren Bowers for building the *only* memorial to the British men of the *Suez Maru* at National Memorial Arboretum for the 70th anniversary dedication.

My sincere thanks to the families of those lost on the *Suez Maru*, who generously supported the building of the *Suez Maru Memorial* at the National Memorial Arboretum in 2013, and are without exception an incredible group of people. *We do not diminish, we grow.*

My heartfelt thanks, *for everything*, to my parents Alastair and Susan, also my family of Friths, nee's and others. To my beloved son *Joseph Alastair* — so that you know truth & honesty.

Finally, and most of all, my unending gratitude is with the men of the *Suez Maru*. For their sacrifice.

WHEN YOU GO HOME,
TELL THEM OF US AND SAY,
FOR YOUR TOMORROW,
WE GAVE OUR TODAY

Kohima Epitaph.

- British Casualties of the Suez Maru -

Service Number	Rank	Name		Age	Wife	Parents/Home
1308868	Cpl	Walter James	Abbott	33		Percy and Miriam Abbott Hayes, Bromley, Kent
D/SSX 15176	Able Seaman	John	Affleck	34	Florence May	Robert and Alice Affleck Whickham, Co Durham
975543	Gunner	John Robert	Agar	27		Mr and Mrs W Agar Etruria, Stoke-on-Trent
539725	L.A.C	Joseph Batty	Alderson	24		Ernest and Annie Alderson Darlington, Co Durham
554863	Trooper	George	Alton	27		Mrs E.E. Alton Brampton, Derbyshire
918239	L.A.C	Eric William	Andrews	23		C and E Andrews Coulsdon, Surrey
858461	L/SGT	Thomas John	Argust	27		
2323853	Driver	William	Arnold	28	Mary Arnold	Middleton Tyas, Yorkshire
1776004	Gunner	John Thomas	Ashby	23		William and Rose Ashby Mill Hill, Middlesex
935929	Cpl	Stanley Glendon	Ashworth			
926840	L.A.C	Ingerson Keith	Badcock	31	Constance Badcock	A and G Badcock New Milton, Hampshire
1491630	Gunner	Leonard John	Bailey	25		Montague and Mary Bailey Tooting, Surrey
1132321	L.A.C	George John	Barber		Marjorie Barber	George and Emily Barber Ilford Essex
1646062	Gunner	Reginald Walter	Barrett	36		Devizes
552028	Trooper	William James	Barson	30		Benjamin and Nellie Barson Botley, Berkshire
1646452	Gunner	Nelson Fredrick	Baxter	29	Macolalata Baxter	Nelson and Ellen Baxter Hampstead, London
1646453	Gunner	Peter Henry	Baylis	31	B.B.Baylis	Edward and Amelia Baylis Fulham, London
883260	Bomb.	Kenneth	Beard	23		Cardiff
626496	Cpl	Maurice Alfred	Beatty	23		Charles and Adelaide Beatty Tunbridge Wells, Kent
3197011	Driver	Thomas	Beesley	32		
1040478	A.C.2	William	Bell	33	Margaret Bell	John and Ann Bell Woodhouse, Cumberland
1555676	Gunner	William John	Bennell	30	Doris Bennell	Byfleet, Surrey
7931567	Trooper	Ellis	Bennett	33	Elsie Bennett	G and E Bennett Hollingworth, Manchester
847141	L.A.C	Alec Henry	Bennett	29		Henry and Jane Bennett Leyton, Essex
515790	W/Offr	Claude Henry	Bere	32	Kathleen Bere	Tiverton, Devon
781554	Gunner	Thomas Edmund	Bessant	33		Pontypridd
1023130	A.C.2	David	Blackwood	26		Helen Blackwood Addiewell, Midlothian
1771730	L/Bomb	Horace George	Blake	38		Chichester
634798	L.A.C	Alfred George	Blakely	22		H and B Blakely, Kington, Herefordshire

2056513	Gunner	James Walter	Bogie	22		James and Lilian Bogie Gosport, Hampshire
654650	L.A.C	Ivanhoe Frederick	Bonner	24	Ethel Bonner	Thomas and Lilian Birmingham
1734919	Gunner	Arthur	Boswell	35	Agnes Boswell	Isiah and Hilda Boswell Heaton Norris, Stockport
1152607	Cpl	Ben	Boulton	30	Eva Boulton	Charles and Ruth Boulton Burslem, Stoke-on-Trent
1545633	Bombdr	Edwin	Bowins	30		John and Ellen Bowins Tackley, Oxfordshire
1808638	Gunner	Sidney Walter	Boyton	22		Walter and Louisa Boyton Hook End, Ongar, Essex
1265463	A.C.1	Phil	Bracegirdle	31		Willis and Annie Bracegirdle
1156249	A.C.1	Joseph Eric	Brant			
47467	Fly/Offr	Alfred Sidney	Brentnall	37	Edith Brentnall	T and E Brentnall Gonerby, Lincolnshire
522691	Sgt	James	Broadhurst	29	Gladys Broadhurst	Henry and may Broadhurst Dogsthorpe, Peterborough
1440802	A.C.2	George Reginald	Brockman	20		C and H Brockman Rainham, Kent
993595	A.C.2	William Forbes	Brodie	29		George and Margret Brodie Rattray, Perthshire
1368857	A.C.1	Thomas	Bromley	22		James and Emily Bromley Barrhead, Glasgow
1231177	A.C.1	Donald Archie	Brooker	20		Archie and Lilian Brooker West Malling, Kent
634480	L.A.C.	Alec	Brookes	22	Evelyn Brookes	David and Elsie Brookes Walsall, Staffordshire
2359179	Sig/man	Ronald	Brooks	23		
524715	Cpl	Leslie	Brown	37		Robert and Martha Brown
950438	A.C.1	Robert Aitken	Brown	25		William and Agnes Brown Glasgow, Scotland
1407313	A.C.2	Victor Lewis	Brown	23		Lewis and Mary Brown Buckland Brewer, Devon
392206	Cpl	Edwin Norman	Buck	43	Emily Buck	Arthur and Ann Buck Hanging Houghton,
T/204369	Driver	Richard	Bumpus	27		
T/3772352	Driver	George Edward	Burns	22		E and C Burns Dovecot, Liverpool
958014	Cpl	Walter	Burt	26	Eva Maud Burt	Hedworth and Mary Burt Doncaster, Yorkshire
814176	A.C.2	George Harold	Burton	21		George and Ada Burton Bircotes, Nottinghamshire
1706299	L/Bomb	William Henry	Butler	30	Lucy Butler	Burslem, Stoke-on-Trent
554363	Trooper	Ralph David	Butler	27		Frederick and Edith Butler Bognor Regis, Sussex
1491669	Gunner	Sydney John	Buzzacott	25	Annie Buzzacott	John and Annie Buzzacott Kentish Town, London
574149	L.A.C.	Geoffrey Meallin	Byng	21		
7905199	Trooper	Charles	Callaghan	26		
991671	Cpl	Joseph Ernest	Carlin	41	Margret Carlin	John and Selina Carlin
1098479	A.C.2	Robert	Carroll			
553865	Trooper	Sidney Albert	Carter	28		

1229958	A.C.2	Sydney John	Chambers			
645028	Cpl	Henry George	Chandler	27		Henry and Daisy Chandler
1059606	L.A.C	William Laing	Chapman	23		W and T Chapman Aberdeen, Scotland
1211362	A.C.1	Ernest Edward	Checketts	21		Mr and Mrs E W Checketts Worcester
2578462	Cpl	William Arthur	Clarke	22		Arthur and Jane Clark
839063	Gunner	Albert Stafford	Clarke	27		Charles and Annie Clarke Pentre, Rhondda,Glamorgan
1700354	Lance Bombdr	Arthur Edmund	Clarke	33	Blanche Clarke	Bradford, Yorkshire.
1011674	A.C.1	Harold Creighton	Clegg			Thomas and Jane Clegg Worsborough Dale, York
1016297	A.C.1	Bernard	Coates	31		Israel and Clara Coates Farsley, Yorkshire
651422	Cpl	Robert Alec	Cole	22		Mr and Mrs H.M. Cole Lostwithiel, Cornwall
1491692	Gunner	George John	Coleman	24		Thomas and Rose Coleman Kentish Town, London
1444944	L/Bomb	David Clifford	Coleman	36	Arlien Coleman	Giles and Sarah Colemen Ystrad, Glamorgan
537707	Cpl	Richard Anthony	Collingwood	25		J and C Collingwood Low Fell, Gateshead
1012371	L.A.C	John Henry	Connett	31		Mrs B.S. Connett Plymouth, Devon
1654011	Gunner	John Harold	Cook	33		Mrs R.T.E Cook Purley, Surrey
7607793	Private	Raymond Hilary	Cooper	26	Lavinia Cooper	William and Kate Cooper Perry Barr, Birmingham
857848	L/Bomb	Michael	Coughlin	30		Mrs H A Coughlin Canton, Cardiff
1706343	Gunner	Thomas	Couley	35		Coventry
1531976	A.C.2	Arthur William	Cousins	44		Mr and Mrs Arthur Cousins Stockport, Cheshire
1444948	Gunner	Raymond William	Cowell	23		William and Ivy Cowell Leckwith, Glamorgan
530013	L.A.C	Thomas	Croston	27		Edward and Nellie Croston Westhoughton, Lancs
T/279213	Driver	Allan	Crowther	31		Walter and Anne Crowther Idle, Yorkshire
979836	Cpl	David Robson	Currie	23		Mr and Mrs Thomas Currie Stirling, Scotland
1136563	A.C.2	William	Daft	29	E Daft	Stapleford, Nottingham
539874	Sgt	Geoffrey George	Darwen	26	Marjorie Darwen	William and Floss Darwen Bridlington, Yorkshire
1719728	Gunner	Richard James	Davenport			
223662	Captain	Harold George	Davey	36		Francis and Edith Davey
1474423	Bomb	John Samuel	Davies	33	Martha Davies	David and Rebecca Davies Ystrad-Mynach, Glamorgan
1779354	Gunner	William Elwyn	Davies	22		William & Gertrude Davies Cardiff
1635984	Gunner	Fredrick George	Davis	32		F and Beatrice Davis Caddington, Beds
1762524	Gunner	Jack	Davis	38	Florence Davis	Frederick and Catherine Parkstone, Dorset

1794622	Gunner	George	Dawson	32	Irene Dawson	Matthew and Lena Dawson Brinsworth, Yorkshire
6918688	Trooper	William Charles	Denyer	27	Thelma Denyer	William and Alice Denyer Danbury, Essex
1226089	LAC 1st class	Sydney William	Dicks			WF and AEM Dicks Isham, Northamptonshire.
552316	Cpl	Robert	Dickson	33		
2357678	Sigmn	John James	Digsby	33		
1161056	A.C.1	Bernard William	Dix	26		Bernard and Beatrice Dix Norwich, Norfolk
1031192	A.C.1	William	Dixon	23		William and Ann Dixon Preston, Lancashire
985788	Warrant Officer	Roy Alexander	Dodds	24		Alexander and Mildred Dodds
954800	L.A.C	John	Donaldson			
1654019	Gunner	Edwin	Dring	31		Edwin and Elizabeth Dring Penge, Kent
1204528	Cpl	Charles Phillips	Dron			Eleanor Dron Whitley Bay
548567	Cpl	Ronald Albert	Dunlop			
7933280	Trooper	Norman	Dunning	31	Emily Dunning	William and Ethel Dunning Rhyl, Flintshire
1265129	A.C.2	Cyril Thomas	Dunphy	32		Thomas and Kate Dunphy
1143310	A.C.1	Colin Stuart	Earl	43	Kate Earl	Cheltenham
903009	L.A.C	Jim	Edis			
2351273	Sigmn	Robert	Edmondson	27	V Edmondson	M and M Edmondson Higher Walton, Lancashire
T/3456500	Driver	Frank	Edmondson	28		
4913355	Trooper	Frederick Ernest	Edwards	28	Violet Edwards	Frederick and Lena Edwards Chadsmoor, Staffordshire
1286282	A.C.1	Thomas Islwyn	Elias	27	Megan Elias	Mr and Mrs Gwilym Elias Swansea, South Wales
1484330	A.C.2	Edward	Ellison	21	Josephine Ellison	Birkenhead
1743083	L/Bomb	Bernard	Ellwood	35	Mae Ellwood	John and Ada Ellwood Widnes, Lancashire
553240	SGT	Alfred William	Emery	28	Catherine Emery	Harry and Emely Emery Crawley, Sussex
1614637	Bomb	Douglas Charles	Emms	30	Kathleen Emms	Charles and Rose Emms Tottenham, London
7608356	Private	William	Entwistle	29		
1004122	A.C.2	Stanley	Entwistle			Sebastian & Edith Entwistle Blackburn, Lancashire
929550	L.A.C	Thomas John	Evans	30		Mr and Mrs Gwilym Evans Burry Port, Carmarthenshire
1082200	A.C.2	Albert	Fairhurst			
1074199	Gunner	Herbert King	Falconer	32		Douglas & Emma Falconer King Warboy's Hunts
550681	SGT	Albert	Farmer	27	Gladys Farmer	York
1165931	L.A.C	Arthur Sidney	Farnell	23		
1434031	Gunner	John	Fawcett	38		Hull, Yorkshire

632931	Cpl	Henry	Fawcett	23		Robert & Florence Fawcett Bearpark, Co Durham
1623465	Gunner	Robert Alfred	Ferguson	33	Elizabeth Ferguson	R and E Ferguson Appley Bridge, Lansashire
1360261	A.C.1	Frank	Files			
1184503	A.C.2	Brian	Filmer	31		Frank and Janet Filmer Willington Quay
1807016	Gunner	Leslie Ernest	Fitch	22		Walter and Bessie Fitch Waltham Abbey, Herts
1090680	A.C.2	John Wilfred	Flavell	24		Mr and Mrs Bernard Flavell West Dulwich, London
1614639	Gunner	Charles Herbert	Foster	30	Ellen Foster	Albert and Matlida Foster East Sheen, Surrey
937854	Cpl	Joseph Renton	Foster	29		J and E Foster Fulwell, Sunderland
1794521	Gunner	Jack	Frith	23		John and Florrie Frith 13 Spring Street, Hyde, Cheshire
905642	A.C.1	Leslie Alan	Frost			
2366953	Sigmn	Alexander F	Fullarton	35	Ethel Fullarton	A and M Fullarton Wood Green, London
1102563	Cpl	Alan	Fulton	28	A Fulton	Walter and Penelope Fulton Wallsend, Northumberland
1609535	Gunner	Walter	Garner	31	Hilda Garner	Benjamin & Martha Garner Edgeley, Stockport
1587840	Gunner	William Alexander	Gay	30		Hubert and Ada Gay
1006617	Cpl	William	Gelder	34	Esther Mary Gelder	William and Eliza Gelder Accrington, Lancashire
1807736	Gunner	William Percy	Gell	22		
1141703	L.A.C	Arthur	Gelling	22		Henry and Louisa Gelling Widnes, Lancashire
1491801	Gunner	Henry Charles	George	24		Henry and Ethel George Marylebone, London
546442	Cpl	Terence	Gleeson			James and Mary Gleeson
T/182497	Driver	Arthur Edward	Glennon			
2370913	Driver	Robert Henry	Glover	22		Elsie Glover Cross Heath, Staffordshire
117803	Fly/Offr	John Henry	Godfree	48	Irene Mary Godfree	Pietermaritzburg, S Africa
1061437	A.C.2	Charles	Goldberg		Shirley Goldberg	Louis and Cissie Goldberg Leeds, Yorkshire
1733525	Gunner	Clifford	Goodier	36		Stretford, Manchester
1056822	A.C.2	Fred	Gorst	23		Edwaed and Ellen Gorst Preston, Lancashire
1646355	Gunner	William Ernest	Gosling	29		Ealing, London
1491824	L/SGT	Maurice Eugene	Grady	25		Thomas and Jessie Grady Ramsgate, Kent
1822265	Gunner	Gerald Lockhart	Grant	35		William and Jane Grant Dumfries, Scotland
611159	L.A.C	James	Graveson	23		G and Kate Graveson Maryport, Cumberland
535963	Cpl	Thomas Young	Gray	33		James and M.A. Gray Maryhill, Glasgow
1491825	L/Bomb	Joseph Thomas	Greaves	25		John and Mary Greaves Streatham, London

116815	Fly/Offr	John Francis	Gregg	40		Revd John and Anna Gregg Armagh, Northern Ireland
2042674	Gunner	James Ypres	Griffin	28	K M Griffin	Annie Griffin Brixton, London
936592	L.A.C	William	Griffin			
955915	L.A.C	John	Griffith	24		William and Martha Griffith Llanllyfni, Caernarfonshire
913137	L.A.C	James Gilbert	Groombridge	37	Eveline Groombridge	J & A Groombridge Crowborough, Sussex
1254212	A.C.1	Abe	Grunis			
1591190	L/Bomb	Harold	Guest	23	Elizabeth Guest	John and Miranda Guest Miles Platting, Manchester
918269	Gunner	Peter	Guilar	21		Peter and Agnes Guilar Edinburgh, Scotland
1706476	Gunner	Arthur	Hadley	25		Smethwick
7625227	SGT	Thomas Freeman	Hall	29		
1480589	A.C.2	Joseph Harbottle	Halliday	22		John and Rebbecca Halliday South Shields, Co Durham
901652	L.A.C	Alan Richard	Hambridge			
626473	L.A.C	James Christopher	Hanley			James and Johannah Hanley
2063179	Gunner	Cecil Hemslie	Harding	23		Samuel and Mabel Harding Loughborough
930495	L.A.C	Robert	Hardy			
1210798	A.C.1	John	Harnden			
1213243	A.C.1	Alfred Frank	Harris			
7894655	Trooper	Victor	Harrison	23		Victor and Alice Harrison Selsley, Gloucestershire
616344	Cpl	Herbert	Harrison	24	Ethel May Harrison	Brackley, Northamptonshire
1235829	A.C.1	William John	Hayes			Percy and Bessie Hayes Bramford, Suffolk
1807575	Gunner	Cecil Thomas	Haywood	31	Ellen Haywood	Mr and Mrs T Haywood Breaston, Derbyshire
1604973	Gunner	Stanley Ernest	Healey	34	Kate Healey	Nottingham
1025956	A.C.2	Reginald Arthur	Heath	33	Lilian Heath	William and Helen Heath Frome, Somerset
156510	L.A.C	William	Hedgecox	43	Florence Hedgecox	Barnsley, Yorkshire
1746331	Gunner	James Michael	Herley	33		Deptford, London
1304949	A.C.1	Walter	Hicks	23		Arthur and Ellen Hicks Hornchurch, Essex
1646112	Bomb	Herbert George	Hillier	30	Queenie Hillier	Herbert and Rose Hillier Street, Somerset
1157359	A.C.1	Archibald Leslie	Holman	27		Henry and Elsie Holman Callington, Cornwall
1252122	Wt/Offr	Howard Henry	Hough			
991586	A.C.1	Frank	Hoyles			
1280482	A.C.1	Patrick O'Dwyer	Hulley	26		William and Evelyn Hulley Lewisham, London
1173380	A.C.1	Jonathan Henry	Hunt	29		Jonathan & Catherine Hunt Barnet, Hertfordshire

1517804	Bomb	Leonard	Hurrel	24		Dagenham, Essex
1870889	Sapper	David William	Hutchins	26		Dorothy Hutchins Harlesden, Middlesex
903136	L.A.C	Roy Smeaton	Hutchinson	24		Mr and Mrs J Hutchinson Plympton, Devon
2351640	Sigmn	George	Hyde	27		George and Margaret Hyde Chester
1587861	L/Bomb	Roy William	James	30		Gravesend, Kent
554343	Cpl	Frank William	Jarvis	27		Henry and Mary Jarvis Buckingham
1443870	Gunner	Leonard Westley	John	35	Chrishilda John	William and Mary John Cardiff, South Wales
1512208	L/Bomb	Thomas Jack	Johnson	24	Hilda Johnson	W & G Johnson Wolverhampton
1580632	Gunner	Lewis	Jones	29	Doris Agnes Jones	Mr and Mrs Garnsworthy King's Cross, London
883016	Gunner	Bernard Walter	Jones	25	Nora Jones	Josiah and Kate Jones Penyrheol, Glamorgan
1459948	Gunner	Joseph William	Jones	42		
1442911	Gunner	Winser	Jones	25		David and Margaret Jones Abertridior, Glamorgan
3439328	SGT	William John	Jones	40	Ellen Jones	Tonypandy, Glamorgan
2367018	Sigmn	Ernest	Jones	30		Ernest and Margaret Jones
978595	A.C.1	Cuthbert Edward	Jones	26		Dewi and Frances Jones Newcastle-on-Tyne
532739	Cpl	Edgar Amphion	Jones	29	M. Jones	Stonehouse, Gloucestershire
575062	A.C.1	Gordon Leslie	Jones	21		Charles and Alice Jones Bath, Somerset
1548354	Gunner	Joseph Harry	Joseph	27		Whitechapel, London
1152011	Wt/Offr	Dennis Albert	Juby	27	Ethel Juby	Lionel and Lily Juby Norwich, Norfolk
1214661	A.C.1	Alfred Leonard	Kaines	35	Maud Kaines	Charles and Annie Kaines Milton, Berkshire
531925	Flt/Sgt	Stanley	Kemp	25	M.H.Kemp	Bispham, Blackpool
534165	Cpl	Stanley	Key	28		William and Lucy Key
1387333	A.C.1	John Thomas	Kidd	22		J.A. and Elizabeth Kidd Bethnal Green, London
7925299	Trooper	Harold Percival	King	37	A.N.King	Frederick and Marion King Bitterne, Southampton
1430241	A.C.1	John Thomas	King	22		Mrs E.M. King Great Brickhill, B'hamshire
1309078	A.C.1	Maurice George	King	34	N.M. King	Lower Kingswood, Surrey
1194884	A.C.2	Henry George	Knight	21		Herbert and Caroline Knight Partridge Green, Sussex
950227	Cpl	George Bertram	Knightley	29		James and Ella Knightley Cheadle, Staffordshire
1134274	A.C.1	William Frederick	Knock	37	Ada Florence Knock	Mr and Mrs F Knock Ingatestone, Essex
1808704	Gunner	Walter Robert	Knowles	23		Ellen Knowles Great Yarmouth, Norfolk
762154	L.A.C	Norman Edward	Lawe	34		Mr and Mrs B E Lawe Stafford
1250653	L.A.C	Neville James	Lawes			

614399	Cpl	Harold	Lawson	32		William and Nancy Lawson Wallasey, Cheshire
1166195	A.C.1	Leslie Charles	Lawson	26		Mr and Mrs W J Lawson New Southgate, Middlesex
979864	A.C.1	Ronald Charles	Leach	27	Flora Leach	Sidney and Winifred Leach Mannamead, Plymouth,
622386	A.C.1	William Alexander	Lee			William and Charlotte Lee St Ninians, Stirling
1286884	A.C.1	Daniel John	Leeper	32	Winifred Leeper	Henry and Elizabeth Leeper Reigate, Surrey
570612	Cpl	Francis Norman	Lees	23		Harry and Mable Lees Wallasey, Cheshire
1164591	L.A.C	William	Leeves	34	Doris Leeves	Jarvis Brook, Sussex
1645999	Gunner	Oscar Thomas	Lewis	23		James and Olwen Lewis Camborne, Cornwall
621301	Cpl	Basil Frank	Lewis			
1022389	A.C.2	Samuel	Lindsay	32		David and Margaret Lindsay Dalmarnock, Glasgow
1563570	Bomb	Sidney John	Lintott	36	Doris Lintott	Mr and Mrs F Lintott St. John's, Woking, Surrey
538172	A.C.1	John	Litherland			Thomas & Mary Litherland Bewsey, Lancashire
1582380	Gunner	John Henry	Lloyd	29		Flint, North Wales
1587717	L/SGT	Charles Alfred	Locke	29	Ellen Locke	Prestwood, Buckingham
1046901	A.C.1	Cecil Frank	Love	38	Annie Love	Ashington, Essex
1286202	L.A.C	Harold Denis	Lowle	30	Margaret Lowle	Ernest and Agnes Lowle West Brompton, London
2370030	Sigmn	Cyril	Lund	30		
1746273	Gunner	Sidney Harold	Luxford	36	Mary Luxford	Mr and Mrs E W Luxford East Grinstead, Sussex
1180421	Wt/Offr	Douglas James	Mackillop			Douglas & Ethel Mackillop Woolland, Dorset
1366673	A.C.2	George	Mair	29		George and Isabella Mair
3385975	Trooper	Edgar Henry	Marriot	24		John and Ellen Marriott Kings Heath, Northampton
1591196	Gunner	James Henry	Marsh	23		Liverpool
1605582	Gunner	John William	Marshall	33	Lillian Marshall	South Shields, Co. Durham
554672	Trooper	Henry Sylvester	Martin	29		Mr J Mernagh St. Helens, Lancashire
958215	A.C.2	John Robert	Martin		Ada May Martin	John and Annie Martin Yiewsley, Middlesex
1205241	A.C.2	Raymond James	Martin	35	Queenie Martin	Hezekiah and Eliza Martin Abbey Wood, London
1794617	Gunner	Raymond	Maskill	22		Castleford
632671	L.A.C	Edwin Henry	Mason	32	Adeline Mason	Edwin and Margaret Mason St Pancras, London
1234797	L.A.C	William Dennis	Mason	22		Sydney and Mary Mason Vennington, Shropshire
979553	L.A.C	David	Maxwell	28	Christina Maxwell	David & Catherine Maxwell Tillicoultry, Clackmanshire
570306	L.A.C	Vivian Foyle	Maynard	22		Mr and Mrs F C Maynard Pembroke Dock,
T/3064085	Driver	Robert	McCallum	30		

550582	Flt/Sgt	John William	McCormack			
1820793	Gunner	David Sage	McFarlane	31	Annie McFarlane	Friarton St Martins Perthshire
978073	A.C.1	Robert	McGuiness	20		James and Mary McGuiness Belfast, Northern Ireland
2346442	L/Cpl	Patrick Joseph	McHugh	29	Mary McHugh	Peter and Mary McHugh Oldham, Lancashire
1056500	L.A.C	Robert Anderson	McIntyre	29		Thomas and Elizabeth Port Glasgow, Renfrewshire
1062210	Cpl	Angus	McLean	30		Angus & Josephine McLean Ibrox, Glasgow
2326759	Sigmn	James	McManus	25		
621000	A.C.1	Thomas	McPhillips			A and H McPhillips Dunfermline, Fife
3856946	Gunner	James	Meadows	23		Wigan
1645950	Gunner	Reginal Percy	Medway	30	Kathleen Medway	Frederick and Lily Medway Exeter
1807626	Gunner	James	Mee	24		Robert and Alice Mee Sandiacre, Derby
1835097	Gunner	David Thomas	Megins	21		John and Janet Megins Maesteg, Glamorgan
117433	A.C.1	Matthew	Metcalfe	23		Leonard and Jane Metcalfe
1807628	Gunner	Henry	Milner	22		Henry and Mary Mansfield, Nottinghamshire
1112966	L.A.C	Frederick Albert	Minton			Caroline Minton Liverpool
5886739	Sigmn	Jack	Mold	24		
980427	L.A.C	Francis Albert	Morgan	22		Caroline Morgan Dublin, Irish Republic
912211	A.C.2	Ronal George	Morgan	23		George and Alice Morgan Streatham, London
552648	Cpl	George Frederick	Morris	29		John and Ella Morris Shrewsbury, Shropshire
1292710	A.C.1	Ernest William	Morris	23		Charles and Maria Morris
527412	Cpl	Rowland Vernun	Morris			
1657365	Gunner	Alex	Morrow	34		Arthur & Margaret Morrow Donegal, N. Ireland
1706536	Gunner	Henry	Mosley	34	Agnes Mosley	Robert and Annie New Stevenston, Lanark
1587875	L/Bomb	Ernest	Moulton	37		E & F Moulton Brighton, Sussex
1190136	A.C.2	Harry Kenneth	Mundin	22		Ernest and Mary Mundin South Wigston, Leics
S/226241	Private	Alexander	Murphy	23		John and Agnes Murphy
1793083	Gunner	James	Murray	23		George and Mary Murray Grasslot, Cumberland
1636090	Gunner	Cooper	Naylor	32	Alice Naylor	Pudsey, Yorkshire
1475012	Gunner	John Louis	Nevill	31		William and Lillian Nevill Hillingdon, Middlesex
1057122	Cpl	William	Nicholson	34		
1234542	A.C.2	Geoffrey Ernest	Niehorster	21		Ernest and Helen Niehorster Enfield, Middlesex
615574	Cpl	Donald Edward	North	25		Edward and Ethel North North Finchley, Middlesex

2354843	Driver	Horace	Oldfield	37		
1646529	Gunner	Reginald Victor	Osborn	29	A L Osborn	Hamstead, London
3184681	Gunner	Frederick Charles	Osborne	35		Frederick & Emily Osborne Bournemouth, Hants
1441079	A.C.2	William Emlyn	Owen			
1627446	Gunner	Edward	Owens	35		Mr and Mrs Edward Owens Dowlais, Glamorgan
7932239	Trooper	Ernest Joseph	Page	33	Beulah Page	William and Daisy Norwich, Norfolk
1643469	Gunner	Albert Frederick	Palmer	32	Winifred Palmer	Albert and Eleanor Palmer St Pancras, London
903290	Cpl	John Eden	Palmer			
1447475	A.C.1	William George	Parsons	36	Lydia Parsons	William and Alice Parsons Gorleston-on-Sea, Norfolk
701363	Cpl	James	Permain			George & Gertrude Permain Freemantle, Southampton
5248434	Trooper	William	Perry	34	Marian Perry	Woodsetton, Staffordshire
6016330	Craftsman	Rowland John	Philllips	23		
929224	L.A.C	Sidney	Philpott	23		Sidney and Violet Philpott Canvey Island, Essex
1012421	L.A.C	Alfred Leslie	Pont	30	Minnie Pont	Northfield, Birmingham
1627486	Gunner	Ivor Aleck	Pope	35	A. M. Pope	Swindon, Wiltshire
631904	A.C.1	Phillip Frederick	Pope	20	Lilian Pope	Hucknall, Nottinghamshire
405502	Cpl	George	Powell	30		George and Maria Powell Woodhouse, Leeds
1284061	A.C.1	Edward John	Powell	26		James and Emily Powell Southall, Middlesex
1017978	A.C.2	John Stanley	Pownall	33		William and Jane Pownall St Helens, Lancashire
402661	Cpl	George James	Preece	34		
1158337	L.A.C	Albert James	Prime	23		Bert and Elsie Prime Lower Cam Gloucestershire
1309574	A.C.1	Charles Henry	Prime			
6897326	Gunner	Victor Gordon	Prior	22		Harry and Elsie Prior Caterham, Surrey
1732105	Gunner	Frederick John	Pritchard	23		
7890060	Trooper	Wilfred	Pritchard	23		Joseph and Martha Pritchard Salford, Lancashire
640281	L.A.C	Joseph Walter	Pusey	23		Frederick and L Pusey Windsor, Berkshire
1177682	A.C.2	Norman	Radford	22		Frederick & Frances Radford Leicester
1808708	Gunner	James Arthur	Ransome	22		Robert and Anna Ransome Docking, Norfolk
1006943	A.C.1	Leonard	Ratcliffe	29	Mary Ratcliffe	Bonus and Emily Ratcliffe New Mills, Derbyshire
649039	L.A.C	Reginald Frederick	Reay	23		Mr and Mrs A F Reay Walthamstow, Essex
1063513	L.A.C	Ernest Montieth	Reid			
1108806	A.C.2	William	Renshaw	25		James and Mary Renshaw Wing, Buckinghamshire

2366447	Sigmn	Hubert Morris	Reynolds	22		
1124266	A.C.1	Arthur	Reynolds			
1137513	A.C.1	Alfred	Richardson	34	Elizabeth Richardson	J & C Richardson Chadderton, Lancashire
1826603	Gunner	Peter	Rigby	29	Hilda Rigby	Peter and Elizabeth Rigby Over Hulton, Lancashire
925034	L.A.C	Frederick Charles	Ringrow	23		Frederick & Ethel Ringrow Rainham, Essex
S/238808	Private	Jack	Roberts	23		John and Daisy Roberts Cambridge
1582438	Gunner	Robert Charles	Robertson			Cardiff, South Wales
1340008	A.C.1	Albert	Robertson	22		Robert and Isabella Robertson
1605469	Gunner	Thomas	Robinson	35		Arthur and Mary Robinson West Aukland, Durham
1019835	A.C.1	John Edward	Robson	31	Elsie Robson	James and Lily Robson Ambleside, Westmorland
1256012	L.A.C	Louis	Romain	28		Jack and Lucy Romain Kentish Town, London
748122	B.Q.M.S	Reginald Hubert	Rowe	38	Gwyneth Rowe	Rupert and Rose Rowe Gelli Pentre, Glamorgan
1807346	Gunner	Cyril Victor	Saban	22		Edmonton, London
1626641	L/Bomb	Norman	Sage	29	Peggy Sage	William and Ruth Sage Upper Norwood, Surrey
654537	Cpl	Reginald Thomas	Sant	21		Thomas and Sarah Sant Middlewich, Cheshire
1751252	Gunner	Norman Eric	Saunders	35	Ethel Saunders	Ernest and Emily Saunders Redland, Glous
1064369	L/Bomb	Henry Thomas	Scarborough	37		Guildford
2579558	Sigmn	Jimmy Ivor Griffen	Sharpe	22		
1019586	A.C.2	Vincent Thomas	Shaw	31	Ida Shaw	William and Agnes Shaw Southport, Lancashire
518753	Flt/Sgt	Leonard	Shimells			
906113	A.C.1	Derrick William	Shouler	23		Frederick and Doris Shouler Torquay, Devon
1074216	A.C.2	Donald Anthony	Shuttleworth	32		T and M Shuttleworth Burnley, Lancashire
803509	Cpl	John Hart	Sim			
1156987	L.A.C	Stanley Richard	Small	28		William and Louisa Small Wandsworth, London
956483	L.A.C	Jack	Smart	25	Gladys Smart	Francis and Beatrice Smart Penyfai, Glamorgan
1826738	Gunner	Kenneth	Smith	37	Elizabeth Smith	William and Lily Smith Rutherglen, Lanarkshire
1261758	Cpl	Arthur Bertram	Smith	21		Bertram and Ada Smith Exeter
1055923	L.A.C	Arthur Hudson	Smith	23		Frank and Ethel Smith Colne, Lancashire
972275	L.A.C	Donald	Smith			
975810	A.C.1	Edwin Francis	Smith	27		
1103013	L.A.C	Henry Llewellyn	Smith		M Smith	Liverpool
1377011	L.A.C	Herbert John	Smith			

1482054	SGT	Leslie Fredrick	Spence	28	Doris Spence	Banstead, Surrey
1319147	A.C.2	Robert John	Sprake	22		Mr and Mrs H R Sprake Bridport, Dorsetshire
573094	Cpl	Peter John	Standley	21		Arthur and Ethel Standley Kingsteignton, Devon
553192	Cpl	William Leslie	Stanford	30	Theresa Stanford	Mr and Mrs W J Stanford Darlington, Co. Durham
925188	L.A.C	Eric John	Staniland			Frederick and Olive Staniland
1770727	Gunner	Sampson Edwin	Stanley	23		Arthur and Mary Stanley Oadby, Leicestershire
1736274	Gunner	Sidney	Stearn	36		Warlingham, Surrey
625564	Cpl	John Walter	Stedman	24	E M Stedman	Henry and Ellen Stedman Romford, Essex
1502670	Gunner	William	Steed	25		J.T. and Jane Steed Walsall, Staffordshire
1439392	Gunner	Edward	Steedman	36	Jessie Steedman	J & C Steedman Edinburgh, Scotland
1549377	Gunner	George Victor	Steventon	29	A E Stevenson	Henry and Alice Stevenson Stockwell, London
543906	Cpl	Edward William	Stigant	37		Edward and Lily Stigant Gosport, Hampshire
1646008	Gunner	Ernest John	Stone	29	Lilian Stone	James and Edith Stone Wevilscombe, Somerset
1807387	Gunner	Stanley William	Stoneham	22		Harrow, Middlesex
1378172	A.C.1	Victor Sydney	Streater	32	Winifred Streater	Horace and Violet Streater Chingford, Essex
3855662	L/Cpl	William	Stringfellow	30		W and M Stringfellow Hindley, Lancashire
627036	L.A.C	Benjamin Walter	Stuart	23		Alexander & Dorothy Stuart Walmer, Kent
747928	B.S.M	Edward	Sumption	52	Florence Sumption	Pentre, Glamorgan
822321	Gunner	Lawrence Henry	Sunley	29	Annie Sunley	Henry and Margaret Sunley Alverstoke, Hampshire
610989	Sgt	Noel George	Swaffield			Richard and Ethel Swaffield Southsea, Hampshire
T/89779	SGT	Ronald Roulston	Sweeney	37	F.O. Sweeney	William and Amy Sweeney Harrogate, Yorkshire
1167039	A.C.1	Raymond Louis	Tanguy			
T/254047	Driver	Ronald	Taylor	23		
577270	A.C.1	Frank	Taylor			
957318	L.A.C.	Freddie	Taylor	24		Edward and Ada Taylor Hindhead, Surrey
1259891	A.C.1	Loftus George	Taylor	23		Loftus and Ethel Taylor East Ham, London
941699	L.A.C	George Norman	Teasdale	25		Clifford and Elsie Teasdale Grimsby, Lincolnshire
1447543	Gunner	William Charles	Thomas	29		William and Ethel Thomas Ton Pentre, Glamorgan
T/157214	Private	Albert	Thorpe	25		
818155	L/Bomb	Charles Willie	Tinsley	32	Rosetta Tinsley	Joe and Hilda Crayford, Kent
1427519	SGT	George Michael	Toole	23		Laurence and Ada Toole Basingstoke, Hampshire

1807700	Gunner	Alfred Ambrose	Toon	22		Elijah and A Toon Leicester
805530	L.A.C	Cyril Geoffrey	Tooth	28	Winifred Tooth	King's Norton, Birmingham
591817	L.A.C	Leslie Raymond	Tozer	21		Mr and Mrs William Tozer Tonteg, Glamorgan
T/68799	Driver	William Joseph	Tregaskis	22		Thomas and Alice Tregaskis Plymouth, Devon
1646054	Gunner	Harold	Tucker	28		Jessie Sly Tucker Chumleigh, Devon
550100	Sgt	William Edwin	Tully	25		Michael and Bridget Tully Sheffield, Yorkshire
3527946	Trooper	Walter Dyson	Turner	26		Alice Greenwood Dukinfield, Cheshire
1208373	A.C.2	Harold	Utting	27		Mr and Mrs S D Utting Romford, Essex
1502708	Gunner	Thomas Edward	Varney	25		William & Elizabeth Varney Derby
944211	A.C.1	Donald Raymond	Vincent	27		Owen and laura Vincent Handsworth, Birmingham
984512	Bomb	Jack	Walker	28		Hereford
1190515	A.C.1	Arthur Cecil	Walker			
1023094	A.C.2	Allan Noel	Walton		Lilah Walton	George and Gertrude Walton Newton-le-Willows, Lancs
1706719	Gunner	Mark William	Wardell	33	Eileen Wardell	Kingstanding, Birmingham
2352277	L/Cpl	Ewart Gladstone	Waring	33		
1287882	L.A.C	Charles Percy	Watson	22		Ethel Watson Ipswich, Suffolk
1458782	L/Bomb	Francis Joseph	Watts	35		Cardiff
1065009	Gunner	Christopher Thomas	Wayman	36	Frances Wayman	William and Sarah Wayman Chaxhill, Glouestershire
833203	SGT	Charles Oliver	Webb	30	Constance Webb	Tenby, Pembrokeshire
1507596	Gunner	Allenby Foch	Webb	25		Mr, Mrs M M Webb Laindon, Essex
611113	L.A.C	Hector John	Webb			
411484	Flt/ Lieut	Grahame Prebble	White	24		Harold and Gertrude White Wellington, New Zealand
1808716	L/Bomb	William John	Whitman	29	Kathleen Whitman	William and Lottie Whitman Leighton Buzzard,
1235505	A.C.2	George Virgo	Wigley	22		George and Henrietta Wigley
1010120	L.A.C	Harry Rourke	Wilcock	30		Harry and Hilda Wilcock Higher Broughton, Lancs
1545761	Gunner	Charles Frank	Wilkinson	29		Maud Wilkinson Neasden, Middlesex
7899863	Trooper	Arnold	Williams	25		Henry and Isabel Williams Chester
405133	Cpl	Ernest Charles	Williams	29	Vera Williams	Thomas and Ellen Williams Folkestone, Kent
1121640	L.A.C	Edward Stanley	Williams	27	Ethel Williams	William and Emily Williams Wolstanton, Staffordshire
629130	L.A.C	Harold Eric	Williams	22		Albert and Elfrida Williams Saltash, Cornwall
626147	A.C.1	John Dewi	Williams			

953620	L.A.C	Raymond James	Williams	23		James and Elsie Williams Leicester
553616	Trooper	Kenneth	Williamson	30		
1794556	Gunner	Frank	Wilson	32	Vera Wilson	Headingley, Yorkshire
1316108	A.C.2	Francis Jesse	Wing	21		Joseph and Fanny Wing Islip, Oxfordshire
7629277	Private	Percy Douglas	Wood	32	Francis Wood	Ernest and Winifred Wood Taunton, Somerset
1555770	L/Bomb	Leslie Harold	Woodman	29		Edgar and Lily Woodman Malmesbury, Wiltshire
511113	Wt/Offr	George Cranston	Wright			
1259752	L.A.C	Wilfred Edward	Yallop	23		Wilfred and Ruth Yallop Beccles, Suffolk
1819219	Gunner	Abraham Larkhall	Yudkin	29	Frances Yudkin	Sam and Anne Yudkin Hackney, London

THEY WENT WITH SONGS TO THE BATTLE, THEY WERE YOUNG.
STRAIGHT OF LIMB, TRUE OF EYES, STEADY AND AGLOW.
THEY WERE STAUNCH TO THE END AGAINST ODDS UNCOUNTED,
THEY FELL WITH THEIR FACES TO THE FOE.

THEY SHALL GROW NOT OLD, AS WE THAT ARE LEFT GROW OLD
AGE SHALL NOT WEARY THEM, NOR THE YEARS CONDEMN.
AT THE GOING DOWN OF THE SUN AND IN THE MORNING,
WE WILL REMEMBER THEM.

THEY MINGLE NOT WITH THEIR LAUGHING COMRADES AGAIN,
THEY SIT NO MORE AT FAMILIAR TABLES OF HOME,
THEY HAVE NO LOT IN OUR LABOUR OF THE DAY-TIME,
THEY SLEEP BEYOND ENGLAND'S FOAM

For the Fallen,
Robert Laurence Binyon, (1869—1943)